Britney
Inside the Dream

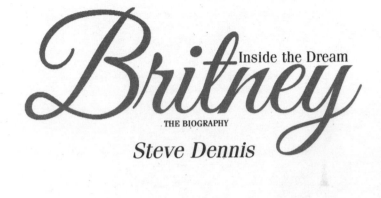

Inside the Dream

Britney

THE BIOGRAPHY

Steve Dennis

HARPER

an imprint of
HarperCollins*Publishers*
77–85 Fulham Palace Road,
Hammersmith, London W6 8JB

www.harpercollins.co.uk

First published by HarperCollins*Publishers* 2009
This edition 2010

1 3 5 7 9 10 8 6 4 2

A catalogue record of this book is
available from the British Library

ISBN 978 0 00 731893 3

Printed and bound in Great Britain by
Clays Ltd, St Ives plc

PICTURE CREDITS:
Section 1: Splash News (top), Disney/Splash News (middle), REX Features
(bottom), page 1; PA Photos, page 2; PA Photos (top & middle), REX Features
(bottom), page 3; PA Photos (top, bottom left & bottom right), REX Features
(middle), page 4; PA Photos (top), REX Features (bottom), page 5; PA Photos
(top), Getty Images (middle), Splash News (bottom), page 6; REX Features
(top & middle), PA Photos (bottom), page 7; X17online.com (top), Getty Images
(middle left & right), REX Features (bottom), page 8.

Section 2: X17online.com (top), Splash News (bottom), page 1; X17online.com
(top), Splash News (middle & bottom), page 2; X17online.com, page 3;
REX Features (top left), PA Photos (top right), London Entertainment/Splash
News (bottom), page 4; X17online.com (top & bottom left), REX Features
(middle), Clint Brewer/Splash News (bottom right), page 5; REX Features, page 6;
REX Features (top & bottom), PA Photos (middle), page 7; Getty Images, page 8.

Character cannot be developed in ease and quiet. Only through experience of trial and suffering can the soul be strengthened, ambition inspired, and success achieved.

Helen Keller, US educator

(1880–1968)

Contents

Introduction:
The Search for Brit-Brit   ix

1: **Home Sweet Home**   1

2: **The Inner Child**   14

3: **Sins of the Father**   34

4: **Bridges to Stardom**   60

5: **The Disney Dream**   77

6: **Teen Pop Sensation**   108

7: **The Making of Britney**   131

8: **Backstage: In the Zone**   157

9: **Love and Loathing In ...**   193

10: **It's Her Prerogative**   218

11: **Little Girl Lost**   247

12: **The Self-Destruct**   276

13: **Through the Lens**   303

14: **Rescue Mission**   330

15: **The Resurrection**   359

16: **Britney ... One More Time**   382

Author's Research Note   401

Acknowledgements   403

The Search for Brit-Brit

'It is so weird how stories are told. There is your side, my side, and the truth. Somebody has to figure it out. I guess we will never really understand or figure out life completely. That's God's job. I can't wait to meet him – or her.'

– Britney, 2007

LOCATION: LOS ANGELES, CALIFORNIA

'You're wanting to do *what?*'

'Understand the *real* Britney … the human behind the brand,' I repeated.

The music-industry man seated opposite eyed me curiously, and his cynical smile suggested he'd already viewed some greenness behind my intentions.

'Like pulling back the curtain to reveal the true Wizard of Oz?' he said, 'As easy as that, right?'

He's among the few who truly know Britney Spears, and was an integral part of her set-up long before the conservatorship became an issue, and long before Sam Lutfi, Adnan Ghalib et al. arrived on the scene. That, perhaps, also explains why he viewed me with suspicion as I fished for co-operation, and he fished for motive.

We're at the Mondrian, an all-white boutique hotel where, apparently, it's hip to be seen off the Sunset Strip in LA. And the sun is indeed setting, dunked by the sky into the Pacific Ocean, 17 miles away, tinting the skyline orange. This used to be a favourite haunt of Britney, with the glass-backed patio of the 'Sky Bar' providing a commanding view from the foot of the Hollywood Hills, overlooking a metropolis fading into night; a darkness that helps mask the ordinariness of the concrete basin which falls away down the hill and stretches to the 10 Freeway and beyond. That same view provided a distraction during an awkward silence, which I broke by saying: 'I want to know her reality.'

Now, he really did scoff.

'Reality as defined by you is incomprehensible to Britney. An artificial world is her normal. Outside of that, she is lost – completely and totally lost. Great kid, great girl – but lost.'

This meeting has taken weeks to set up and the door into Britney's world is merely ajar, with the chain still on. And this is just the outer-ring to an understandably cagey group of people who guard Britney Corporation Inc as if it were the one bank that can never be allowed to fail. But I'm determined to keep my foot in the door in this attempt to get closer to understanding a fragile colossus within the music industry. Her image might well be a parade of many revitalised masks, and the headlines may have echoed the management's talk of 'comebacks', but the smoke and mirrors of show business shouldn't lull anyone into a false sense of believing everything is suddenly okay again. The act may be back, the persona rescued, but the human being inside remains as brittle and vulnerable as ever. Behind the hype is a woman who is searching for direction, screaming to be understood, listened to and allowed to breathe as someone other than Britney Spears the Performer.

There is a barely concealed fragility to this free spirit, who finds herself encased within a micro-managed structure built by her own dreams. To all intents and purposes, she is a robotic brand functioning on remote control; steered by managers Larry Rudolph and Adam Leber in consultation with Jive Records, controlled as a person – and by order of the courts – by her father, Jamie Spears.

This is her recent reality, cocooned within a legal 'conservatorship' – a guardianship where responsibility for all corners of her life and decision-making rest with her father, in consultation with others. It is, of course, the consequence of a very public meltdown, effectively being made a ward of court under the guardianship of adults who 'know best' because Britney was not deemed to have the mental capacity to make compos mentis choices in life, according to a judge. In her 28th year, she seems to enjoy all the rights and freedoms of a twelve-year-old; an adult woman forced into a child-like situation, policed by her own father. In 2008, she was granted 'pocket-money' and 'allowed' a credit card of her own. Dad Jamie was even permitted to comb her mobile telephone bills, checking who she's called or texted. He still does.

In any other life, these would be the traits of a possessive controller. But under a court-appointed conservatorship, this is the permitted interventionist control exercised to

ensure the life of an iconic figure remains on track. Its juxtaposition is hard to fathom alongside the pop superstar who
has sold 84 million records worldwide, and has been crying
'freedom' since 2004.

In late 2008, the terms of her conservatorship were made
indefinite, as her dad was made permanent guardian. Britney has struggled with this set-up as it further reinforces
her belief that fame has become her prison. We are told
conservatorship is a price she must pay for her own welfare
and to redeem a career that was spectacularly imploding
throughout 2007–8. Hers was an infamous 'meltdown',
played out in agonising slow motion on the public
stage before being dissected, shaken and tipped upside
down by the world's media. Britney Spears seems to
perform, live and self-destruct within a commercial snow
globe for the entertainment, prurience and profit of others.
But what cost to her soul? What about the human being
inside?

The man I'm speaking with at the Mondrian leans
forward, seeking to educate me.

'People get it so wrong. Look, she has a huge heart and is
so sweet. But there's also a dark side, and it's not of her
making. The girl's got shit going on and everyone's dealing
with it the best they can. Tough love harms no one when all
they can do is harm themselves. So you want to find the real
Britney? Good luck, bro'! Even the woman herself ain't
found that one out yet.'

To be fair, he didn't say much more, but his impassioned
testimony was typical of the consensus encountered over
the past eight months traversing the show-business landscape of Hollywood, the southern terrains of Louisiana,
then Florida, and the roads of a chaotic childhood.

People were keen to assist with the depiction of a 'true
soul'.

'No one's troubles should reflect on who they really are,' said one backstage ally from the MTV Video Music Awards, 'but the problem with Brit is that her troubles went public, and that projected an image that was a travesty to the essence of who she is.'

Wherever I go, she is talked about as someone who is immensely likeable and great fun. It seems the harsher judgements passed down on Britney were, in the main, generated by media commentators and faceless bloggers. Such is the consequence of the human spirit when constructed into a brand that people view as faulty product. But the one thing I've learned is that no one is tougher on Britney than Britney herself. Within the privacy of her own counsel, she sits with self-berating judgement, keen to learn lessons and remind herself to 'keep thinking positive'. Positive thinking is her shield from the dark moods that can consume her.

There is also an emotional depth to Britney that few appreciate. She might not be someone who can easily articulate herself, and she may just be a simple girl from a small town, but in her own mind she finds a simple connection with words, lyrics and poetry, which she expresses on paper. It is her way of making sense of the madness. In moments of quiet, she'll analyse *everything*, then toy with words, which she scribbles in her journals in looping handwriting, attempting to reflect her mood of the moment. She is passionate about maintaining a journal – it's her one true confidante.

Britney is today a young woman and mother-of-two searching for an identity away from her music and fame. And yet she's searching for her own sense of self, while simultaneously fighting back to redeem the brand.

Hollywood celebrates 'comeback kids' who once stared into the abyss, like actors Robert Downey Jr. and Mickey

Rourke but few redemptive stories are as compelling as the rise, fall and fight back of Britney Spears. Her life has commanded a level of curiosity that refuses to loosen its grip or avert its gaze. In 2008, Yahoo announced she was *the* most popular name entered into its search engine – in a year that saw the momentous election of Barack Obama. It is evidence, if such were needed, of a fascination of Princess Diana and Marilyn Monroe proportions.

'She is by far the most powerful celebrity on this planet,' was how she was once described by ABC's chat show host and American Music Awards compere Jimmy Kimmel.

Anyone with an ounce of compassion cannot help but wish Britney all the best in her current resurrection. She has clawed her way back from the edge, pulled by the rope of people's good wishes. No doubt such public empathy is drawn because an entire generation has grown up alongside her music from 1999 onwards. In America, the pre-teen set of the nineties shared its pubescent years with her as she broadcast daily into their front rooms via *The All New Mickey Mouse Club.*

Most likely, her ardent following is because Britney embodies the dreams within every girl who has ever posed with a hairbrush for a microphone in front of the mirror that becomes a TV camera. She represents a billion dreams with which those dreamers identify. And then, of course, there are the boys who became men, entranced by the girl in school uniform whose provocative image enticed their equal adulation.

Within the enduring brand that is Britney Spears, the canny marketing that mixes innocence with seduction has ensured that here is an artiste who has been shaped, sold and viewed as all things to all people. She has seemingly transported everyone on a journey into a collective fantasy about her dance with the devil called fame.

But it's also the tale of that old adage, 'Be Careful What You Wish For ...' because no one, let alone a teenage girl, is sufficiently wired to cope with such impossible expectations, not to mention the rabid attention of the paparazzi. Few families would be strong enough to sustain without injury the 'tornado' that leaves 'debris scattered all over' as mum Lynne Spears described it in her memoir, *Through The Storm*.

As Vanessa Gregoriadis wrote in the February 2008 edition of *Rolling Stone* magazine: 'More than any other star today, Britney epitomizes the crucible of fame for the famous: loving it, hating it and never quite being able to stop it from destroying you.' Such nightmares seemed impossible at the start of a story where the précis is simple enough: an angelic teenager from Kentwood, Louisiana, bursts onto the pop scene with '... Baby, One More Time' in 1998. A fledgling career goes meteoric and she is crowned the world's princess of pop. Fame and fortune take their toll and the wheels fall off a once unstoppable juggernaut after Britney marries and soon divorces an ex-dancer called Kevin Federline, mothering two sons, Sean Preston and Jayden James.

Devastated, Britney numbs the pain by keeping occupied, transforming herself into a party girl. She starts to court the paparazzi and rebels against her family, which leads to an infamous head-shaving incident, a mean-looking umbrella attack on photographers and a custody battle with her ex-husband. She then loses her custodial rights until the rock bottom moment plays out on our television screens: Britney being strapped to a gurney and loaded into the back of an ambulance, looking lost and bewildered as TV-news helicopters beamed spotlights from above and paparazzi trailed in pursuit. Cornered by her own demons, she had nowhere to turn but the psychiatric ward of an American hospital. It was a physical and mental breakdown not afforded the usual rights of dignity, like a bad episode of the *Jerry Springer Show*.

But it is the underlying causes, the elements not readily visible, which drive this story and provide an insight, which in turn helps us understand much of what has been played out. It is these hidden factors which this book attempts to explore within the unravelling story: where Britney came from, what drives her, what makes her tick, what has rendered her so fragile and what circumstances ultimately conspired to de-rail her. It is a raw story so no one should expect the saccharine taste of brand-driven publications. There are no villains in this story – and there are no heroes either. But I sincerely believe there's a huge amount of people wishing for a happy outcome to this endless saga and it is within this collective hope that the redemption of Britney Spears is rooted – and this book was born.

LOCATION: KENTWOOD, LOUISIANA

The hit song is in full-stride: 'I'm runnin' this like-like-like a circus ...' Six men sit at a bar, barely noticing Britney's lyrics. Two somewhat inebriated women close their eyes and sway on the empty dance floor, paying homage.

The song continues: 'Yeah, like a what? Like-like-like a circus ...'

I'm inside The Dub bar room in the Louisiana backwater of Kentwood, Britney's hometown, where there are no hip places to be seen. Outside, there's just pitch darkness. Inside, Billy and Sue from Starlight Entertainment are giving 'Circus' their best shot.

'Y'all wanna know Britney?' shouts the man at the bar, 'The sweetest kid, sweet as pie. She's alright, she's alright. She knows where home is.'

If anywhere is rooting for her, it is Kentwood. It is here that she relaxed ahead of the launch of her 2009 'Circus' tour in New Orleans, and it is here that she'll head once an expanding worldwide tour wraps. Then, somewhere between here and Los Angeles, Britney will retreat to consider writing an autobiography first teased in the MTV documentary, *Britney: For The Record*, in December 2008: 'I'll have a good book one day ... a good, mysterious book.'

Discussions have already taken place with publishers but plans remain on hold. Whether it happens sooner or later, one can only wonder how truly candid such a memoir can be under the control of the brand and the policing circumstances that come attached to her conservatorship. If her expressed attitudes of the past are any measure, Britney might feel like a prisoner writing a letter to the outside world, only for the guards to first check its content.

A true life story is always measured but the written word must be allowed to breathe with honest self-expression. I have some knowledge of the autobiographical market because, ordinarily, I'm a ghost-writer – that person who collaborates with a subject to translate their life into words. In that part-symbiotic, part-parasitic professional relationship between 'ghost' and 'subject', I'm granted an all-access pass to get under their skin, look through their eyes, get into their heads and capture their voice. It's been my job for six years now, and has transported me into the world of royalty, sport and music as a detached observer who has vicariously witnessed life and media storms from within the 'fame bubble', always able to walk away yet often stunned by its intensity and ferocity. It is a perspective which has taught me the vast difference between the sold or reported 'image' of a celebrity, and the truth of the actual person; the distinction between reputation and true character.

There is, of course, a sliding scale of 'celebrity' from A through to Z-list. But Britney's profile belongs in another stratosphere entirely, entering the realm of the iconic, where very few names reside. As much as many high-profile individuals talk about fame, few know what this level entails. It attaches twenty or thirty paparazzi lenses to your coat-tails, every day of the week, following and scrutinising your every move; a Home Office curfew-tag that diminishes personal freedom to such an extent that the only place to find true sanctuary is corralled by the four walls of your home or hotel suite.

Fame zooms in and magnifies every expression, foible, flaw or mistake and holds it against you for life. It clocks every bad skin day, every dimple of cellulite or extra pound on the hip or thigh. If you beg, scream or cry to be left alone for just one moment, it captures this and turns it into a headline of weeping, crisis, heartache or woe. Victoria Beckham once summed up this reality during a conversation at the World Cup in Germany 2006 when she said: 'It is like a jacket that's stitched to your back forever. Once you've put it on, there's no taking it off.'

As a ghost-writer I hope to bring about an empathy that belongs more on the celebrity side of the fence, informed by the books I have written, the environments in which I have found myself, and the trusted circles into which I've been invited. As I've discovered, Britney's circle is harder to get invited into but I have met her once, for about ten seconds, back in October 2003.

She was a guest on Channel 4's *Richard & Judy* show. A client had just finished recording that afternoon's programme and we were in the Green Room for after-show drinks. Both Richard and Judy, and executive producer Amanda Ross, were on their toes, awaiting the arrival of the pop princess herself, ready to present her with a pink designer handbag and matching bracelet. I found myself waiting, both fascinated and curious, with a small group of pre-teens at the window overlooking the car park. I knew she'd arrived when a presidential-like cavalcade swept in, and this 22-year-old stepped out of an SUV with what can only be described as a 'Ready Brek glow'. Her star-like radiance was somewhat obscured by the rolling bubble of hefty bodyguards in which she was cocooned. I moved into the corridor near the front entrance and she couldn't have been more gracious with everyone. I said 'Hello', she said 'Hi' and that was the full extent of our memorable chat, which in my world has gone down as The Day I Met Britney.

I wasn't the only one rendered giddily star-struck that day. Just ask former US Secretary of State Madeleine Albright. She, too, had been a guest, promoting her memoir. But when she saw her dressing room was adjacent to Britney, Bill Clinton's hardened chief diplomat suddenly came over all soft. She asked that a photo be taken of her door nameplate next to that of 'Britney Spears' to impress her grandchildren. Such was the power of Britney's fame.

With this book, it is my intention to reach behind the curtain and into that dressing room: to peel off the mask and discover the person inside. But a true understanding of character requires an expert analysis of both Britney's childhood and life, and I'm no expert in such psychological matters. With this in mind, I have consulted a psychotherapist known for her spiritual and compassionate approach in dealing with clients in Hollywood. Like actors, psychotherapists are ten a penny in this town. But within the quantity, I've found quality via informed recommendation. This lady, who has clients in the entertainment industry, cannot provide an in-depth and 100 per cent accurate analysis that would ordinarily be derived from one-on-one sessions. However, within the discoveries embedded in

Britney's life story and the information gleaned from discreet sources, the insights that emerge will, I hope, encourage a compassion that gets people thinking about this story in terms of Britney the person, not Britney the act.

For four hours a week, for three months, I sat on the psychotherapist's couch 'as Britney' in an attempt to get inside her head, and look through her eyes, based on all the information that was collated. Therapy, by its nature, is challenging because it often faces a wall of denial in the truth that it asks individuals to face. One thing I can state categorically: therapy – and the insights it stirs – provides more hope for Britney than returning her to the stage.

Of course, in Hollywood, it is the entertainment value that counts. Publicists and promoters are retained to prop up the facades. These are the 'The PR Generals' employed to defend, mitigate, deny and obfuscate when human frailty starts to unstitch a carefully woven celebrity image. Britney's cry for help in 2007–8 meant her image fell apart at the seams. No longer could she maintain the act, leaving behind elements of truth that only a psychotherapist can properly discern.

For obvious professional reasons, the psychotherapist has asked not to be identified. It is, she says, the insights that matter, not the messenger. As you read on, you'll notice her guidance and opinion throughout, marked by indented paragraphs, and in italics. This differentiation is deliberately designed to set apart my voice and that of the expert.

Aside from her couch, I have also sat with and interviewed the people who best know Britney, having worked with or shared friendship with her, witnessing the person at close quarters backstage. You'll note, too, that many discreet sources have asked not to be identified. Such is the level of paranoia within Britney's controlled world. But through their eyes and unique accounts, I hope a better picture emerges of the girl still struggling to be a woman as she continues to hold our fascination.

Britney wants to be loved and is desperate to be happy. If she can't say it out loud, she expresses it in the big heart shapes that she doodles on paper and the large smileys she draws. That's her one aim in life: big hearts, permanent smiles. In her 2002 publication, *Stages*, she said that if anyone really wants to understand who she is, they should go talk to the people who know her best.

With this in mind, I set off for America to explore the life of the idol that friends simply refer to as 'Brit-Brit'.

Steve Dennis
Venice Beach 2222
Los Angeles 2009

Britney
Inside the Dream

Home
Sweet Home

'Kentwood's in my heart. I'm a country girl.'
– Britney, 1994

They call it the 'Boon Docks' – the middle of nowhere. It is only when you have stood in the rural remoteness of Kentwood, in the vastness of Louisiana's pinelands, that you begin to understand two things: the very obscurity from which Britney Spears was plucked and the sheer determination required to even get noticed by the show-business radar. Britney might as well have screamed her dreams from the middle of the desert.

The entertainment worlds of Los Angeles and New York seem light years away on the country roads and when walking beside the creeks. This region is a flat, sparsely populated landscape of pastures and woodland, broken up by little pockets of hamlet towns, connected by narrow backroads; sandy veins webbing across endless greenery.

Modern-day life is serviced by Interstate 55, running north from its starting point on New Orleans' outskirts in a 70-minute drive to Kentwood, transporting visitors deep in-land. The 55 is the 'hurricane evacuation route' out of the city that remains haunted by Hurricane Katrina but aside from such emergency circumstances, there seems little reason to even contemplate a visit – unless you're a die-hard Britney fan or a member of the paparazzi.

Louisiana is a state sandwiched by Texas to the west and Mississippi to the east – a thick, giant 'L' on the Gulf of Mexico coast, with stifling summer heat that can reach 38°C (100°F) within 90 per cent humidity. Kentwood lies on the top ridge of the L's lower section. There, it relaxes in its rocking chair on a state-line porch, with Mississippi out front and Louisiana out back, minding its own business in the twilight zone between states. Stay too long, not far from the Mississippi River, and you'll dream of Huckleberry Finn wandering by, thumbs braced in dungarees, spitting dust into the dirt. Set against Britney's conservatorship case, it is something of an irony that Huck himself searched for freedom away from the guardianship of Widow Douglas.

First-time visitors almost certainly rock up with preconceived notions of *Gone with the Wind* and then struggle to match the reality with the fiction, or fathom the idealised version of what Britney Spears' home town is supposed to be like. Kentwood is part of the Britney legend, the first facade encountered. Over the years, its projected image is that of a clean-living, God-fearing, conservative-church town, which upholds the strictest Christian values. Such a description conjures up an image of a joyous Britney running down the hill in her Sunday best, like Laura Ingalls in *Little House on the Prairie*. But the truth is a little different.

In fact, Kentwood's roads travel a surface-deep reality covered with asphalt PR on one hand – and then the more raw, less polished under-belly; the scratched truths before the gloss is applied. This is the beginning of a thread of a noticeable show-don't-reveal pattern, from grass roots to celebrity pedestal.

Kentwood is home to just under 600 families, according to the last consensus. The Spears are one of them. Population is barely above the 2,000 mark, the average income is estimated to be around $17,000 (about £12,000) and the average house price is $70,000 (about £40,000). It is a hard-working, low-income town – deeply human, truly organic.

If you blinked coasting north along Interstate 55, you'd miss its entry point off Exit 61 – the last exit before the border with Mississippi, 5 miles away. Liverpool lies to the left, Kentwood to the right, turning onto the local Route 38. In many respects, it's like driving into a location that time forgot; a place caught between the interstate and the tracks of the Central Illinois railroad that cuts through en route to Chicago.

Three budget stores – Dollar General, Family Dollar and Super Dollar – come up on the right, alongside a local supermarket and volunteer fire station. Further into town, there is Kentwood Cafe, Connie's Jewellers, Schillings Pharmacy and two small banks. There is a store that sells guns, ammunition … and toys, and then a truck and tractor parts shop. Almost all retail shops are metal-fronted, constructed of corrugated iron with metal roofs. It is a cheaper, quicker way to build, and these roofs will better withstand the storms that often threaten. Residential streets don't have names, but letters of the alphabet: Avenue A, Avenue B, Avenue C, Avenue D and so on, with not a two-storey house in sight. Most homes are set back from the roads on scraggy grassland: ranch-style bungalows, 'double-wide' mobile homes or 'cracker-shacks' – rickety-looking structures built from plywood and elevated on brick-built stilts. Everyone else lives on farms or bungalows within the mass acreage of Tangipahoa Parish. Wheel-less cars and truck shells have taken root where they rust. It becomes instantly clear that this is the lower-end of the socio-economic spectrum in the rural US, and the poor relation to Hammond (26 miles away), McComb (15 miles) and Amite (10 miles).

Two main roads dissect Kentwood: the 38 travelling east to west and feeding off the Interstate, and Highway 51 running south to north to the state line with 'Ole Missy'. Their meeting point creates the only crossroads with a single over-head stoplight that sways in a stiff breeze. A traffic jam is when four cars wait on red. It's at this crossroads where the paparazzi loiter with intent.

'It's not hard to pick out the Spears' family,' said one snapper. 'You see Lynne's white Land Rover or a Lexus on roads where everyone else has a GMC or Chevrolet truck, compacts or rust-buckets.'

Turn left at the lights and first right into Main Street and Kentwood's true decay becomes all too evident. This was once the hub-and-buzz of the parish with a drive-in, cinema, bars and restaurants.

'People used to come here just to be seen but what y'all seeing now is Kentwood's slow death,' said one veteran. He remembers a thriving dairy industry that once supported 200 farms but the arrival of Wal-Mart in surrounding towns soon put milk-plants and dairies out of business. Only 10 dairies are said to survive and for the past 20 years, the town has been in gradual decline. Today, Main Street is the thoroughfare of a ghost town. Not one shop has survived along its 100-metre stretch. Every window is broken, buildings and roofs have crumbled, the gable-ends collapsed in a pile of brick and debris. Amid this dilapidation and neglect, one starts to question whether the pop princess really does originate from here. It is hard to marry such glaring decay with the impossible wealth of its famous daughter. But then, by way of confirmation, the visitor is confronted by a Disney-like sign on the town's outskirts reading: 'Kentwood – Home to Britney Spears'. On first impressions, it seems the towns-folk are mighty proud of their girl who, along with bottled Kentwood Spring Water, put this parish firmly on the map.

Not that it seems to have done much good.

No one has yet been entrepreneurial enough to launch the 'Britney Tours' guide but it would be easy enough to organise by following the footsteps that trace back to an ordinary past. What used to be Granny's Deli is on the street corner where Britney once assisted on weekend mornings; also the First Baptist Church where she sang in public for the first time; her favourite restaurant – Nyla's Burger Barn; the bungalow of Kentwood Museum which celebrates her roots within its own memorabilia exhibition and then her former childhood home: a brown-brick, ranch-style bungalow with three bedrooms and two bathrooms.

It is tucked away off a side-road, backing onto dense woodland, and lies behind the immaculate Greenlaw Baptist Church, where the family attended Sunday service. There is the backyard where Britney's trampoline was housed and a driveway where her brother Bryan practised basketball on the hoop above a carport. Often Britney came barrelling out the front door as she performed cartwheels and back-flips on the front lawn, putting on a show for her neighbours, the Stricklands and the Reeds. On the adjacent land, a large, high barn stands derelict in overgrown grass.

Times have, of course, changed and Britney's fame and fortune allowed her to build her mama a property called 'Serenity' and this is where Lynne Spears continues to reside, 6 miles away. There is also a detached guest-house for when Britney visits. Serenity is a piece of Beverly Hills built in a backwater of Louisiana, providing a permanent reminder of the dreams that can exist beyond Kentwood's horizons. This immense home would be an ostentatious eyesore if it were built in the town's centre, but it is discreetly hidden away in 7 acres of pine woodland, set off a narrow country road.

It also proves one truth about Kentwood life for the Spears clan: no matter how successful life might appear, there is no leaving this foundational bedrock. Here, they are tethered by generational roots that have grown deep into the red earth, bound by a sense of community that makes everywhere else seem distant and foreign. Whatever glamorous façades are erected, whatever the trappings of wealth afforded, they remain deeply ingrained as country folk.

Behind the church, Britney's childhood home is tenant-occupied these days, but it's still the place visitors seek out. Kentwood's proximity to the state border is evidenced by the property's very location – a short run, hop, skip and a jump to Mississippi, where the homey pavilion of Nyla's Burger joint sits on the main road and celebrates its near-neighbour with an entire room decorated in memorabilia. Even the menu boasts: 'Britney Spears' favourite family restaurant'.

Then there is Kentwood Museum, a converted funeral parlour near the relic of Main Street, where curator Hazel Morris showcases Britney's career to date. It was first opened in 1975 to honour veterans of war and Britney's grandparents take pride of place – Jamie's dad June Austin Spears, a former sergeant in the US Air Force in the Korean War; and Lynne's dad Barney Bridges, a technical sergeant with the US Army during World War II. With 66 headshots to a frame and 15 frames around the walls, Kentwood's contribution to America's freedom is evident.

In another section of the room, among these men, are reminders of 'The pin-ups who went to war': Veronica Lake, Lana Turner, Vivien Leigh, Jane Russell and Barbara Stanwyck. It seems apt that the door adjacent to this display leads through to the area celebrating the modern-day icon: Britney Spears. She dominates three separate rooms and everything the eye sees used to hang on Britney's walls until dad Jamie decided to loan to the museum in 2000: platinum record plaques, framed magazine covers, family-framed photos, childhood dresses and awards – MTV Awards, American Music Awards, a CD: UK trophy, and awards from *Smash Hits* and *Hollywood Reporter*.

If visitors are not arriving as fans, this town is automatically on the back-foot. The official speed limit is 35mph, but locals drive 25mph so anyone travelling that 10mph faster provides the giveaway that an outsider is in town. Heads turn and beady eyes take note. If the local sheriff spots the number plate of a rental car, the 'suspicious' invader will be asked to pull over and some searching questions will be posed.

Locals have one another's backs covered, and everybody knows everyone's business. It is the essence of a close-knit community that many city-dwellers would find alien. But if your intentions are good, and you tread respectfully, then people shake your hand and give you the time of day, consistent with good old southern hospitality. These are down-to-earth, hardworking and honest folk, the working rather than educated type. There's no tolerance for idealising, moralising or posturing but there is warmth to their simplicity and an enviable contentment. Here, working life is authentic, insular and raw. Its small-town sensibilities don't contemplate the filters that would ordinarily check conversation that might shock and offend. The social rules are simple: if you don't like it, keep moving on through.

Whether or not they know you, questions will always be respectfully answered in a thick southern accent – 'Yes, sir' or 'No, ma'am'. They will address you as Mister or Miss, as a title attached to your Christian, not surname. If an 'Alan Jones' wanders into town, he'll be greeted as 'Mr Alan'. Should his wife Mary join him, she'll be 'Miss Mary'. The vernacular and attitude belongs to a bygone age.

In Britney's younger days, there used to be at least six drinking holes but now there's just one: a rough-and-ready pavilion, once called the VFW (Veterans of Foreign Wars) but, now decommissioned, it is known as 'The Dub'. From the outside, it resembles a mini-warehouse with its window-less, corrugated iron structure. Local laws mean it has to hide its neon-Budweiser signs inside. The Dub is the community gathering point and it's the kind of joint where all eyes turn to the door when an outsider first enters and walks into a wall of automatic wariness. It's the same at Country Boys, a bar 14 miles away in another cultureless land, attracting people from both Mississippi and Louisiana, and it's a tribal feel that becomes a recipe for regular brawls: 'Mississippi's in tonight,' one local warned, 'it's going to break.'

For many men in these parts, decompressing after six days' hard graft on the land or faraway refineries, the week is not complete without several beers and a good fight. They are not afraid to tell you that fighting is regarded as a release of pent-up energy. Men – and women – will even fight among themselves when bar banter is fuelled by alcohol, spilling outside into the gravel parking lots. The next night, those same combatants will sit down, share a beer and recount the incident with laughter.

Until recently, each patron had to sign in at the front door of The Dub, but it still remains advisable to walk in with someone with whom the locals are familiar, otherwise you'll be invited into that same parking-lot and asked what your business is. Those who 'don't belong' include lone outsiders, the paparazzi and African-Americans. Locals regard The Dub as Kentwood's white-bar. The black-bar, 'The Sugar Shack', is further into town.

At Kentwood High School, only a handful of white faces can be seen in a predominantly African-American enrolment. White families tend to send their children out of town: to Amite's Oak Forest Academy or Park Lane Academy in McComb, Mississippi – Britney's former school. Both these private schools, which come with relatively affordable fees, have good educational standards but there is no escaping the fractious attitudes concerning race. State segregation may be illegal now but segregation from choice remains a way of life. They will tell you it's no different in countless other areas of middle America.

All around the town, frank conversation about colour and creed is not for the ears of the easily offended because there is an unapologetic use of the word 'nigger'. It forms an everyday part of many people's vernacular; the legacy of generational hand-me-downs which has left a deeply-entrenched mind-set among people who don't care for worldly experience, or what the world thinks. But it seems to be a powerless mind-set, as indicated by the 2002 election of the first non-white mayor, Harold Smith, erstwhile assistant principal at Kentwood High. Now there is talk of a new dawn and increased integration.

Smith is the Barack Obama of Kentwood with a Herculean mission to alter hearts and minds. He travelled to Washington to witness the President's inauguration in January 2009 and returned to write a piece in *Amite Today*: 'It revived my spirit and motivated me to return home to share the necessary ideas and feeling of hope and change to benefit all people, regardless of background ... because there is no place like home'.

A mother who knew Britney from school, and still talks to the star's cousins, is quick to point out that, 'Britney knows how people talk but she don't agree with it. She's had black friends, management, dancers and bodyguards. It don't matter the colour of a guy's skin.'

It would be unjust to apply a broad brush and say this one issue sums up Kentwood. In fact, whites from Mississippi are viewed with just as much suspicion as blacks But it remains a social indicator of the background in which Britney has grown. Inevitably, her fame has broadened her own perspectives and afforded her a life education that few will sample. But Kentwood is also where she feels safest and most known. In her 2008 MTV documentary, *Britney – For The Record*, she referred to her 'meltdown' and wondered out loud why she didn't seek out its sanctuary and serenity of home: 'You would think that I would have gone home … I think back now and I'm like, "Why did I, in that fragile state, why didn't I just up and go to Louisiana?"'

Her aunt Chanda McGovern, formerly married to John Mark Spears, explains: 'People here love Britney for Britney, and nothing else. People see past all the fame and celebrity, and accept her for who she is. Kentwood is where people have got her back covered, where she has all the love and support she needs. Whatever the image of Britney, she is a country girl and Kentwood's own.'

Kentwood takes its name from Amos Kent, an early settler who established a brickyard and sawmill to kick-start the lumber industry that survived until the early twenties He was also a confederate rebel, jailed for not swearing allegiance to the US during the American Civil War; a leader of a unit within the 12,000 Louisiana infantrymen who served the Confederate Army of Northern Virginia. Kent was one of 'Lee's Tigers', which earned the sobriquet 'The Fighting Tigers' because its soldiers were rowdy, fearless drunks whose behaviour was tolerated because of their immense achievements in battle, according to historian Arthur Bergeron. That work-hard, play-hard, fear nothing attitude is just as prevalent today and the 'stars-and-bars' of the Confederate Flag fly just as proudly in this town as Uncle Sam's stars-and-stripes.

There is little to do for children growing up there. They become accustomed to a southern life of playing and hunting in the woods. Basketball and football are the main pursuits for boys and the girls' focus is basketball and also cheerleading before settling into early domestic bliss.

The roads are so remote that fathers will ride with their children sat between their legs in the car, in front of the steering wheel; they ride with children on their laps in the same way as many dog owners do with their pets. When Britney became a mother and attempted to transfer this practice to the roads of Malibu in 2007, she soon realised a Louisiana way of life won't wash elsewhere. But that incident served to highlight the conditioning influences spilling over from her childhood.

Kentwood is a hunt-shoot-fish town but it's not 'country life' in the same fashion as England's tweed jackets and picnic hampers, or Balmoral shoots. Men throw a rifle and ice-packed beer in the back of their trucks and hunt for deer and rabbit, sitting in 'deer-hides' – wooden shacks where they sit to hide from the deer. They'll then return home and throw a 'crawfish boil party', thanking God for the catches they've snared.

For God is one of the chief grandfathers of this 'Bible Belt' town. His presence is observed in the community and in locals' vernacular. The Spears family merely had to walk across the road from their home to Sunday service. Christian values formed the backbone of Britney's upbringing and education. The way that Mum Lynne explains it is that they are not a religious, but deeply spiritual family and yet they are strongly tied to the Christian faith.

As a child, Britney kept a prayer journal and was encouraged to have discussions with God and confide in her local pastor. Of course, as a child, it is easy to nod one's head in blithe acceptance of a faith that perhaps holds more of a worship indoctrination than actual *meaning*. Britney almost certainly found pleasure in the 'performance' and rituals – the ceremonies that would ultimately allow her to showcase her talents. Yet, regardless of meaning, she was obviously influenced by the beliefs instilled in her by her elders.

What she was told, she believed. So, when Britney went to bed each night, she believed God was watching over her and that everything happened because of His higher reasoning. He was her mainstay. Indeed, this is illustrated as she grew up and found her dreams coming true, blessing Him for the opportunities she had, acknowledging His guidance in the albums she made and believing He places obstacles in our way to make us stronger. Britney's early-stated philosophy on life was that: 'He has a hand in everything, good or bad. It's all part of God's plan.'

In a book penned by Britney and Lynne together, called *Heart to Heart*, Britney wrote: 'I pray all the time. I find a lot of comfort and strength in knowing I can talk to God and He's listening. That's the way we were raised.' On the wall above her bed, she hung a cross-stitch of the 18th-century prayer:

Now I lay me down to sleep
I pray the Lord my soul to keep
If I should die before I wake
I pray the Lord my soul to take.

Each night before bed, Britney wrote down her thoughts for 'God to read'. Her jottings complete, she kneeled at her bed and prayed, hands steepled in prayer. Then she reached under the blue, glass-plated bedside lamp and turned out the light to disappear into dreamland.

2

The Inner Child

'Dancing and singing all the time …
Like a little girl should.'
– *Britney, 2007*

Kentwood may well have counted as home, but Britney was a girl who yearned for faraway places. She was, say friends, 'always different' and came across as a day-dreaming introvert, absorbed in her own thoughts.

Often she found places to go that were a million miles from her woodland playground, running toward secret locations where she felt happy and in control. This is something Britney learned to do from a tender age: to step into self-created bubbles that distracted her and denied access to insecurities she didn't yet understand; allowing her to avoid a confrontation with a childhood far more distressing than has previously been acknowledged.

In getting to know Britney, one soon learns that it was in such day-dreamy places that the escapist performer was born and as will become clear, her hunger to perform was as much a coping mechanism as a desire to entertain. It was in a corner of her vivid imagination that she first located *Klickitat Street*, a place where '… growing up was the slowest thing there was'. All she wanted was to sing and skip, and say: 'This is a great day … This is a great day!', wanting to be universally popular. It was a make-believe world that she dived into, as created by children's author Beverly Cleary. Britney immersed herself in the adventures of her protagonist Ramona Quimby, a brown-haired girl with brown eyes and no cavities, perfect in every sense. Britney was, in her own words, 'obsessed' and cites her favourite book among the titles as *Ramona the Pest*, who '… struggles to make a place for herself in an uncomprehending world'. Just like Ramona, Britney Spears always wanted to fit in and be accepted.

Ensconced in her bedroom, lying prone on her bed, with her legs in the air, she jumped into the pages and then rushed into the bathroom – directly opposite her door, on the other side of the hallway – armed with her doll collection and teddy bears. There, behind the locked door of this mock VIP room, she lined up twelve dolls and six bears in the sitting position as her pretend audience; she perched and stood with the bath's edge as her stage and then performed before a giant mirror on the wall (her television camera), using a shampoo bottle as a microphone. In a town where everyone listened to Dolly Parton, Randy Travis and Reba McEntire, she belted out hits from Mariah Carey, Whitney Houston and Madonna. In that box of a bathroom, she was, she said, 'the biggest star in the world – bigger than Madonna.'

At the age of five, Britney set her sights high and 'rehearsed' in that little room for hours on end, cut off from – and unconcerned about – the rest of the household.

'Brit-Brit, please keep it down, baby,' Mum Lynne pleaded from the wood-panelled kitchen.

'BRITNEY! You'd better shut up this minute!' yelled her brother Bryan from the couch in the wood-panelled living room.

Whether Dad Jamie heard her at all was debatable, but the bathroom door remained locked and Britney kept entertaining her dolls, focussed on the world where her singing blocked out everything and everyone else. In that zone, she found her entrance to a Narnia-like world of music, applause and uninterrupted bliss. That perhaps explains why, even to this day, she'll sing in the bathroom, usually while soaking in the tub surrounded by candles, because, she says, you can't beat the acoustics. It is the same in elevators, minus the candles. A lot of what Britney experienced and was influenced by as a child would continue to make its impression known in adulthood, from the trivial to the emotional, to the deep psychological imprinting which effectively began from the moment she was born.

Britney's official birthplace is actually 15 miles away, across the state border in McComb, Mississippi. She was born Britney Jean Spears on 2 December 1981, a daughter to boilermaker Jamie Spears and wife Lynne, who worked as a day-care supervisor; sneaking into the world six months after a certain Lady Diana Spencer married Prince Charles in another fairytale that was just beginning on the other side of the Atlantic. The royal marriage didn't merit a mention in the *Kentwood News*, unlike Britney. When she was eight months old she made her first headline: 'BABY OF THE WEEK: A Scoop of Happiness'. A black-and-white photo showed Britney, wide-mouthed with a baby's laughter, above a caption that read: 'Happy Baby! That's me!'.

Dairy farmer's daughter Lynne couldn't contain her excitement over her 'extremely active, precious bundle of joy' – her first daughter and a sister for four-year-old son Bryan. Family lineage on both sides had always produced boys so she'd yearned for a girl, no doubt to repeat the mother-daughter bond shared with her English-born mother Lillian Portell, who emigrated from London in 1946.

'You can imagine how excited I was,' Lynne recalls in *Heart to Heart*, 'an adorable baby girl to dress up like a little doll! A daughter to have little tea parties with!' It seems a strange, child-like reaction for a mother to have, recognising the accessory and companion before the actual child. There is no doubting the genuine joy Lynne felt, or the doting adoration she heaped on her second child, but embedded within that natural reaction is the first sign that Britney was unconsciously regarded as an object or a possession; an attitude that would follow her through life. She was a living doll back then as much as she remains a commodity today. Such an unintended insight suggests Britney was objectified from the moment she was born. As the psychotherapist consulted says:

> Lynne reveals much with her response to Britney's birth because when people don't have a sense of self, they tend to objectify others and babies can be viewed as 'dolls' to fulfil a parent's need to be merged with their child, and to be in control of love. But when this happens, there tends to be trouble ahead. It's almost as if Lynne was telling Britney, 'You're going to be my love object, and all my needs are with you.' And she wanted everyone to know how happy this first daughter made her, showing her as 'Baby of the Week'.

The honey-coated pedestal was already being prepared. Around the same time, Lynne's sister, Sandra Covington, also gave birth to Laura Lynn. Though cousins, she and Britney grew up side by side as if they were twins, sharing the same crib by day, wearing matching outfits, and attending dance recitals together. The family photo albums are filled with pictures of Britney and Laura, always hand in hand, wearing identical dresses, nightgowns, tutus, shoes and hairstyles. The girls played dress-up, and often did so with garish make-up and adult attire, all dolled-up to the mutual delight of their mothers. They even had the same toys and gifts to open at Christmas, so that they wouldn't feel as if they were being treated differently. But Britney *was* different.

The family recognised her precocious talent and, within their community, friends and neighbours commented on the little girl's gifted voice and rare agility. At friends' houses or the farm of Lynne's brother Sonny, a three-year-old Britney often showed off a dance routine acquired through watching a toothpaste commercial on television.

'Go on, Brit-Brit, show 'em what y'all can do!' encouraged her mother, uncles and aunties.

'I'm convinced that baby was born with a microphone in her hand!' said museum curator Hazel Morris, who has known Britney since she was born, 'she really was the sweetest of children, who shone from day one.'

From an early age, Lynne was both curious and perplexed by the bundle of energy that she sometimes struggled to contain. Britney was 'the doll' that wouldn't sit still – jigging, singing, dancing or cartwheeling around the house, on the trampoline in the backyard, in the back-seat of the car or across the front lawn. She only ever seemed to stop to watch favourite TV shows, *Growing Pains* and *The Wonder Years*, or to continue the adventures of Ramona Quimby.

Lynne's best way of harnessing that irrepressible energy was to find suitable outlets: the Renee Donewar School of Dance in Kentwood, and gymnastics lessons in Covington, 55 miles away. Her daughter attended classes three nights a week and every Saturday.

Britney's first dance class was at the age of two and her first solo on-stage recital came at four. Dance teacher Renee Donewar described her as: 'unusually driven, focussed and a perfectionist.' Here was a girl, who for some inexplicable reason, was determined to perform and throw her heart and soul into being the best by turning in foot-perfect recitals. If there was a new technique to master, Britney mastered it; if there was a new dance routine, she owned it. She was clearly one of those potentially annoying, but gifted children who wanted to outshine everyone, with a poise, intent and concentration that belied her years. It therefore surprised no one when she often earned the Best Attendee in Class awards. As she grew older, Britney would write out scorecards and judge her own performances with marks out of ten. Then, as now, she was her own worst critic.

In gymnastics, she walked away with trophies and medals for impressive floor shows, and went on to win her junior level at the State Louisiana Gymnastics competition, performing a triple back-flip followed by a somersault in her lucky, all-white leotard. From the age of six to nine, Britney excelled, and different coaches suggested she had what it took to go all the way; a budding Shawn Johnson of her time. But when such high hopes led to more gruelling practice, and when the fun of performing became secondary to the need to work, her enthusiasm popped.

'Mama, I don't want to do this anymore. It's too hard,' she said one day. Gymnastics never provided the same buzz as performing, she later admitted.

For Jamie and Lynne, this represented a dilemma because they had witnessed the excellence of their daughter's talent and agility, and felt she was abandoning great potential. But they saw how fed-up it made her, compared to how her face lit up when she danced or sang. Even though it went against their better judgement at the time, they backed her decision. They didn't wish to push her down a particular road, regardless of pleadings from coaches.

Nor were the Spears keen to push their daughter down the road of that showy American culture: the beauty pageant. Ever since the 1850s, these competitions have provided a somewhat cosmetic approval-bar. It is a culture which encourages dressing six-year-olds up as adults, with full make-up, building up an emphasis on image and beauty. One sour experience was enough for Lynne to realise the 'horror' of the system when Britney, who was painfully shy when not engaged in performance mode, lost out and finished almost bottom in a local 'Little Miss Something' contest.

Lynne was adamant her daughter would never again be made to feel ugly or rejected by the values of image and image alone. She always wanted Britney to know that it is someone's qualities and attitudes that make them beautiful, not their looks. If there was one person in the world who could wipe away Britney's tears and put her back together again, it was her mama. The irony, bearing in mind what she would ultimately be marketed as, was that the Spears family had vehemently railed against a pageant system primarily built on beauty as a commodity. Yet that's exactly what their daughter would become: a marketable, image-led commodity; dressed up like a doll for the pop industry. Then again, Britney wouldn't finish near the bottom of the table in the music industry as she did at the pageant. The Spears would argue that her success as a pop star was based on talent, not looks alone; that she is a performer, not a walkabout prop.

In recent years, a lot of emphasis has been placed on the fact that Britney was more performer and dancer than strong vocal talent. That suggestion seems hard to accept based on people's recollections and what is evident in archive footage. It seems more like a well-embroidered argument promoted to mitigate the fact that the modern-day Britney lip-syncs when singing live; that she is more entertainer than great singer. But anyone who witnessed her sing as a child – and during 1999–2001 – can feel rightly perplexed because she literally blew audiences away with her voice. On-lookers couldn't help but get the chills when she sang as a child, with a mature quality and depth. She might not have come near the natural ability of a Christina Aguilera but she was nevertheless impressive. Let no one say Britney cannot sing live. She can. Or, more pertinently, she *could* … back in the early days.

She first stepped up to the plate in public at the First Baptist Church, aged four, holding a microphone bigger than her own forearm and immaculately turned out in a floral, conservative-church dress. It was Christmas 1985 and she sang the carol 'What Child Is This?' to the melody of 'Greensleeves'. The congregation was stunned by the voice that emerged from the youngster. Lynne was told that her daughter was 'Broadway-bound'.

Of course, she was as proud as punch but no one actually believed the toddler would get anywhere. No matter how talented, no matter how powerful, this voice would always be lost within the vastness of Middle America. Lynne simply did what any proud mother would do: she encouraged Britney to keep on singing.

Mum scoured local newspapers for talent competitions. If everyone was telling her that her daughter had a talent, then Lynne felt an urge to show it off. After all, Britney had given up on a natural flair for gymnastics and her mama didn't want another talent to go begging.

One year later, Britney ended up winning a singing and dancing competition at the Kentwood Dairy Day Festival. She went on to win another competition in Lafayette, a two-hour drive away, singing 'Sweet Georgia Brown', and soon added first prize at the Miss Talent Central States contest in Baton Rouge. Soon enough, talent-contest rosettes, certificates and trophies vied for space on the mantlepiece with gymnastic medals and golden statuettes. Britney's sense of self-worth was being pampered with much attention, admiration and acclaim, albeit on a local scale.

Aunty Chanda – who was in Britney's life from 1991–8 through dating and then marrying her uncle, John Mark Spears – fondly recalls her niece's voice: 'Oh Lord, she was better back then than she is today. She needs to recapture her natural voice because that child could sing, let me tell you. She had a gorgeous voice, one that sent chills through everyone who heard her. She was breathtaking, and don't let people tell you no different.'

Britney was the star turn at Chanda's wedding to John Mark in 1993, at the Nazarene Church in Magnolia, Mississippi. Wearing a floral frock, she took centre stage to sing the Naomi Judd hit 'Love Can Build A Bridge'. Chanda said: 'Actually, she sang it better than Judd. It was a special day to have my niece singing to me, and there were tears rolling down people's faces. Guests who didn't know her were in awe, saying, "That young one's going somewhere."'

Even Britney was recognising her abilities. She recalls that she deliberately chose songs that 'highlighted my range and how powerful my voice was.'

Steve Hood, a dance instructor in Baton Rouge who worked with eight-year-old Britney, remembers: 'I didn't exactly meet her the first time she came to our dance studio, but I certainly heard her. I was coaching one of her friends in a group class when we suddenly heard this powerful voice echoing through the building. When I went to check, there was Britney in the middle of the corridor outside our class, singing her heart out. Why? Because she felt like it, I guess.'

The more her daughter's voice was heard, the more Lynne was impelled to do something about her talent. She has always sworn that Britney's '… real … astonishing … powerful sound' could blow the roof off a house in the days before she was given a 'super-produced pop voice'.

As Lynne scoured the south for fresh opportunities, Britney simply kept plugging away, almost nonchalant to ambition. Despite numerous talent show triumphs, she wasn't transformed into a petulant brat demanding success. Quite the opposite, she remained humble, impeccably well mannered and always responded to elders with a respectful 'Yes, ma'am' and 'No, sir'. Oddly enough, when she wasn't performing, Britney acted more like a shrinking violet; she seemed only comfortable in groups of people she already knew.

She was a diligent and well-behaved kid who was 'a fine example to her folks,' according to local consensus. 'She was raised right by her mama, and knew right from wrong,' said Aunty Chanda, who has since divorced John Mark, 'Britney was a kind-hearted, down-to-earth country girl who liked to kick around in her bare feet and play. I can still see her wrestling with the other kids, giggling and laughing on the grass. I'll tell you, she was as good as gold and respected her elders – she was the model child.'

What becomes clear is that Britney placed as much faith in adults as she did in God. What her elders did, she watched and learned; what they told her to do, she did. She was someone who always seemed eager to please.

This trust-all-elders mentality was imbibed at her private school, Park Lane Academy, further down Highway 55 into Mississippi where Britney, dressed in a red-and-blue uniform with a 'P' as its embossed emblem, would take the yellow school bus or jump in a neighbour's car, for the 25-minute drive. It was some drive to take each morning but Jamie and Lynne were determined their children would receive a good education. Jamie, a former pupil of Kentwood High, wanted better for his kids.

Park Lane is a one-storey building of corrugated iron with an impressive football pitch and bleachers, and it has a strong reputation in the area. It cost around $200-a-month to enrol Britney as well as Bryan. Rules were aplenty in the wood-panelled classrooms, where teachers stood at pulpit-like wooden lecterns adorned with a crucifix at the front.

Red rulebooks were issued each term, instilling Christian values and beliefs, and teachers issued guidance such as: 'Thank God for all your many blessings. He gave you a brain and expects you to use it!' or 'Give God your best and he will help with the rest'. For Britney, such teachings merely mirrored her mama's beliefs. Already she had learned the power of the Lord at home and so it wasn't surprising for her when each school day started with a Bible reading and prayer.

There was nothing particularly extraordinary about the young Britney. She happily joined in with others and had a healthy number of friends. Always diligent with her homework, she kept her textbooks immaculate and non-creased. Her recreations outside school – aside from singing, dancing and gymnastics – revolved around go-karting and basketball.

The dirt tracks and sprawling plains is where Britney, like every other child in the area, could be found bombing about in her own motorised go-kart buggy. Where most people grew up riding bicycles, most kids in Kentwood had go-karts or ATV quad-bikes, zipping around the community in little packs.

'She'd join all the kids out in their go-karts, seeing how fast she could go and how much mud she could get on her!' recalls Aunty Chanda.

The family would often convene at Jamie and Lynne's for two reasons: first, Jamie was known for cooking up a mean crawfish boil party and second, whenever bad storms knocked out the electricity, they were the only ones with a generator. But on Sundays after church service, it became a family tradition in Britney's early years for everyone to visit the home of Jamie's dad, Papa June, who built his all-wood property with his own hands. He had a reputation in the area for tearing down old houses and 'making 'em beautiful'.

It resembled an afternoon at the Waltons when the Spears and the Bridges, and all their children, gathered around a wooden, oval table for early Sunday dinner. When the meal was finished and the plates cleaned, everyone knew the routine: Papa June would make little Britney climb onto the table and sing his favourite song, 'Amazing Grace'.

'I can see her now,' recalls Aunty Chanda, 'stood in the middle of that table, singing just beautifully, and everyone was woo-hooing. Then she'd climb down and run outside to play.'

Another place to find Britney was the local basketball court on summer evenings. She played point guard for her school team, wearing the No. 25 shirt: 'I loved it,' she said, 'I could play basketball all night long, but would have to be up in the morning to help out at Granny's Deli.'

Lexie Pierce, Britney's great-grandmother, ran the deli. The place is now a lawyer's office and she has since passed away but Britney turned up at 9am on weekends, eager to work, shelling crawfish and crabs before manning the cash register and cleaning tables. Locals can still visualise her to this day: expert at shelling, singing while she worked, and her hands in a bucket of crawfish, pulling off the legs and heads, preparing them. There was great demand for Granny's crawfish and Britney was the eager assistant.

She was meticulous in everything she did, not just preparing crawfish and performing. Within the home, she strived for perfection, too. She made her own bed and kept her little bedroom pristine by folding and stacking clothes into neat piles. Her school uniform was laid out on her day bed for the next day and she organised her doll collection into well-ordered groups. These twelve collectibles were a prized and well-groomed gathering of pale-faced porcelain dolls, vintage looking with blonde, Annie-style ringlets and sparkling glass eyes. Lynne bought her one each birthday for twelve years. She had one Cabbage Patch doll but no Barbies, and there were six teddy bears, brown or white.

Dolls and bears filled a table and chair plus all shelves of a white wooden bureau, where she sat to pen her prayer journal. It was a small, box-sized bedroom, all white with a single yellow rose on each top drawer to her bureau, dressing table and chest of drawers.

Britney herself was immaculately dressed, pristine as any one of her dolls. Family photographs from the early years are quite telling, depicting a girl who couldn't relax for the camera, but instead felt a natural compunction to pose with the grace of a ballerina and a smile that seemed more exaggerated than natural; a child on her toes, being perfect. Praised when she danced; praised when she sang; praised when she back-flipped; praised when she posed; praised for being such a good girl. Britney grew up to the sound of applause – and no one applauded louder or prouder than her mama.

'Lynne always knew there was a big wide world out there beyond Kentwood. It was the English blood in her! She wanted to be like her mama and Britney's grandma – a true lady,' said a life-long friend of the Spears and Bridges.

This man doesn't only know Jamie and Lynne but has a fond history stretching back to a friendship with Lynne's parents, Barney and Lillian. During three different meetings, he talked of a family pedigree and its influences that offers intriguing insights into Britney's make-up.

The matrimony of dairyman Barney Bridges and his English war bride Lillian Portell means that Lynne Spears and her two siblings were half-Louisiana, half-London. Among the locals, there was a sneaking suspicion that such extraction left Lynne with a natural air of being 'slightly better than the rest of us' and that opinion wasn't expressed in a bad way.

'It's in her genes!' laughs the family friend.

In deepest Louisiana, the sound of a British accent bestows on any such visitor the automatic assumption that one is classy and sophisticated; quintessentially proper. Unlike New Orleans, New York, LA or Orlando, Kentwood is no tourist hot spot. The sight or sound of someone from England remains alien to locals, as if they've just wandered in from the set of a romantic movie. Talk, and they break out in a smile. English people are viewed as a mesmerising delicacy from a faraway land. If that is the case today, imagine the reaction that Lillian Portell received when she stepped off the boat on Barney Bridges' arm in 1946, with papers stamped in Tottenham.

The lifelong friend recalls: 'We thought British royalty had arrived. She was like Princess Margaret. She dressed and talked proper, and always called tea at four o'clock. She was a novelty but a wonderful lady.'

Lillian had been a typist at the Law Stationery Office when she met US soldier Barney at a dance in London. As he swept her round the floor in full uniform, he wooed her and projected a new life away from blitzed London, where he owned land in a little place called Kentwood. No one could have blamed Lillian for equating mass acreage with wealth back then; Louisiana's equivalent of the landed gentry. But all romantic visions of *Gone with the Wind* must have died the moment she arrived at the farm, where everyone toiled and sweated in the intense heat of the Deep South.

The family friend remembers her arrival: 'If she hated it, then she said nothing. She might have seen land but it was worth nothing. It was dirt land, and the house was no more than a big shack. This was the great new life she'd left home for. That girl pined for home, but she stuck with it and worked damn hard.'

Lillian's sister Joan Woolmore views the situation some-what differently, sensing that Barney was a 'domineering' man who wouldn't allow his wife to return to Britain because of the fear she might never return.

'Mr Barney didn't encourage visits, let's put it like that,' says the friend, 'but they had a dairy to run and there was no time. Lillian didn't whine. She loved Barney, and she stuck around to raise a family and raise her calves.'

There is no one in Kentwood who would deign to say a bad word about Lillian. Her Englishness and warm heart are fondly remembered. One lady, who often visited the dairy to share afternoon tea, remembers Lillian causing whispered disdain at Sunday church service when it was discovered that she breastfed Lynne: 'Back then, breastfeeding was a no-no. It was not thought appropriate and was frowned on, but Lillian's attitude was, "If it's good enough for England, it's good enough for Kentwood!" and she just carried on.'

Breastfeeding wasn't the only aspect of British life that she introduced: 'She brought Lady Di into our lives. When she married Prince Charles, Lil had us all sat around a television watching the wedding. It took a lady to know a lady. Lil's English accent was better than music,' she laughed.

Lillian introduced words like 'bloody' and 'blooming' into Kentwood's vernacular, and people were fascinated with her intonation of certain words. 'God' became 'Gawd' and expressions of surprise such as 'Oh My!' became 'Good Lawd!' Even though she was from London, her accent might as well have been from Windsor.

According to those who knew Lillian, young Britney was fascinated by her grandma's accent. She was forever taking it off and disappearing into an English accent; it was all part of her repertoire. Lillian's old friend said: 'Britney thought there was something proper about being an English lady and, because of Lil, she listened to all those stories about Princess Diana.'

What's telling about this insight is that when Britney's troubles were witnessed in 2007, paparazzi and television footage recorded her 'speaking in a bizarre English accent.' It was reported as a worrying indication of mental illness; Britney was somehow losing the plot. People in Kentwood smiled at such reportage: 'Britney's been doing that since she was a kid, putting on the old English.'

'She's an impersonator – it's what she does,' said the life-long friend. Perhaps this also explains why, in later life, Britney would have a terrier dog called London.

Those who remember Lillian suspect that she believed that her children – Sonny, Sandra and Lynne – should do better than she herself had done. In many respects, this is a normal wish for any parent, but Lillian's belief was flavoured by her sure knowledge that there was more to life than Kentwood, the place that had failed to match her dreams.

Back to the friend, and the opinion is clear: 'Lynne was born with a silver spoon up her ass because she was English. She's a great girl but she always wanted better, and that's got a lot to do with Lillian. That belief must have filtered down.'

Only Lynne and her siblings will truly know the influence of the private encouragements that were given, but when Lillian's somewhat limited circumstances are taken into consideration, it rings true that their mama might have whispered a bettering belief in their ears.

Naturally, when Britney was born, Lynne instilled in her daughter that she was capable of anything if only she had the passion to follow it through; if she wanted it badly enough. 'There is nothing you cannot achieve' was the message being gently drilled into Britney because 'There is more to life than Kentwood' was the subtle message Lynne herself had received.

Lynne was exceptionally close to her mother and forever longed for a similar mother-daughter relationship. It is not surprising therefore that she was never far from Britney's side in a bond that was inextricably fierce. One was lost without the other. Lynne could 'never be without' her daughter, and vice-versa. Indeed, Britney always wanted her in close proximity; needing to see her through the window of the gym-hall door, eager to catch her encouraging nods of approval in the wings at talent contests. Britney, it seemed, could only perform under Mama's enthusiastic wing. When her routine was complete, her eyes darted to catch the only gaze that mattered. In return, Lynne's face beamed back with pride.

It is in this parish, and from that past, that a snapshot picture of Britney starts to come into focus: a typical Southern belle who carried the Bible's teachings within her innocence. She was a mother's pride and joy, with a shyness that belied her need to perform; the bashful, all-American girl, who could not have seemed happier or better behaved. It's doubtful there was a more talented, picture-perfect, sickeningly content girl in the whole of Louisiana.

At least, that's the rose-tinted version of Britney's childhood. But first appearances can be deceptive. Because all that excitable energy, early perfectionism and those regular retreats into a self-created, make-believe world spoke of something much deeper being stirred within the child, especially when viewed alongside the demonstrative talents so eagerly displayed.

The sweetest child, it seems, had learned to indulge in a constant mode of performance: singing loudly in the bathroom, in the backyard or on the trampoline; being Little Miss Perfect at dance recital; the trophy winner in gymnastics; the perpetual first place at talent contests and the voice that amazed people whenever she sang.

All these images form a performing montage that brought attention and approval, and it was that attention that soothed the young Britney, allowing her to feel good, to feel extra-loved. Why the constant mode of performing, though? As the psychotherapist queries:

> As with most personas presented to the outside world, they tend to be a front to a hidden story of what is actually stirring beneath the surface. From the moment we are born our behaviours are influenced by environments into which we arrive. And

if a child's behaviours are not the result of being taught but are instinctive, then it is most likely a reaction shaped by what the psyche has experienced, both before birth and in early childhood. So where Britney was described as a bundle of energy, I'd query whether observers were actually witnessing a bundle of anxiety in a girl whose energy had its origins in nervousness, not excitement. Where we see a child so young striving for perfection and being so tidy, I'd suggest she was trying to control the outside of her life because she felt so out of sorts on the inside. Where we see a child disappear into a self-created, make-believe world, I'd examine the domestic reality she was trying to escape. And when someone is seemingly engaged in a perpetual performance, I'd wonder what unconscious needs are motivating that need to perform, and for whom the performance was aimed to please – Britney or her parents?

Such questions become valid when we go beyond the surface-deep reality of Britney's upbringing: the deeper truth and the roots to our understanding lie behind the slammed doors of the family home.

Britney was not born into a stable home. She was born into a dysfunctional disorder created by a father whose heavy drinking turned him into an alcoholic whose rages primed a family to live on its nerves. This created a bundle of nerves within Britney that others, including her own mother, would then mistake for natural excitement or energy. In fact, it was more likely the reaction of an anxiety-ridden child in need of constant activity to block out the unholy din and drama surrounding her. Though too young to realise it, here was a girl whose need to perform masked such imperfections, allowing her to escape the distress.

But what isn't known is that Britney almost wasn't born at all. Lynne had already given up on her husband and marriage, and filed for divorce in 1980. And it is those legal papers that provide the backdrop to the flip side of Britney's childhood, offering insights into the adult she would become, and the father who would become her legal guardian under the 2008 conservatorship.

3

Sins of the Father

> 'Mama, do you want to live like
> this for the rest of your life?'
> *— Britney to Lynne Spears, 2000*

Through the Storm was the title of Lynne Spears'
memoir about coping in a world of fame and tabloid
headlines. Perhaps it would also be an apt label to
sum up the strife and struggle within the household as Britney grew up. Indeed, in the year preceding her conception,
it was already evident that Lynne was emotionally and
psychologically defeated by her husband's behaviour.

In her memoir, she admits filing for divorce before Britney's birth, without detailing why. The clear impression is
that her reason was solely because of Jamie's drinking. Yet
this masks the true background; a history that Lynne clearly
isn't keen on forming part of the Britney Spears' story.
Instead, after acknowledging the 'wrecking balls' and upset

Jamie's drinking created, she reflected that the first five years of their marriage were 'an oasis of calm and happiness in our often turbulent life together.' But that's not the story contained in the legal papers she served just three years and six months into their union.

Lynne filed for divorce on grounds of adultery. This, perhaps, explains why she had no desire to reveal the finer details, going no further than mentioning gossip about his 'flirting' at bars. Intended or otherwise, by not mentioning infidelity as the reason behind her divorce petition, the focus remains on Jamie not her; on his addiction, not her desirability; his irresponsibility and not the humiliation she felt when he chose to have sex with someone else – and in their marital home.

According to the petition, Jamie committed adultery on the evening of Christmas Day, 1979. Heartbroken and livid, Lynne wasted no time in consulting local attorney Lou Sherman. Eight days later, and on the first working day after New Year, she submitted a detailed petition to the courts It was this stormy prelude that foreshadowed the 'dysfunctional marriage' that Britney was born into and, as will become clear, this would prove to be a highly relevant event.

For Lynne, the betrayal followed a prolonged period of enduring her husband's 'benders'. In her book, she lays bare his alcoholism and told how he'd gone missing on Christmas Day morning as she and two-year-old Bryan waited to open gifts. When he didn't show, she packed a bag and went to her mother's. There must have been a furious row because Jamie clearly realised he'd be spending Christmas alone and that Lynne had deserted him. If she didn't know what her husband would do, she soon found out.

In her petition, she makes allegations of cheating, and told how Jamie was seen entering one of his regular hangouts, a

Kentwood bar called Baby Tate's. But he went in with a local woman who Lynne named. Inside, it was claimed, he was 'observed hugging, kissing and fondling this woman throughout their stay'. From there, she writes, they went to the Spears' trailer, 'where he committed adultery ... during the late evening hours of December 25th and the early morning hours of December 26th.'

And therein lies another truth that has never previously emerged: the origins of the Britney Spears' story can be traced to a trailer park where the family had their first home. Simpson's Trailer Park, located off Highway 51 in Kentwood, two minutes from the state line with Mississippi, was where matrimonial life began for Jamie and Lynne. Lot No. 13 housed a cramped but cosy trailer that Lynne had helped fill with appliances and furniture; it was their first purchase as a couple along with a 1979 Chevrolet, a 1978 Dr Lincoln Continental and a 4-wheel drive pick-up truck. One trailer and three vehicles represented their humble beginnings. It was here that the family lived with their only son, and it was here that Jamie was alleged to have marked Christmas with his lover.

A friend who has known the Spears since they married said: 'Y'all must understand. Miss Lynne is mighty proud. Image and reputation matter, especially since she's become known as Britney's mama. She don't want to be seen as "white trailer-park trash" because that ain't Miss Lynne. She's always wanted to be viewed as a lady.'

Just like her English mother, Lillian.

Trailer-park homes and little shacks on the roadside are the norm in Kentwood and no one bats an eyelid over such realities, but perhaps its juxtaposition alongside Britney's stardom felt uncomfortable for Lynne Spears. Britney wasn't to spend a single day of her life in a trailer, but if anything, these beginnings further enrich the family history.

From a trailer park to 'Serenity' is far more inspiring than from ranch-style bungalow to 'Serenity'. It illustrates how far the Spears have travelled in the past 30 years.

According to the legal papers, the trailer belonged to Lynne. In fact, she was greatly worried that Jamie would damage it, and her furniture, when he learned she was filing for a divorce. She clearly feared his temper and she even alluded to what he was capable of when drunk. In that same petition, her attorney said: 'She fears the defendant will become angry when served with these papers; that he will harass and/or physically harm her, especially if he has been drinking alcoholic beverages, as he has done in the past.'

Those words, 'as he has done in the past', form the first-known mention of Lynne going further than saying that her husband was merely an alcoholic. Here she was, telling a court that Jamie had harassed and/or harmed her previously. She was also making it clear that she sought the court's protection and Lou Sherman sought a temporary restraining order.

The use of restraining orders would become something Jamie would utilise to protect Britney in later life but back in 1980, his own wife sought to exercise those same powers against him. Indeed, if this was the extent of Jamie's temper, it might go some way to explaining some of Britney's reported reluctance at him being installed as her conservator in 2008.

Lynne was loath to leave Jamie because she dearly loved him and she'd been vehemently opposed to divorce, living in a less nonchalant era when the very idea was frowned upon within a Baptist community. So the fact she actively sought a decree nisi illustrates how desperate she had become. Her friends have suggested it was an overreaction in the red mist of betrayal but in that January of 1980, it could not have seemed more final. She sought a custody order over Bryan; $200-a-month child support and $400-a-month alimony; and declared to the courts an intention to find her own place. Jamie was ordered to attend a hearing on 1 February to explain himself and state his case.

For Lynne, this sad episode marked the end of the fairytale in which she'd described their union as 'the Barbie and Ken of Kentwood'.

It was a fairytale that began in the spring of 1976. Lynne's maiden name was Bridges and she was a 20-year-old student at a community college renamed Southeastern Louisiana University in nearby Hammond. She was an education major who met Jamie Spears, 23, at a local swimming pool in July 1976, after skipping summer school. He was relaxing from his 'tough-ass job' as a boilermaker – a trained craftsman who fits, welds and constructs steel plates and sections on projects as diverse as bridges to blast furnaces. By then, he was used to going where the contracts were: from Louisiana to New York, Missouri to Memphis.

Spears was considered as quite a catch by the ladies: it wasn't just that he was regarded as 'high, wide and handsome', he was renowned for being one of the region's finest athletes, basketball and football players; the all-round sportsman whose abilities are still remembered to this day.

'He could shoot the basket with one step over the centre-line, let alone the shooting zone. Let me tell you, when you've got black basketball players complimenting the skills of a white basketball player, then you're somebody special – and Jamie *was* that man. He was also a mean quarterback. That big son-of-a-bitch would have had some career if someone had punched him between the eyes and made him focus,' said one ex-peer, who believes, 'the reason for Jamie's ultimate downfall was Jamie himself'.

Another friend who has known Jamie since schooldays said: 'He should have made the big-time. He was one of Kentwood's finest but could have been much more.'

Lynne was smitten, swept off her feet by either the man or her romantic ideals. However, the same could not be said for her parents, Barney and Lillian Bridges, because they knew what everyone else knew: Jamie had been married before. In Baptist Kentwood, getting together with a once-married man could bring a shame that was community-sent. But local archives prove it was much more complicated than a blotted copybook, and 'Mr Barney and Miss Lillian' could be justified for harbouring real concerns for their daughter's welfare.

Lynne has since described her husband's first marriage as 'a brief union that was over almost before it began' but Jamie married a 'real beautiful' woman called Debra Sanders in December 1972 and it lasted a good three years. Jamie was said to be head-over-heels in love, but he inexplicably upped and left on 10 May 1975, according to legal papers served by Debra. She claimed he 'abandoned' her despite the fact she'd been 'a faithful wife, given her husband no cause for mistreating her and always tried to make him happy.' He denied abandoning her. Friends say he felt 'suffocated'.

One year later, with reconciliation unlikely, Debra sought to terminate their marriage. It is interesting to note that Jamie denied all her allegations and said that he 'pray[ed] that the demand of the plaintiff be rejected.' He submitted his denials to the courts on 14 July 1976 but the following day, the divorce was granted.

Fifteen days later, on 29 July, Jamie Spears married Lynne Bridges.

On the evidence of these concrete dates, they met, dated and married within the space of two weeks. The only other possibility is that they met while Jamie was still technically married but that was surely never the case in their Baptist community. Whichever way it is viewed, this headlong rush into a union will have been frowned on regardless.

No wonder the Bridges were alarmed. They always felt their daughter could do better, not to mention the fact that she was in the middle of her studies, with one year left at college. The family were 'good stock' and 'Miss Lillian' felt her daughters Sandra and Lynne deserved quintessential gentlemen who knew how to treat a lady.

Sandra's husband Reggie, a financial wizard who went into banking, won their approval. Jamie, the once-married boilermaker, did not. He was known in the community for his 'crazy' ways; the work hard, play hard type, and it is highly unlikely the Spears' and Bridges' clans would ever have sat down to dinner together. It was the combination of chalk and fine cheese as far as Kentwood was concerned.

That might explain why Lynne chose to elope to New York and marry in Oswego, where Jamie was working a short-term contract. She sacrificed her fantasy of a fairytale wedding for a quick registration formality, without parental consent. In an action that Britney would copy in later life, she was defiant and rebellious. Nothing would come between her and her man.

In her mind, she was being responsible, choosing to be a mother and set up home with the local hero who, in her eyes, was capable and solid.

Nine months later, their only son Bryan was born.

Lynne was a mum aged 21, and couldn't have been happier. But the arrival of their first child triggered something within Jamie and his capable mask began to slip.

All boilermakers will tell you that the unforgiving work and hours in intense heat require the reward of a cold beer to unwind afterwards. But Jamie's cold beers turned into drinking binges. He often staggered home with a tongue poisoned by alcohol to belittle and berate Lynne. His slurred insults and frightening temper chipped away at his wife's confidence as he criticised her efforts around the home and mocked her intention to finish the studies interrupted by Bryan's birth. Then, in the mornings, he'd sober up and tell Lynne he couldn't live without her. He would change, he promised; he would quit, he insisted. Lynne, demonstrating the classic response of a co-dependant, believed him.

Her need to retain this man in her life was no doubt aided and abetted by the grief she experienced over the loss of her father, two years into the marriage. Barney Bridges was killed on the family dairy farm when his milk truck rolled over. It crushed him as he attempted to jump to safety. Jamie's response to the tragedy was to disappear for a week. But even then, and understandably, Lynne didn't have the will or strength to let go of the only other man in her life. Grief conspired to pin her to the spot, despite the protests of her sister and mama.

She soldiered on as a mother and student, finally completing her education diploma in 1979, leaving Bryan with his widowed grandma by day, but it was obvious to everyone that she was living in an intolerable set-up. Lynne covered up and excused her husband's behaviour. Her big heart misguided her into thinking that compassion was enough to save him but she was as much in denial over the truth as Jamie was about his drinking. Lynne felt a need to take care of her husband more than she wished to take care of herself, thereby drawing her into his web of addiction.

Then came the Christmas of 1979, and the adultery cited by Lynne.

After taking refuge with her mama, she seemed determined to make a fresh start going into 1980. For two weeks, she stood her ground and then took Jamie back. This meant he didn't need to appear in court to respond to her divorce petition and it was officially withdrawn on 26 March 1980. It was a legal irony that the attorney's daughter Jody Sherman went on to marry Jamie's brother Austin, ten years later.

Such is life in the small town of Kentwood.

Under their marital reconciliation, Lynne found it hard to contemplate turning over a new leaf in the trailer-home where the hurtful tryst apparently happened. Jamie had eyed some land further down the road from Simpson's Trailer Park, locating a property in need of improvement behind Greenlaw Baptist Church. By July 1980, no doubt flushed with his good earnings from short-term contract work, the young couple took out their first mortgage on the bungalow and an extra plot of adjoining land for a total of $34,750, putting down $18,580 in cash. This is the property that would become Britney's childhood home.

Lynne describes those first twelve months back together as 'a year of peace', and she happily fell pregnant with Britney. A new start and a new addition to the family became the redeeming factors in rebuilding the marriage, but it seemed hardly a stable set-up to those who looked on with concern. The emotional wounds caused by Jamie's infidelity can hardly have healed in twelve months; in fact, Lynne's suspicions were never slayed. Inevitably, from the moment Britney arrived in the world, she had an expectation unwittingly heaped on her shoulders.

Britney the Saviour had been born … Born to save her parents' marriage.

Britney was born into a loaded situation. From the moment she was conceived, she was charged with the unconscious purpose of saving the marriage. She was not entering a healthy environment; she was entering a fragile truce. Whatever the underlying reasoning, this marriage's hopes of happiness rested on Britney's shoulders. That unwittingly placed on her an agenda no one will have been aware of, but one that will have left its load imprinted on her psyche. 'Britney is here … this time things will be different!' was a hope projected onto her.

It's sometimes hard for the layperson to take in, but a baby picks up messages and detects every experience through the mother's own psyche, heartbeat and nervous system, and all that information is imprinted. Even during pregnancy, Britney will have 'felt' whatever anxieties Lynne faced. Was she right to give Jamie another chance? Would he keep his word? Would he be the father she needed him to be? Would he start drinking again? So when she's born, she's automatically at one with Mum, tuned into her anxieties. This would explain their intense bond. This inherent anxiousness would go a long way to explaining much of the nervous energy Britney exhibited, and the anxiety she would carry throughout life.

The family would mostly be unaware of these factors. Unconscious influences are responsible for many human actions and behaviours, though.

Britney has always said her childhood memories make her such a 'family person'. She once wrote on her website that she remembered watching movies with her family and 'feeling so at peace'. At other times, she has recalled her father's crawfish boil parties – Louisiana's equivalent of a barbecue – and her mama's specialities: chicken spaghetti and homemade ice cream. For breakfast, it would always be a southern favourite, cheese grits – 'breakfast for champions', according to Jamie. It would be inaccurate to suggest this was a continually unhappy childhood; clearly it was not. For Britney, this domestic environment represented the norm and undoubtedly she would have cherished those times when Jamie was present, loving and attentive, together with Lynne.

Indeed, Jamie was determined to embrace his second chance with Lynne, keen to be a better father and husband.

Friends of Jamie Spears describe him as 'a man with a big heart, a good soul but a stronger liver'. One lifelong friend in Kentwood, who wishes to remain nameless, jumps to his defence and says: 'If that man gets the chance to put things right when he's screwed up, he'll do all in his power to make amends. He'll do it to prove it to himself, to prove it to God and to prove others wrong. Whether he succeeds or fails, he gives his best.'

The general consensus is that Jamie is a 'stubborn son-of-a-bitch' with flaws he's all too aware of, but this 'does not make him mean-spirited by nature'. The distinction drawn is that between the great guy who is sober, and the crazy guy when drunk. Back in 1981, Jamie focussed on being that great guy.

There is a saying in Kentwood – 'Getting Right With God' – and Jamie repented of his sins, rededicated himself to God and undertook voluntary work at the family church. Prior to Britney's birth, he decided half his problems were caused by the stresses of work that took him away from home. So, with the money that work had earned, and after moving into the new family home, he and Lynne decided to build and open what she has referred to a 'health spa'. It sounds impressive, conveying images of a Champneys of the eighties. In actuality, it was a large barn with a metal-structured extension at one end, built on a plot of land adjacent to their home. Called 'Total Fitness by Jamie', the sign, in white lettering, was nailed to the double doors. To help fund this venture, they took out a further mortgage for $50,000 in 1981 and, suddenly, Kentwood had a gym with the latest running and weight machinery, a hot-tub and a steam-room. In truth, it was more gym than health-spa.

Nevertheless, it represented a brave move at a time when the concept of healthy living and wellbeing was in its embryonic stages, but Jamie had a vision. His life-long friend comments: 'Jamie worked out, and was entering and winning bodybuilding contests. The man was built like a house and he thought he could turn his business into the next Gold's Gym.'

For $300 a month, locals had somewhere to work out and, at one time, the venue attracted around 120 members. Initially, all seemed well but much as Jamie felt ready to meet his new responsibilities, he simply wasn't capable of doing so. Alcoholism's demons proved too strong to conquer alone and soon he was drinking again. As with Bryan, Britney's birth seemed to trigger this return to the bottle. Twice he had been ready to be a father, and twice that joyous event had sent him over the edge.

From this moment on, son and daughter witnessed regular slanging matches between their parents. Tensions were not helped when brothers Austin and Willie Spears moved in for a spell, sleeping in a treehouse that Jamie had built for the kids.

Jamie's friend has commented that sometimes it got 'nasty' between Jamie and Lynne: 'They were always at each other's throats, fighting like mountain lions. 'Course it was traumatic for the children; it had to be.'

In the family, Jamie earned the nickname 'Captain Red-Ass' because of his temper: 'He was the sweetest man and good as gold one minute but once you've pressed the wrong button, you best run and hide – and Lynne knew how to press the wrong buttons,' said Britney's Aunty Chanda. She

witnessed many storms pass through the Spears' household because, for a two-year spell, she lived with her
husband John Mark, Jamie's brother, in a trailer on land
near the house. Her observations are worrying and instantaneously remove the perfect-family image promoted
when Britney first shot to stardom. The truth is that what
Britney witnessed will have been deeply traumatic for a
child.

When the fights happened, Britney sought refuge in
Chanda's trailer. Her aunt paints a picture of a sweet, but
timid girl – it seems an environment of constant hollering
and verbal abuse rendered Britney quiet and withdrawn;
that's until she had to perform.

Aunty Chanda said: 'She stayed with us quite a bit to get
away from Jamie's drinking. It scared her. Jamie and Lynne
would fight about anything and everything, and the same
pattern would happen: she'd take off to her sister's or
mama's, come back, Jamie would quit drinking but then
he'd start again.'.

One night Aunty Chanda vividly remembers is when
Britney's brother Bryan was sleeping over at the trailer with
two friends. Jamie and Lynne's place was already full
because Austin Spears was temporarily staying over. The
next thing Chanda knew was a rapid knocking on her trailer
door – and there was Lynne, sobbing: 'Apparently, Jamie
came in after drinking, shouting and screaming at her.
Austin stuck up for Lynne, and then him and Jamie started
fighting. Lynne then took off and came to our house.'

Chanda McGovern points out that these were not
sporadic incidents. Far from a blessed home, the domestic
situation seemed blighted by the self-hate of an alcoholic's
love for drink and the reactionary dramas of his co-dependent wife. In the middle ground stood Bryan and Britney.
Now it becomes clearer why Britney often escaped to her

bedroom and the bathroom to dream of faraway places. 'All the kids would cling to Lynne, and I can see them now, wrapped around her or clinging to her legs. As long as they stuck close to their mama, they felt safe,' Chanda recalls.

To exacerbate matters, Jamie neglected the gym business and bills went unpaid. The situation reached a point where Lynne had to beg and borrow money from friends to keep afloat. It didn't help that Jamie was playing poker. Kentwood folklore states that one night, when a millionaire was in town, Jamie 'skinned' him for £3,000. This went down as the occasion when the boilermaker chased the rich man's ass out of town. But often, Jamie lost, and he lost heavily and then drank heavily to make up for it. His usual bar crawl involved visits to many bars that no longer exist: The Uptown Lounge, Baby Tate's, The Foxes Den, Tic-Tok and The Mulberry Bush.

The full extent of the Spears' poverty has never fully come across, but things became so bad that Britney would go to the fridge and find it bare. This wasn't just a family with money troubles. They were broke and often financially desperate. Britney has since told friends that 'people don't realise how broke we were'. It reached the point where Jamie had to wander into the woods behind the home and hunt food for dinner. On occasion, as Britney herself has revealed, that meant eating rabbit and squirrel. Against such desperation, tensions were understandably heightened. Britney's Uncle Willie – Jamie's brother – bore witness to some ugly incidents, including once at a family crawfish boil.

'Jamie was drunk and then tried to drive off with Britney in the car. She was no more than five years old. I tried to stop him, so I reached into the truck to grab the keys from the ignition and he punched me. We got right into it there by the car, fighting in front of her. Britney was jumping up

and down, crying. Lynne had to run out to get her inside.
We Spears men are known for fighting. If Britney happened
to be there, so be it. It's sad but it's what happened,' he said.
The true sadness is that no one realised what it was doing to
the children:

> If Mum is distracted by an on-going battle with her husband,
> can you imagine how that focus on Jamie, and all that time and
> energy spent fighting, will have affected the attachment with
> Britney? When both parents are 100 per cent committed and
> engaged with the upbringing of their children, a sense of value
> and strong sense of self is allowed to grow. But when the dad is
> emotionally and physically distant, and when the mother is the
> co-dependant consumed by his same troubles, it makes it
> tremendously hard for either of them to be 100 per cent present
> for the children, however much they think they are. As Britney
> matures, she will have especially asked herself of Lynne: 'Why
> did you put us through such misery?' or 'What made you so
> blind?' or 'Why weren't you stronger?' The truth is that Lynne
> probably struggled being on her own and was emotionally
> invested in a fantasy, trying to keep together the family she'd
> always envisioned. Back then, the deeper ramifications will not
> have been apparent to Lynne. She and Jamie were too imma-
> ture to understand the wider implications of their behaviour.

If there was one person aside from Aunty Chanda that Britney could count on amid the chaos, it was another aunty,
Sandra Covington: Lynne's sister and mother of cousin
Laura-Lynn. Aunty Sandra was a second mother and true
rock.

Throughout the mayhem of Jamie's alcoholism, and his
daughter's world fame in later years, Sandra was the safe
and wise harbour where both Britney and Lynne found
strength and eternal support. She was the lynchpin within

the family, and her role and importance in Britney's life cannot be over-estimated. Whenever Britney returned home when she became famous, her first stop was always Aunty Sandra's house. But she was as powerless as everyone else to do anything about Jamie's alcoholism. Inevitably, the family home – with Bryan and Britney at its centre – became an energetic field of pain, rage, and anxiety, all competing against the genuine love the parents had for their children.

Two undisciplined adults attempted to be parents within a self-created emotional chaos that enjoyed small windows of sobriety and calm. Lynne, by her own admission, lived on her wits end in a vortex of uncertainty and insecurity. Yet the enabler she became tried in vain to manage Jamie's alcohol intake, allowing him to drink only beer, not spirits, or suggesting days when it would be okay to drink. Many a night, when he was still out, she cried herself to sleep, worried whether he was with another woman, still plagued by his deceit of 1979.

Bryan and Britney witnessed everything: Dad's hollering, and Mama sat crumpled on the kitchen floor; Dad begging for forgiveness at her feet and Mama giving him yet another second chance. Such evident disorder and anxiety would have been transmitted into the very fibre of Britney's being as an impressionable girl who, together with Bryan, witnessed the example set by her two chief role models.

Jamie's brother Willie has also recalled a time when Britney called him to fetch her. 'She said, "They're fighting again – please come get me." It was rough, but the sad thing is that it became normal life. Once, I was over at the house and Jamie walked in drunk and called Lynne a bad name. She was in the kitchen drinking water and he grabbed the glass, walked into the lounge and just hurled it. At first, Britney was a scared child and you'd catch her crying but she reached the stage when she just walked off, as if it wasn't happening. As she got older, she would scream and curse at her parents, trying to get them to stop fighting.'

Considering the non-disciplined environment in which Britney was raised, this allows us to make better sense of the out-of-control self-destruction that she, too, would exhibit in adulthood. It also casts light on the present conservatorship where the contrasts are painfully ironic: the man who set an out-of-control example to his daughter and handed down the worst possible lesson in discipline is now the same man exercising control over every aspect of Britney's life, expecting her to show discipline.

But one thing is also certain: it is Jamie's own realizations about the father he was, and the mistakes he made, that are now driving him to make amends. His friends are unanimous: he is trying to save Britney from the same 'craziness' that marred his own life; he doesn't want her making the same mistakes that he made in his twenties. For him, the conservatorship grants a second chance to be a good father, and Britney one last chance to bring order to her life.

No one is more aware than Jamie and Lynne that all their children should have been spared such distress. With the wisdom of their years and the benefit of hindsight, in her memoir Lynne accepts that they fought too much in front of the kids and failed to contain the volatility of their relationship. She knows she should have dealt with such matters behind closed doors. Perhaps what she hasn't realized is that the long-term effects on Britney are untold:

When a child is caught in the middle of such rage and volatility, that child feels abject terror, and constant anxiety. It would have left Britney with a sense of always living on the edge, always zinging her nervous system. From within this unmanaged set-up the parents act erratically, impulsively and recklessly with one another. And this is the lesson handed down to the child. Such traumatic domestic environments don't feel safe to a child and they often emerge from the chaos as impulsive individuals with little concept of consequences, suffering from low self-esteem, great anxiety and trust issues. Also, the child's loss of respect for its parents, and the later resentments it can cause, cannot be over-estimated.

From all the domestic chaos an angelic little Britney would rise from the dust-cloud; the performer whose singing and dancing provided the one happy respite. From an early age, she would have felt the positive impact she brought – when she performed, her parents stopped fighting. Daddy was proud and her mama looked happy, no longer crying.

Through Britney, through her performing, this family found highs, triumphs and a distraction that they couldn't find on their own. Britney had found a way of stopping the rows that were disturbing, bringing everyone else out of their craziness and into a place of agreement. Performance became the answer, and she became the spark plug to light up the family with her talent – and her hope. So, instead of having an authority figure she could look up to, Britney's talents became the one thing that shone. As for Britney, as she asks, 'Who can I look up to in all of this?' She would have had to look outside the family and look to God, Madonna, a relative or a teacher.

Within this environment, it becomes clear that Lynne wasn't so much pushing Britney's talents but viewing them as an outlet for happiness; almost living vicariously through her daughter. A constant treadmill of dance recitals, gymnastic classes, vocal lessons and talent contests – and ultimately *The Mickey Mouse Club* – removed both mother and daughter from a house regularly filled with trauma,

distress and tears. Little wonder Britney's blossoming potential preoccupied Lynne because her romantic notions of
family life were going in the same direction as her mama's.

As for Britney, she discovered that performing was her
sole coping mechanism to shut out the quiet pain she must
have felt. It was in her self-made bubbles that her persona as
a singer and dancer was developed as a defence against the
anxiety inside the home:

> If mum and dad's life was so out of control, how could any child
> feel secure within that environment? So performing became
> Britney's one reliable source of pleasure and coping strategy.
> When she was in the 'performance', she felt free and safe; it
> provided a place which allowed her to disconnect from her real-
> ity. Consequently, to this day, performing will be her go-to place
> to which she can connect, avoid pain and find freedom. But in
> adulthood, in a mirror to her childhood, when she steps out of
> performance-mode, she's in disarray and confusion, and feels
> lost. Flash forward to 2007, and what shocked the world was
> that when Britney's façade fell away, she could no longer hide in
> a performance, or hide how out-of-control she really was on
> the inside. And we can trace that back to an out-of-control
> home.

It would be easy for people to pin the blame at Jamie
Spears' door, and judge him based on the raw evidence of
his alcoholism. But few hit the bottle for fun, and there's
almost always an underlying trauma that causes the addict
to find an anaesthetic to suppress their own pain. Often,
the root cause is some kind of trauma that the person has
never found a way to come to terms with.

In her memoir, Lynne wrote how people asked, 'if there
was some sort of trigger, a traumatic event' that pushed
Jamie into drinking. 'The answer is no,' she said, referring

to the duration of their marriage. On the surface, nothing was readily obvious. But it's accurate to say that each time he was 'dry', his return to drinking coincided with the births of Bryan and Britney. Fatherhood triggered something. And it is there, in his distant past, the most likely trigger-point can be found in a traumatic event that would break him as an individual and ultimately shape the world Britney was born into.

The 31-year-old woman had selected her perfect spot to die.

She had left the family home and driven to a cemetery three miles east of Kentwood. She parked her car before walking between the different burial plots, stopping at the graveside of a baby boy who had lived only three short days. Calmly, this mother-of-four sat down and rested against the small gravestone before removing her right shoe, revealing a bare foot. She splayed out her left leg across the grave and then checked the 12-bore shotgun was ready and loaded with a single shell. Satisfied and sure, she turned the gun inward, pressed it against her chest and pointed the barrel's end to the heart.

Then, using the big toe of her right foot, she pulled the trigger.

Emma Jean Spears – Jamie's mum and the grandma Britney would never know – had long imagined and planned this suicide. It was shortly before 4pm on 29 May 1966, the baking sun was out and she'd simply wanted the pain to end, having never come to terms with the loss of her baby son, Austin Wayne, nine years earlier in March 1957.

She had fought depression ever since, while trying to maintain a home for her three other sons and a daughter, and her husband, a former juvenile officer with the Baton Rouge Police Department. Britney's grandfather, Austin Spears Sr, told the local coroner that his wife grieved the loss of their son and had attempted suicide on three previous occasions.

The suicide made the front-page of the 10-cents-a-copy *Kentwood News* on 2 June 1966 under the headline: 'Find Body at Grave of Infant Son'. No one in the community understood how Emma Jean could take her life to be with the three-day-old baby boy she'd lost, leaving her four other living children, including Jamie, then aged fourteen, without a mother.

Although the tragedy took place fifteen years before Britney was born, it provides an insight into the man and father Jamie would become. In finding compassion for him within this event, there is opportunity to understand why he was so incapable of being a loving father and husband, no matter how much he wanted to be.

Can you imagine how broken Jamie must have felt? The sense of worthlessness and rejection is beyond ordinary comprehension. We don't know how close he was to his mother, but her leaving him in these circumstances would be a significant trauma. How could he not take such an event personally?

Pure, healthy maternal love is ordinarily the most important love from the primary caretaker, but his mother's love abandoned him. So his auto-response was likely to be: 'If Mum can leave me like that, what does that say about me?' It sends a misleading message that he's not loveable and not worthy, and becomes a source of great pain. Not only that, but if his mother was depressed for the nine years since her baby's death, she may have been emotionally and physically distant from the time he was six; as Jamie was emotionally and physically distant with Britney. Is this the reason why?

When a trauma like this happens, then future relationships can be affected because Jamie associates love with this trauma. Being attached to a woman could make him fear loss again; that if his mother could drop out of his life, so could his wife. This would leave him in a perpetual state of anxiety. The births of both Bryan and Britney trigger the memory of the birth of the brother who died – the event that led to his mother's suicide. He'll therefore equate birth with death, and this is what most likely tips him over the edge. In many respects, his responses were borne out of an intense fear of losing Lynne and his children. It wasn't the absence of love that meant he couldn't show up as a father or husband; it was the presence of immense pain. His behaviour, therefore, requires compassion because it was an addiction with its roots in a tragedy that wreaked havoc within him.

For a good time after the birth of their third child, Jamie-Lynn, Jamie was 'dry'. His exertions were applied to the gym. It was also here that Britney would wander in. Men in mid-work out, pumping iron to the sound of country music, still remember her switching the music to pop, dancing on a mat. Members objected but Jamie smiled, letting her be. As for the piece and quiet of the steam room, men would be sitting in their swimming trunks when Britney entered in her bikini. One ex-member recalled: 'She knew how to empty that room! She was doing vocal coaching at the time so she'd screech opera notes. It was like listening to someone gurgling water!'

Jamie's friends believe he deserves compassion, not judgement. When he drank, there was no stopping him but his sacrifices for the good were, they say, equal to his flaws. His life-long friend said: 'It all started going wrong again when Lynne and Britney went to Orlando. He backed it all the way but he was left alone and became frustrated.

Instead, he occupied himself with nights out in Hammond with a bunch of 25-year-olds. That man worked damn hard but never had a grip on his life.'

Jamie Spears lets few people close to him. He is a strong, impenetrable southern man. But one acquaintance, who knows him from LA, believes the focus on his alcoholism – as first detailed in Lynne's memoir – blights the truth of his love for Britney: 'No-one more than Jamie knows that he messed up, but he believes God gives people second chances. He's a decent, stand-up guy who refuses to deal in bad business and he doesn't really care what people think about him. He's faced tougher battles than contending with people's opinions.'

According to this friend, Jamie's home is a shrine to his daughter with her childhood photos reflecting a father's pride, and perhaps a regret for times lost: 'You want to see how his face lights up when he speaks about her. He'd spend all day showing you photos, if he could. His favourite memories are the vacations taken in Tennessee. When his mind goes back there, he has a massive grin on his face, and I've seen tears well in those eyes of his. He can't put back what's gone, but he can make amends.'

The Spears' family photo albums, and the recollections found within two books by mum and daughter – *Heart to Heart* and *A Mother's Gift* – bury the pain of Britney's childhood. They were published to run parallel with brand Britney, assisting the Stepford perfect image that was constructed.

When the cracks did show in 2007, and Britney imploded Lynne Spears was already writing a book on her own: *Through The Storm*. In total, she has co-written two books with Britney, and one on her own, no doubt making her the only mother in showbusiness to pen a memoir *before* the star herself. It is therefore hard not to draw the conclusion that Lynne is incapable of withdrawing into the shadows.

Perhaps when Britney's fame turned sour, Lynne felt the need to set the record straight, no doubt in response to a collective media question that asked: 'Where are the parents in all this?' Indeed, her memoir provides many rebuttals to the myths she wished to slay.

One such 'myth' is that she was the archetypal stage-mom, who pushed Britney into the spotlight. In this regard, she can rightly feel aggrieved. Britney's 'performing' and talents were self-created. Lynne was simply the mother who decided to trust the direction her daughter wanted to go, and hang onto the magic carpet.

But Lynne was always overly keen to publicly celebrate her special mother-daughter relationship. A showy declaration of a mother's love and pride is not only contained within the pages of three books, it was the very subtext behind Britney's childhood; a mother who lit up in the light and attention reflected off her daughter's talents. And this satisfaction would have filled the hole left by her disintegrating marriage.

What Lynne didn't feel as a wife, she felt as a mother. By her own admission, she says motherhood kept her sane. Her children were her salvation, reinforcing the burden unwittingly placed on young shoulders, and especially Britney's.

It's almost as if Lynne felt it was her purpose to find success for her daughter because she felt she'd failed in her own life. Britney was the hope amid the hopelessness. But the danger is that Lynne may have recognised Britney the performer, not Britney the child – her real self. Lynne, quite rightly, would say that she absolutely adored her daughter, provided all the love in the world and raised her correctly. That is not in doubt. What we are referring to here is the unconscious elements found in the undercurrents and the emphasis Lynne placed on Britney as a performer.

If the approval, the applause, and 'look everybody' attitude is what greeted Britney's talents, then that's the only value Britney will have associated with – the value of being 'seen' as the performer. Britney will have noted the sparkle in Mum's eyes and that would have been the validation she'd sought. In Britney's mind, performing provides an illusion that solves everything: it makes her feel stable and makes people around her happy. In turn, all this brings love, praise and hugs. But that mind-set actually becomes a burden because it turns Britney into a performing doll, performing to keep peace and happiness, as an antidote to the chaos.

The problem is this: Jamie and Lynne had no idea who they were as people and so cannot pass down any sense of self, or what that means, to Britney. One of the big ways we all form a sense of self is through mirroring our environment. Accordingly, she is being taught to identify with being a performer and builds a false sense of self. But what is home and who is she when not performing? This will be the source of Britney's confusion and the cause of great anxiety.

Lynne, too, will have realised that she felt good about herself for the first time in ages.

The unmet needs of an adult relationship can lead to a parent going to the child to receive those needs, and that child then feels responsible for those needs. There was almost an unconscious trade-off between Britney and Lynne. The vibe between both of them was, 'When I'm with you, I feel better'. Britney had another unconscious agenda placed on her – as the source of pleasure, and this further strengthened the development of a performer's persona. Mum placed her on a pedestal in her own mind, and within the community. I would simply ask, 'What other aspect of Britney was developed and encouraged away from the performer and her talents?'

Propelled by so many invisible forces, and the personal dream she held, the young girl with the cheesy smile and bright innocence was destined to push beyond Louisiana's borders. Something always whispered to Britney that her destiny belonged somewhere other than Kentwood. What no one could know was that Mickey Mouse was soon to extend a hand that would pull her to the next level, away from the disorder and towards 'stardom'.

4

Bridges
to Stardom

'It's just my time to express myself.'
– Britney, Stages, 2007

For one gloriously over-the-top but proud minute, it seemed as if Kentwood would declare a national holiday, such was the genuine excitement around town. But the Council Mayor settled for announcing an official 'Britney Spears Day' within the locality. Its talented daughter had been chosen as one of the performing 'mouseketeers' for the Disney Channel's *The Mickey Mouse Club*, a more razzamatazz version of Britain's *Why Don't You?*.

She had been selected from 20,000 hopefuls after her talents clearly stood out at an audition and judges issued an immediate instruction to sign her up. Such recognition would catapult Britney from Louisiana to Orlando, Florida, where the recording studios were located at Disney World, and where she'd reside alongside Mickey, Minnie, Pluto and Donald Duck, to name but a few.

Few locals could comprehend that one of their own had been chosen to star in the 30-minute television show, broadcast daily into homes throughout America. It created a distinct sense of occasion, and Britney had her first taste of merchandise produced in her name: one local made up T-shirts with a Hollywood movie clipboard emblem declaring 'Britney Spears Fan Club'. An artist hung an ink-portrait of child Britney in a shop window under a 'Congratulations Mouseketeer' banner. And a cardboard cut-out Mickey Mouse was posted in the same window, with a cartoon bubble saying, 'Presenting Britney Spears!' All around Kent-wood, shop owners displayed messages on their mobile bill-boards: 'Disney or Bust!', 'Congratulations Britney – We're Proud of You!', 'Disney-bound!' and, at Buddy's Seafood Place, 'Kentwood's Mouseketeer'.

There was a distinct carnival feel in the air as local news-papers and television covered Britney's achievement in a starry reflection on Kentwood itself. A special ceremony was held on the local sports field, where a large crowd gathered. Britney sang the national anthem and then, according to a report in the *Kentwood News*, '… brought tears to the eyes of all those present when she sang, "I Will Always Love You" by Whitney Houston. The Rotary Club's James Allen presented her a bouquet of roses, and the Chamber of Commerce's Gerald Broussard presented her with a commemorative plaque. Town mayor Bobby Gill went as far as issuing an official proclamation, which read:

WHEREAS the Walt Disney Corporation has, for the past 30 years, searched the United States for talented young people to become part of the organisation.

WHEREAS this year, for the first time, the state of Louisiana has had a participant chosen, and she is one of ours. We have watched her grow and her talents mature ... given with such warmth and noticeable enjoyment.

WHEREAS the people of Kentwood and surrounding area wish to give tribute to this well-deserving young lady as she continues her work in Orlando, Florida.

Therefore, I, Bobby Gill, Mayor of the town of Kentwood, do hereby proclaim, Saturday April 24 1993 BRITNEY SPEARS DAY, and invite everyone to applaud her accomplishments and wish her great things as she takes this next exciting step in her promising career.

Britney was just eleven years old, but long before that momentous day, there would be setbacks, tests of character and leaps of faith, together with hour upon hour of repetitive practice. Whatever propelled Britney, however, turned her into an unstoppable force, breaking down Kentwood's frontiers.

But before Mickey Mouse, there would be Broadway. Before Broadway, there would be a television talent show. Before the TV show there would be training. And before training, there would be rejection. Looking back in rewind to the journey of Britney's rise to fame, it all makes sense now: a line of stepping stones that would ultimately lead to the bridge from rural Louisiana to the intensity of that fantasy place called 'Stardom'. The first stepping-stone was in Atlanta when Britney was eight.

It was 1990 and word reached Kentwood that there was an open audition for *The Mickey Mouse Club*. Buoyed by her talent contest whitewashes, Britney pleaded to take her chance. Lynne couldn't say no, despite being heavily – and accidentally – pregnant with her second daughter, Jamie-Lynn – taking both parents' first names. After an eight-hour drive across the 500 miles, Britney and her mum pitched up in Atlanta, and she'd rehearsed her old favourite, 'Sweet Georgia Brown', all the way there. They waited a further eight hours as she lined up to take her turn before theatre and casting director Matt Casella, a talent scout for Disney, who travelled America with his video camera and tripod looking for new 'mouseketeers'. Britney joined 2,000 other hopefuls to take her three-minute opportunity, wearing a black-and-white striped leotard.

The oh-so-shy Britney – the girl too timid to even sit on Santa's knee in Christmas grottos – was nervous. It was the same before any contest: her body quivered slightly, her knees knocked, but she maintained focus. Here was a fascinating dichotomy within the young Britney: the painfully shy and seemingly subdued little girl, who needed Mum to be near, versus the little dynamo who had the presence, gusto and confidence to perform out of her skin.

Within reassuring eyeshot, Lynne sat behind Matt Casella, offering constant reassurance. But the moment Britney walked out and took to the floor, the energy shifted within. From a humming generator of nervous energy, she burst into a livewire of performing electricity. She transformed from shy to dazzling in an instant, as if someone had flicked a switch. Like the fictional Billy Elliot, it felt like electricity in her body.

Years later, in her *Stages* publication, Britney described this switch-moment in her own words: 'There's something that comes out of me – like this energy or force. It's just my time to express myself, to feel the lyric and the rhythm, to go with the music and the moment. I'm running on the adrenaline and the excitement – and the electricity of the audience.'

Britney's Aunty Chanda was often a fascinated observer of such transformations and said: 'She just went from this shy, reserved girl who was scared to talk to a stranger, to someone who was on top of the world. It was a like a light turned on inside her.'

The psychotherapist offers an explanation as to why someone can so effortlessly switch from withdrawn to livewire:

> Children raised in traumatic environments where there is a lot of shouting and yelling are withdrawn because it is a learned behaviour not to exist too loudly. A child doesn't want the pain it sees being directed in his or her direction. I suspect that Britney would tell you that she tried to be impeccably behaved or invisible – until she was performing because that's when she was guaranteed to bring happiness.

In Atlanta, Matt Casella was blown away by what he witnessed, referring to her 'amazing triple threat' – an industry term for those capable of a multi-professional discipline in singing, dancing and acting. 'Britney was the most talented eight-year-old I ever auditioned,' he says on his MySpace page. 'She was a one-of-a-kind kid with the singing, dancing and acting. She did it all and then threw in gymnastics at her final video taped audition for me in Atlanta, just to make sure she showed me all that she could do.'

When her performance stopped, Britney bowed, stood still and then became all coy again, her eyes unsure whether to leave the video camera before darting to catch her mum's proud gaze. Matt's video still catches this awkward, yet modest moment as Britney starts to twiddle her long hair, between thumb and forefinger.

'Great. You always bow?' Matt is heard asking his protégée. She nods, unsure.

'Who taught you that?'

'My mama,' said Britney, letting her hair fall free. 'She just told me every time I sing, just to bow.'

Matt Casella would have signed up Britney there and then, but after consultation with Disney executives it was felt that, even though she was almost nine, she was too young for a show where the average age of a 'mouseketeer' was twelve. The same thing ultimately happened to another nine-year-old in Pittsburgh: Christina Aguilera. It was their first taste of rejection but it was hardly a brutal fall because Matt's belief and enthusiasm cushioned the blow and he urged both of them to return. In Britney's case, he reassured her that he would be making a life-changing call on her behalf.

The offices of the Carson-Adler talent agency are somewhat anonymous-looking on West 57th Street, New York; situated high above a Gap store between 8th Avenue and Broadway and yet forensic officers would be able to follow a trail of stardust stretching back almost 30 years, from the revolving doors of Hollywood and Broadway to the elevator that takes you to one of the most respected agencies in the industry, on the twentieth floor of the Fisk Building. This is where child stars come to learn, grow and find guidance.

Names such as Ben Affleck, Matt Damon, Mischa Barton and *Sex and the City*'s Cynthia Nixon have all passed through here as children, wide-eyed with expectation and dreams. And Britney Spears joined their ranks when she arrived for a meeting with Nancy Carson, the agency's owner, after Matt Casella's over-the-phone recommendation persuaded her to meet with the little girl from Louisiana.

This mother hen of Broadway was the ideal rep for the Spears, who were already lost and uncertain within the vastness of their daughter's mere potential. Nancy's experienced but maternal tenderness was extremely reassuring. Indeed, she would go on to write a parental guide for young hopefuls called *Raising A Star*, promoted as a 'guide to helping kids break into theater, film, television or music'. She looks for youngsters driven by an inexplicable but burning desire to perform; a child who will drag their parent into her office, not vice versa. And that was Britney, always pulling on Lynne's arm to allow her to perform. It was Britney who was propelling her destiny, contrary to popular opinion.

Lynne, with the detached support of Jamie, may have facilitated the dream, but she never invented nor pushed it. If anything she was excited by the prospect of her child bettering the life that she'd had, as family friend Joy Moore told an NBC *Dateline* special in April 2008: 'Lynne just had such high hopes, you know? That her kids were going to have it better. It was just these wonderful dreams.'

Lynne had already spoken to Nancy over the phone, and submitted a raw videotape showcasing Britney's talent as she belted out 'Shine on Harvest Moon' and Sinead O'Connor's haunting 'Nothing Compares 2 U'. It was then that she invited them to New York. Within the community of Kentwood, Jamie and Lynne could see the frowns from those who felt they were opening up their daughter to crushing, inevitable rejection. And even if she made it, they would be denying her the riches of childhood, it was argued. The consensus was that the Spears shouldn't allow their child's schooling to be interrupted by far-fetched dreams. It was, says Lynne, indicative of 'a small-town way of thinking.'

Dance tutor Steve Hood explained: 'The only thing kids were encouraged to do here was go to church, leave school and get married – anything else simply wasn't an option. Singing and dancing was something people did on television and it wasn't for the likes of us Louisiana folk. No one liked change and everyone did exactly what was expected of them – until Britney came along.'

Undeterred, the Spears kept going, so emotionally invested were they in Britney's dream, and they headed to New York in February 1991. Unable to afford the airfare, they made the 1,400-mile journey by Amtrak, travelling the No. 19 train from New Orleans Union terminal direct into New York's Pennsylvania station. The travelling party was Britney, Lynne, Jamie, brother Bryan, his friend Hunter, Aunty Jeanine (Jamie's sister) and cousin Tara. The average journey time is 30 hours, so the family bunked down in a two-bed sleeper carriage and booked one hotel room for all of them once they'd arrived in the Big Apple.

The country folk pitched up in Manhattan slightly bewildered by its density. Horizons were compressed into the narrowing funnels of the avenues, and the sky could only be seen by looking upward. Britney's first question was to ask where the cows were. It must have been an odd experience for a child to be transported from the remote roads of trundling trucks to the bedlam of Manhattan, where bumper-to-bumper cars and yellow cabs are seemingly strung together in neverending loops of traffic.

In Nancy's office, Britney was wide-eyed with excitement. Removed from her parents, and seemingly okay to be without Lynne's presence, she exuded all the attributes the agent was looking for: motivation, imagination, expression, obvious talent and a winning look. 'I liked her instantly. Britney is a terrific person, and she was a remarkable child,' said Nancy, speaking from her offices, 'she and her mum are honest people, and I still know the family well today.' She still gets the chills thinking about the young

Britney, whom she has described as 'unique' and among the best she's seen at such a young age. She also told the *Pittsburgh Post-Gazette*: 'She walked through the door, and she was shy. But the moment she was asked to perform, this amazing little performer just started up. She evolved on the spot.'

All Jamie and Lynne wanted to know was the answer to one burning question: did their daughter have what it takes or were they wasting their time? Nancy was honest, imparting her view that their daughter had something that could be honed with professional training, but there are never any guarantees in show business. Sensing the same opportunity as the gymnastics, Jamie and Lynne somehow knew this was more than parental belief – they shared an instinct, and they wouldn't be the ones to stand in Britney's way. Their love knew no other option but to back her. Britney, in her tenth year, was New York-bound to be both schooled and professionally trained.

On 4 April 1991, Britney's younger sister Jamie-Lynn – another bundle of nervous energy – was born. By the May, both newborn and a recovered mum joined Britney in a tiny apartment in the heart of New York's theatre district, off 48th Street. Bryan, then fourteen, was left with Jamie, aided by assistance from their neighbours, the Reeds.

The Manhattan apartment was an ideal location because of its proximity to Professional Performing Arts School, where Britney would spend three summers attending educational classes, as well as receiving vocal and acting coaching. She was back and forth between New York and Kentwood, returning to her roots and Park Lane Academy in between her performing arts studies.

The arts school, which has also assisted Alicia Keys, had only opened the previous year to meet the needs of young students whose ambitions were fixed on the arts. Its mission statement is to offer personalised teaching, 'to develop, refine, and showcase students in dance, drama, and vocal music whilst providing a rigorous, meaningful academic curriculum'.

It was here, it is said, that Britney mastered her 'more breathy' signature vocals, as well as polishing her moves at the Broadway Dance Center off 45th Street, just off Times Square. If someone had tracked Britney in those days, her Manhattan was virtually contained within a twelve-block parameter, from 45th Street to Nancy's agency offices in 57th Street. The sight of Britney and her mum pushing a stroller around theatre-land, and taking in theatre row in 46th Street, was a regular occurrence. Lynne was convinced the bright lights of Broadway would be where Britney would end up.

But she would have to settle for less starry surroundings in the beginning, and it was on one of her return visits to Louisiana that Britney first sampled what it felt like to draw a crowd – at an annual spring arts and craft on a former sugar cane plantation on the banks of the Mississippi. It was March 1992, and Lynne had been looking for venues where Britney could sing, when a local in Kentwood suggested a new festival held in Vacherie, about a two-hour drive away. Britney's 'stage' was the spectacular setting of the Oak Alley plantation, so-called because of a quarter-mile canopy of oak trees with contorted branches that reach over to form a natural archway leading to a classical antebellum home. It is an immensely popular festival in the Deep South, attracting 8,000 tourists, artists and crafters from Illinois, Kansas, Texas and Tennessee, and it was Britney's biggest test to date.

There is probably not a more picturesque location in the whole of Louisiana and yet these beginnings could not have been more basic. Britney's venue among the 150 stalls was a 60 × 60ft tent filled with picnic tables and chairs, where visitors could find shade and escape the sun. The stage was a square of wooden flooring. Backing music came courtesy of a little sound system borrowed from the son of a groundsman. Most of the crowd was busily shuttling between stalls when the little girl, wearing blue jeans, a buttoned-down white shirt and a trilby, walked anonymously onto stage with a microphone in her hand. In front of Britney, about twenty people sat at the tables on the grass, and that included mum Lynne, and family friends Jill Prescott and Felicia Culotta.

Outside the tent was a moving sea of people. The music piped up, and Britney started to sing, confidently, loudly, brilliantly. Slowly but surely, that empty tent filled with an estimated 200 people. Britney remembers the moment for the 'amazed look on Mama's face'. One of the festival's organisers recalls the day vividly: 'I remember people commenting afterwards, saying what an amazing and powerful voice she had. No one had heard of Britney Spears back then, but her voice literally drew people into the tent.'

What surprised this particular observer, who had met Britney and her family on arrival, was the difference between the performer and the timid girl who showed up: 'She was quiet, shy, almost withdrawn. She wasn't a child performer who was full of herself, at all. Then she sang and became someone else. We were like, "Wow – she's got some talent!" We booked her to return the following year.' Britney also walked away with her first-ever performance fee – $50 in cash and some food coupons. Lynne treated her to a new doll from one of the stalls.

Britney had come on by leaps and bounds on the back of intense vocal and dancing coaching, both in New York and at home, and now she was ready for the stage. But television would beckon first: an appearance on a talent show called *Star Search* which, after being devised in 1983, was the forerunner to such modern-day shows such as *America's Got Talent* or *American Idol*. The format was a face-off between two acts, presided over by four judges who rated each performance with full stars, quarter-stars or half-stars before presenter Ed McMahon announced the scores. It was a show which produced a stellar crop of future stars, including Christina Aguilera, LeAnn Rimes, Rosie O'Donnell, Tiffany, Justin Timberlake, Usher and, oddly enough, Sharon Stone as a 'spokesmodel'.

When it came to Britney's 'star turn', she breezed through initial episodes, notching up regular three-and-a-half and three-and-three quarter scores out of a four-star maximum 'perfect'. With Kentwood cheering, she progressed to the final in a head-to-head with a boy called Marty Thomas, and the winner was to be crowned the 1992 Junior Vocalist Champion. Countless documentaries on Britney have shown the archive clip of her big moment, singing Naomi Judd's 'Love Can Build A Bridge', and Britney herself has often cringed at flashbacks to the conservative black dress and Minnie Mouse-style bow in her hair. It was a powerful performance and she couldn't have felt happier.

She had become used to the dramatic anticipation of awaiting the judge's scores and then hearing her name as the winner. But her face fell when Ed McMahon declared Marty Thomas as the champion, winning by the narrowest of margins: a quarter-star.

She had to settle for the silver medal and was noble in defeat, hugging her competitor and smiling bravely. But, as the credits rolled and she walked off stage, she burst into tears, and ran heartbroken into Lynne's arms. In Britney's mind, there were no second bests. She had striven to be best at *everything*, and felt she'd let herself and all of Kentwood down. But that very public defeat delivered a positive outcome when the phone in Nancy Carson's office rang soon afterwards.

The producers of a new off-Broadway production, *Ruthless! The Musical*, were looking for a youngster with 'triple threat' capabilities who could play an eight-year-old at the 248-seat Players Theater in Greenwich Village. Britney was approached to be understudy for the lead role, played by first choice Laura Bell Bundy. The irony contained within this opportunity lies in the musical's Hollywood spoof storyline: promoted as a tale about '... a precocious little girl, Tina Denmark, who will stop at nothing to reach her goal of becoming a star, whilst encouraged by an equally obsessed mother.'

The opening line of the play is delivered from agent Sylvia St Croix:

> Talent! Where does it come from? Is it a product of one's environment ... Or is talent something you are born with? Something passed down from generation to generation, something in the blood?

Lynne Spears, watching in the wings with Britney, would say it's in the blood; her English blood. For the roots of Britney's talents can be found on grandma Lillian's side of the family. Her sister, and Britney's great-aunt Joan Woolmore, now 80, told the *Daily Mail*: 'We came from humble beginnings. We didn't have a great deal ... but what both Lillian and I loved to do was dance and play music. Our father saved up and sent us to dance classes and piano lessons. During the war, we used to go dancing in Covent Garden where they had turned the Royal Opera House into a dance hall. We could jitterbug with the best of them!'

It's also obvious that Britney's talents spoke to a dormant dream within Lynne because her own mother, Lillian, reminded her that she, too, would sing and dance as a girl. 'It must be in Britney's genes,' said the grandma, 'music runs in our blood.'

Britney joined the cast at the end of August 1992 and rehearsed her lines like a pro. She was at rehearsals from two o'clock and remained, in costume, backstage each night until the end of every performance just in case the lead fell sick. But Laura Bell Bundy hardly missed a show. Broadway veteran Donna English, who played the role of the fame-hungry mother, rehearsed with Britney on a few occasions but the only thing that sticks in her memory, according to a broadway.com Q&A, '… was that she had a big voice.'

Donna doesn't remember Britney ever taking the stage but in actual fact, she stepped in when Laura Bell Bundy took a brief sojourn to film a small part in the movie, *The Adventures of Huck Finn*. Consequently, the role of Tina Denmark fell to Britney, appearing like a version of Annie in a pink polka-dot dress with lace hem and collar, and a giant bow in her hair. There were no critiques of her performance but agent Nancy said she was 'a natural'. But Laura Bell Bundy returned, and Britney fell back into the shadows.

Success, let alone stardom, must have felt light years away for both Britney and Lynne during those long days and nights, confined backstage in a quaint theatre and then cooped up in a tiny apartment, which they wouldn't reach until gone midnight most days. Suddenly, the reality – and odds – of 'making it' whilst treading the boards didn't match Britney's great expectations. As with gymnastics, the fun was being drummed out of the experience by the tedium of routine and the frustration of playing second-fiddle.

As Christmas neared, Britney began to pine for home. She gazed at the spindly miniature tree decorated with sparse tinsel in their apartment and imagined the scent of the large evergreen that Jamie brought home each year; she looked ahead to a bleak Christmas Day morning, and then imagined missing church one more time. And that's when she turned to Lynne to ask: 'Mama, can we go home?'

That was all her mother needed to hear. Neither was particularly enjoying the experience anymore, and Lynne's absence wasn't helping a deteriorating marriage. Agent Nancy rang the producers and they found a replacement in child actress Natalie Portman, who would grow up to win international acclaim in movies such as *Leon, Closer* and *The Other Boleyn Girl.* As Nancy says today: 'Three little girls – Laura, Britney and Natalie – went on to great things in their own rights so the casting director for *Ruthless!* clearly had a good eye!'

Britney returned to the bosom of Kentwood, cushioned by Disney casting director Matt Casella's reassuring message: 'You'll be back'. That remained the opportunity she was holding out for. Britney's faith was pinned to the map at Central Florida.

Everyone was home for the Christmas of 1992, and Lynne returned to become a second-grade teacher at Silver Creek Elementary School. But the New Year would bring exciting beginnings. Disney executives knew Britney would be ready, transformed into a slick and edgier performer because of her New York experience.

Out of 20,000 applicants, she was selected as one of 24 contenders to fight for seven places as a new 'mouseketeer' at a three-day audition camp at Disney/MGM studios in Orlando. Inevitably, she shone and her performance earned her a B+ mark with the reported comments: 'Very good ... nice girl! Sign her up.'

She was announced as one of the all-new seven mice to join the established 20 members of *The Mickey Mouse Club*, aka *MMC*. This time, Kentwood didn't just hang out the bunting and bang its drum; it went on a hi-tech spending spree. Local demand soared for cable television installation so that the community could tune into the Disney Channel for its half-hour daily broadcast. Buddy Powell, from the Golden Corral restaurant, said Britney was living proof that anything was possible and described her as a walking inspiration to everyone in Kentwood to follow their dreams.

After all the television coverage and the town mayor's proclamation of a Britney Spears Day, the family posted a message at the council buildings:

Dear Kentwood,

Britney has many memorable moments to remember in her short, little life. But April 24th 1993 has to be the most sentimental moment yet. It is so exciting to have these wonderful experiences but what makes it so wonderful is to have so many loved ones you can share them with.

Thank you Kentwood for your support and encouragement.

We love you – The Britney Spears Family

If you asked either Britney or Lynne at this time, this was probably as good as it got: handpicked for the televised *Mickey Mouse Club*.

People have since questioned why Lynne said yes to the opportunity, taking her daughter out of mainstream schooling so she could be thrust into the limelight. Britney would never know a normal junior high education, and it's not as if Lynne wasn't warned by Kentwood locals who counselled against such an upheaval. It does seem that what Britney wanted, Britney got. But who could blame Lynne? She was no different to the proud dad who felt his young son could go all the way to Old Trafford, or the parents convinced their classically trained musician child could one day play for the London Philharmonic. Besides, *The Mickey Mouse Club* would take responsible care of Britney's educational needs. And when your child is hell-bent on a dream, it is hard for any parent to deny them when opportunity knocks. It is presumably why hundreds of thousands of youngsters line up, with parental consent, to take their chances on *American Idol* or *The X-Factor*, never once considering the ramifications of the fame they are chasing.

In Britney's case, *The Mickey Mouse Club* seemed a natural opportunity to embrace and she'd no longer need to invent her own make-believe world. She was about to become an integral part of a Disney fantasyland. It was, by any stretch of her furtive imagination, a pinch-me dream come true in its own right.

But it was only the beginning.

5

The Disney Dream

'She always wanted to learn,
always wanted to better herself.'
— *Choreographer Myles Thoroughgood on Britney*

'I'll be honest, I didn't see instant star quality and I worried about what would become of her. I walked away, thinking, "This business is going to eat her up,"' said Chuck Yerger. He is seated on the patio of his Floridian home, and has just cast his mind back to an initial one-on-one meeting with Britney as she arrived for her first day on the Disney lot, with Lynne pushing a stroller that carried a restless Jamie-Lynn, aged two.

It was in the sunshine state that Britney first basked in the national spotlight as a 'mousketeer', dressed in a brown Mickey Mouse jacket with yellow arms. Chuck didn't pay much attention to this side of the new recruit because his perspective was obtained behind the scenes, with Britney off-duty. He, more than anyone at Disney, was the monitor of Britney's educational progress as a child, with a vested professional interest in her development as a girl, not a talent.

Chuck was lead tutor and principal at the 'Mickey Mouse School', located in a bungalow building near the costume department, a 100ft walk from the sound stage where production was based. It was under his tutelage in 'bungalow No. 4' that Britney attended class to ensure her education didn't suffer. But it wasn't her academic abilities that concerned the 'mouseke-tutor' that first day in May 1993; it was the patent innocence and naivety writ large on the face of a child who looked more like an intrigued tourist than a star in the making.

For a moment, Chuck might have been forgiven for believing that the mother and two daughters had wandered in by mistake from the Disney-MGM theme park in the Lake Buena Vista division of Orlando: 'I look at this kid – the sweetest, cuddliest, huggable little thing you could imagine – and I think to myself, "She's tiny – what is this cutesy doing here?" Nothing about her gave the impression that she was ready for any of this,' he said.

'She stood before me looking more like someone who should be riding a bike back and forth to gym class, not showing up for *Mickey Mouse Club*. She seemed out of place. Everything she radiated was that of an innocent babe in the woods.'

On that first day, parents and new recruits were allowed to wander freely around the lot in an exploration of their new world when a smiling Britney wandered into the classroom where Chuck was on hand to meet and greet. As she walked in happily, he first noticed her tiny frame, but then something else struck him: the way she found a diversion in her sister, Jamie-Lynn, in the stroller: 'She was so solicitous of her baby sister. She fussed her, attended to her and bent down, grabbing her little finger. It was strange, almost as if she was emulating her mum, mimicking what she would do.'

This young starlet was not, as was the norm, bursting into his classroom with passion and child-like vigour. What Chuck observed was more the passive curiosity of a shy visitor. In his mind, he tried to match the reality of what stood before him with the sure knowledge that all seven new 'mice' had come through a rigorous and exacting audition process. As he explains: 'I thought, "How did this little sweet thing survive that process?" The way she looked, filled with wonder, made it appear as if someone had just plucked her from Louisiana and placed her down at Disney and she's going, "Wow!"'

He knew that Britney must be enormously capable to get beyond the likes of Matt Casella, but physically, 'she was an eleven-year-old who looked eight' and her tiny frame and evident fragility made him privately question whether she was sufficiently equipped for the industry as a whole: 'Though she had a basic talent, I did not know if she had the sophistication necessary that made many child-stars stand out.'

It says a lot about Britney's raw innocence that Chuck so easily detected her vulnerabilities on first impression, *without* even understanding that here was a girl whose unconscious definition of performing was rooted in attention that brought approval, that in turn equalled love. And there was Lynne, still happy and supportive, so everything remained normal, stable and okay in Britney's mind.

It's highly unlikely any potential pitfalls crossed either mum or daughter's thoughts in the manner that they crossed Chuck's. Indeed, he knew they had entered an image-conscious arena and such awareness would only be magnified as Britney neared the threshold of puberty, a time when facial and bodily features are liable to dramatically change. Whether parents realised it or not, Disney's prerequisite for wholesomeness meant that the camera needed to keep liking the face and that the physical structure projected 'the right image' to a young audience. For instance, a flat-chested twelve-year-old wouldn't be retained if she suddenly turned inappropriately voluptuous. Britney's look encapsulated the sweet and innocent image Disney was all about, but she hadn't yet entered puberty.

'Talent alone didn't carry them through,' explained Chuck. 'I had been at *MMC* four years when Britney arrived and had seen four kids get cut out because they did not look right; their appearance changed as they developed. I saw Britney's bright eyes and trusting smile, and thought she'd never cope with such rejection.'

One wonders how this truth sat comfortably with Lynne's stated vehemence against the harsh vanities of the beauty pageant system to which she was so fiercely opposed. Had this Disney truth emerged, would she then have withdrawn Britney from this Mickey Mouse Club dream? But Lynne would not be aware of such expectations.

Indeed, based on the first-hand account from the experienced tutor, she appeared as naive and wondrous as her daughter: 'Lynne was as awed and overwhelmed as Britney. I looked at the three of them and I could not understand how they got here. I thought, "This business is going to be too much for people like this." It was impossible not to like them because they are wonderful, kind-hearted folk, but it was also hard not to worry for them. Not because of *The MMC* – because it did things the right way and really took care of its kids – but because of the industry they were choosing. Britney had a talent; she was capable and conscientious, but I never became convinced that she was ever equipped or prepared for the journey ahead. I thought the industry would destroy her, not make her,' he admitted.

But Britney had proved she was more than capable, earning her stripes three months earlier at the 'audition camp' where she'd first met fellow novices Justin Timberlake, Jessica Simpson, Christina Aguilera and Ryan Gosling, who would grow up to become a Hollywood actor known for his roles in *Notebook, Fracture* and *Lars and the Real Girl.* Only Jessica Simpson would be rejected, falling short with a seven-and-a-half out of ten mark for her vocals. Executives believed she 'wasn't ready'. But Britney impressed across the board, earning an eight-and-a-half for both acting and dancing, and a clear eight for vocals.

It was an excellent score, eclipsed only by the vocal tally of Christina Aguilera, whose extraordinarily unique sound earned her a near-perfect nine-and-a-half and an eight in both acting and dancing. Justin Timberlake wasn't so hot when it came to his acting score (seven-and-a-half) and his dancing was marked half a point lower than Britney; he, too, scored eight for vocals. But the all-round talent of the new crop was obvious and each would help the other to become more polished performers.

Mickey Mouse Club choreographer Myles Thoroughgood, who was responsible for whipping their dancing talents into shape, said: 'Each one of them brought their own range of talents. Vocally, I think Britney learned a lot through others but she also taught others a lot about dance because she arrived fully trained and with lots of ability.'

The new 'mouseketeers' developed a three-musketeer philosophy, sticking together and helping each other within their newfound Disney family. Britney was tightly bound throughout every step of the experience with Justin, Christina and Ryan. She couldn't believe her luck. And 'luck' was how she viewed it. She didn't believe it was her

right to be there, she simply felt blessed to be granted the
opportunity. In pre-teen America, being selected as a
'mouseketeer' was the child's equivalent of 'getting to the
Olympics', according to Disney acting coach Gary Spatz.

Lynne's wisdom was vindicated: belief and focus brings
about achievement in alignment with God's providence.

Chuck Yerger was not, at first, aware of how far Britney
had travelled: 'I didn't know she had studied and rehearsed
in New York and then done *Star Search*. But that's because
nothing carried over from those experiences to suggest she
was a seasoned pro. There was no sense of "I've been to the
wars". Nor did I see a passion in the eyes or drive that so
many child stars have, the one that says, "I'm doing this to
get ahead in life". My evaluation was that she saw the mouse
club as an adventure.'

But Britney was there to take her chance and this particular opportunity combined two dizzying fantasies: to
appear on daily television, but also to be part of the Mickey
Mouse story from a theme park where the promise of a
two-week vacation was normally sufficient to send kids wild
with excitement. For the girl from a low-income town in
Louisiana, just visiting Disney World had always been a far-
fetched dream. But she was now installed as another incar-
nation of the Mickey Mouse mantra which encourages all
children to *believe* in their dreams, with a pip-squeak voice
that, on all Disney parades, quickly adds: 'Gosh! Everybody
can imagine …'

<hr />

When the curtain went up on Season 6 of *The All New
Mickey Mouse Club*, Kentwood was glued to its newly
installed cable channels, watching Britney make her
onscreen debut in the fall of 1993. The show's cheerleader-

esque theme tune cued in the seven new recruits, along with the more established, older stars, with the catchy lyrics that spelled out Mickey Mouse's name: *'Who's the leader of the club that's made for you and me? Emm-Eye-See … Kay-Eee-Why … Emm-O-Yew-S-Seeee!'*

And there, flashing up onscreen as the music continued, was a girl with a full, brushed fringe, excitedly announcing herself as 'BRITNEY!' alongside the other notable recruits announcing their arrival: 'JUSTIN!' … 'CHRISTINA!' … 'RYAN!'

As with every show's opening, 'mouseketeers' bounded and skipped onto the set of an American diner before a studio audience made up of giddy children. The staple diet of the family-oriented content for these half-hour variety shows comprised comedy sketches based around school and home life, or parodies of family game shows. Its skits were classical Disney – promoting messages of sharing, goodness and kindness. The upbeat tempo of pop music song and dance was weaved around a theme-for-the-day. It was colourful, bubbly, fast-paced and fun, appealing to the milder sensibilities of the early nineties.

Looking back now, the show smacks of low budget but this was an era when cable television was a premium and video gaming hadn't completely entranced children with the now-seemingly basic Sega Genesis game system and the Nintendo Game Boy. 'Mouseketeers' reached into living rooms throughout America, inviting viewers to be part of the Disney family and allowing them to relate to the like-able, everyday personalities of the kids who had brought *Mickey Mouse Club* back to life in 1989, reviving a format first launched by Walt Disney himself in 1955, before ABC dropped it after a four-year run.

In 1993, the show was aired Monday to Thursday at 5.30pm. It was the most-watched afternoon series on the

Disney Channel, which reached 5.6 million cable subscribers and its popularity was reflected in the mailbag: an estimated 250,000 fan letters were received during its modern-day run. But that popularity created a punishing schedule for Britney and friends, with demands that would be asking a lot of a seasoned pro, let alone an eleven-year-old. A real graft lay behind the ever-happy smiling faces in weeks that comprised three days of rehearsals followed by two days of filming.

They were long, intense days, demanding three dance production numbers and two on-location music video-shoots each week, alongside the comedy skits, parodies and promotional work. And all educational needs had to be accommodated, too. Britney lived like this for the four months between May and September filming, and then returned to Kentwood in time for the show's airing. What amazed both her tutors and coaches was that she kept smiling throughout. There were many backstage dramas, as might be expected with a bunch of pre-teens and adolescents working together in a creative environment. But Britney is not remembered for being crabby or throwing tantrums. Choreographer Myles Thoroughgood says: 'What struck me was her attitude: it was exemplary. She was a true workhorse with a great energy. If I remember anything about Britney it was her intense focus – and her smiling face.'

For the first time, Britney learned on the job about working with TV cameras, lighting and top musical directors and choreographers. She grasped the concepts and imagery applied to dance routines and how they were intended to relate to the audience at home; she became ever more mindful of the connection between artist and audience; that the folks at home needed to relate to the themes within each routine or music video. If the likes of Britney, Justin and Christina walked away with one creative message it was, quite simply, 'Know your audience and relate to them'. This in itself, as would become clear with her first hit single '… Baby One More Time', would provide an invaluable education for the years ahead.

Disney policy also dictated the kind of things that were appropriate to say and laid down rules about good conduct. 'Mouseketeers' were expected to uphold the same squeaky-clean behaviour as Mickey and Minnie. They were told that projecting the proper image was essential and that their public conduct reflected on Disney's image. Here was Britney's first lesson in commercially minded PR: wholesome, clean, butter-wouldn't-melt-in-the-mouth behaviour. She was listening to her elders and doing exactly as she was told; being trained in how to sing, dance, hold herself; conduct and help 'sell' a corporate image. The unspoken message was clear: behave this way, follow the rules, keep everyone happy and success will follow.

As Chuck explained: 'Everything had to be very wholesome and exemplary. She practised how to sign autographs, how to flash the right smile, how to answer questions. These kids would be sent out into the theme park to do "meet-and-greets" with adoring fans and so they underwent training in the Disney technique, as young ambassadors of Disney.'

A picture starts to emerge of Britney as an eager-to-please, malleable young girl who auto-responded to whatever direction she was given; an actor in her own life receiving offstage direction. Believe in God, and you will be protected. Perform for Mum, and you will be secure and make her happy. Sing, dance and cartwheel, and the talent contest shall be yours. Conduct yourself accordingly and you, too, can become part of the Disney magic. She was continuing to grow and be shaped by an environment with constant directions from outside of her. It's unclear, if not doubtful, whether anything in Britney's development emanated from her core, naturally and authentically. It seemed that everything was invested in the reverence she displayed towards adults, and the performance she created.

Chuck Yerger noticed this was a tendency that carried over into her school work: 'She was absolutely insistent about doing everything the correct way, in line with what her teachers expected back home. The reverence she showed towards teachers was striking.'

In the US, he says many teachers adhere to 'procedures' and 'ways of doing things', such as essays having to be written on specific lined notebook paper; punch holes should be three, not four for a ring-binder; all submitted work should not only carry a name but the period of day that the piece was written; blue pens for this, black pens for that. It is an educational code of discipline that fusses over small details. Life at Park Lane Academy was clearly no exception – and Britney was adamant about honouring it.

Chuck further explained: 'She knew what pen should be used, and in what ink; where her name should go and the precise width of the margins. I asked her why it was so, and she said, "I have to do it this way. My teachers will not like it, if not." She was very much aware of her teachers' expectations and her goal was to please them. So we learned to trust Britney and followed the requirements she gave us.'

Britney the pupil was forever punctual, perky, polite and pleasing – and never slacked on her homework: 'She always delivered. The very idea of not doing homework and giving an adult the chance to say, "Tut, tut, tut – you've disappointed me" was unthinkable to her,' said Chuck.

However, such conscientiousness doesn't suggest Britney was a teacher's pet wanting to impress with an academic brilliance. What Chuck observed was more of an unquestioning trust in her elders. This was also mirrored in her compliant performance mentality.

Chuck recalled: 'In all that she did, Britney gave the distinct impression that if an adult says do something, you do it. She truly felt that all adults and people in authority were good people, who had her best interests at heart. If a responsible adult says, "This is how it should be" then she believed that person. It really was that inconceivable to her that anyone could steer her wrong and she carried that mind-set into her early performing life.'

All this most likely stems from being raised in an out-of-control environment so all these unconscious behaviours are an attempt to feel in control. She can't control her feelings or her parents so she chose to control her pens, the way she wrote, the way she does things. It brings order. Children really do need boundaries and limits, and I would think Britney was trying to be good because she wanted to be liked, because she wanted peace. She was looking for an authority figure but there wasn't one at home so she looks around her other environments. Her reverence is a need to look up to someone, someone in authority, someone who gives her instructions and control. It's not as conscious as that – more of an impulse as a response to what had happened around her but it makes her especially open to the instructions of anyone around her in a position of trust. From properly representing the image of Disney to adhering to rule systems from school, Britney would have been so mouldable because she didn't have a developed sense of self. Consequently, you are liable to become what people ask of you. She would be the sheep that followed, as reared in childhood.

It all confirms Chuck's initial impression that this Kentwood lamb could be in trouble in the entertainment industry. 'What hope did she have when, in her heart, she invests all that unquestioning belief in those who say "This is good for you" or "Follow this advice, trust us"? All I ever saw in her eyes was a trust that required guidance, as opposed to a selfish and driven passion.'

Life at Disney also taught Britney to be without Lynne: parents were not allowed on set except on the two days of the week when the show was taped. Lynne, together with the other parents, would laze poolside or go shopping at the malls.

Meanwhile, Britney found herself in the thick of life at 'showbiz boot-camp'. She loved every second; she told family and friends that being chosen for *The Mickey Mouse Club* was 'the best day of my life'.

Britney had been bitten, and the entertainment industry was now working its way into her bloodstream – the nerves, the pre-show adrenaline, the highs of performing before an audience, that euphoric release that she couldn't quite put her finger on. It was no longer a dream but a priceless education towards an unknown adult career. What she didn't perhaps realise back then was that with each show, 'Britney' was fast becoming a familiar name and face throughout America; a face that would be on television for two seasons in four-month blocks. This platform and audience recognition would play its part in a phenomenal success, and fan-base, that she did not yet know.

In fact, the environment she was already immersed in was surreal enough and still relatively new to Orlando. The 135-acre Disney-MGM Studio site (now known as Disney's Hollywood Studios) opened as a backlot studio theme park in 1989 to provide the East Coast with an experience that already existed on the West, in Burbank, Los Angeles. Britney's world is best illustrated within the park's opening dedication that Disney CEO Michael Eisner created for tourists:

The world you have entered was created by The Walt Disney
Company and is dedicated to Hollywood – not a place on a map,
but a state of mind that exists, wherever people dream and
wonder and imagine, a place where illusion and reality are
fused by technological magic. We welcome you to a Hollywood
that never was – and always will be.

An eleven-year-old from Louisiana suddenly landed in the
twilight zone between fiction and reality, working in close
proximity to *Residential Street,* where faux home facades
provided backdrops for *The Golden Girls, Adventures in
Wonderland* and *Ernest Saves Christmas.* Around the corner,
in this land of movie sets, were the replica locations of *New
York Street* and *Washington State Park.* Just around the
corner from Britney's school bungalow was the 'bone yard'
where old props lay scattered about as discarded relics from
earlier productions such as *Roger Rabbit* and *Star Wars.* An
Alice in her own Wonderland, Britney even rehearsed and
performed in 'Mickey Avenue' – the street address for the
sound stage. It was here that she had to grow accustomed to
being one of the theme park attractions because the famous
'Back-lot Tour' provided tourists with an access-all-areas
insight.

The very concept of providing people with a snoop
behind the scenes turned the tour into a hugely popular
attraction and honoured the premise of allowing visitors to
immerse themselves in the sensation of being attached to
the Hollywood experience. For *Mickey Mouse Club* fans, it
allowed them to jump into their television sets and 'belong'
to the club, which had so entertained them during week-
days. Consequently, gaggles of giddy tourists would enter
the soundstage via a raised, glassed-off walkway that
allowed them to look down on the *MMC* set and watch
rehearsals and live performances as they happened. Britney

found herself swimming in this aquarium, flashing a smile, waving to fans; a mermaid with cartoon ears. As fellow 'mousketeer' Tony Lucca told an *E! True Hollywood Story* documentary, they were '… performing even when we weren't performing.'

Seemingly unfazed, Britney made the adjustment effortlessly. Privately, she entertained insecurities about the way she looked; she wanted to look as 'perfect and beautiful' as her 'mouseketeer' role model – the porcelain-faced, curly-haired, sixteen-year-old Keri Russell. She would grow up to be an actress best known for starring in the 2008 movie *Bedtime Stories* and playing college girl Felicity Porter in the award-winning prime-time series *Felicity*, a role which earned her a Golden Globe in 1999.

Britney apparently used to blush in Keri's presence, feeling self-conscious with what she considered to be her own gawky face, flyaway hair, crooked teeth and a nose she thought too big. She also suffered from spots and feared they would break out into rampant acne. Each night before bed, she foamed her face with Dove soap and applied Clearasil to her spots. Britney was entering an industry where image mattered and she wanted to look perfect. By her own admission, when she looked in the mirror, she felt like an ugly duckling. That self-image wasn't helped when she had to wear braces to correct her teeth. Chuck says she was more 'cute and adorable' than noticeably pretty or striking. Even to this day, that ordinary pre-pubescent look has imprinted itself on Britney's psyche. 'When I look in a mirror, I'm still very self-critical. All I see is a goofy girl,' she once admitted.

As a pre-teen on television, there was no hiding place for her insecurities. Of course, she had a professional hair and make-up department to rely on, but they could do nothing about the nose she hated or the teeth that needed a retainer-brace. But the experience is credited with helping her confront a low self-esteem that was no doubt responsible for her shyness, when not performing. In this respect, *The Mickey Mouse Club* wasn't just a good training ground for a professional career, it was a confidence-boosting environment, encouraged by the more outgoing, gregarious types, such as TJ Fantini, Ryan Gosling and the irrepressible, but charming cheek of a young Justin Timberlake. Within her newfound family of fellow performers, she was comfortable in the same way she'd felt accepted within the small community of Kentwood. And the sound of applause from a weekly audience was yet more confirmation of the happiness she was giving others.

Christina Aguilera shared Britney's admiration for Keri Russell, who had what the two girls wanted: the star-status, the car and the perfect man – her teenage boyfriend, Tony Lucca. Both harboured a secret crush on the young Tony and vowed 'to be big, grown up and famous just like Keri one day!'

Indeed, Christina one day let slip that the younger recruits made a secret pact. Nikki DeLoach, an older 'mouseketeer', told an *E! True Hollywood Story* documentary: 'Christina had told me that a couple of the younger kids had made a vow to become stars one day, and promised each other that they were going to do this.'

It is almost certain Britney was a co-signee to this pact because she and Christina were inseparable, always hanging out with one another, walking and skipping hand-in-hand around set. Wherever Christina was, Britney wouldn't be far behind. Their training mirrored the same parallels that their careers would follow, and these roots of friendship would defy a media-invented rivalry, which both girls would find themselves playing down in later years.

'Britney was someone I used to hold hands with all the time. We were silly little girls together on *The Mickey Mouse Club*,' recalled Christina, when promoting her 2008 album, *Keeps Getting Better.*

Britney and Christina would go round to each other's apartments for dinner because mothers Spears, Timberlake, Gosling and Aguilera all lived in the same condominium, about a 15-minute drive from the set. At the end of each day, a coach would transport them back to the apartment complex, where there were swimming pools and hot tubs. Aged eleven or twelve, this was the height of luxury and a taster of the star treatment.

Lynne became good friends with Christina's mother, Shelly Fidler, as well as Justin's mother, Lynn Harless. As the mothers cooked, the daughters would bathe in the evening heat, rehearse or play on a Sega Genesis game system.

Lynne had always raised Britney to be a good sport, and to respect her peers, and Christina was raised with the same attitude, so there was never any jealousy or overt competitiveness between the two girls though it was accepted by the elders and coaches that Christina had the better voice. In that regard, she belonged in an exceptional league all of her own. Even Britney has since admitted: 'I wish I had a voice like Christina's.' Post-series, they might not have remained close friends, but both have nothing but a mutual respect and admiration built on fond memories back at Disney.

❦

Park Lane Academy and Britney's parents supported her sojourn into show business because they both recognised the opportunity, and because they had been reassured by Disney that schooling was never allowed to become secondary to performing. It fell to Chuck Yerger to ensure that a sound education ran parallel to the great dreams that a bunch of talented children projected onto the blank canvases of adulthood. In his time, he has steered many a child-star's education through the travails of show business, including actress Melissa Joan Hart. Chuck, whose amiability and gentleness shouldn't disguise a schoolmaster's sternness, was regarded as 'the teacher of teachers' in his former home state of Pennsylvania, where he worked in education for 17 years.

He moved to Florida, where, upon the recommendation of an ex-student, he began work for New York-based On-Location Education (OLE), which co-ordinates the tutoring of young performers on-set for those children working in film, television and theatre productions or the recording industry. In Orlando, he soon found that both Disney and Nickelodeon wanted to tap into his esteemed expertise, bringing a steady discipline to child performers who, without proper guidance, were in danger of believing that an education in performing was all that mattered. He was a stickler in honouring the strict legal requirements – governed by the Screen Actors Guild (SAG) and the American Federation of Television and Radio Artists (AFTRA) – ensuring an educational excellence was maintained, both in terms of the hours schooled and the consistent continuance of a child's individual curriculum in tandem with their respective schools. Walt Disney and Chuck Yerger obsessed about the high quality of education for everyone, regardless of the show's need to be a ratings success.

For Britney, this meant her fundamental, Christian-based curriculum was maintained on location in Orlando. Even though she was in another state, her education had to mirror teachings in accord with the strict curriculum back in McComb, thereby allowing her to slip back into normal class easily, without being behind or ahead when the filming stints concluded. This meant that, for 1993 and 1994, Britney was part-educated by the teachers who knew her, part-educated by Chuck and his four other members of staff, but all of them working from the same page. Typically, the 'Mickey Mouse School' covered the last 10 weeks of the school year, allowing filming to continue into the summer break.

The new recruits were left in no doubt that Chuck Yerger was a powerful man indeed – the man who could make or break their fledgling careers. *MMC* executive producer Dennis Steinmetz gathered all parents and new 'mouseketeers' in a conference room; children and parents sat around a large oval table. As the top man delivered a serious welcome message with much joviality, the tall, bespectacled authority-figure of Chuck Yerger stood just behind, awaiting his introduction.

'This,' said Mr Steinmetz, 'is the most important man you are all going to meet today because he's the one who tells me if you're allowed to perform. So, let me make it very clear: if you don't keep your schoolwork and grades, it will get noticed and you won't perform.'

Chuck smiles at the memory today, because this power played on the minds of the children, who only ever wanted to perform. He'd wield this influence subtly, gently issuing an over-the-shoulder reminder that if their homework or grades didn't improve, 'then I will have to tell Dennis'.

'They knew that I could pull them out of the show,' he said, 'It was the ultimate sanction that cleverly maintained a focus on their education. The idea of being barred from performing made them think, "Oh My God, that can never happen" and so they would knuckle down and do the school work that was required.'

To some parents, it mattered equally that their children's performing and long-term careers were not adversely affected either, but Lynne was not one of them. Chuck says her 'stage-mom' label is a myth: 'Believe me, I've had parents in the past who have made it very clear that this opportunity represented their kid's career and I best understand that. Lynne was never like that. What mattered most was Britney's education. I can't remember her asking a single question about how the schoolwork was going to impact her career plan. Never once did I detect from either Lynne or Britney that *The Mickey Mouse Club* was calculated to advance a long-term career. I honestly felt that they turned up without a plan.'

In previous seasons, producers had wanted school out of the way before filming began, meaning that all tutoring took place in the mornings, and filming in the afternoon and early evening. But all that changed when Britney et al. arrived, so there was a constant stream of kids, going back and forth between school and studio, as dictated by the shooting schedule. Strict regulations meant that each child had to be in school at least 15 hours a week, 3 hours a day. Not even the principal knew the school timetable until 7am each day.

On a typical day, Britney – with English, Maths, History, Science and Geography studies transferred from the Park Lane curriculum – would, for example, find herself in class from 9–10am and then tape or rehearse a show segment from 10.10–11.30am; then 11.45am–12.45pm in class, followed by lunch, and then 2.30–3.30pm vocal training, before resuming studies between 4–5pm. With the constant shuttling to-and-fro, it must have been exceptionally hard for the young performers to split their focus.

Indeed, one wonders what they were actually learning in such small time blocks. After all, these were performers savouring the anticipation of performing. But that's where the 'Dennis warning' provided the blinkers and Chuck's opinion was that the top grades achieved speak their own truth: 'The only times we had problems with getting the kids to concentrate was if they had been on stage in front of a live audience, or were due to perform live. That would present some difficulties because, naturally, they were either gearing themselves up or coming down from the high. But most of the time, they adapted well, like little professionals.

'We must have been doing something right because in the four years I was there, I never needed to pull out one "mouseketeer". I maybe had to issue the threat on six or eight occasions to two main culprits – and Britney wasn't one of them!'

Naturally, she was far too attentive to be anything other than well behaved, just as her mama had raised her. 'I'll never forget Britney sat on a chair, looking around, perky and smiling. She was so small that her legs dangled off the front, and her toes couldn't touch the floor,' recalls Chuck Yerger.

He still holds dear Britney's report cards – an 8 × 11in sheet of paper that was prepared to send to Park Lane Academy, which allowed teachers to track her progress from afar. What they saw was mainly straight As across the board.

On face value, such grades seem impressive but Britney was only an average student in terms of academic ability. Her A-grades were a relatively easy reach within a 6th and 7th Grade curriculum regarded as somewhat fundamental: basic maths and vocabulary lists, and memorising basic science, geographical and historic facts.

'There was a lot of filling in worksheets and learning long lists and facts,' said Chuck. 'Britney's strength was learning all this like she was learning lines. She was great at memorisation, great at direction and great at reeling off lists of words, without really exploring what it all meant.'

.The very ethos behind her Christian school's curriculum was that it provided children with basic literacy and numeracy skills and also armed them with essential facts and knowledge. What was taught was factually based. There seemed little opportunity for a higher order of thinking that could question, interpret or analyse. During her time in Orlando, Britney wasn't given a single essay to write or asked to think about anything outside pre-established facts.

'Britney's education was very much oriented to a fact and skills memorisation curriculum with not a lot of thinking required,' recalled Chuck.

There was also a strong religious thread running through the themed teachings, bound with a religious framework. Mathematical equations were based on brain-teasers along the lines of: 'If Jesus had four loaves and cut each one into eight pieces, how many pieces in total would there be to hand out?' Grammar lessons became a modern version of the Bible, asking children to correct spelling and grammatical errors. And history lessons were built on pure creationism – the Christian fundamentalist belief that God created the cosmos and there is no such thing as evolution. Indeed, this is not surprising in a country where the theory of evolution was omitted entirely from school textbooks until the sixties. But in places like Louisiana, such ardent beliefs held firm and give us a true idea of the zealous religious programming that influenced Britney.

This is not simply a matter of a girl who attended church every Sunday and prayed before bedtime; it goes to the core of Britney's entire thinking as a child, influenced by a fervent belief that was drilled into her bones.

She even turned to God when it came to exam time. Chuck remembers the day when Park Lane sent a vocabulary-list test through the mail. Britney was sitting at her desk wearing little crucifixes as earrings when Chuck approached. He recalls: 'When I announced that I'd received a package from Park Lane containing a vocabulary quiz, she looked at me, put her hands together prayerfully in a steeple, looked up to the ceiling and said, "Oh Lord" so earnestly. It was so worshipful and yet strange because most kids her age would have said something like, "Oh crap!" or "Oh Gawd" but not Britney. It was almost as if she was pleading, "Oh Lord, please help me with this!".

Educationally, the most sophisticated subject matter she was challenged with in class was a copy of Ernest Hemingway's *The Old Man and The Sea*, but Chuck never did get the chance to explore with her its lost causes, themes and symbols because time at Disney would expire. It's doubtful Britney got the chance to finish that literary classic, let alone time to understand its story, nuances and meanings.

'Britney was wonderful to teach, and she had such a pleasing manner. There was a sense of "This is school time and I must do what I'm told" so she put her head down and studied hard. She was a great kid,' said Chuck.

What he didn't appreciate back then was not only how phenomenally famous Britney would become, but that *The Mickey Mouse Club* of 1993–4 would rank as a veritable Who's Who of the stars of the future: 'It's hard to believe it now, but as Dennis Steinmetz addressed the room on that first day, I looked around and took in the fresh faces of Britney Spears, Christina Aguilera, Justin Timberlake and Ryan Gosling. Who'd have reckoned on the magnificent achievements they would all make? It's incredible when you think about it, and it makes me feel immensely proud.'

Britney's potential as a performer was blossoming. Weekly vocal and dance coaching took raw talent and applied a show-business polish. She was also undergoing a crash course in on-camera professionalism and 'hitting her mark' – industry speak that refers to hitting a precise position to be captured in focus, in frame and in the best light. Everything we see in television production is lit for what the camera sees through the lens, and so Britney was learning, for the first time to sing, dance and act while respecting each camera's position within a five-camera production.

Chuck Yerger remembers watching Britney one night on the Disney Channel: 'Tutors didn't see too much production because they liked to keep us separate. So I was very surprised when I saw Britney the performer on television – there was a maturity to her moves and it seemed incongruous that this little girl in class could do these amazing things on stage, as if she was mimicking an idol. It was the difference between night and day.'

As a trained dancer, previously she'd only known how to honour the audience before her. Now she had to play to the camera, rehearsing routines while simultaneously remembering which camera to address for different lyrics and verses. Suddenly, it would all become second nature to hear instructions as she sang and moved: 'Looking down the line to camera 3 … Up to an overhead wide-shot camera 5 … Now close-up camera 4 …'

Sometimes the lyrics, the choreography and camera positions would have to be rehearsed in windows as narrow as 90 minutes. When they were putting routines together, the dance studio was hardly ideal: it was a double wide trailer with mirrors down one side and a dance floor in the middle. There, routines would be shot on VHS and then played back for the director so that he could translate the performance to the set.

Choreographer Myles Thoroughgood remembers: 'I used to say to them that, "You're never going to work harder than this" because the days were difficult and relentless but the schedule and the training is what would turn them into pros.'

Jean Wiegman, artistic director at *MMC*, always felt that Myles' 'technical skill and clear direction' maximised the talents of all 'mouseketeers' and Britney was among the chief beneficiaries. Some routines required four full takes to ensure every move was captured by the five different camera angles.

Taking a break from his current schedule in Orlando, Myles said: 'I had maybe four hours of rehearsal time with each song and sometimes only 90 minutes. Everyone had to learn to work together very quickly – and Britney took to it like a duck to water.' He describes her as a 'dynamic dancer, who was an incredible turner and had a great kick'. What her performances lacked was 'a connection to the camera' but that would come with time and arm her with an invaluable knowledge for her music videos.

'She always wanted to learn, always wanted to better herself,' recalled Myles, 'and she always wanted to be involved. I remember her coming to me and saying over and over: "I really would love to be in more numbers." One thing I'll say about Britney is that her ability certainly added to, and enhanced, any dance number that included her. Whatever we gave her, she took it and owned it. She was a performer who shone.'

Sometimes, she radiated a little too much for the camera and tried too hard. Young Britney soon learned her natural state of performing could be marred from being over-zealous. After certain taped rehearsals or live shows, Myles would be handed notes from the producers about aspects that needed improvement next time: 'One note referred to

Britney and it pointed out that, occasionally, she would make this face whilst dancing – an expression we called "a rat's face". Basically, it was an overdone smile. It was a smile you'd associate with a beauty pageant and it made her eyes squint and her nose all crinkled. I had to tell her to relax and vary her expressions. But bless her, I couldn't criticise her because that over-zealousness was just the joy she experienced when dancing. I could tell, just by watching her, the genuine pleasure she derived from dancing and performing.'

Among the cast, the voices of Chicago-born Rhona Bennett and Texan Jennifer McGill were regarded as the most accomplished (even taking into account the blossoming Christina), but Myles regarded Britney, together with Keri Russell, as the best dancer. Ultimately, he would oversee 300 production numbers for *The Mickey Mouse Club*, having joined in Season 4, and he would become a chief influence in the soon-to-explode Britney career.

The dance moves that wowed the world in her early music videos were strongly flavoured by what other 'mousketeers' would call the 'cool Myles Thoroughgood effect'. The man himself modestly dismisses such credit, referring to the abilities that Britney already arrived with: 'There was already gold in that girl and I utilised what she had, and channelled that into the interests of Disney. I was exceptionally proud of the performer she would become,' he said.

Through his eyes, it's also possible to glean a better understanding of Britney's creative mechanism. Many people, including Chuck Yerger and future observers, speak of a painfully shy little girl who went into performance mode like a click of a switch; from off to on. They do not describe a noticeable fire burning beyond those eyes. While Myles Thoroughgood agreed that this was unusual for a child-star, he doesn't believe that it suggests a lack of hunger: 'I think what people witness is someone with a concentrated focus: quiet, seemingly passive but absolutely centred.'

It was in another trailer-turned-studio that Britney underwent vocal coaching with Robin Wiley, someone else who has received little credit for her role in the careers of Britney, Justin Timberlake and Christina Aguilera – someone she described as being blessed with 'an Aretha Franklin voice.'

Robin, a producer and singer-songwriter from Seattle, would later work with *NSYNC, writing hits such as 'I Thought She Knew', 'No Strings Attached' and 'Home for Christmas', becoming an integral part of their success story. Justin Timberlake's background singers used her CD for vocal warm-up techniques prior to his performances. Known for what her producer friend Matt Shaw described as 'gorgeous arrangements with serious jazz harmonies', Robin died from cancer, aged 45, but her legacy is everlasting in the careers of so many. Myles Thoroughgood said: 'Robin was a genius and I think it's fair to say that Britney found her true voice under her coaching. Britney was cognisant of her strengths and weaknesses, and Robin worked hard with her. Britney never had a voice like Christina, but the voice that she did have was improved beyond measure by Robin Wiley.'

Matt Shaw, Robin's long-time friend, said: 'Robin taught all the musical arranging and vocal coaching, and was almost regarded as "House Mom". She took care of those kids and she was influential in teaching them all about voice technique: with Britney, for example, how to sing a pop song. Robin raved about Britney, saying she was a happy, bubbly girl.'

Season 6 turned into Season 7, but the show was running out of steam and changes were made. 'Mouseketeers' were simply to be known as 'cast members' and the show was renamed *MMC* to make the brand seem 'edgier, hip and less Disney'.

Executives realised even pre-teens didn't think it cool to be associated with Mickey Mouse anymore. An album of rap, R&B and hip-hop was released to move with the times and help salvage a show that, behind the scenes, was fighting increasing costs and changing trends. The cosmetic revamp was designed to present the cast 'as a wholesome version of that Beverly Hills bunch from the 90210 zip code,' according to the *LA Times*.

In an interview with that same newspaper, Tony Lucca bashfully acknowledged that he was regarded as more of a heart-throb and less of a mouse without ears. A sexy image was drawing screaming girls and he was reported as saying: 'That's what's selling! You've got to get on that "sexy" bandwagon.'

But it was hardly Disney. A wholesomeness that perhaps belonged in the fifties was no longer relevant in a street-smart teen generation that was becoming more individualistic. The sexualisation of society was about to wash over the TV, music, advertising and media industries, while a nineties culture would embrace the shock, sex and voyeuristic values of reality television. There was also a noticeable increase in sex, violence and swearing in dramas, resulting in the introduction of a nine o'clock watershed.

In the music industry, Madonna had parted the sea to create the female pop-star powerhouse, teasing audiences with provocative lyrics and raunchy videos. The one-time male domination over the teen pop market, once seen with the likes of Duran Duran, Spandau Ballet, A-Ha, and Wham, was now a bygone era that could be boxed-up and placed in eighties' attics. Madonna the dominatrix and the

Spice Girls, who formed in 1994 with 'girl power', would make their commercial presence felt.

Despite the ubiquitous presence of those two female acts, there would still be a missing piece in the market; the absence of an act that teens could actually relate to. Strong as the messages might have been, and as contagiously popular as their music was, Madonna, Mel B and Posh Spice were not teenagers; never 'one of us' but 'women we'd one day like to be'. The softer, bubblegum, eighties acts of Debbie Gibson and Tiffany were as outdated as Mickey Mouse was becoming, but their edgier, sassier, modern-day equivalent had yet to be invented.

In June 1994, Disney executives knew the *MMC* was pushing beyond its sell-by-date. Britney was among the cast members called into a room to be told the show was being axed. They were told that it was time, 'to move on with Godspeed'. Most of the older cast members had been itching to find new challenges but the novelty still hadn't worn thin for Christina and Britney. With only two seasons under their belts, both were devastated. The thirteen-year-olds couldn't contain their upset and broke down in tears, leaning into one another and feeling deprived of the continuance of a golden opportunity.

Christina returned to Pittsburgh, and Britney to Louisiana. Justin Timberlake didn't let the grass grow under his feet, contacting fellow 'mouseketeer' J.C. Chasez to discuss the formation of a boy band. Two years later, in 1995, this germ of an idea ultimately led to the creation of *NSYNC, together with Chris Kirkpatrick, Lance Bass and Joey Fatone. After being launched under manager Lou Pearlman in Germany and landing a recording deal with RCA Records in 1977, the boy band took America by storm. Christina Aguilera would follow suit, landing her own solo recording deal in 1998 with RCA, after recording

'Reflection', a song for the Disney animated feature *Mulan*.

Back in Kentwood, Britney returned to 'normal' life and Park Lane Academy. She attended the school prom and homecoming dances, and was voted 'Junior High Most Beautiful'. She helped Lynne run aerobics classes at the family gym, turning her dance moves into a keep-fit routine. She went shopping and enjoyed nights out at the cinema in nearby Hammond with her closest friends – cousin Laura Lynn Covington and school buddies Cortney Brabham and Elizabeth Jensen, who all remain friends to this day, reminders of a grounding, ordinary era.

But Britney's landscape had changed; her horizons had broadened, her expectations grown. Over the next 18 months, such normality bored her. She had matured into someone whose professionalism and focus belonged in a career-minded adulthood, not junior high. Now she had risen above playground politics and undergone master-classes in marketing, PR and proper conduct. She wanted to move forwards, not back. She recalled her training under Myles Thoroughgood and Robin Wiley, and wanted to take her newly acquired knowledge to the next level. Life in Kentwood no longer challenged her. Now the most exciting thing on the horizon was the much-anticipated opening of a local Burger King.

During this time, Britney had consulted an entertainment lawyer named Larry Rudolph at the New York-based Rudolph & Beer entertainment and media law firm, established in 1992. She had first met him with dad Jamie when she was thirteen, arranging a meeting on the back of an audition that came to nothing. In her eyes, Larry was a powerful figure in the industry, a no-nonsense man from the Bronx, who cuts to the chase. His clients included The Backstreet Boys and Toni Braxton so he oozed pedigree as well as a knowing authority.

In his presence that first time, Britney was so painfully shy that she came across as 'introverted', he told the *Hollywood Reporter*. She shuffled in her seat and wouldn't look him in the eye, answering his questions with her stock 'Yes, sir', 'No, sir' politeness. Even after all her *Mickey Mouse Club* training, Britney as a person, not an act, found herself bound within a shell; there was no strong presence about her. And yet Larry Rudolph says that he knew she contained 'a certain inexplicable quality'. Besides, she was only thirteen at this first meeting and he sensed a ripening talent would blossom in later years.

Often called Larry in the industry, his letter-headed paper was not so informal. It read: 'Laurence H Rudolph Esq'.

Larry Rudolph, as well as Britney Spears, was clearly going up in the world. A music industry source described him as 'more rock than dorky lawyer' and added: 'There's something rough around the edges but he's sharp, level-headed and fancies himself as a bit of a visionary. Let's face it, he recognised something in Britney when others could be accused of missing it. He's that mix of cutting-edge and safe pair of hands.'

Back in Louisiana, the Spears decided they would do all they could to focus on their daughter's singing career. She was experiencing a 'comedown' in which her unhappiness clouded her smiles. They regularly held 'family meetings' and it was at one of these that Jamie promised to work longer hours and arrange loans from friends to help fund Britney's career plan. The family fitness business was struggling financially and money was exceptionally tight, but Jamie vowed to anyone who would listen that his Britney was going to make it, and he'd do whatever it took. His own limitations were never something with which he wanted to curse Britney. It was also decided that Britney should be home-schooled, using her mum's teaching expertise that would guide a Christian-faith based educational correspondence course from the University of Nebraska.

As Britney approached her fifteenth birthday, her career focus intensified and she was looking beyond the frontiers of Kentwood, searching for the next opportunity without needing to name it.

She is, she says, someone who 'gets off' on pushing her boundaries and challenging herself. During this time, she continued to take dance classes, now in New Orleans, but as she explains it: 'Back home, I got bored and wanted to sing again so, with my lawyer in New York, I called him up and said, "Is there *anything* I can do?"'

6

Teen Pop Sensation

'I really hoped and dreamed that all of this would come
to reality, but I really did not expect it to come so fast.'

– Britney, 1999

Venice High School sits with Art-Deco boldness on a
boulevard a short drive from the Pacific Ocean and
looks no different than any other public school in
the Los Angeles district. But it modestly conceals a starry
history, not wishing to alert vanloads of tourists to its show-
business anointment. Not everything and everyone seeks
attention in Hollywood.

Indeed, even some of the most informed locals don't
seem to know the trivia-quiz answers contained within its
corridors. Most remember, of course, that this was the
public school also known as 'Rydell High', where John
Travolta and Olivia Newton-John danced around the football bleachers in *Grease*. But few realise that its corridors

should be registered in the annals of music history as the setting for what became the iconic music video that launched Britney Spears into orbit with her first hit, '... Baby One More Time'.

It was here, in a first-floor corridor and science classroom, that Britney and Larry Rudolph found something for her to do: become the new solo 'teen sensation' or, as many newspapers would label her, the teen 'pop tart'; someone with whom adolescents could identify – the girls for wanting to emulate her, the boys for wanting to date someone just like her.

Britney, the shy, cosseted, teenager from unworldly Kentwood, was about to be transformed from 'mouseketeer' into a highly marketable hybrid of sweet cheerleader and naughty St Trinians schoolgirl. The journey from Kentwood to New York to Orlando suddenly moved to the production line of the music industry. Production lines manufacture and create product to be packaged and marketed, and Britney Spears – all-innocent, trusting and dreamy – had potential mass market written all over her. Like a wannabe stepping through the dry-ice smoke of the *Stars In Your Eyes*' doors, she emerged as someone new, remodelled into an adolescent who was as much about naughty-but-nice as sugar-and-spice; the all-American girl-next-door with a hint of rebel within.

Britney Spears the commercial living doll – and brand – was born.

The music industry ripped away the conservative church dresses, floral prints and pretty bows in the hair and replaced them with a white blouse, knotted at the midriff and unbuttoned at the chest to reveal a black sports bra. When completed with grey school skirt, plaited pigtails and knee-highs, she was portrayed as the innocent provocateur, whose breathy voice and fresh appeal would take a catchy song to No. 1. The schoolgirl fashionista look, coined by characters like Amber in the teen movie *Clueless*, was taken up a notch or two.

Britney also had a definitive edge over rivals Madonna and the Spice Girls because she could actually say to fans that she associated with what they wanted, felt and dreamed; she belonged to the very demographic that was her target audience. Her high-energy choreography and 'coolness', combined with teen-life themes and lyrics, would create an act that the Anglo-American music scene had never seen before in the youth pop-cult. As one critic at the time described her: 'She was the Sandra Dee of the nineties', but she blended fifties wholesomeness with the sexier undertones of the nineties.

The prelude to this breakthrough took place when Britney sent Larry Rudolph a raw demo cassette tape, following up her disillusioned call from the dreariness that was Kentwood.

From the moment she licked that envelope containing one single cassette tape, she sealed her fate. The pop industry's Venus flytrap opened, inviting in the dreams of a bored girl. The age of teen-power had arrived and the marketing geniuses had found their all-performing muse and a gap in the market.

It's hard to distinguish the true details behind the origins of the demo that would change her life. In Britney's version of events, as explained in *Heart to Heart*, the book she penned with Lynne, she made the tape after Larry advised Lynne to 'just hold a tape recorder and let me sing into it', karaoke-style. In Lynne's memoir, *Through The Storm*, she mailed Larry a tape of Britney singing at a wedding.

Whichever version is correct, the demo was sent with a couple of photographs that included one of a more grown-up Britney sitting on a blanket, stroking a dog. The last time

Larry had seen her was when she was thirteen and she hardly said a word. Since then, Britney had clearly blossomed. She was now fifteen.

'I was convinced she was the real thing. She was the most beautiful girl any record label could hope for,' Larry remembered in his contribution in *Heart to Heart*.

But he knew that he needed something more polished and so, with the assistance of a producer-client, he sent her an unreleased Toni Braxton song that had been discarded because it sounded too poppy. There were two versions: one instrumental, the other with Toni singing the lyrics. It was Britney's task to copy the way she sang it. Once she'd mastered that imitation, she hired a local music studio and recorded her vocals over the instrumental version. This would become the formal demo track that Larry submitted to record labels, with photos attached.

Larry reeled out his fishing line, and got instant bites.

Once again, there seems uncertainty in the Spears' camp as to the finer details surrounding this memorable breakthrough. In *Heart to Heart*, Britney says: 'two music publishers and four labels' were interested. While in Lynne's *Through The Storm*, meetings were arranged 'with a couple of record labels'.

What can be established beyond doubt is this: there were definitely three record labels interested – Jive, Mercury and Epic. Larry flew mum and daughter to New York to showcase his new discovery and meetings were lined up before the respective A&R teams. The term 'A&R' stands for 'artistes and repertoire' and it's these scouts who have an eye for discovering talent. Once an artist is signed, then the 'repertoire' is to take charge of their careers and promotion, fulfilling their maximum potential.

Britney's '*American Idol*' moment had arrived, and Larry prepared her for the fact that she would be walking into offices with anything from four to fifteen individuals staring back at her. She prepared three songs, all from her Whitney Houston collection: 'Jesus Love Me', 'I Have Nothing' and a cover of the hymn, 'Amazing Grace'. The song she sang for Grandpa Spears after church service on Sundays now became her calling card to the music industry.

In each office, singing to karaoke tapes, she re-enacted her earlier childhood: slipping into a focus, taking the floor and then giving it her all. When the music ended, Britney couldn't help her conditioning – and she bowed. Then she stood, with Larry by her side, to receive the questions thrown at her. It was a scene straight from *Billy Elliot*.

Recalling this time during interviews in 1999, Britney said: 'It was sort of nerve-wracking because I'm used to singing in front of big crowds, and I went in there and there were these ten executive people sitting there staring at me. I was like, "Oh, my goodness, I'm just going to close my eyes and do the best I can do!" And I sang.'

Initial reactions were not promising. At Mercury Records, an executive reported back that they 'just don't see it'. And at Epic Records, they were equally unimpressed. Vice president of A&R at the time was Michael Caplan, an industry veteran, who would later co-found indie-label OR Music before being headhunted by Columbia Records because, according to its executives, he was a 'visionary with unrivalled artistic instincts and acumen'. Asked what he looks for in a talent, Michael replies that it's 'that ephemeral "it".' Larry Rudolph, in his inimitable style, convinced him Britney had 'it'.

Today Michael remembers: 'What you've got to know is that Larry Rudolph is a good guy and great lawyer, but he's also the master of hyperbole. He always sold people as the newest and the best. He did it with Britney, saying, "I've got this girl from *The Mickey Mouse Club* ... She's the next big thing ... She's amazing ... She's so beautiful." He was giving me all that and so we were genuinely interested.'

Michael gathered in a small office in the Sony building at 550 Madison in New York, together with Polly Anthony, then senior vice-president of promotions at Epic. More significantly, according to Michael, she had more of an ear for the pop sound.

Larry led Britney into the room. Immediately, Michael's instincts flared. He recalls that moment with a brutal honesty typical of those within the music industry, taken straight from the Simon Cowell book on frankness: 'I don't mean any offence but here was this "next big thing" who was cosmetically challenged, had no presence and, for me, showed no hunger. I was expecting a true artiste ... and in walked a shy little girl.'

Clearly, Britney did not have the ephemeral 'it' that he was looking for: 'She came in, warbled, "I Will Always Love You" and I couldn't wait for it to end. Her complexion wasn't great, her voice wasn't great and when the song ended, it was Larry, not Britney, who did all the talking. Seated beside me was Polly – more the pop connoisseur – and I don't think she was impressed either, so we passed,' he said.

Next stop was Jive Records and Jeff Fenster, vice-president of A&R. He took a drastically different view. The former music lawyer, who is credited for putting the careers of Jane's Addiction and The Backstreet Boys on the map, was impressed by the demo tape. When he saw the photos and listened to the sound, he said he 'heard something from the voice ... and the delivery' despite Britney singing off-key. If the teenager backed up in the flesh what he saw in the photo, he had a star in the making.

Finding the songs would be easy – that's why he'd previously retained Swedish writer-producer Max Martin, someone recommended to him to use in collaboration with the

Backstreet Boys. But first, he wanted to look into the windows of Britney's soul and see if she had what he refers to as 'the eye of the tiger'. Previously, throughout a shy and reserved childhood, no one had ever seen Jeff's prerequisite of tiger-like hunger in her eyes. Both Jeff and his A&R colleague Steve Lunt sat back and watched the audition.

When she stopped singing, Britney remembers she was 'met by complete silence'. Steve Lunt had detected she was nervous: 'Her eyes were rolling back in her head and I thought, "This isn't going to look great on video." Then I realised her eyes were rolling because she was about to pass out!' he told the *Daily Record* in 2000, 'But even at that point, her star quality was obvious.' And, despite all previous testimonies that run to the contrary, Jeff Fenster says Britney really did have 'the eye of the tiger' and 'her vocal ability and commercial appeal caught me right away.'

Michael Caplan produces a discreet, wry smile when reminded of that appraisal but he maintains his sure stance. Some would, perhaps, accuse him of sour grapes but he insists his principles as an A&R have never regretted passing on Britney Spears: 'I believe in artistes, I believe in the art within music. Call me old-fashioned but I'm looking for true talent and a hell of a voice. I'm not looking for someone I can reinvent in the age of the celebutante that seems to have transcended the musical artiste.

'Jeff saw the same hand puppet that I did. He wanted to do something with it; I did not. Bottom line in my opinion – it could have been any number of girls stood in her shoes in the right place at the right time.'

In today's music industry, and especially since the advent of social networking sites such as MySpace, solo artistes and new bands tend to build their own platforms and make their own EPs in a bid to get noticed or, in the words of Michael Caplan, 'make some noise.' Artist development nowadays seems to be a sole perk of television talent shows, and even those fifteen minutes of fame don't necessarily guarantee huge success or royalties. But back in the mid-nineties, getting a record deal was still viewed as the holy grail of the pop star wannabe, and Britney's dream was about to materialise.

She returned to Kentwood, and prayed every night, writing down her hopes into her prayer journal. Two weeks later, Larry rang with the words: 'We've got a deal!'

According to those who know him, he was just as excited as Britney.

Jeff Fenster wanted to snap her up: 'She had no material, she didn't write, she was fifteen. We went out and found songs and producers,' he says. It was, he admits, a 'classic A&R job'. He had, in collaboration with Larry Rudolph, unearthed an uncut stone from Louisiana's soil and now they were going to polish, set and sell it on as a diamond.

Initially, Britney signed a development deal with a 90-day 'get-out' clause. In that time, Jeff introduced her to producer Max Martin, then twenty-seven, in New York in the early Fall of 1997. He left them in his office, and when he returned hours later, the starlet and record producer were bouncing ideas off one another. Britney felt instantly at ease with Max and he recognised an evident dedication; Jeff knew something exciting was cooking.

Britney, fifteen-going-on-sixteen, was to be in the vanguard of a new pop culture about to assault the chart stranglehold of R&B and hip-hop. If LeAnn Rimes had been the child star of country and Brandy the child star of R&B, then Britney Spears was about to be crowned not just the princess of pop but the newcomer whose presence would have a universal impact on the entire industry – and charts worldwide.

It all could have turned out so differently, had Britney taken the Girls Aloud route.

Post-*Mickey Mouse Club*, and long before the likes of Cheryl, Kimberley, Nicola, Nadine and Sarah would take Britain by storm, she was approached by Justin Timberlake's mum to join Innosense, an all-girl band that was in development. Spurred on by her son's newly formed boy-band *NSYNC, Lynn Harless started forming ideas for a girl-band equivalent. She felt one of the five slots was tailor-made for Britney and fellow *MMC* member, Nikki DeLoach.

Justin's mum rang Lynne Spears and laid her cards on the table, and it couldn't have seemed more timely. Britney was looking for her break in the weeks before she'd sent the demo tape to Larry Rudolph. Indeed, the family sounded out Larry and he reminded them that The Backstreet Boys were huge and there was no female equivalent, except for the Spice Girls back in Britain. Britney was definitely interested, and she and her mama felt that God was opening one of his doors of opportunities.

Matters progressed as far as management papers being drawn up and detailed discussions were held. Indeed, Lynn Harless and the forming Innosense group truly felt that Britney was fully on-board. But 48 hours before Britney was due to put pen to paper, the Spears held one of their family discussions, where it was collectively realised that her dream had always been to become a solo singer like Madonna or a Whitney. Despite everything being set, and having *NSYNC manager Lou Pearlman prepared to provide financial backing, Britney pulled out even though, back then, she had nothing to rely on save for a 'strong hunch'. Mum, father and daughter agreed she would go solo – and it proved to be the wisest hunch.

As Jive Records' newest solo artiste, Britney found herself locked onto a fast-track treadmill in 1998, destined for recording studios in both America and Europe to cut the single and album, '… Baby One More Time'. The fun would turn into a gruelling schedule, far more exacting than pressures she faced at gymnastics and during *Ruthless! The Musical*. This time, she wouldn't ask to quit because she had, as she said, 'found my job in life'.

The signing also meant returning to live in New York, and neither parent could join her. Lynne was a second-grade teacher with a five-year-old Jamie-Lynn to consider, while Jamie was struggling to keep the gym afloat. Indeed, they couldn't tell Britney the dire state of their financial affairs because they didn't want to detract from her required focus.

But the truth was miserable. The family business had proved a fad that Kentwood couldn't sustain. Not enough money was being generated and so Jamie left staff barely eighteen years old in charge while he travelled to towns such as Memphis and Jackson on construction contracts. At one point, he swallowed his pride to ride the tractor on his brother-in-law Sonny's farm. As he over-stretched himself, the 'Total Fitness by Jamie' venture was neglected and its young employees ended up not being paid. The Spears had no option but to file for bankruptcy. Official records showed debts included the sterling equivalent of £31,000 in unpaid taxes. Their Ford Probe car was seized by the local sheriff with £7,000 owing on an unpaid loan, and they had also defaulted on an outstanding £26,000 mortgage on the land where the gym was built. On top of all that, the family phone-line was disconnected. It reached a point where Lynne had to resort to a $500 line of credit from a local store so she could afford Christmas gifts for the children.

The lifelong friend of the Spears, mentioned previously, has heard the tales laying the blame at Jamie's door but contends: 'The business went down because him and Lynne spread themselves too thin. Jamie worked his knuckles to the bone because they had this thing about trying to better themselves but they took too much on: the gym, the boiler-making, the construction, the teaching. Basically, years of working every hour God sent to fund Britney's dream caught up with them.'

No doubt Britney was oblivious to the strife as she prepared for New York. Lynne wanted to make sure her daughter wasn't alone in New York and Europe. That's when another lynch pin in 'Team Britney' was found – the woman who'd accompanied them to the Oak Alley arts and craft festival: Felicia Culotta. Then aged thirty-two, she became Britney's 'substitute Mama' and they clicked imme-diately, so much so that the chaperone-come-assistant would later be described by Britney as 'like my right arm'. She called Felicia 'Fe'. In turn, Felicia called Britney 'Boo'. Lynne described Felicia as 'the angel' watching over her daughter.

For a mother and daughter who had been inseparable since birth, Britney's departure was a wrench. In many respects, Fe would become the mutual comforter – for Brit-ney when she'd cry for her mama, and by ringing Lynne morning and night to assuage her worries. One thing that Fe learned was that Britney may have had a talent, but she had been hitherto tied to her mama's apron-strings and so, in those early days, a lot of surrogate mollycoddling was required. Indeed, as a reminder of home, Britney even packed one of the dolls from her treasured collection.

It seems almost an irony that Fe's previous job, as well as working as a dental hygienist, was as a professional nanny. But her soothing presence, combined with her patience and measured advice, was deemed priceless by both the family and management company. 'Home' for the two of them would become a Jive-owned penthouse, which commanded impressive views of the Manhattan skyline and where, in between her recording work, Britney continued her educational correspondence course.

First stop on their travels was New Jersey to work with renowned producer and songwriter Eric Foster White, who had previously worked with artistes such as Whitney Houston, The Backstreet Boys and Hi-Five. Then, it was on to Sweden to work with 'super-producer' Max Martin, who had recently collaborated on The Backstreet Boys' album *Millennium*. The square-jawed, blond-haired Swede is a workhorse and an absolute perfectionist: 'I want to be part of every note, every single moment going on in the studio. I want nothing forgotten, I want nothing missed,' he told the *LA Times*.

His dedication matched that of Britney's, and if anyone was flagging at the end of the sessions, it was Fe Culotta. Max said he found a perfect synergy with his new talent, and not only praised her work ethic but her talent, saying that "she takes things to another level."

Sweden was where '… Baby One More Time' was created but it didn't always have Britney's name written all over it. From his Stockholm studio, Max had specifically written that number for four-times Grammy award-winning group TLC: Lisa 'Left Eye' Lopes, Rozonda 'Chilli' Thomas, and Tionne 'T-Boz' Watkins. But, as the story goes, the R&B trio's producer Dallas Austin rejected the track and allowed Max to place it elsewhere. That composition sat on a shelf in Sweden for a whole year until the young girl from Louisiana walked in and made it her own.

In both New Jersey and Sweden, Britney had thrown herself into an exhaustive schedule, which started around noon most days and sometimes stretched beyond midnight. When Jeff Fenster heard the reports – and sounds – coming out of New Jersey and Sweden, he tore up the 90-day 'get-out' clause and signed Britney Spears to a permanent record deal with Jive, nowadays part of the Zomba Label Group. The entire label was abuzz about the prospects for the new artiste the world had yet to discover. With the album recorded and packaged, a massive promotional blitz was orchestrated to spread word of mouth throughout Middle America in the early summer of 1998.

Britney was sent on a 26-city tour of shopping malls from East to West, supported by two backing dancers in a four-song set. This was her 'making a noise' on the marketing front. On the back of this wave, radio stations were sent '… Baby One More Time' for their playlists, to be launched one month ahead of its official US release, slated for November 1998. The idea, from hitting the shopping malls and getting the song out there on the airwaves, was to seep this catchy number into the public unconscious, to build the wave.

The determined promotional push was enhanced by the arrival of another addition to 'Team Britney' – Florida-based manager Johnny Wright, who was brought in to work alongside Larry Rudolph, bolstering the management team with a true industry heavyweight. Johnny had previously worked with New Kids On The Block, The Backstreet Boys and Janet Jackson. His addition was evidence of the serious intent behind the Britney campaign, and he set to work on organising her first solo concert tour. Someone who knew Johnny socially – when he went on to manage *NSYNC – says of him: 'He is a super cool guy, very suave, very centred. He has a meticulous eye and is so orchestrated about everything. He has everything covered but maintains this calm about him. Whether he was looking out for *NSYNC or Britney, his attention to detail was second to none.'

'Team Britney' now comprised managers Larry and Johnny, Jive's A&R men Jeff Fenster and Steve Lunt, and assistant Felicia, with mum Lynne hovering on the periphery as a constant presence. But this impenetrable inner-circle would later evolve to include make-up artists Fran Cooper and Julianne Day, stylists Tanya Tomboran and the dynamic partnership known only as 'Kurt & Bart', and choreographer Wade Robson, not to mention a ring of bodyguards led by Robert Finn, also known as 'Big Rob'.

With the official US-release date nearing, it was time to shoot *that* music video and invite someone else into the fold: LA-based British director Nigel Dick, who shot the Band Aid video for 'Do They Know It's Christmas'. It was his third video for Jive Records, but the director's debut with Britney would be his true triumph, strapping both Britney and the song to a rocket that was just starting up its engines.

As Britney strolled with assistant Felicia into Venice High School on Thursday, 6 August 1999, she experienced a sensation she wouldn't yet realise was strange: she felt anonymous. She had little under three months left of what could be termed 'ordinary personal freedom'. It was a clear summer's day and many students were milling about because it was summer school. Britney was unrecognisable, save for the fact she was a Louisiana teenager wandering amid predominantly Mexican-Americans. Crew trucks parked kerb-side as lights, cameras and tracks were unloaded for a three-day shoot. To any passing motorist on Venice Boulevard, it looked like any other on-location set-up, an everyday occurrence in LA.

For director Nigel Dick, it was just another video shoot, and Britney was just another hopeful: 'Whilst everything was being set-up, I remember her sitting around with the other dancers, as an equal. No one knew who she was; she just blended in. I look back now and wonder if she remembers how that even felt, to blend in with everyone else.'

He had met Britney some weeks earlier in New York, having been flown in by Jive. When he listened to the song, it surprised him, and not just because he normally plays shred-guitar to heavy rock, and listens to Led Zeppelin: 'I thought, "This is a great song!" It had *Top of the Pops* written all over it. Then I met Britney, and there was something refreshing about her because she was easy-going, without a hint of arrogance. So I said, "Okay, I'll do it."'

Nigel – who would go on to direct more than 300 music videos for a range of different artistes – returned to LA to draw up some ideas. Britney remembers those first sketches being 'some bizarre Power Ranger-thing'. In promotional interviews, she said she didn't like it, instead preferring something to which schoolgirls could relate: 'We're all in school and bored out of our minds so I thought it would be really cool,' she said. It was she, so the legend goes, who came up with the Catholic schoolgirl theme.

At first glance, this seems incredulous, asking the public to believe that this compliant teenager with a reverence of her elders had, on her first video shoot, spoken up and risked the disappointment of the record label. Indeed, many have scoffed at the claim, suggesting it's a concocted story for promotional purposes. But Britney is justified, in part, for taking some of the credit, as the director himself explains: 'Britney hated my idea, and Jive hated it, so they rang me and passed the phone to Britney. She said, "Let's do a video where I'm a girl in school looking at lots of hot boys."

'I'm sitting in my car, on the cell-phone, thinking, "Good God, I'm a grown man taking instructions from a sixteen-year-old girl about something I wasn't sure about. But then I had this moment of clarity – she knows more about this world of girls and boys than I do. So I swallowed my pride, got what she was saying and wrote out the idea that became the video. But yes, the kernel of the idea came from Britney.'

Nor does this surprise *Mickey Mouse Club* choreographer Myles Thoroughgood, who immediately recognised Britney's hand in the video the moment it first aired. It mirrored a concept both he and musical segment producer Sarah Elgart devised: five dancing girls dressed in Catholic school uniform, with Christina Aguilera as the lead. This on-set production number, filmed for Season 7 of *MMC*, was set to Aretha Franklin's less energetic 'Think' and, because it was *Mickey Mouse*, the girls buttoned up with a tie and wore tights, not knee-highs. But the Catholic skirts and the pigtails were on full display as Christina sang lead vocals with Britney as one of four schoolgirl dancers.

Myles has no doubt that Britney took her inspiration for this number, and could actually picture her speaking up for herself: 'You've got to remember that part of Britney's education with us was to always ask herself: "How can I relate what I'm doing to the audience?" She was conditioned to think creatively. She took that lesson away and translated it into her own career. People forget that Britney was trained to think that way and, when she feels confident within her group or with someone, she absolutely asks questions and speaks up.'

The filming of music videos on location can be a notoriously pressurised environment for both artiste and crew working to an allotted time schedule and budget. Director Nigel didn't know what to expect from this newcomer on day one, when the 'Britney-in-car' scenes were shot. With everything ready to go, he set the cameras rolling and said out loud: 'Looking at the camera ... Here we go ... Enjoy everyone ... See you on MTV!'

'And she just did it!' he recalled, 'I would like to say that the reason she did great was because of me, but I can't. She nailed it and she was the one thing we didn't have to worry about.'

Once more, Britney's Disney training came to the fore.

She was happy when the people at Jive created a distinct look and style rooted in the schoolgirl image. This image creation was specifically designed to provide an 'authenticity' schoolgirls throughout America could derive both an association and an identity. In terms of the video, Britney's acknowledged input was evidence of her growing confidence.

The single and album sleeves for the '... Baby One More Time' single couldn't have been tamer: Britney sat on the floor with legs tucked either side of her, looking up to the camera, against a pink background. It resembled a cover-shoot for *Jackie*. Then there was one of Britney, hands clasped almost in prayer, against an all-white background. They even manufactured an eleven-inch doll version of Britney, which mimicked the knotted blouse, knee-highs and pigtails. Finally, the doll collector had become someone to be collected, dressed-up ... and objectified for real.

But Britney's focus was on the song's prospects: 'Every night, I had a Bible book that I prayed in and every night I would pray: "I hope my song plays on a certain radio station that's really big" and it would happen. Then I'd be like, "I hope the video is wonderful" – and it was. Then I was like, "I hope they play it on MTV" – and they did. I am totally blessed,' she recalled to the *Daily Mirror* in 2000.

Nigel Dick was a happy man, too, but the reaction to his video – both then and since – amuses him because when he and colleague Declan Whitebloom cut the piece, there was nothing sexual or iconic about it: 'Everyone has obsessed about this video and the media made it something it never was in my book. It's not as if we set out to make an iconic video, and it wasn't even raunchy. It grew from nowhere, and became iconic.

'What's funny is that we were relaxed about it, and Jive were hardly jumping up and down. In fact, they were like, "We don't like what you've done in the middle eight" and we had to change a few things, but the end result was taken completely out of context. I'm proud of it for another reason – because I'm a British guy who went to a boys' school with no idea about American schools, and yet people said we captured the American school atmosphere. I'd successfully recreated a life I didn't know about – that's why I'm proud of it.'

Privately, as the Spears played the what-if game with the single's prospects, they collectively pinned their hopes of Britney's debut single making the Top 40. A dream outcome, they agreed, would be if they managed the Top 10.

With Britney away from home and preparing for the single's release, Lynne kept herself busy in Kentwood. When she first heard the song on the radio, she burst into tears. For Britney, that moment came when she flew into Louisiana and, as she settled into Lynne's car, she heard the song on 104.1 New Orleans: 'I let out such a scream!'

Back in the day, as a child strapped into the back seat, a little Britney would sing along to the radio that her mama used to crank up loud; mum and daughter singing together. Only this time, it wasn't Madonna or Whitney Houston but Britney herself. It was one of many pinch-me-I'm-dreaming moments to which she became accustomed.

The single '... Baby One More Time' hit the stores on 3 November 1998 and debuted in the Billboard Hot 100 Chart at No. 17, pushed by constant video re-runs on *MTV's Total Request Live* (TRL) show. Nigel Dick witnessed the wall-to-wall playbacks and couldn't quite believe the stir it was causing: 'I had given a sneak preview of that video to someone in the industry and they seemed completely unmoved, virtually dismissing it. So I didn't have great expectations. But then MTV start playing it and my phone didn't stop ringing. It was only then that I suspected we'd started something.'

To continue the gathering momentum, Britney was installed as the warm-up act for *NSYNC on its American tour, reuniting her with ex-'mousketeers' Justin and J.C. Chasez. As initiations go, she could not have found better allies and more familiar company.

'It was probably the funniest thing I have done since I have been signed to Jive,' she said at the time, 'I had the advantage that I wasn't the main act and I was able to do my little show and get back on the bus. I didn't have all that pressure on me like they did.'

That was a brave spin on the harder reality of a girl – one month from her seventeenth birthday – having to enter an arena of similarly aged teenage girls, who were there to scream and cry for their boy idols, not some unknown girl from Louisiana. Britney had been to a Backstreet Boys' gig where the support act was drowned out by chanting: 'I was like, "Oh my goodness, I hope that doesn't happen to me! I got really stressed about it.'

On her debut night, she could not have been more nervous. At first, she remembers a few boos ringing out but as her 20-minute set continued, she silenced the crowds and received an accepting, if not a rapturous reception.

'I just got on stage and did the best I could, and it turned out really well. After that first show, I felt really comfortable and there was always a good energy.'

Reviewing the act, Gemma Tarlack in the *Milwaukee Journal* observed: 'Spears' amiable voice and solid stage presence were more than enough to carry inane material about crushes, and her 20-minute set was full of hints that a more interesting vocalist may one day break through her sugar shell.'

In those pre-iTune days, the song also previewed on a free-toll phone number while Sunglass Hut chief executive John Watson agreed to his first merchandise tie-in, issuing a free CD with every $80 sunglasses purchase. Such deals would become a huge generator of wealth for Britney as she signed a lucrative arrangement with Sony Signatures to exercise her worldwide licensing and tour merchandising rights.

The combined effect of a relentless marketing campaign and touring with *NSYNC meant that, by the time Britney celebrated her seventeenth birthday that December, '... Baby One More Time' had climbed to No. 8 in the US charts. In January 1999, the dreamscape was complete when both her debut single and debut album simultane-ously hit the No. 1 spot – a feat never before accomplished by any artist in the Nielson SoundScan era, the system that tracks sales of music and music video products throughout the US and Canada.

Released in the UK in February 1999, it became the best-selling single of the year and held its No. 1 spot for two consecutive weeks. It also became a No. 1 single in 13 other territories including New Zealand, Australia, Canada and throughout Europe. It was nominated in the Best Female Vocal Performance at the Grammys, won 'Best Single' at the Teen Choice Awards and 'Best Female Performer', 'Best

Breakthrough Act', 'Best Song' and 'Best Pop Act' at the 1999 MTV Europe Music Awards in Dublin. That night, giddy with excitement, she thanked, 'Jesus Christ and my family … and just the world for accepting pop again.'

In total, the single '… Baby One More Time' sold almost 4 million copies worldwide, and the album of the same name went on to sell a worldwide 25 million. Such a staggering achievement was testimony to a brilliantly executed promotional campaign. Ultimate success in the music industry depends on many factors coming together and hitting a simultaneous crescendo. A record label is its own orchestra, all working from the same hymn sheet to impact the marketplace. This re-modelled pop-creation that sashayed onto Jive Record's platform had become the de facto 'next big thing' – just as Larry Rudolph predicted. Britney's failed auditions were instantly irrelevant. What mattered was the performer who had blossomed beyond recognition.

Britney was doing much more than living a personal dream. Her success sent a potent message to teen America and Britain: that it is possible to be plucked from obscurity and become an 'American Idol'. Her vault to success sowed the seeds in a youth culture that would become enthralled by fame. Her fulfilled fantasy created fantasies within others, spawning a classless idea that everyone with a dream 'could do a Britney'. It's this very attitude that continues to fuel the talent show format that has made the likes of Simon Cowell a fortune.

The days of anonymity at Venice High School were over. She was the 'overnight phenomenon' launched into an intense media and chat show tour. For the uninitiated, such promotional slogs can be a rude awakening, with back-to-back radio, television, newspaper and magazine interviews. Some days would include around 40 interviews, starting with breakfast shows in the morning and late shows at night. But she handled herself like a pro.

On *Access Hollywood*, she was asked if she saw herself having the staying power to be more than a mere one-hit wonder. She answered: 'I think this is what I want to do for the rest of my life, definitely ... All you've got to do is make great music and make music the audience wants to hear and you will be around for a long time – and that's what I intend to do.'

The speed of her success and fame took everyone by surprise. ABC television host Regis Philbin described it as a 'Britney Spears explosion' and the media vernacular testified to the overnight force of her impact: SPEARS RAPIDLY ASCENDS AS NEW POP POWERHOUSE declared the *LA Times* and there was the usual tabloid excitement heralding 'the Queen of Teen', 'the teen phenomenon' and 'the red-hot pop star'. Britney didn't really have the time to think about all the 'weird craziness', as she described it, because it was all a blur.

In that late winter of 1998 and initial months of 1999, it seemed that she was on every TV and radio station throughout America and then Europe. Observers couldn't help but be impressed by this likeable, mild-mannered, softly-spoken newcomer. She had a habit of sitting on her hands during interviews, and smiling awkwardly when a presenter's banter led her away from a framework of usual answers. Whenever a fan or interviewer paid her a compliment, she'd turn all embarrassed and say: 'Awwwwww, that's so sweet, thank you!' She was 'walking the walk and talking the talk', becoming the pitch-perfect spokesmodel. Once again, it was a fine example of her Disney training.

She looked her most relaxed on the *Rosie O'Donnell Show* and she couldn't have come across any better, seemingly solid, unfazed and with her feet firmly on the ground.

Perhaps that's why Rosie imparted some motherly advice as they wrapped the interview before going into a commercial break: 'Well, you're a level-headed young girl and I hope you stay that way – and I think you will. Stay in Louisiana … it's a very nice place … and it will keep you grounded.'

7

The Making of Britney

'I don't like being a role model.
I'm not perfect, I'm human."
– *Britney*, **Rolling Stone**, *2001*

In 1927, the Hollywood actress Mae West was arrested by police following complaints about her 'suggestive' performance as a prostitute in a play titled *Sex*. Its content caused consternation among the Society for the Suppression of Vice and she was accused of 'corrupting the morals of youth'. As she was led away amid an explosion of paparazzi flashbulbs, she recognised the value in the controversy. 'This will be the making of me!' she declared to waiting reporters.

Britney Spears is no Mae West, and nor could she be accused of corrupting morals with her arrival on the pop-scene, even if the Baptist Church may not have wholly approved. But fame was to teach her that media coverage, with all its distortions, exaggerations and hyperbole, was an essential element in her transformation from country bumpkin to pop princess. She, too, learned that there was no harm in being 'suggestive' and the hype surrounding the release of '... Baby One More Time' demonstrated the truth that 'there's no such thing as bad publicity', at least not in the days when controversy was confined to the superficial issues of image as opposed to her mental wellbeing.

In the same way that controversy helped turn Mae West into the highest-paid woman of her day, Britney entertained a controversy that helped create a fame and fortune beyond the comprehension of most people, let alone a bankrupt family from Kentwood. But her Mae West making-of-me controversy wasn't confined to three minutes in a fairly tame music video. The media furore that she endorsed was a cover-shoot for *Rolling Stone* magazine in April 1999.

The arresting image – designed to capture both Britney's allure and innocence – showed her in her bedroom, lying flat on a purple satin sheet, holding a telephone to one ear with her left hand, and cuddling the purple Tellytubby 'Tinky Winky' under her right arm. As she lay there, looking up to the camera, she allowed a white cardigan to gape open and reveal a black push-up bra and polkadot briefs. The nudge, nudge, wink-wink elements of her publicity campaign were suddenly elevated to a code-red of media excitement and moral debate.

America's Bible Belt – Britney's own conservative roots – was outraged. But this was the starting point for a common theme that was to be forever stitched through her career: sexuality, tease, shock, provocation and suggestiveness would soon overtake the boy-meets-girl romanticism within her early lyrics. That said, as *Rolling Stone* magazine pointed out, the title of her first hit, '... Baby One More

Time', had already used ellipsis to allude to a breathless 'hit me one more' with its spank-me subtext.

Journalism was complicit in generating the sexualised hype that defined this teenager. If Jive Records lit the fire, the media arrived with the petrol. It cannot have been an accident that photographer David LaChapelle, a man renowned for his nude portraits and exaggerated depiction of personalities, was booked for the shoot. Then there was magazine correspondent Stephen Daly, whose introduction to the text mentioned how Britney 'extends a honeyed thigh across the length of the sofa' and how her T-shirt is 'distended by her ample chest' while her shorts 'cling snugly to her hips'. In pointing out that he is falling into the alluring trap made for the youth-generation, he wrote how his interviewee cocked her head and 'smiles receptively'. Between them, both record label and magazine cooked up a storm.

The rest of the media followed this lead by inventing labels such as 'Louisiana's Lolita' and 'vampish seductress', and provided a platform for the moral extremists to speak out. Scotland's *Daily Record* spoke of 'blatant exploitation' and asked in its headline: 'Why is this God-fearing pop star posing as Lolita?' Tom Connelly, spokesman for the Scottish Catholic church, said, 'People like Britney should not be allowed to be people's role models.' The Church of Scotland's Board of Social Responsibility expressed concerns that Britney was promoting a destructive message. And an article for the University Wire publication, posted as part of its Iowa State Daily coverage, said, 'the trend of sexualizing teenagers sets a dangerous precedent.'

It added: 'When it comes to the under-18 set, there needs to be some limits on how sexy these children should be. Spears may be on top now, having the time of her life, but one day she will look back and see what the rest of us see: a moderately talented girl, whose body is the main event.'

Rolling Stone traditionalists were not amused either. This American institution in the magazine world, which had first launched the careers of Tom Wolfe and Hunter S. Thompson, had lowered its standards, argued the purists. But the magazine's publisher Jann Wenner had always kept the magazine at the cutting edge of the market by reflecting society – and society was clearly fascinated by the young Miss Spears. The bottom line was that everyone was chasing the dollar and Britney was the commodity up for grabs. Substance and worthiness could be left for another day.

Jann Wenner's acumen was rewarded when *Rolling Stone* had a circulation-busting cover that became iconic, and Jive achieved publicity that dollars simply couldn't buy. It responded by turning the magazine cover into a poster that was mailed out to the media to provide a backdrop for future television interviews.

Everyone was a winner, including Britney Spears the performer, if not necessarily Britney Spears, the humble teenager from Kentwood. This was more to do with reputation-building. The character building challenges would come much later.

There is an innate quality within Britney that appealed to both record executives and fans alike but the disparity between the conflicting images was causing confusion among the youth culture. No one knew exactly what ground Britney occupied. Did she represent the Church? Or sex? This deliberate enigma was recognised by The Centre for Parent-Youth Understanding in Elizabethtown, Pennsylvania, and it issued a research paper on the mixed message: 'Spears pulls no punches when it comes to talking about her Baptist faith. She speaks of praying nightly and her love for God. But, in true postmodern fashion, her verbalized commitment doesn't mesh with the sexual messages of her visual image.'

The paper didn't necessarily criticise the singer because it cited her songs as the chief reason why Britney was 'a darling of so many parents'. But it stressed that she was promoting 'a subtle and seductive image of female adolescent sexuality'. That contradiction was causing 'confusion' among children, it said.

Britney wasn't offering any definitive answers. If anything, she seemed equally confused. Privately, she considered the media reaction to her magazine shoot to be 'demeaning and degrading' because everything focused on the sexual connotations, not her talent. In her mind, she was acting, playing to the camera – as taught.

One year later, again in *Rolling Stone*, Britney aired this frustration: 'It was about being in a magazine and playing a part ... It's like on TV, if you see Jennifer Love Hewitt or Sarah Michelle Gellar kill someone, do you think that means they go out and do that? Of course not.'

Bearing in mind her insular background and cloistered upbringing, it's understandable why Britney was bewildered, but some commentators believed 'playing along' constituted fully informed knowledge and awareness; that the wagging of one's tail indicated a deeper understanding of the meanings and subtexts. The *Guardian* newspaper, for example, asked us to believe that Britney had become some kind of marketing mogul; that overnight success also equated to overnight intelligence. An article by Hetti Judah tagged the teenager as 'an astute marketing woman'. But this wasn't Britney being clever; it was Britney returning to a mode that was second nature: disappearing into her bedroom to perform and become someone other than herself. She was playing dress-up, and she was the doll.

A source working with her at that time said: 'It was obvious to everyone that she was not the most tasteful girl in the world but she was striking so it was recognised that her songs and image would do most of the talking.

'Britney was not very clued-up about the business back then; it was all new and she was so trusting. She worked hard on that video shoot and the publicity, and back then, she believed it was all about talent and being taken seriously. The promotional stuff was "acting" and her singing/dancing was "performing". It was as simple as that to her.'

If that sounds incredibly naive, then that truth starts to accurately portray the image of a lamb that had just wandered into a lion's den. She may well have known what themes relate to her audience, but there's nothing to suggest she was so sexually aware or cognisant of the deeper meanings and subtle nuances. In Orlando, her *Mickey Mouse Club* tutor Chuck Yerger watched from afar and heard the echo of a girl who never thought her elders would ask her to do anything that was deemed inappropriate.

It was her first photo-shoot, organised by her record label, and everyone was present, including parents Lynne and Jamie and manager Larry. The shoot also took place at her home. In that environment, it would have been contrary to her nature to object.

But if Lynne Spears' account is accepted, then everyone was as green as Britney. Hundreds of photos were taken around the family home in different locations, but when it came to the bedroom scene, parents and manager were shut out because there wasn't enough space inside.

According to Lynne, the first she knew was when Larry popped his head round the door and abruptly called a halt to proceedings. Lynne hurried in to see what the problem was – and there was Britney lying on the bed in her bra and pants; a startled teenager caught doing something she shouldn't have been. No photo approval was agreed by her management – 'Larry was also new to this managing business'. Not for the first time, no one was taking control in Britney's childhood home.

Aunty Chanda, who was by now divorcing Britney's Uncle John Mark, remembers the Spears discussing the front cover when it was published. A copy was lying on the kitchen top, and Lynne was visibly upset, saying: 'Things went much further than we realised.' Aunty Chanda said: 'That was her baby lying there, half-naked. She felt proud, but also embarrassed. She wanted Britney to be out there as Britney, not in the way she was portrayed. Even back then, I remember Lynne saying, "I've got no control" and everyone was telling her it was okay, it was just a look they were achieving. And Lynne was like, "Okay, I guess so." When they saw stuff like this happening, they wanted to pull the ropes back a little bit, but never knew how.'

Lynne's account is also supported by a source close to Jive Records who says: 'At first, everyone thought, "What the f***!" but the reaction was great and so Jive ran with it.'

All parties seemed momentarily overwhelmed by the snowball that was turning into an avalanche. One can only wonder if anyone caught up in this maelstrom took time out to ask Britney: 'Are you okay with this? How you doing?'. With the speed of events, it would be debatable whether anyone had the chance to properly discuss anything other than the PR implications.

But there was no doubting the ingenuity behind the PR strategy. It was almost as if someone from Jive had studied the late Simone de Beauvoir, the French philosopher and novelist, who suggested that men deliberately create a sexually-charged mystery around women: 'The young girl's purity allows hope for every kind of licence, and no one knows what perversities are concealed in her innocence. Neither child nor adult, the virgin is one of the privileged exponents of mystery ... on the other hand, the figure of the prostitute gives scope to the grand play of vices and virtues. She belongs to no man ... but lives off such commerce.'

And whatever the unseen eyes of men make of Britney, she retains her purity, come what may. It was, in terms of raw, ruthless marketing, a masterstroke. Once she was dressed-up, all she had to do was look into the camera lens and sear her image on the audience; both redundant, but everlasting.

In Britney's mind, there was nothing to think about. This is what she wanted to do: to sing, dance and perform. It was as simple and as straightforward as that, and for the first year at least, that mind-set meant she was constantly high, disbelieving the dream. It simply didn't seem to dawn on her that she was effectively being 'sold' as part sexual commodity, part innocent schoolgirl. Both teen magazines and influential periodicals sat up and took notice. Within six months of being in the spotlight, she was elevated to teenage role model on the back of one record.

Ask Britney now and she'll say she never wanted to be a role model. She always wanted to be a pop star, not a guru. No one asked her whether she wanted to be a role model, and no one knew whether she'd be anything more than a one-hit wonder. But this enforced responsibility became an automatic consequence of the success that lifted her high and held her aloft – to be both denounced and adored. At times like this, the pressure gets to her and she is someone who can get lost in a mind of racing thoughts without, as she puts it, 'honouring her soul'.

One year later, in a second interview with *Rolling Stone*, she said she liked to be viewed as a kid, 'because people expect so much out of me right now.' Behind the smile and promotional gloss, what would be the psychological impact of this role model status?

Once more, Britney is answering to the expectations heaped on her shoulders. She is suddenly the objectified role model, the saviour of the pop industry. It continues the arc of the 'performer' born to make people happy.

Her performances first made her mum happy, then her wholesomeness is perfect for the Disney smile, then she's the next big thing for Jive Records and then she becomes a pop star-role model whose performances keep the world happy. It doesn't matter whether she's performing for her mum or her fans, she sees the same applause and happiness and equates it with love. It doesn't matter whether she's performing at a talent contest or on the world stage, she sees the No. 1 position and equates this with acceptance and approval. All this is being programmed on an unconscious level and the burden on Britney is tremendous.

Now, she's fulfilling a commercial demand. It's almost as if people look at Britney and ask: 'What can you do for us?' And it feels okay to her because this makes her feel special and important. She automatically thinks, 'Wow – I make people happy!' She's derived value from that since day one, without realizing that her performing more than likely stems from a need to feel connected and in control. All Britney saw, and therefore processed, was that whatever she did, everyone applauded, sending messages that say, 'Keep up the good show, keep on going, look at the happiness you bring'.

Someone has always told her how to be, how to look, how to dress, how to behave, what standard to set. And all the time, deep down, there will be a part of her that, one day, was always going to say, 'Enough – I'm done'. It was always likely with this pattern that Britney would grow sick and tired of performing, and sick and tired of being the person everyone wants her to be. It's a recipe for a backlash in later life and a resentment at being moulded, instructed, steered and directed. But just as significantly, this malleable nature also left her open to being

easily influenced in later life, being overly trusting of others
and susceptible to bad influences.

Such psychological seeds wouldn't pop until much further
down the line, but this insight alone helps explain that her
ultimate rebellion and collapse was already being stirred.
The scale of fame that Britney was being asked to deal with
would test the most stable and centred adult. It is hard to
imagine someone even with a strong sense of self having to
hold up a role for the world.

The deeper impact on Britney will have been invisible,
and it would have taken a highly aware individual to understand – and cater for – the deeper effects that such an
intense commercial drive could have on her. But since when
has Hollywood, or the music industry, considered the
consequences of fame? It is the showbusiness version of
Gulf War syndrome. No one dare tell its soldiers of the realities that might lie ahead.

In Britney's case, it is doubtful anyone would have seen
any pitfalls in a teenager so strongly identifying with being a
performer. As that one-dimensional identity grew, to the
awe and wonderment of the watching world, this blonde
creation basked obliviously in fame and fortune. But behind
the convincing mask of the performer, the *real* Britney
would have become increasingly lost – already the real Britney was eclipsed by the brand. Never again would there be
such a thing as 'normal': The psychological legacy is hard
to define but:

> The role model, her portrayal of a commodity, and the adulation
> all feeds what we call the false self – a false identity. The results
> of Britney's performances provide her with a temporary fix, a
> feeling that everything is going to be okay. But it also means
> she has no idea who she is outside of performing because that

side to her character has never been allowed to develop. As a result, the human inside is so lonely and lost. The magnitude of this isolation within herself would become overwhelming in later years.

I would also question how easy it is for Britney to be alone without feeling terrifying anxiety? I would guess that she'd probably make friends with the janitor if she had to, as long as she's got someone with her. Her performing is so tied to keeping a secure attachment to her mum – and maintaining order – that anything outside of that mode will leave her extremely agitated. Remember, performing is almost the same as her comfort blanket. She's needed it as a go-to place since childhood. Without it, then it's highly likely that she will have been scared by life.

It is perhaps telling that in those initial months of stardom hitting home, Britney has admitted to suffering anxiety and found comfort in sleeping with Lynne in her bed. 'Louisiana's Lolita' didn't wish to be alone in her own room and wanted to be close to Lynne within a process that was increasingly taking her away from home. Management and Jive Records had ensured that Britney returned home every six weeks, and they did all they could to maintain a balance for this mama's girl, but the facades needed to be maintained. After all, she was a media-nominated role model. But within the four walls of her childhood home, Britney slept as close and as tight to her mama as she'd ever done.

In her waking hours, the reaction to her first single educated her into believing that a thousand words dressed around one image were capable of generating star-making publicity. The Mae West lesson was dawning.

Controversy and debate kept Britney in the spotlight for some considerable time. First, there were questions as to whether she'd undergone breast augmentation. Speak to people who knew her in Kentwood, and at *The Mickey*

Mouse Club, and they are all unanimous: the tiny-framed, flat-chested Britney suddenly became noticeably voluptuous. They are all convinced Britney's chest was enhanced to enhance her image, but there was talk of the procedure being reversed 'when she realised that her new breasts restricted movement during dance routines'. A definitive answer was never given but perhaps a smarter question might have been: 'Britney, did you have breast implants and have them *reduced*, not reversed?'

Britney herself described the debate as 'retarded' and always denied ever having surgery. After all, books like *Heart to Heart* had promoted the message that young girls should accept their bodies as they are. But the stir created a did-she-or-didn't-she? media coverage that Jive Records could not buy. Media generated or media manipulated, the end result was the same: Britney maintained her presence in the newspaper and magazine columns.

Then another question emerged: the has-she-or-hasn't-she? on her virginity. Britney soon learned nothing was sacred when one becomes famous; that in between records, the media must have *something* to keep the pot boiling, so the world suddenly switched its focus from an image-conscious discussion to a moral debate, eager to know if the Baptist teenager had ever enjoyed sex. This seemed to be answered when Britney made it clear that she was saving herself for marriage, consistent with her Christian values.

In Kentwood, such a straitlaced answer brought snorts of derision. On this occasion, Britney was honouring the official line from her management but there was also a deeper reason: she didn't want her mama to think she'd had sex before marrying. The truth, as told to her backstage allies, was that she'd lost her virginity in Kentwood before she became famous. But the promoted insistence that yes, she was a virgin, flew nicely in the face of the smouldering sex kitten, creating another deftly executed contradiction to maintain further mystery.

The virginity-card has long been played in the pop industry to promote the appeal of the wholesome star. Labels seek to appeal to 'silver ring teens' – those who abstain from sex until marriage. Research shows that these children want their idols to mirror their values. Virginity clearly sells, and especially when the female artiste happens to be portrayed as a siren fighting temptation. Such hot resistance sets the girls an example while allowing the boys to fantasise about being 'Britney's first'. Presumably that's what led to one businessman to contact Jive Records and make his indecent proposal quite clear: a reputed $10m to take Britney's virginity. She responded by telling the media it was 'disgusting' and he should go take a cold shower.

Undeterred, the media then wanted to know if Britney preferred women to men. At a press conference in Montreal she was asked whether she was a lesbian or bi-sexual? Had she ever had sex with a woman? Britney remained as confused as she was over the *Rolling Stone* cover: 'I was like, "What *are* you talking about?"'

She continued to frown and wondered aloud whether maybe people just wanted something to talk about. For that initial year, she could perhaps be given the benefit of the doubt, but 1999 represented a steep, eye-opening learning curve. Regardless of the ramifications on Britney's subconscious, there was no denying such a baptism of fire had created one sure equation: controversy brings attention that results in number one status. Experience was informing her that only from attention can one prosper. In addition to this, one of her role models since childhood had been Madonna, a star whose image screamed, 'You can be as sexually outrageous as you want'.

Nevertheless, in the early days it was important to maintain the wholesome image because longevity as an artiste depends on room for reinvention further down the road. For as long as Britney remained a teenager, the values of chastity would be defended with the skill and belief of a politician. The attention she basked in would become something she'd crave, like a fix. From that moment on, the heralded pop star from Louisiana would always evoke a curiosity and a passion, love or loath her.

In that first year of world pop domination, Britney's schedule was fierce. No one at Jive wished to take their foot off the accelerator, seeking to harness the momentum and success that exceeded all calculations. The singles 'Sometimes' and '(You Drive Me) Crazy' – which both reached the top five in the UK – were released in 1999 to capitalise on the gains made and keep reminding people of the artiste who was planning her first headline tour in 2000. The only real down-time Britney enjoyed was in February 1999 as a result of a knee injury sustained when rehearsing her second video 'Sometimes', again with Nigel Dick as director.

She'd been at rehearsals and was practising a routine in front of the mirror when, with one kick, she put her cartilage out. It was, she said, God's way of telling her to take a break.

During that recuperation, part spent in LA and Kentwood, evidence of change was apparent. She not only had a driver hired by the record label and a bodyguard installed in the shape of a man called 'Big Rob', but there was also money in the bank. One day in California, when she was bored, she asked the driver to take her in her wheelchair to the local Jack-in-the-Box store for a burger – and then

Cartier: to try on a $80,000 ring. It's doubtful whether many Cartier customers would arrive via Jack-in-the-Box, but no one at Cartier recognised her. That's because, by her own admission, she looked 'nasty', hadn't showered for two days ... and she was wearing her bedroom slippers!

For her 18th birthday, she didn't quite manage the Cartier ring, but Jive Records did buy her a diamond necklace. Previously, the most Britney had ever had was a treat from Connie's Jewellers in Kentwood. Now, she had real diamonds around her neck.

By the year 2000, and having recorded her second album, *Oops! ... I Did It Again*, it was time to shoot the video for the single of the same name. Having directed 'Sometimes' and '(You Drive Me) Crazy', director Nigel Dick was recruited for the fourth time. They first worked together in August 1998 and now it was March 2000. With each video, Britney's creative contribution was always considered but Nigel observed some notable shifts taking place. She was, most definitely, becoming the 'star' with a sure confidence and a voice that carried weight.

As before, she'd produced the kernel of an idea for the video: Britney wearing a red cat suit on planet Mars when she falls for a 'hot' spaceman, as filmed at the Universal lot in LA behind the *Backdraft* stage. Nigel said: 'Her idea was great and everything was ready on day one but she suddenly came up with a completely new, crazy idea and I had to say, "No, Britney, we can't do it" because we had too much to achieve in too little time already. Her input was great because it showed how spontaneous and versatile she could be, but it just wasn't possible.'

Britney returned to her trailer, determined not to be outdone. With polite insistence, she offered up a new outfit for the shoot, but the director didn't approve: 'What she wanted to wear was ludicrous, like something a stripper would wear. It was sexy, but in a cheesy way. I turned to the person from Jive and asked: "Are you happy with this?" and they were like, "No, no, no, not at all!" But then everyone looks at me as if to say, "Well, you're the director … *you* sort it out!'.

He remembered how easy-going Britney had been when they first met in New York and how receptive she'd been to advice. But on this occasion, he 'saw how people stood off her now.' A straight-talking Yorkshireman is rarely swayed by the vanities of Hollywood and so he went to talk it through with Britney in her trailer. Whether anyone realised or not, he was making a point about what he felt was appropriate for an 18-year-old to be wearing, even if the punchline to the song's chorus was 'I'm not that innocent …'

'Look,' he said, 'I'll go to strip bars with the rest of them but I felt such an overtly sexy number was not what she should be wearing at that point in her career. I wanted it to be tasteful, and was trying to protect her, but I'm not sure that was fully appreciated. In her eyes, I was just some old bloke telling her what to do. But I was employed at some level to have an opinion, so I expressed it.'

In the trailer, Nigel says they reached an agreement that was 'a happy compromise' and Britney selected an alternative outfit – a less revealing white outfit that she wore for verse two, lying on her back, looking up at the camera. Here, in May 2000, was Britney executing the lessons learned from the *Rolling Stone* controversy; no longer bewildered, but actively pursuing shock and awe.

Of course, in her mind, she was only dressing up and acting the part again, but this time the attempted 'risque' was at her behest. She was beginning to stamp her mark on all she did. The little girl was growing up fast. Among some personal piercing choices, she'd chosen to have her navel pierced. This new attitude was perhaps carried in the lyrics from the *Oops!* album and the song 'What U See (Is What You Get)' when she sings: 'But now you think I'm wearing too much make-up/That my dress is too tight … I can be nobody else/And I like the way I am'. Parents, handlers and video directors had been warned that this attitude now meant business.

In the end, filming between 17 and 19 March could not have gone better, and the video went on to be nominated for Best Female Video and then Best Pop Video at the 2000 MVAs (Music Video Awards). Britney even survived a small injury when a piece of camera equipment fell on her head, requiring her to have five stitches. After four hours of rest, she completed the video and then flew to Grand Rapids, Michigan, to perform the following day. That injury incited mum Lynne to pen a message on Britney's official website, saying: 'These are the times that I worry most!' and listed her worries – Britney pushing herself too hard, freak accidents on set, working crazy hours, and flying too much.

With the video wrapped, director Nigel had his own concerns. During the two-day shoot, he'd witnessed a change far more worrying than Britney's spontaneous creativity and wardrobe preferences. Every time she emerged from her trailer, there was a phalanx of camera crews, plus photographers, that included an MTV crew filming a 'making of' special. He was so concerned that he recorded his thoughts in his online blog on 19 March 2000. His views now read as wise foresight rather than clever hindsight:

NIGEL'S BLOG: 'It's probably 18 months since I first met Britney in a dance studio in New York. She's gone from being a cute unknown who could sing and dance into a multi-million selling singing sensation; from being a bubbly kid into a young woman.

What's more frightening to the casual observer is the way the world has changed around Britney.

'When we shot "... Baby One More Time" at Venice High, Britney could walk around the campus unnoticed. Today she can't so much as poke her nose out of her Winnebago without three video crews descending upon her. The abiding memory of this shoot was a moment when I turned around and saw Britney coming on set. In front of her, cameramen were walking backwards as they pushed their lenses in her face. She was bathed in the glare of hand-held lights as she walked, talked and tried to sign an autograph. I try to allow an artist the space to relax and prepare before they go in front of our cameras to do their thing. For someone like Britney this is just not possible anymore. I have spent two and a half days hanging out with Britney this time and there has not been a single moment for personal reflection between the two of us. No chance to say "How are you doing?" "What's really happening in your world?" It's not Britney's fault or the fault of those around her – it's us, the consumers, that are ultimately to blame. We all feel we need a slice of Britney ... and God forbid that our idol should be tired or in a bad mood when we thrust that grubby piece of paper in their face and ask for an autograph. I always wanted to be a star when I was a teenager ... but now I'm so grateful that when I was 18, wearing loon pants the size of a small tent, experimenting with rather ridiculous facial-hair options and exploring the wonders brought upon by too much alcohol, there was no-one following me around with a camera or a tape recorder.'

As Nigel reflects on those words from his LA home in 2009, he still feels the same: 'I remember it clearly. I said: "We need Britney on set" and I look across and see sixteen guys walking backwards, with cameras, lenses, lights and Britney penned in the middle. I'm watching this charade and I'm thinking, "You poor girl". We're not on the street, we're on set, and it seemed so unfair on her. This is why I've so much sympathy and understanding in regard to her current situation.'

The director then asks us to visualise the scene, as if in Britney's shoes: 'Imagine it. How would you feel, opening your door and walking directly into a scrum that is walking backwards with you at its centre, hemmed in? The faces before you are silent, but recording everything, in your face, up close. You can't see ahead and they're overwhelming you.'

The sad thing is that what Nigel observed would, in later years, become an everyday occurrence at the hands of the paparazzi, with 30 photographers and video-men trailing her every move.

Nigel's concern is not only qualified by a director's experience but because he's also worked as a music PR, handling the media for, among others, eighties group Madness and Ian Dury. Having worked a two-year stint for Stiff Records in London, he understands the world of 'media manipulation and media control'.

'I watched Britney in the middle of that lot and thought it was all so unnecessary. There was no one there saying "Stand back, lads ... Take five!". It was like, "Here's the meat, let them at her!" At least, that was my observation.'

Britney's aunty Chanda was also concerned by the first roots of stardom witnessed in 1999: 'Even then, it was as if Britney was torn between the person she was to us and the person she was being made to be. From her first few hits, she slowly started drifting away, and I think she started to lose who she was.'

No-one is suggesting that Britney's sweet essence was changing for the worse. Her gentle personality and respect for others still remained. She was more sucked up and pulled away. But Nigel Dick's observation is that Britney remained unfazed and a true professional: 'She was such a trooper, dealt with it all and got on with the job, even though it was obvious she felt enormous pressure. The thing that's always impressed me about Britney is that she always worked really, really hard. She was there for rehearsals on time and always worked an extra hour, saying, "Let's do it again!". She was all over it, totally dedicated. She had an amazing work ethic and I use her as an example to young stars I work with today.'

After 'Oops! ... I Did It Again', Nigel never did work with Britney again: 'Maybe it was because I told her what to wear? The bottom line is that she wanted to have her own way more and more, and that's common and I respect it. She'd become successful, with millions in the bank, and I wished her all the good luck then – and I still do now.'

Those 'millions' were beginning to trickle in. Britney's success and financial rewards were akin to a family from a working-class town winning the lottery jackpot and not having a clue how to handle it. Everyone may wish for it, but there are no how-to guidebooks in the dizzying world of fame's fortune. The Spears were, quite simply, under prepared and overwhelmed.

Their lifelong friend recalls: 'Britney's earnings took that family from zero to millions, and it blew their minds. This is a family that had been bankrupt and all that money scared the crap out of them!'

As a Disney 'mouseketeer', Britney was paid a weekly fee of $1,000, 15 per cent of which was placed in trust under the Jackie Coogan Law (otherwise known as the Child Actors Bill), safeguarding that portion of earnings for later life. The bill was passed in 1939 after child actor Coogan discovered that most of his $4 million fortune had been squandered by his parents. Not that Britney needed to worry about an insecure financial future. By 2008, she would, according to official court documents, be earning $737,888 a month to top up a personal fortune estimated at $60 million, of which £33 million in cash was accumulated in six high-interest accounts. Forbes went on to list her in its 20 richest women in entertainment. Over the years, Britney would become a generous charity donor, making sizeable contributions to the charity relief funds after the 9/11 terrorist attack and to her home state, following Hurricane Katrina in 2004.

In 1999, Britney was discovering that agents, managers and record labels were not banks, and she needed a true financial advisor. That's where her ever-reliable Uncle Reggie came in. The husband of Lynne's sister Sandra and father to Britney's virtual twin, Laura Lynn, was an executive at the Bank of Greensburg, a small institution with just five branches in Louisiana. The joke in Kentwood was that the bank, serving its customers since 1904, had been one of the few to survive the Depression but 'might not know how to cope with the millions of Britney Spears'.

Reggie Covington, small-town banking executive, suddenly found himself appointed agent with power of attorney, charged with the responsibility of wisely investing his niece's money. Friends say that he charged a 1 per cent administration fee by way of commission. Set against the usual agent commissions of 15 to 20 per cent, that fact alone shows that here was someone in Britney's life absolutely not in it for any financial gain. Uncle Reggie, a quiet, decent man, was simply interested in ushering in some sensible prudence: 'I don't think Britney's ever come across somebody ever again who was there simply to look after Britney for Britney. She was always in safe hands with Reg,' said the family's lifelong friend.

One of the first things that Britney wanted to do with her money was turn around her family's fortunes. Now the young girl, who had often seen no food in the fridge and the utilities disconnected, could do what every child wishes they could do: pay back her parents for the sacrifices they had made. It was Britney's sole decision, without interference, to financially rescue her family. If ever there was one benefit to fame, this was the one outcome that provided her with true joy.

Together with her Uncle Reggie, she had spotted seven lush acres, six miles out of Kentwood, on which she would build a dream home. She purchased this premium land from Ted and Barbara Lewis, spending $29,000. This first investment was made for 'building a new house for my mama', she said in *Heart to Heart*, published the following year.

Taken on face value, this decision, without mention of her dad, appears to be a reward and punishment all at the same time. But the truth is more complicated. For when Britney made it clear that she wanted to 'gift' Lynne the keys and deeds when the house was built, alarm bells sounded. The realisation dawned that the moment this sizeable asset was transferred into her ownership, Lynne would be tied to the bankruptcy and financial debt of her marriage. This conundrum led to many calls between management, financial advisors and attorneys because Britney was adamant: this had to be a new start for her mama.

In Louisiana, bankruptcy and bad debt sticks to the community property co-owned by man and wife, and Lynne found herself handcuffed to her past. Therefore, had she remained married and taken ownership of the mansion, Jamie would also have had a legal stake and, consequently, his debtors – past and future – could have laid claim to a home whose official assessed value in 2008 was $747,000 with a market value of $1.3 million. This, to Britney at least, was a horrifying prospect. Under no circumstances could anyone envision Jamie's name being anywhere near those deeds.

This was not necessarily a reaction against her own father but an inescapable practicality. Britney had spent a childhood watching her parents rob Peter to pay Paul. Therefore, it meant the world to her that her fortune could make such a difference and turn their lives around. Her understandable concern was focused on protecting a sizeable asset against creditors.

Once again, this is a situation on which the modern-day conservatorship – which now exercises control over Britney's fortune – casts an ironic light. But in January 2000, Lynne was in a flux: caught between her daughter's generosity and a hitherto inability to release herself from her marriage.

In her memoir, Lynne writes that she realised her marriage had long been over and it was for that reason, and that reason alone, that she 'unchose' Jamie. Years of cruel words and 'alcohol's evil' had taken their toll. It was Britney, she said, who sat her down in 2000 and challenged her by asking: 'Do you want to live like this for the rest of your life?' Lynne then made the hardest decision: to separate from Jamie after 24 years of marriage. She says he was furious when he found out. His friends say he 'understood why it was necessary and fell on his sword'.

On a date in February 2000, at a time when Britney's fame was incandescently hot, and in a court in the parish of Livingston, an exceedingly discreet court hearing took place before a judge to decide 'the approval of a matrimonial regime of separate property'.

As all lawyers in Louisiana will know, this in effect is a pre-nuptial agreement struck in the middle of a marriage and it is a rare circumstance that hinges on a judge's discretion. The outcome, after a hearing held in camera, was that the judge agreed the terms of the separation that would precede a divorce.

What was significant about this legal agreement was the clause stating: 'Jamie Spears assumes 100% of any and all debts due, or alleged to be due' throughout his marriage to Lynne, as she did.

The happy coincidence of this decision was that Lynne could take ownership of the land that Britney had bought four months earlier. That single separation contract freed her from all debt liability. Not only would the new property have an impressive wrought-iron gate around its perimeter, it was also legally ring-fenced to ensure no debtors could grab it. Lynne became sole beneficiary, complete with a brand new Mercedes. Assistant Felicia Culotta was also given a brand new car. Neither did Jamie lose out because Britney wiped away all his debts and mortgage, and got to keep the family home behind the Baptist Church.

Whether Jamie's bad debts finally forced Lynne's hand is something only she can know. She maintains her decision to leave him was not related to Britney's fame or newfound fortune. We are therefore asked to believe that she awoke from her co-dependent, submissive state at the same time that Britney intended to build a mansion in the woods. Two years later, Lynne proceeded to divorce her husband.

But the legal separation paperwork also throws up another curious element. In their joint legal declaration, both Jamie and Lynne swore they 'were married on 29th day of July 1976 in the State of Louisiana ...' In Lynne's withdrawn divorce petition of 1979, she quite properly recorded their marriage as taking place in Oswego, New York and in her memoir of 2008, she also made it clear that she eloped to the East Coast.

But in the year 2000, at a time when the media focus was intensifying and a squeaky clean image counted for everything, the location of the marriage was inexplicably stated as Louisiana. This re-write of history, intended or otherwise, covered the marital tracks lest any zealous news hound discover that the pop star's parents had once eloped from a Baptist community.

Friends of Lynne were surprised to discover that the February 2000 hearing was told that Jamie and Lynne were married in their home state. How could anyone forget how this young couple had eloped so dramatically? But perhaps the explanation is a simple one: that in the upset over the separation, neither party properly read the standard boiler-plate separation contract which had assumed that Spears wed in Louisiana. That has to be the only explanation. If Jamie and Lynne had gone through the document properly, as they are supposed to before declaring all facts to be true in a court of law, then the glaring omission would have struck home. If it did, neither said anything to their individual attorneys.

Certainly, it wasn't an omission that would stand in the way of the separation. The outcome was that Jamie found himself not only separated from his wife, but sidelined and without a voice within her growing empire. For any father, that lack of control must have been disempowering and disconcerting. It must have felt like he was almost cut out of the picture, but at least Uncle Reggie could keep an eye on affairs.

He oversaw the construction project of the new property, from start to finish. His sound advice to go for the land has already paid off handsomely because Britney's $29,000 purchase has multiplied in value more than 25 times. But perhaps there are further hidden treasures because the cash deed papers reveal that he had power of attorney 'to make

and execute mineral and royalty rights, including unitiza-
tion and pooling agreements for the exploration and development of oil, gas and other minerals …'

Britney's giving nature is something that everyone who
knows her speaks of, and this one purchase was probably
her happiest achievement, above all the accolades. Fame
had allowed her to make a difference. Lynne had given 24
years of her life to a marriage that had been volatile and
distressing from its third year. She hung in there for many
misguided reasons, out of desperate hope, and because,
aside from all the dramas and upset, she truly loved the
man.

It seems fitting that the person who would give her the
final push of courage was Britney herself, the child who had
been so deeply affected by much of what she'd witnessed.
As a child, she had used the distraction of 'performance' to
escape the emotional trauma in the house and make herself
feel safe. Now, as a pop star, she was using the wealth generated by 'performance' to finally allow her mum to escape, to
a refuge they both agreed would be called 'Serenity'.

8

Backstage: In the Zone

'Do I know my life is weird? It's all I've ever known.'
— *Britney, MTV* **For the Record, 2008**

Britney's own idea of serenity is not a house in the pinelands of Kentwood, but a place where the floors are polished wood, the walls are mirrored and there's a stereo in a corner, its speakers throbbing away.

The dance studio is her constant go-to place. In an all-consumed concentration, nothing and no one reaches or disturbs her; she's the whirling dervish caught within the blurred embodiment of choreography. Britney describes this place as being 'in the zone'.

'Dancing is a huge part of me and who I am. It's like something my spirit just has to do. I would be dead without dancing. Anytime I can go to a studio, dance and put chore-ography together, it's like a spiritual experience,' she told the 2008 MTV documentary, *Britney – For The Record*.

Her 'zone', from 1999 until the current day, is usually created at the 'sanctuary' called the Millennium Dance Complex, located near Universal Studios, North Hollywood. In the beginning, as she prepared for her first headline tour in 2000, this is where Britney spent eight hours a day for four months solid, turning practice into flawless precision. Even then, there was a good chance that she would find a chink in the choreography she'd master mark-by-mark, nuance by nuance. If there is an over-riding essence to Britney then it is her 'obsession' with dancing, repeating and rehearsing a number until it feels natural and seemingly effortless; a creative state of auto-pilot.

The zone into which she disappears is hard to imagine for non-dancers, but her ritual is something that *Mickey Mouse Club* choreographer Myles Thoroughgood identifies with, as he witnessed in Orlando: 'She goes quiet within herself, mentally preparing. I suspect that even to this day she'll ask for quiet time before a concert. She's rehearsed, she's ready and finds an intense focus. For her, it will be like there's nothing going on inside, but she's actually going through everything in her head. She becomes so rehearsed that she could do it in her sleep. The focus puts a lid on the adrenaline and conserves her energy for the moment and for the audience. Then she steps up, and then she's on.'

Before reaching that stage of readiness, Britney often rehearses at Millennium. From the outside, the building looks nothing special. But inside, its walls are stained with the sweat of some of the biggest names in music; a veritable Who's Who lined with framed photographs and signed thank yous from Alicia Keys, Janet Jackson, Christina Aguilera, Missy Elliott, Avril Lavigne, Pussycat Dolls, Jewel, Pink, Justin Timberlake, *NSYNC and J-Lo, to name a few. It also happens to be one of the places where a certain Michael Jackson held his dancer auditions, strictly by invitation only.

And it was Jackson who inadvertently had a hand in shaping the performing career of Britney Spears.

She was already a highly accomplished dancer for television and video, mainly thanks to the work of Myles at MMC. But management felt she needed to be taken to the next level for the stage. Manager Johnny Wright knew exactly the man: Australian choreographer Wade Robson, someone who owes his break to Jackson.

Wade was just five years old when he entered a Michael Jackson dance contest and won the coveted first prize: to dance on stage with the legend himself on a leg of his Australian tour. Michael was 'so impressed' that he sponsored the boy to move from Brisbane to Los Angeles. Aged just six, the little boy found himself taken under Jackson's wing. The relationship between mentor and protégé was scrutinised at Jackson's 2005 child molestation trial, which ended in an acquittal. Wade was compelled to testify and said that he sometimes shared a bed with the singer at his Neverland mansion but he insisted they slept on opposite sides of the bed, like best friends on sleepovers.

It was an unfortunate sideshow that ignored the incredible talent of Wade, who had found himself working out and rehearsing with Jackson at Millennium. His development proved so exceptional that, just four years later, he was installed as a dance teacher at the studio … aged just ten years old.

Robert Baker, director at the Millennium, said: 'Everyone was looking around, wondering who's the kid? You should have seen their faces when they realised it was the teacher! When he started to show them what he could do, chins hit the floor. Few can dance like Wade – and it was he who took Britney to another level.'

The innate perfectionism of Jackson, Robson and Spears combined to create the high-energy hip-hop jazz moves that became Britney's signature. When she first ambled into Millennium, Robert Baker hadn't heard much about her, but he became a fascinated observer as Wade and Britney got to work. Soon enough, he found himself with a front-row seat on the development of an iconic performer. Robert is one of the 'Britney camp', who has been there from the beginning, through good times and bad, and he's regarded as both a professional associate and a dear friend.

In those initial days, he watched in wonder as Wade meticulously honed Britney's choreography, instilling in her that every little move mattered: 'Every pointed finger, every head-turn and every gesture had to be just right, not a second out. Wade's stuff is not easy to master and demands sweat and toil, but she nailed it. A lot of singers say they can dance but that girl *can* dance, with a passion and dedication beyond none. Dance at this level requires a deeper level of commitment than just turning up and rehearsing moves. I said it back then and I say it now – it's programmed in her DNA to succeed.'

Britney will certainly have felt at home at Millennium. Its mission statement, as written by Robert's wife and co-founder Anne-Marie, echoes what she herself tries to achieve: 'by connecting with our world more deeply by connecting more deeply with ourselves'. And then the following words: 'We have made our own world within these walls, driven by music, strength and love. Create what you will.' Over the next few years, Britney created routines that would wow an international fan-base.

In the background, mum Lynne and assistant Felicia watched mesmerised, and breaks would be taken at Starbucks down the road. By now, Lynne had quit teaching to be with her daughter. As well as being the mama-on-the-road, she also ran Britney's official website, earning more money than she could ever have hoped for from teaching.

But the main benefit was that mother and daughter were back together again, day in, day out. With Lynne not far away, Britney was able to give her all; she made other people tired just from watching her.

'People need to understand the stamina required to sustain eight hour days of rehearsing,' said Robert Baker, 'it requires sustainable energy and discipline that is beyond most people's comprehension. But it was Britney's joy.'

Like everyone who'd first met the pop star, he witnessed the same transformation from quiet, pleasant, good-natured girl into a manic livewire who birthed entertainment: 'To hide the choreography and make it appear so natural takes skill. Brit emoted what she danced, and made you feel it, not see it. She literally transcends the choreography. The only other person I've ever seen manage that was Michael Jackson. When people doubt her talent, I'm like, "You must be blind or crazy".'

What Britney *feels* when she dances is also what she expects to see in those who audition for her tours. Anyone curious about what she particularly looks for was given insight by the woman herself in the 2008 MTV documentary: 'I look for pizzazz, like a fire; something that just stands out. They can be the best technical dancer there is, but if they don't dance with passion and fire … that something that makes you want to look at them take over the stage. That's what I'm looking for.'

But Britney is also checking out a dancer's attitude during auditions. She wants to be able to get along with her crew because dancers invariably form her close-knit circle. Those with arrogance, airs and graces need not apply. She is looking for easy people, with whom she can hang out, even if her management and parents might nowadays check such a suggestion. In their eyes, as will become apparent, dancers

could be a social distraction. It is one thorny area with
which Britney disagrees. But, internal politics aside, if a
dancer is accepted into the fold, he or she stood to earn
around $3,000 a week for joining her on the road in 2000.
Her favourite dancer in the early days was a young man
called Trey James Espanoza, who had been by her side since
the shopping mall tour of America to promote 'Baby …
One More Time!'

A source exceptionally close to Britney said: 'She called
her dancers her best friends, saying, "A girl can never have
enough best friends", but T.J. was her absolute star. Whatever was good enough for Britney was good enough for her
dancers. She saw no separation between artiste and crew.
But T.J. was the special one. He was that close to her that he
earned the nickname "T.J. Spears". He was irreplaceable in
her eyes.'

But T.J. wasn't irreplaceable in her management's eyes.
As Britney's fame grew, so did her choreography requirements and, as much as she personally fought to retain T.J.,
he was surplus to requirements in the eyes of those controlling the ship. Having shared the exhilarating ride into
another orbit, this great friend was released and had to start
work at LA's Saddle Ranch bar on the Sunset Strip. An integral part of her inner circle had gone and Britney was grad-
ually realising one thing: when it came to the hiring and
firing of dancers, she didn't exactly have the final say. In this
regard, Larry Rudolph held considerable sway.

As for T.J., he was able to walk away with a treasured
keepsake: a Tiffany heart bracelet from Britney.

By now, even more people had jumped on the Britney
fan bandwagon, and her 'ultimate' album, *Oops! … I Did It
Again*, knocked country star Garth Brooks from his perch to
become the fastest-selling album in the US, shifting 1.3
million copies in its first week after its May 2000 release,

according to SoundScan. It went on to shift a total of 10 million in America and just under one million in the UK. Britney became the only female artist to receive platinum status based on first week sales, and it went straight to No. 1 in the UK. Her tour was due to hit the road that June with a 58-city schedule in America alone, and brand Britney took off, securing product endorsements with Clairol hair, McDonalds, Tommy Jeans, Polaroid, America's 'Get Milk' campaign and Pepsi. She would even end up shooting the most expensive broadcast commercial in history for Pepsi in 2002, costing a reputed $5.4 million.

Many close to Britney felt everything was happening too fast, not giving her the chance to catch her breathe, let alone find an inner balance. But Britney herself seemed happy and content, not even questioning where the emergency chain was located. From the distant vantage point of Millennium, Robert Baker could only hope that the sweet-mannered girl would be resilient enough, but privately he worried.

'This business makes you stand there and scratch your head at the best of times,' he said, 'but when it's all coming at you so fast then it's a blur. This was a girl and a family from a rural town who found themselves at the mercy of a machine that couldn't rewind, couldn't stop and only knew how to go into overdrive. All they could do was hang on, hope for the best and trust. Lynne was just as bewildered as Britney and they had no option but to put on their best faces and smiles for the cameras but, inside, they had no idea.'

Robert's perspective is a unique one because of the stardom that has passed through his studio, but he has rarely witnessed the meteoric rise of someone like Britney. The girl that walked through a door was wide-eyed with awe, but clearly unprepared: 'She is such a heartfelt person and wants to love everyone. There's not a bad bone or ill thought in her body. Now take someone like that, from Louisiana, and put them in Hollywood, and you've just placed the lamb into a pen with a pack of wolves. Then fame goes "Boom!" and says, "Now deal with it",' he said.

Behind the scenes, Britney was struggling, come the year 2000. In New York, after an MTV special, she and assistant Felicia were mobbed by fans and herded up against a brick wall. In *Heart to Heart*, she recorded that moment, but wrote philosophically about the realities of stardom, seemingly willing to accept that, 'You do have to sacrifice your freedom when you're in this business.' At least, that was the official response in the interests of the brand. But when the tour went to Europe and pitched up in London in October 2000, her off-the-record reaction wasn't so restrained. Britney had looked forward to the UK leg of her debut tour because, in her mind, it would be in memory of grandma Lillian and she couldn't wait to visit all the 'cute and quaint English stores'.

'Team Britney' stayed in the Royal Garden Hotel in Kensington and, on this particular day, she was promised a shopping expedition after lunch in Covent Garden. All was going swimmingly until the entourage exited the eaterie only to run straight into a wall of awaiting paparazzi. At that time, long before the advent of 24/7 Internet news and the demands of New Media, there was nothing more startling for a celebrity than a run-in with the British tabloid press. It was a different beast to whatever she had previously faced in America. Within a matter of a few disorienting seconds, Britney was being jostled amid a scrum of flashbulbs with everyone shouting her name: 'Britney! Britney!'

It caught everyone off guard. No one had seen them enter the restaurant and so they walked completely unawares into the scene outside. Bodyguard Big Rob, a 300lb African-American boulder, bundled Britney into the team's van as camera lenses clattered against the vehicle's windows, swarmed by bellowing paparazzi. As the van sped away, Britney freaked out and went as white as a sheet.

From that moment on, the paparazzi would be forever tagged to her coat-tails, but such restrictive realities were not quite dawning: 'She just started crying,' said a source exceptionally close to Britney, 'She was unable to get why she couldn't go shopping like normal kids. She kept saying, "What's happening?", "Why's this happening?".

Britney was struggling to realise that she was no longer classed as 'normal'. This wasn't a talent contest she could simply walk away from. From this juncture, she would continually bemoan the fact that she couldn't do 'normal' things like 'normal' people. The very word 'normal' would be constantly uttered, yet its definition would be forever alien. Britney's dream had led her away from the life she'd never ever know – or own – again. To calm her down and offer reassurance, her camp made comparisons with Madonna and the late Diana, Princess of Wales, who had died three years earlier and had suffered similarly at the hands of the paparazzi.

'But I'm *not* a princess … and I'm *not* Madonna!' Britney protested.

The same source added: 'That's what was so sweet about her – she didn't see how big she was becoming. She just kept asking, "Why? Why me?". Britney never felt anything more than a girl from Louisiana. The whole media thing bewildered her at first.'

Nevertheless, Britney would register the Diana comparison. Clearly, the PR officers at Jive Records had already thought about it, because a fanciful story circulated Fleet Street to greet her UK arrival: that Britney had a secret crush on Prince William. Not only that, but they were due to meet after exchanging emails. In newsrooms around

Britain, it sounded like the innovative flair of an editor desperate for any old story to fill the front page. Its PR benefits were obvious: Prince William was nearing his 18th birthday and America's teen sensation was heading to Britain. Such potential synergy was hard to resist, and so a publicity wave was created to carry Britney into town. It was a classically orchestrated, and executed, 'rumour' that everyone was happy to swallow.

'I WANT TO WED WILLS, SAYS BRITNEY' cried the *Daily Record*; 'QUEEN OF POP – AND ENGLAND?' asked *NME*, and even the extremely sober *Independent* newspaper waded in with: 'WILLIAM, MARRY ME – BRITNEY ASKS'.

Such coverage was fuelled by Britney seeming to confirm that she had contacted William – with the extra tease: 'Who would not want to be a princess?'. At this time in her life, Britney was keeping secret her relationship with Justin Timberlake, so the Prince William script was a convenient diversion offered by a blatant publicity stunt, but after a while even Britney was confused.

She told GMTV's Ross Kelly: 'I've never met him. We exchanged some notes but that was it.' But by October 2000, she was telling the media: 'I really don't know where these stories come from. I've never met him or contacted him.'

In *Heart to Heart*, released that same year, Lynne Spears got equally carried away, asserting, 'We were invited to meet him in London … can you imagine being asked to go to Buckingham Palace?' She said the Royal meet was cancelled due to a foxhunt. If this episode shows anything, it demonstrates that Britney and Lynne were putty in the industry's hands, happy to go along with anything that promoted her.

Lynne herself would admit in 2008 on NBC's *Today* show that the honeymoon stage of fame was a mixture of excitement, shock and awe. Their naivety is nothing more than one would expect from such an unworldly family, but old hands at Buckingham Palace were not amused. It issued a statement, saying Prince William 'had received no correspondence with Britney Spears at all, either by letter or email.'

There were informed reports that William, one year younger than Britney and Eton-educated, was upset at being exploited in such a manner. And he said so.

Wherever Britney travelled on the *Oops! … I Did It Again* world tour, the plush luxuries of stardom were intended to make her feel as comfortable as possible. When one is schlepping from city to city, country to country and hotel to hotel, home comforts become prerequisites.

In the touring convoy that hit the road, she had her own bus. Britney got to taste what life was like living in a trailer, even if it was worlds away from Simpson's Trailer Park. The super-star deluxe version came with fitted cabinets, leather couches and a sumptuous bedroom in the back. This was the world she exclusively shared with Lynne and Felicia. Behind them, followed the crew bus, dancers' bus, band bus and equipment trucks. It was a travelling circus long before 'Circus' became a concept for 2009.

At different arenas and stadiums, there was no mistaking Britney's dressing room. All one had to do was follow the waft of scented candles. Walk down the corridors, follow the aroma, open the star door and visitors entered what observers described as a locker-room transformed into 'the cosiest, girly set-up you can imagine'. Drapery bowed and waved along the ceilings, while curtains and lamps provided that 'homey' feel. The consistent theme, from America to

Europe, seemed to be candles and greenery. Britney's dressing room often resembled a Jo Malone store, complete with large plants and potted trees, sometimes decorated with fairy lights – all lights and wicks burning and flickering for the star's arrival.

But Britney was certainly no diva. There were no outrageous pop-star demands to fit the stereotype. She 'never wanted to be seen to be asking for too much' and she remained the 'Yes, sir', 'No, ma'am' type. Indeed, her demands read more like the polite requests of a teenager being treated to star treatment for a day: fresh white tuna, baked chips, a mix of Altoids mints, French Vanilla coffee, one vegetable platter, a bag of Doritos and, last but not least, two boxes of Pop Tarts. The artiste labelled the 'pop tart' actually requested Pop Tarts frosted, doughy-biscuits. One would be tempted to say you couldn't make it up but, in the world of Britney Spears, such parodies were just happy accidents.

Always, there were two 6ft leather couches to recline on, but Britney's only time for true relaxation was back at the five-star hotel suites that she'd be lucky to spend more than six hours enjoying because of her schedule. Whenever she snatched small windows of down time, she loved nothing more than a frothy bubble bath, surrounded by burning candles. She preferred taking a decadent bath than a quick shower any day of the week and this was how she spoiled herself.

It was always the simple things in life in which Britney found contentment. Because of her fame, she became accustomed to using aliases as a firewall to fans attempting to ring her room. Over the years, she would accumulate many aliases, but her favourites were always 'Ms Alotta Warmheart' because 'she had such a warm heart'; 'Ms Diana Prince', in honour of Diana, Princess of Wales;

Left: 'Born with a microphone in her hand' – Britney performed from a young age. Here, she is seen, aged eleven, singing at the wedding of her Aunty Chanda.

Above: Performing on *The All New Mickey Mouse Club* in 1993/4 and a memorable duet with a young Justin Timberlake.

Left: Britney (bottom right) is unveiled as one of seven new 'mouseketeers' together with Ryan Gosling (bottom left), Christina Aguilera (behind Britney) and Justin (rear, far right).

Above left: The 'mouseketeers' grow up to become pop stars sharing the same stage, vying for the No.1 spot in the charts. Above right: At the 1999 MTV European Music Awards in Dublin in November, thrilled to receive four awards: Best Female Performer, Best Breakthrough Act, Best Song and Best Pop Act.

Above left: With her 'Prince Charming' and true, first love Justin Timberlake before the romance turned sour. Above Right: Performing her raunchy hit single 'I'm a Slave 4 U' at the 2001 MTV Video Music Awards.

Live on stage at the MTV Super Bowl half-time show alongside Mary J Blige, Justin Timberlake and Steven Tyler of Aerosmith, January 2001.

Performing 'The Way You Make Me Feel' with Michael Jackson at his 30th Anniversary Celebration concert at New York's Madison Square Garden, September 2001.

The highlight of the 2003 MTV Video Music Awards: the moment when Madonna and Britney kissed live on stage during their opening performance with Christina Aguilera.

Britney and childhood friend Jason Alexander inside a late-night Las Vegas wedding chapel following their spontaneous marriage, January 2004. The marriage lasted a total of 55 hours.

Frolicking on the beach in Santa Monica with her then boyfriend Kevin Federline, June 2004.

Below left: Taking a tumble, and once again being scrutinized as a mother. New York, May 2006. **Below right:** Britney and Kevin – now married with one child together, February 2006.

THERE MAY BE TROUBLE AHEAD

Lindsay Lohan, Britney Spears and Paris Hilton spotted leaving Paris's house in Hollywood at 7am, November 2006.

Below left: After requesting a private room at a Las Vegas club, Britney stripped down to her bra and shorts and danced for her entourage.
Below right: Enjoying another night out with Paris Hilton.

LITTLE GIRL LOST

Shaving all her hair off with a pair of clippers in a Los Angeles hair salon …

… and attacking a paparazzo's car with an umbrella, February 2007.

Below left: My baby girl – Britney under the protective wing of conservator and daddy, Jamie. **Below right:** A host of ambulances and police cars gathered outside Britney's home, January 2008. Later that night she was rushed to hospital for psychiatric evaluation.

THE COMEBACK BEGINS: 2008

Backstage with *X Factor* host Dermot O'Leary and judges Simon Cowell, Cheryl Cole, Louis Walsh and Dannii Minogue, November 2008.

Above: Performing an energetic dance routine live on *Good Morning America*, December 2008.

Left: Back on top, performing her hit single 'Womanizer' on ITV's *X Factor*, in her first UK appearance for five years.

THE RESURRECTION: 'The Circus Starring Britney Spears', New Orleans, March 2009.
Below left: On stage with Madonna on her Sticky Sweet tour, LA, November 2008.
Below right: Something to smile about – a happy Britney clutching her awards back-stage at the MTV Video Music Awards, September 2008. She made a clean sweep of all her nominated awards.

'Queen of the Fairy Dance' because she was the dancing
fairy and 'Ms Abra Cadabra' ... for no apparent known
reason.

When one steps back and observes this world – five-star
hotels, private jets, tour buses complete with bedroom and
all the pampering a girl could desire – such a dream set-up
sounds enviably glamorous. But then it must be checked
with the stark realisations of an incessant schedule that
demanded she climb into a golden hamster wheel and start
running. The illusion of fame creates the delusion that all
the star has to do is show up, enjoy and smile. The truth,
and the stamina required, is rarely acknowledged.

It takes some imagination to grasp the demands heaped
on a twenty-year-old Britney, none of which she will have
factored into the dreams that manifested this reality. But
Larry Rudolph was always on hand to remind her of the
responsibilities and obligations that came with the territory,
and the schedule itself shouted its instructions lest the star
forget.

By way of example, it went something like this: Showtime tonight, Britney! But first you've got a meet-and-greet,
say about fifty people, then an on-camera interview, then a
two-hour press junket, then it's prep for showtime. Then
we head to the next city, leaving midnight, arriving say 4am,
check in new hotel, and then tomorrow it's showtime, Britney! But first you've got a meet-and-greet, say about eighty
people, then a few on-camera interviews plus radio, then a
three-hour press junket, then it's prep for showtime ...' and
so the loop continued.

Britney, usually sat in her sweats, hair wrapped in towel
and knees tucked to chin, listened while chewing gum;
always chewing gum – the Alex Ferguson of the pop world.
In an endless procession of perfunctory promotions and
parades, she yearned for it all to stop; wishing to take time

out to gather herself or to enjoy a full-day, not a snatched hour or two sightseeing the Europe she would never get to properly view. Fame propelled her into obligations that provided little everlasting personal bliss. The only true thrill she experienced was the pre-concert build-up and the 90 'spiritual' minutes found on stage, riding the euphoria she felt from within and emitted from the audience.

But the ever-amenable Britney kept on smiling through the duties and necessities, confiding only in those closest to her just how tedious she found the whole process.

'I'm not feeling it,' she'd say, 'I'm just not feeling it.'

'Meet-and-greets' were especially challenging. These were the moments when local dignitaries, sponsors, label executives and VIP groups would arrive pre-show as an excited ensemble of adults and children. Britney would be wheeled out to meet the chosen few. Except it was rarely a few. Usually numbers were anything from 15 to 50, and it was the pop princess's own royal receiving line at every venue she attended. It could take an hour to smile, auto-graph and pose with each individual. Nobody could have been more outwardly gracious or professional, but for someone who has never felt comfortable in the presence of strangers, they were difficult moments.

The source close to Britney said: 'She always asked, "Why do I have to do all this?" and Larry said it was important. So she had to go be Little Miss Perfect, regardless of her mood. These were the times when she felt like a robot. All she wanted to do was perform. I don't think she felt comfort-able doing anything else. She said it was nothing getting on stage in front of thousands but she struggled with small groups. I'm not sure whether it was social anxiety or just boredom.'

But 'pressing the flesh' was all part of the pop star's duties, and Britney had to get used to it.

'All you saw was Britney being whisked here and whisked there,' said the source, 'and *everything* was planned, from the moment she woke up to when she went to bed. Her entire days were straitjacketed. For someone who's spontaneous, it was strangling. Even award shows in Europe became in-and-out hurries: hitting the red carpet, sitting down, taking the award, posing for photos and then out a back door – always smiling.'

Robert Baker understands the pressures that fame and adoration bring, having witnessed it vicariously from his studios, but he believes that, as much as Britney may have voiced concerns to others, she 'bent over backwards' to make time for her fans. The distinction quite clearly rests on Britney's freedom of choice to partake, and being instructed what to do, and when to do it: 'From where I stood, there's no one more gracious,' said Robert, 'she always found time for people because she is altruistic in the way she operates.'

Once royal duties were out of the way, Britney was typically led before a horde of media and this rigmarole could last up to three hours. Then she'd be taken to the stage for a sound-check. Before she knew it, the clock was running down to showtime.

Welcome to Britney's Groundhog Day – a term she was still using in 2008.

Observing her on these occasions was like watching an actor slip into a role when prompted. In the moments before the 'reveal' to media or guests, her face would be dead-pan, illustrating someone lost in thought or lost in the monotony, still chewing gum. But then, when the lights came on or the velvet rope lifted, the gum was discarded and her face lit up with evident delight, leaving people with a memorable impression. Britney, once again, was turning it on at the flick of an internal switch; the difference between night and day – but even night and day began to merge.

After each concert, 'Team Britney' decamped from a venue around 11.30pm and the convoy would make the 2–4 hour drive to the next city or country. Britney flaked in her bus-bedroom but, on arrival at 4am, she'd be woken to check-in to her new suite in a different hotel, to then return to the land of nod until noon. Inevitably, the exhaustion and demands took their toll.

'She would sometimes be in tears after meet-and-greets and junkets because she was so frustrated, so tired and there was no end in sight. Then she'd pull herself together, wave her hands to stop the tears and say, "Aww, I'm just being silly. I'm fine. I'm fine,"' said the same source.

The rare down times when she was able to go sightseeing with Felicia brought yelps of delight and excitement, like in Amsterdam, Paris and Germany. In shops, the simple sight of dolls or figurines held her spellbound, and her generosity focussed on buying everyone gifts. But there were many occasions when the media hype meant it was crazy outside, and often it was in her best interests to be on 'lock-down' in the hotel.

This enforced containment wasn't helped by an unspecified death threat during the European leg of the tour, and it was one that had to be taken seriously. It was kept from the star so she rarely understood the need for 'lock downs'. The source said: 'She would ask, "Can't I even go out and get a coffee?" She didn't realise that even something so ordinary created a circus outside. She was bummed out that she couldn't do normal things like go for a walk down the road without getting mobbed.'

The ever-present protector in Big Rob went everywhere with Britney, sticking to her like glue as per management instructions. On the occasions it was deemed safe to venture outside, Britney felt his presence always attracted attention. This was the double-edged sword that always

drove Diana, Princess of Wales to the verge of stifling claus-
trophobia: the unsolvable dilemma between protection and
freedom. Like Diana, Britney often tested the system
around her, sometimes sneaking off to see how far she could
get, but rarely did she get very far. Grand hotels became the
home that a rebellious teenager sought to flee and her fame
was starting to feel like a self-made prison. Britney yearned
to clock in and clock off but there was no such mechanism.
Slowly, but surely, the reality of fame and the simplicity of
her expectations were being exposed.

If there was an upside to the privileges, then it was
contained in the attendance at industry awards that Britney
had time to stay and enjoy. In her initial years, she got to
meet her idols: Madonna, Michael Jackson, Olivia Newton-
John, Celine Dion and Janet Jackson: 'Being famous doesn't
make you any less affected by meeting stars,' said the
source, 'and Britney was like a little girl. She idolised these
people, and it was funny seeing the star act like fan.'

Meanwhile, Jive Records and A&R man Steve Lunt were
determined to turn Britney into a similar mega-star. In an
interview with the *Daily Record*, he explained the strategy:
'What we are trying to do with Britney is cover all the bases
with all the people who like her. We're trying to make every
song count to capture her personality. That's what makes
Britney a star; we don't want her to be just a teen thing.'

If someone had then asked Britney if she wanted to
become a megastar with world domination, the answer
might have been interesting to hear, once the realities and
the pressures dawned.

Back in her hotel suite, Britney often re-enacted her childhood and disappeared into an imagined land. Only this time,
she fantasised about a normal life and opening a little coffee
shop or a bead store where she'd serve people and chat all
day. She wanted something simple, not complicated, and

spoke aloud about owning a 'normal' business in Venice, a beach community near Santa Monica, and running it with assistant Felicia.

Those who humoured this dream observed how animated she became as she visualised it.

'It'd be sooooo cute!' she said.

Britney's pre-concert routine is a buzzing build-up of joy and adrenaline. The two hours before showtime and her time on stage were the hours in which she thrived. She happily embraced the thought of getting out there, day in, day out, and entertaining the masses, once describing the feeling it gave her as 'like having a birthday every day.'

Her days typically started when she rose at noon and then she immediately headed to the gym for an hour-long workout. Whenever Britney was asked how she kept in shape, she said the choreography routines were a workout in themselves – and they undoubtedly were. But the secret to those killer abs lies not only in three trips to the gym every week but an obsessive habit of daily stomach crunches. Each day, without fail – and *after* the gym – she simply had to do 800–1,000 crunches. That was in the morning. Then, as she prepped for show-time, she'd do another 800–1,000 in her dressing room. Any less than that and she wasn't satisfied. Crunches were part of a daily ritual and she became incredibly toned, assisted by a high-protein, high-carb diet (discounting cheese grits for breakfast and Pop Tarts as snacks).

One hour before showtime, her dressing room door would shut and Madonna's *Ray Of Light* and, later, *Music* album were heard blaring from her stereo. From 2001, if ever there was one pre-concert motivational song, it was the single 'What It Feels Like For A Girl', a song Madonna often dedicated 'to all the pop bitches out there.'

Backstage, crew always heard that song playing with the sound of playful shrieks emanating from the other side of the door. Only the soundman was ever allowed access to mike her up as the gable-end of Big Rob's frame stood guard. Otherwise, it was only Britney and a trusted côterie of assistants and stylists, having fun, feeling invigorated.

As the clock ticked down, the dancers limbered up and waited backstage. In the now-packed arenas, an expectant audience demanded her presence:

'BRITNEY! … BRITNEY! … BRITNEY!'

Then, the stomping of the feet began. As the princess of pop emerged from her dressing room, she was beaming. She was 'on' … preparing to go 'in the zone'. But not before honouring a ritual that seemed to have been fashioned from Madonna's 1991 tour documentary, *Truth Or Dare*. Madonna's influence was everywhere one looked in Britney's developing world.

'Gather round y'all!' Britney said to crew and dancers.

In the shadows backstage, artiste, dancers and members of the team formed a circle, holding hands high, and Britney said a prayer out loud: 'Please God, let's make sure this show is great!' The circle then broke up amid high-fives and loud encouragement. Britney hugged every single one of her team.

Then, taking a breath, she gathered herself and mentally prepared. She walked to position, strapping herself into a fake magic carpet or a silver ball for her grand entrance. Many times, she'd look back at her crew, smile and wink. The wide smile on her face told everyone how much she revelled in these moments.

Back in the arena, the lights dimmed, darkness falling on the screams of anticipation. Seconds passed.

And then came the roar.

The 'Oops! … I Did It Again World Tour 2000' was a huge success that established Britney as a showman-type performer capable of creating a live spectacle. She was a fire that swept the stages she owned.

Her fans seemed more concerned with seeing Britney 'live' than the mechanics, and those mechanics centred on a question that would evolve into a larger issue: is Britney singing live or lip-synching? It was this tour that first focused on Britney's lips.

Lip-synching has become the new 'Gotcha' of media coverage and the debate asks whether audiences pay to see a live concert or a live show, Las Vegas-style. In 2009, there increasingly seems to be an expectation for authentic enter-tainment and the manufactured days of teen-pop seem to be making way for the age of the singer-songwriter. Emerg-ing talents and true voices from the likes of Meiko, Missy Higgins, Leona Lewis, Adele, Duffy and Kate Perry are in the ascendant.

But, at the turn of the new millennium, the focus was on the spectacle of pop-acts, so it was inevitable that Britney's first headline tour would attract close scrutiny. Many observed that the video projection screens were out of sync with the music but that was explained by a time-delay, and Britney insisted she was 'singing my ass off'.

But the reality was that, during the live shows, some of the high-energy dance routine left her so breathless that she needed 'assistance' from the sound desk, on a coded signal. In an age when everyone became obsessed with media-image – from pop stars to politicians – the lip-synch debate seemed an illegitimate controversy, the revealing of a trick of the trade that had been used without fuss – or without realisation? – since the seventies. 'Canned' performances and taped backup have long been a behind-the-scenes truth. To say this industry ploy is a 'cheat' is the same as accusing record producers of artificially enhancing and improving the voices of artistes from the studio. But once the curtains are pulled back to reveal this sleight of hand, the magic somehow seems tainted and that awareness becomes irreversible, like the shattered illusion of Santa Claus.

In the Britney camp, no one could understand the big deal. It didn't matter that it was 2000 or 2009. In their eyes, Britney 'singing' to a backing-track of her own voice guarantees the audience what they came for – entertainment.

Britney started reading the first book in the *Conversations with God* series, over and over. The *New York Times* bestseller, a constant in the charts for 137 weeks, was written by Neale Donald Walsch after he conceived his work during a low point in his life. He wrote an angry letter to God, seeking answers, and the answers apparently came in a form of dialogue. These became the conversations from which Britney drew comfort as she contended with her newfound fame and hotel lock-downs.

She'd also find inspiration and guidance from verses and wisdoms borrowed from many books, or something she'd heard someone say that day. Additionally, she consulted the heavens and star-gazed with astrologers, seeking answers about love, direction and the true self. In many respects, she was, and remains, the archetypal lost soul searching everywhere for meaning and a true connection within the disorientation she undoubtedly felt.

'Everyone can associate with that feeling when you're momentarily disoriented,' said the close source, 'when you wake up not knowing where you are or become absent-minded for a second or three. Britney felt like that for long periods, not moments. Outside of the schedule framework, she was often all over the place.'

Britney was desperate to find her bearings, and the *Conversations with God* book was a constant companion. She'd write down its messages and learn lines that resonated. But she struggled with its *meanings*: 'She explored, and wanted to know more about life, but big words were lost on her, along with the nuances of the deeper meanings,' said the source. This one fact would not surprise her *Mickey Mouse Club* tutor Chuck Yerger. He'd always noted that her education was rooted in fact memori-sation, not the interpretation of meaning.

What is interesting about this period is that this is also when Britney started to question her Christian faith. She wondered if God's house was simply the Baptist Church, and whether there was a right or wrong way anymore. But she truly believed in the after-life and spoke of a reassur-ance that spirits were guiding her. Such spiritual talk was soothing ... until she reached certain ancient buildings converted into hotels in Europe and believed the rooms could be haunted.

The more she openly questioned spirituality and reli-gion, the more mixed messages and confusion she found. Britney was known for over-analysing everything and got herself into all sorts of mental knots. She even searched for the fate behind her fame: 'Why is this happening to me? There *must* be a reason? What does it all mean?' she asked out loud.

But the surface realities never changed: she had contractual responsibilities to be 'Britney Spears the Performer' for the sake of everyone else – management, label and, most expectantly, her fans. She was the pillar to the Britney Spears' temple.

It seemed that was the only *meaning* she needed to know.

Within that temple, the real Britney could often be found. The source close to her said: 'When no one was around and the promotional duties were done, she was the most natural, silly, upbeat person you could know. With the crew and dancers, it felt like one big happy family on the road. There were so many good times with Britney at the centre of them. But I think she *needed* us around her. She needed a support network – she hated being by herself.'

Britney would also seek the wise counsel of others, bouncing ideas and thoughts off those she trusted: 'She was curious about everything, but that meant she analysed everything to death: life, love, God and people's motives. She'd take what someone said or did and turn it inside out, wondering what they meant. She was deep about so many things, but struggled defining things and finding meaning. She's someone who has great flashes of insight, not prolonged periods of meaningful reflection,' said the source.

Britney often sat in her hotel suite, pouring emotions down into her journal, trying to shape her thoughts into lyrics that could later be inserted into songs. But in her deep reflections, she sometimes 'visited some bad, dark places'. Ask for further expansion on this from the source and 'brooding moods' are mentioned, but they would never last for long. Soon enough, Britney would announce gleefully that she had never felt better or happier. Central to that, no doubt, was assistant Felica, who Britney described as 'the happiest, most positive person in the world.'

There were also the shoulders to cry on of mum Lynne, and her Aunty Sandra – the wise owl of the family. Britney often said that she got her strength from Sandra. But in the year 2000, her aunt was diagnosed with ovarian cancer and Britney took the news hard.

Once again, she questioned her Christian faith, asking God why such illness happened. As well as conversations with God, she also shared another conversation with *Rolling Stone* magazine, one year on from its 'Lolita' cover-shoot. This time, the focus of the interview with Chris Mundy was about life on the road. The discerning writer-now-turned-television-producer was perceptive enough to see through the promoted facades when they were at their strongest and the interview of 2000 now reads as a somewhat prescient insight into her troubles.

In his one-on-one with Britney in her hotel suite, she asked for his opinion of her. He told her that she seemed 'very lonely'.

Britney said he was correct.

She asked him to keep going, feeling that this stranger somehow 'got it', that he was nailing something that had been niggling her and now here was the explanation. Chris continued, pointing out the very dichotomy that exists today: that she wanted a normal life, but normal life bored her.

Spot on again, said Britney.

In that moment, she was acknowledging the very wedge that fame and fortune forever placed between where she stood and where she started. In Kentwood, old school friends' dilemmas revolved which town they should venture out to on a Friday night: Hammond or McComb? Or what should they do about problems at the office? In Britney's world, problems involved tour schedules, catching private jets and whether a single would reach No. 1.

Perceptions are all relative but Britney would soon realise that she could never return 'home'. Her flux was that she could inherently identify with Kentwood but could no longer associate with its way of life, and nor could anyone understand hers.

Chris Mundy asked if she was scared that by wanting her current life, she was alienating people closest to her.

'That's so right, it's scary", Britney said.

She also conceded her anxieties had been crazy.

Agitated nerves were a common characteristic of the private pop star. Chewing gum was always a good distraction and she'd forever bite her nails. Stylists would be in despair when Britney would emerge from a manicure with false nails. The source said: 'Brit needed to chew on something – gum, her nails, even her toenails. It grossed out everyone, but I guess it showed how supple she was!'

Britney referred to her stress-outs as her 'inner demons'. Her one way of dealing with these troubling issues as they cropped up was to swallow them, as she explained in an interview with *Glamour* magazine in 2001: 'You're going to think I'm crazy, but we all have inner demons ... and I just picture them and put 'em in my throat. I use a different demon every time – like, if I'm stressed out about something ... or if I miss my mom."

Another stress-buster was a game played with assistant Felicia: impersonating famous people, including Ashley Judd and Lenny Kravitz. It's not surprising that here was Britney using 'performance' to regulate her anxiety, as she did when younger. When the crowds and autograph hunters became too much, she even invented a coded alert with her constant shadow, Felicia.

She was the perfect assistant – knowing something before the subject knew it herself. Whenever the time came for Britney to be pulled away, the star would hand back a fan's pen, pose for one final photo, then smile convincingly and turn to Fe with a smile, and say: 'It's getting stormy outside.'

> The onslaught of fame will no doubt have made Britney feel trapped, and there was an intense burden on her. No longer did she feel the burden of having to keep her parents happy. Now, she had to keep millions happy. Fame has almost become the authority-figure she must respond to, but it obliterates any sense of normalcy. It means she has to subjugate her own needs to respond to a wider commercial need. The bigger the fame, the more it swallows your own needs, and the more pressure there is. This can create a co-dependency with fame itself, entering a relationship in which Britney must become the performing doll to fulfill the needs of others: 'It's not about me, it's about responding to a force that's bigger than me.' And because of how she responded as a performer when she was a child, she identifies with this force as a force for good. I suspect that Britney thinks that she never had a choice, and always felt propelled by events she had no control over, from inside the home to inside the record label. But it's a show that brings happiness to others, so she responds, feeds off it and holds fame in reverence, as if it were a teacher, providing her with a value and validation that she cannot live without.

By the time Britney turned 21, she had sold 37 million albums worldwide. She lost out at the 42nd Grammy Awards when, ironically, her ex-*Mickey Mouse Club* friend Christina Aguilera took the title 'Best New Artist', but Britney could hardly be disappointed.

She was listed in the *Guinness Book of Records* for having the best-selling album by a teenage solo artist in … *Baby One More Time* as it went on to sell 13 million copies in the US alone. She would also be registered as a record-breaker for being Yahoo's most searched-for item on the web, a status she still holds today. The awards just kept coming in: American Music Awards 'Favourite Pop/Rock New Artist'; World Music Awards for World's Best Selling Pop Female Artist; Billboard Awards 'Album Artist 2000' and 'World Record Breaker of 2000'. She swept the boards at the Smash Hits Poll Winners and the Teen Choice Awards, including accolades for 'Most Fanciable Female' and 'Best Hottie'. Britney would even become one of the youngest people to have her name and star added to Hollywood's Walk of Fame: her name set in stone – in pink. At 21, she was the youngest ever person to accept such an accolade, tying with actress Melissa Gilbert, the girl who played Laura Ingalls in *Little House on the Prairie*.

Barbara Ellen, in the *Observer*, reported: 'While other little girls were putting posters on their walls, Britney was wanting to be the poster on the wall. Whereas other children develop at their own pace, Britney was developing at a pace set by the ferociously competitive American entertainment industry.'

It seemed there was little else she could achieve, except for the one thing that most people arriving in Hollywood do: make a movie. In this regard, Britney was keen to follow in the footsteps of Whitney Houston and, of course, Madonna.

When the princess of pop ventured into movieland, she would face a choice: a career-building breakthrough as an actress, or a commercial vehicle for Britney the performer. In an ideal world, Britney wished to follow the example of Will Smith, the rapper turned actor, who spun a successful solo music career while simultaneously starring in a series of films. Many scripts came and went, but she couldn't have been more excited when a script with Steven Spielberg attached as a producer landed in her lap.

At that time, it was in development but it promised a film that was a cross between *Dirty Dancing* and *The Flamingo Kid*. Producers were even prepared to insert extra dance sequences to showcase her talents. Here was a chance to blend her passion for dance with the challenge of acting, something she'd not done since her *Mickey Mouse Club* days. As Britney read the script, her excitement was obvious; it even had the backing of Larry Rudolph.

It is not known what happened to that opportunity. What is known is that the camp opted instead for a film that revolved around her as the main star; a vehicle for the brand. Britney went commercial after all. When in Hollywood, think like Hollywood. Screen-writer Shonda Rhimes was drafted in to make it happen and the end result of this collaboration was *Crossroads*.

There was no 'based on a true story' qualifier and the camp insisted the debut movie was not, in fact, autobiographical. But in summary, art unmistakably mirrored Britney's life. The protagonist 'Lucy' was a Little Miss Perfect, who lives in America's Deep South (Georgia) and wants a career in music. She's an eighteen-year-old virgin who pretends to be Madonna in her bedroom. Together with two friends and one love interest, she takes a road trip to LA, where she auditions in a talent contest sponsored by a record company, and wins.

In interviews for the movie's release in February 2002, Britney insisted 'Lucy' was nothing like her: 'She is very different from me. I think she's a perfectionist and everything has to be perfect and done her way. I think I'm a little bit more … carefree.'

She was asked if she was aware of her responsibilities as a role model. By now, this was becoming a particularly thorny issue, but ever the diplomat, she replied: 'As far as the children are concerned, it's a beautiful thing that they do look up to me, but at the same time, their parents should explain to them that when I'm on stage or when I'm doing a video, that's not me.'

Increasingly, Britney wanted off the pedestal that came with a ready-made halo; she couldn't understand why she was the figurehead of the celebrity tribe her fame had created.

Crossroads was a moderate success. Reviewing it in the *Washington Post*, Ann Homaday's appraisal seemed the fairest: 'Can Britney act her way out of a Kate Spade bag? Not really, although she cannot be accused of overreaching … acquitting herself if not admirably, at least not shamefully. But let's be real: Streisand she ain't.'

Other critics panned it as a 'shameless promotion' vehicle with characters drinking Pepsi and holding close-ups of Polaroid snaps. The movie also provided a platform for the new album, called *Britney*, and showcased the single 'I'm A Girl, Not Yet A Woman'. And, inevitably, Britney was seen parading around in her pink bra and panties. At least on this occasion, she could say, quite justifiably, that she was acting.

Distributed by Paramount, *Crossroads* achieved its aim, and made money. It grossed $61 million worldwide against a £12 million production budget. In terms of pop stars making film debuts, Britney emerged with credit as the 13th best-ranked box-office performance. Not quite in the same blockbuster league as Whitney Houston (*The Bodyguard*) and Eminem (*8 Mile*), but a creditable effort. Sadly, she was also awarded 'Worst Film of the Year' and 'Worst Original Song' at the 2003 Razzies, which celebrate the worst achievements in film prior to the Oscars.

The movie certainly didn't harm screenwriter Shonda Rhimes' fortunes, either. She went on to create and

executive produce the hit ABC series *Grey's Anatomy* and
then *Private Practice*.

Britney came out and told the world she was a slave. Not in
so many words but within the lyrics to her raunchiest
number yet, 'I'm A Slave 4 U', described by *NME* as 'funk
the way God intended – hypnotic, insistent, mysterious,
suggestive.' This hit was heralded as her coming-of-age
moment.

It's not known whether Britney's hotel scribings were
incorporated into the lyrics by writers Pharrell Williams and
Chad Hugo but, on reflection, two lines at least suggest art
was imitating life. In the first verse, she sings: 'All you people
look at me like I'm a little girl/ Well did you ever think it'd
be OK for me to step into this world?'

Asked about the song's meaning, Britney was reported
as saying: 'It's talking about me just wanting to go out and
forget who I am ... That's kinda where I am right now.' It
coincided with her trying to convey a private message to
both her parents and management: she needed to be cut
some slack. Britney felt controlled in many aspects of her
life, even down to the company she kept. Lynne especially
worried her daughter was susceptible to bad influences
within the crew and dancers with whom she made friends.
She was concerned by those individuals who dabbled in
drugs and partied on the back of pot and Ecstasy, fearing
Britney could get sucked into the wild and seductive scenes.
Indeed, it seemed to many on the periphery that anyone
who came exceptionally close to Britney was worthy of an
unforgiving scrutiny. Britney already felt that fame was
laying siege to her door without having the beady eyes of
her parent and management on her 24/7.

Later, in an interview with *Seventeen* magazine in 2004, this sense of restriction was obvious when she said: 'Your parents have to let go of you and let you mess up because it allows you to learn who you are. You can't live in a prison.'

Those mess-ups would come in time, and it was clear that Britney's patience was wearing thin over the role she was being asked to honour. Fame was defining the person she was becoming. Her biggest complaint, heard more and more, was the cry: 'I just want to do what normal people do!'

The source close to Britney said: 'She is a born performer and wanted this life to a large degree but she also started to rebel against it. Her star was bigger than she could cope with. When Britney got her first million in the bank, she was like, "Oh my Gawd!" and her joy came from knowing that she could now take care of her family. She hadn't considered other stuff and was beginning to feel out of control with it all.'

Robert Baker looks back on many conversations shared with Britney, and he always knew her heart was in the right place, even if her head spun with the pressure: 'She understood that she was the person who was going to make sure everyone in her family was financially okay; that was her goal. Outside of that, she didn't understand much else,' he said.

Of course, the 'performer' kept the controversies and attention-grabbing stunts coming in one faux shock after another: the 'kiss' with Madonna at the MTV Awards 2003 followed the python around her neck at the MTV Awards 2001, when she performed 'I'm A Slave 4 U'.

Phallic symbols and pretend lesbianism seemed like one big yawn to most people by 2003; the only people who seemed giddy about a 21-year-old girl open-mouth kissing a 45-year-old woman were Britney and Madonna themselves.

In an interview with *Out* magazine, Madonna said she'd explained to her daughter that this was 'the mommy pop star and she is the baby pop star. I am kissing her to pass my energy on to her ...'

Shock, awe, and controversy had become Britney's learned behaviours and 'performance' was the only mode in which she found a form of identity. Taken at the age of sixteen, she had undergone the full celebrity make-over. It was by now the only skin in which she both felt comfortable – and uncomfortable. She saw herself only in the projections of others, aided by a world of fashion, make-up and stylists who built, on a daily basis, a look that was a million dollars.

Britney now derived both a purpose and approval from the very identity she put out there, as well as the things she did. Grant any self-conscious woman with low self-esteem such star treatment and she'd gladly discard her old self and jump into the new, bedazzling suit that fame provided for free. Within that intoxicating promise lies the promotion of a fake self but Britney was too far down the road to ask for a reversal. Fame, she was learning, is not a breast implant.

Ever since childhood, she'd never disobeyed her elders so downing tools was not an option. Britney's compliant nature would ensure she remained in the position she'd occupied since a teenager. Personally, the idea of letting down anyone in authority still unsettled her. Obedience and respect was in her blood and now her responsibilities were vested in the expectations of a watching world.

Robert Baker said: 'She became tired of playing the person everyone wanted her to be. Everything was on her. She was carrying the ball to make the touchdown for everyone else. But within in all of this, she was asking herself: "Who am I in all of this?"'

The emerging answer was that she had little idea when removed from the stage and the spotlight. To borrow a phrase from Peter Sellers, Britney was the star already saying: 'I do not know who or what I am'. The person behind the mask was beginning to wobble. Whether that realisation was conscious within Britney is doubtful. Certainly, she was experiencing an immense pressure that no young girl is equipped to sustain.

Many from the world of 'live performance', regardless of fame, would speak of the invigorating high that comes from entertaining an enthralled audience. Britney said: 'Being on stage makes me the happiest person in the world.' Those performances reinforced the pleasure she'd always felt as a child but now instead of seeing the one happy face of Lynne, she felt an adoration reflected by 10,000 fans each night. This euphoria therefore flooded an already over-active nervous system, now feeding off the crowd's mania. 'In the zone' Britney couldn't have soared any higher: the problems came with the post-show comedown.

Performance was becoming akin to an addiction for Britney because, like most addictions, it filled the emptiness she felt as a private person. The pleasure and connection felt when performing creates a mistaken belief that this is who she truly is. This is the problem if people become famous and have no sense of self. The fame, the performance, it starts to define them. So Britney will constantly crave the fix of the next performance because it propels her to a glorified status that provides that intense high which, in turn, supports a false self. And it grants her control. But it's artificial and never lasting.

This creates a split within Britney: someone with a strong identity on stage and then someone who feels lost when not performing. She drops back into reality and feels removed from her bearings, and this induces anxiety.

As the 'Oops! … I Did It Again World Tour' reached Europe in that winter of 2000, Britney started suffering 'massive anxieties' in the middle of the night.

The source exceptionally close to her said: 'She didn't exhibit the classic "I'm-about-to-die" panic attack but her anxieties did overwhelm her. She had trouble sleeping and had these crying fits. She was turning extremely restless and agitated. Night-times were the only times she was truly alone and she struggled with that.'

On tour and when back in LA, Britney started to sleep fitfully and had urges to do something, regardless of the hour. She called dancers in their rooms and, on occasion, reached out to Justin Timberlake. If anyone could soothe Britney, it was the young man who could associate with her unique position.

'She often just wanted to talk, and saw nothing wrong with ringing anyone in the middle of the night. I think it was loneliness and anxiety in the night,' said the source.

But this was darker than mere loneliness. If anything, it signalled an inability to be alone. Britney talked about feeling depressed and the agitations she exhibited started to concern her camp. 'When nothing was happening, it drove her crazy,' said the source, 'She was impulsive, spontaneous and random, and no one was ever sure what satisfied her. Only exhaustion would eventually knock her out.'

Contrary to the impressions in the tabloids, such anxiety was not drug-induced. This was Britney's natural state and natural nervous energy, as exhibited since birth, but it was now heightened by the ingredients of fame. Her moods started to swing noticeably, high and happy one minute, sad and brooding the next. She wept deeply, then instantaneously stopped and became happy, dismissing her behaviour as 'silly ole me!'

Britney's anxiety will have become louder when she's alone or unoccupied; she's so big within her fame that she cannot tolerate being by herself. She will be someone who needs people around her. When the performance is gone and only anxiety is left, this creates many fearful, negative thoughts and erratic moods. She is struggling to deal with the enormity of her fame and loss of freedom but has nothing to hold onto outside of it. She is caught in the middle ground between both states and two worlds, unable to cope with either fame or the confusion she feels when alone.

Such was the level of concern that Britney was prescribed the drug Prozac – used for obsessive disorders, depression and panic attacks – but she treated the pills like headache tablets, taking one only on the days when she awoke depressed. Both her reliance on, and erratic use of, the drug seemed to make her only more manic. There were also, at this time, other prescription drugs but she kept those discreetly hidden away. It seems only assistant Felicia and manager Larry knew what they were. Outside of Prozac, the only other way Britney could rise above her manic state was to get out on stage and perform.

What this illustrates is that as early as 2000, the writing started to appear on the wall. Outwardly, all seemed perfectly happy and the mask never slipped. Inwardly, something was clearly amiss. It seems the world didn't question Britney's mental wellbeing until 2006, but the depressions, the anxieties and unhappiness took root far earlier, and long before any marital breakdown or custody battle.

Behind the scenes, and for those with awareness, the warning signs were already present, but awareness is such a subjective animal. The juggernaut was going too fast to stop, with the world's eyes watching every stage of its journey. What proper mental evaluations took place, and whether they took place at all, is unknown. But it was inevitable that something, someday, would give.

What is known beyond doubt is that one person definitely did pull Britney to one side to ask whether she wanted to continue – and that was her dad, Jamie. A story was published in the tabloid magazine, *The Star*, that she'd been doing cocaine with members from her entourage in a nightclub in Miami. These allegations were nebulous and never cited anyone actually *seeing* Britney snorting lines. The story was vehemently denied and her management threatened, but didn't execute, legal action. Back in Kentwood, Jamie and Lynne read the reports, disbelieving the content. But that's not to say they were not seriously worried about bad influences around their daughter. It must be remembered that, as far as they were concerned, she didn't even smoke.

Jamie was concerned by the whirlwind that he witnessed from afar, with his daughter at its epicentre. According to a source in Kentwood, he shared a brief conversation with her on a short trip back home. When Jamie spoke one-on-one with Britney, his voice cracked and tears welled up in his eyes as he said: 'My baby girl, I love you so much. You can come home any time you want. You don't need to do this.' But Britney just laughed and told him not to be silly: 'I'll be fine, Daddy,' she said.

She knew, as everyone else knew, that the show must go on.

9

Love and Loathing In ...

'As much as you love is as much as you hurt.'
– Britney, 2003

'Success and awards meant more to everyone else than her,' said the source who had Britney's ear. 'There was lots of excitement about the constant push for No. 1, but it started to mean less and less to Britney.'

When 'Laurence H. Rudolph Esq' – aka Larry – first broke the news to Britney that she'd become the first female artist in history to have a single and album simultaneously reach No. 1 with '... Baby One More Time!' the childlike screams could be heard from east to west. But constant success tends to desensitise the euphoria. As the saying goes: 'Savour the first time you have a "first" because it doesn't come around again'.

The source exceptionally close to Britney said: 'Larry always got excited. In the beginning, Britney was like

"Wow!", but she became jaded at being the hit-maker. I don't think she ever tired of performing; she loved that part, but the accolades became "just another day at the office" and her "Wows" turned into "Okay … cools".'

When one witnesses a glimpse of Britney the private person, the needs of the superstar seem out of sync with the wants of the country girl. Nor are these the only differences. Away from the spotlight, an off-duty Britney talks in a much thicker southern drawl, goofing around, sitting cross-legged, laughing out loud, pulling faces and sometimes amused by puerile things such as burping; a girl freed from public parade. Observing her relax in this carefree fashion, in company that soothed her anxieties, the sensational veneer is removed to show an immensely likeable, ordinary girl-next-door; the kind of girl other girls would want even more to be their BFF.

'Britney Spears the performer' is reduced to an impersonation, as if her technicolour dreamcoat has been left in another room. She couldn't appear less like a pop star if she tried. Instead, she is the essence of mischievous sweetness and, while taste is always a subjective matter, it could be argued there is little sex appeal. The branded 'seductress' fails to smoulder. Instead, she is returned to apple-pie cuteness.

Such are the divides between image and reality; human versus brand. What increasingly mattered to Britney was not album sales and No. 1s but a yearning for normal life. 'Normal' was a word she used incessantly; such 'normal' goals included the quest for true love, and building a family. The white-picket fence of the home-making wife with husband and two children – as depicted in her 2009 *If You Seek Amy* video – was, with all its paradoxes, the life that Britney had long visualised.

'Britney has never been a celebrity who is like "Where's my f****** jet?" and "Where's the limo?"' said the source, 'because the trappings of wealth were never important. She sincerely appreciates the little, ordinary things in life – and wanted the picket fence and 2.4 children, not the entourage.'

'I would love to have five or six kids and have a beautiful home,' she admitted on C4's *Richard & Judy* show in 2003, when asked to consider her life aged forty. 'I do believe there's a Prince Charming for everybody and I hope I find that one day.'

The search for that prince began in Kentwood. Her first boyfriend was a local boy from McComb, Mississippi, when she was fourteen. She met Reg Jones after returning home from *The Mickey Mouse Club*. As with most high-school sweethearts, Reg was Britney's first introduction to matters of the heart and she said they were 'head over heels in love'. But it is hard to place too much significance on this puppy love because it was hardly a formative one. Of course, when Britney made headlines at seventeen, it took on an elevated meaning to mirror her heart-tugging teen-love lyrics. But to place emphasis on this relationship, and to suggest it shaped Britney in a deep way, would be flawed.

In Britney's mind, Reg Jones represents names scratched on tree trunks and on the bottom of pencil cases, together with blushing recollections of the fumbling discoveries that Lynne was never supposed to know about. He was the hook on which Britney hung the answer that most reporters asked her when she first set out: 'How does a seventeen-year-old girl relate to such serious love songs?' Cue-in Reg as she sighed: 'I don't think I'll ever love somebody like that again. I just woke up one day and click, it was gone.'

Reg can justifiably claim to be the inspiration behind Britney's fifth single and love ballad 'From the Bottom of My Broken Heart', written and produced by Eric Foster White. The lyrics recall Britney's 'first love' and the video depicts her moving away from the Deep South, knowing she'll miss her boyfriend. As the boy rushes to wave her off, he literally misses the bus and she's gone, lost forever.

These days, Reg is still working hard, drinking his beer and shooting pool in the Country Boys Bar, located somewhere between Kentwood and McComb. He's a modest, likeable man whose photo albums will always bear testimony to the quiet boast that he was Britney Spears' first boyfriend. Today, he'll wistfully remark that the girl he knew was 'pulled away from the people she identified with'; lured by the promise of stardom. When her recording career took off, 'they decided it wasn't good for me to be part of the picture anymore,' he said. Ask him for a deeper reflection, and he'll simply ask to beat you at pool one more time.

He knew his days were numbered when, not long after they watched *Titanic* at the local cinema, an excited Britney phoned him from LA and squealed: 'Guess who I've just beaten at ping-pong? Leo DiCaprio!'

As Reg rightly says: 'How do you compete with that?'

Britney knew it was over when he rolled up with a clearly drunk Jamie Spears to a concert in New Orleans when she was supporting *NSYNC. When she smelled beer on their breaths, she was livid. If Reg was trying to win points by ingratiating himself with the man of the house, it hopelessly backfired.

Thankfully, she had the arms of Justin Timberlake to fall into – and it's this partnership that can properly be defined as Britney's formative relationship, where its true love and harsh lessons would have great impact.

The Britney Spears–Justin Timberlake romance was the Brad Pitt–Jennifer Aniston story of its time, a showbusiness couple that had everyone rooting for eternal happiness. That it was destined to end is a sadness that harbours the same wishful thinking: that one day, both parties may yet get together again. It's debatable which pairing would generate the biggest cheer if either scenario were ever to materialise.

There was always a question mark over when Britney and Justin actually 'got it on'. The truth is that they started dating when Britney was seventeen.

This relationship's promise grew at *Mickey Mouse Club*, and if Reg Jones can boast that he was Britney's first boyfriend, then Justin can boast that he stole her first kiss, during a game of Truth or Dare. 'Mouseketeers' sat in a circle at T.J. Fantini's apartment and the spinning bottle settled on Britney. The dare was to kiss Justin.

He had always described himself as her biggest cheer-leader and, in a 2002 television interview with Barbara Walters on ABC, he admitted: 'I was pretty infatuated with her. Looking back, it definitely had this *Great Expectations* vibe to it.'

Britney and Justin first became close during her support of *NSYNC's tour in November 1998, and they were most definitely a couple by end January 1999, in between the release of her first single and the knee injury. Of course, no one was allowed to know about it because Justin, as a boy-band member, had to maintain his status as hot, free and single. Likewise, Britney, as the solo sex kitten, needed to appear accessible to her following. First and foremost, the fantasies of the fans must be honoured, and both of them were under strict instructions to perpetuate the myth of singledom. The more Britney's star was in the ascendant, the more imperative this became. Love and romance were also placed into 'lock down'.

Britney viewed this denial as a role and became a master deflector by insisting: 'I'm not dating Justin; I'm not! I really don't have time for a boyfriend.' Meanwhile, Justin mocked the rumours by laughing them off.

But in their social circle in Los Angeles, it was an open, albeit well-protected 'secret'. Britney snatched moments at *NSYNC's regular haunt, Le Montrose Hotel, and each Monday night they both joined a regular crowd, including Justin's band-mates, at an upstairs nightclub called Dublin's, off Sunset Boulevard. Brent Bolthouse staged the evening alongside a fellow promoter nicknamed 'Pantera Sarah'. To this day, both these names are synonymous in LA with the ultra-exclusive, need-to-be-seen-at club scene. If these two names touch it, then A-listers and celebutantes flock to it. In early 1999, Dublin's on a Monday was one such select venue. It's also a place touched with irony because the Irish whiskey bar would also become one of Kevin Federline's favourite hangouts in later years.

But back then, it was Britney and Justin's main haunt, as '... Baby One More Time' climbed the charts in the US, and awaited its UK release. It was here, around the booths at Dublin's, that Britney shared conversations with *NSYNC's J.C. Chasez about one day getting their own songs written and produced.

It is within this social circle, as it discreetly moved around select bars and hotels in LA, that one is afforded a glimpse of the record labels' forbidden love. Indeed, such was the paranoid over-protection that even their arrivals and departures had to be carefully choreographed to ensure they were never seen together. When the Hollywood factor interferes in relationships in LA, one of two things tends to happen: one, it is either an 'arrangement' where the soul is traded for the purposes of promotion when two people are set up to appear – or sometimes stay – together (a ploy often used to disguise a man's homosexuality and protect his image); and two, when real love exists but it's not good for the image to be seen together, publicists bend over backwards to ensure such love is never allowed outside. Britney and Justin obviously fell into the latter category.

Britney was just one of the 'secret' *NSYNC girlfriends – including two actresses – who used the cloak of Dublin's to be with her man. When it was time to leave, it fell to promoter 'Pantera Sarah' to chaperone Britney out the door, ensuring she was 'seen' to be alone. It is because of the protection that stars are afforded that the names 'Pantera Sarah' and Brent Bolthouse remain so dialled-in and instrumental on the LA social scene. Indeed, nowadays, 'Pantera Sarah' is such an influential name, even on the political front, that she's even dialled-in to none other than Barack Obama. The journey from protecting a pop princess to canvassing for an American president has been a rewarding one for some in Hollywood.

Today, in another exclusive club on the LA scene, a female source – who was regarded as being affiliated on Justin's side of the fence – looks back with nostalgia on those Monday nights of 1999, and recalls the anticipation she felt at meeting America's newest teen sensation. Her perspective illustrates once more the distinctions between what the public expects and what the reality actually is: 'My first impression was gleaned from the video for "… Baby One More Time" so I was intrigued to meet this girl. But then I saw her sat in this booth with Justin and she was as quiet as a mouse. She kind of sat there, so close to Justin, not saying very much and I'm like, "Is this the same girl?!"'

A picture emerges of a young girl whose body language remained tight with Justin, more looking up to him than being an equal, and she kept a lit cigarette hidden below table level, as if it was a vice no one should find out about.

Surrounding Britney was a raucous and gregarious crowd, and there was certainly no holding back Justin. When he got up, Britney remained seated, chatting quietly with other girlfriends: 'He was up dancing and circulating a lot, joking around and being really engaging but honestly, she looked uncomfortable. Maybe she was keeping it under the radar, but if you'd not seen her video, you'd have thought she was the unconfident girlfriend hanging on. She couldn't have been more polite and was never rude, but there was nothing "superstar" about her. It all seemed a real effort for her.'

Over the coming weeks and months, this first impression was only solidified at different venues: 'After a time, I started to see that here was a girl put together with popsicle sticks and glue. You didn't worry about Justin – he was screwed on and a wise old soul. But you looked at Britney and thought, "This kid's f*****!"'

Even back at *The Mickey Mouse Club*, Justin was the savviest one, as principal tutor Chuck Yerger bore witness. As Britney and Lynne Spears resembled Charlie and his granddad in Wonka's chocolate factory, Justin and his mum Lynn Harless readied themselves for the journey ahead:'My clear memory inside the schoolhouse was Britney seeing where her desk was, and Lynne and Lynn chatting. I remember Lynn Harless talking about Justin, saying he was trying to decide what his stage name would be,' said Chuck. In the end, Justin settled on 'Timberlake' and not his middle name – Randall.

But even Justin can appear nothing like his image, if the experience of video director Nigel Dick is anything to go by. He was filming the 'Crazy' video when Britney introduced a fresh-faced boyfriend on set and told her director: 'This is Justin' before rushing off.

'So I'm left standing there,' said Nigel, 'and I came out with "Hi Justin, what do you do?". He says, "I'm in a group" and I'm like, "Are you? What group's that then?" and he goes, "NSYNC." It was embarrassing, especially for a music video director! I knew the image of Justin Timberlake but the boy stood before me as Justin didn't look the same.'

There was not a hint of the prima donna about either of them, and Justin appeared at video rehearsals as any ordinary, supportive boyfriend would. Even when Britney's parked car was blocking someone and she was asked to move it, he grabbed the keys and moved it for her: 'I thought, "How great is that?"' said Nigel, 'but that was typical of what I witnessed – two great people as great friends in a relationship, and they'd have done anything for one another.'

Even the separation of demanding schedules couldn't keep Justin and Britney apart for too long. When she launched into her debut tour in 2000, Justin liaised with Lynne and Felicia to orchestrate and then spring secret visits. Britney wouldn't have a clue until she'd decamped from the dressing room and walked onto the tour bus expecting another uneventful journey – only to find Justin waiting inside. Her face always lit up.

The female source that knew Justin at this time said: 'That boy was romantic slush but in a creative way, always trying to dream up something original. He was all about rose petals, candles and springing the great unexpected. He adored Britney, and she thought him so clever and talented, raving about how he played the guitar *and* the piano. It was so sweet hearing her talk about him.'

On one occasion, Britney arrived in one of her dressing rooms to find a piano with Justin at the stool, 'playing her in'.

'That boy made her so happy, but it was more than that,' said the source, 'because he also provided her with the balance she craved. He knew her and she knew him, and in Hollywood, that "knowing" is priceless.'

For one birthday, he presented Britney with a diamond music box that she wore around her neck. When she opened the locket-like box, there was a diamond pink bee resting inside.

But it remained young, naive love for two people discovering life in the heady environment of fame and Britney was still waking up to the realities of attracting male interest, something a self-conscious girl still found difficult to accept. Within all of this, the hallmarks of this relationship were numerous: intense, passionate, romantic – and some jealousy, especially on Britney's part.

She became suspicious that he was having an affair with one of the All Saints after he was photographed leaving a club with the British girl-group. 'Why would you leave the club with them?' Britney demanded of Justin. 'Where were you going?'

But All Saints had toured with *NSYNC and Justin insisted he was innocent, but this seed took plant and led to some strained long-distance phone conversations. Britney was also bothered by one of Justin's exes, Veronica Finn, who was a member of the girl band she pulled out of joining: Innosense. Britney often sized herself up against Veronica, wanting to know that she was prettier, slimmer and better. Whatever the truth, Justin nodded encouragingly just for the quiet life. In Britney's defence, these insecurities were more born out of a fear of losing something precious than anything else. It's obvious that the dramatic and unannounced walkouts by her dad during her childhood had left their insecure mark.

A source exceptionally close to her said: 'Britney was so in love, and she was convinced this was the guy she would marry. There were actually three pregnancy scares but it didn't freak them out because this was her "forever". If Britney and Justin didn't know where the condom shelf was, they sure knew where the pregnancy kits were located.' The mere suggestion of a baby on the way from a couple whose love was PR-censored would have been enough to induce fainting fits at the record labels but, as it was, nothing came of these 'scares'.

By late 2001, the Britney and Justin love story was permitted and became common knowledge. Now, the speculation moved onto the issue of potential marriage. Britney bought a Spanish-style house in a cul-de-sac in the Hollywood Hills, above Sunset Boulevard. Cut into a hill, there was a steep bank and a clubhouse behind the house and boyfriend and girlfriend would sit with champagne under a blanket on chilly Californian nights, watching sunsets over LA. Justin technically moved in, and marriage seemed certain.

Then came a heart-breaking discovery.

There has been much speculation, and many versions, about the reasons behind the collapse of this seemingly perfect relationship. Indeed, Justin publicly made it clear that she betrayed him. Britney would only admit doing something 'technically' but insisted it was never quite so black-and-white as first suggested.

The truth, as corroborated by a source from both camps, is that Justin discovered a handwritten letter at the house and this intimated 'something' had gone on between Britney and her choreographer Wade Robson. When Justin confronted Britney, there 'was a blazing row and many tears – but no apology'. What made the betrayal worse in Justin's eyes was that Britney seemed to rationalise everything. Wade had also been great friends with the *NSYNC star, working together on the album *Celebrity* in 2001, and so Justin felt he had suffered a double-betrayal.

The source exceptionally close to Britney didn't wish to clarify the origins or content of the letter, but defended Britney: 'She was young, discovering life and saw no harm in a kiss that went no further. But I'll tell you for sure – she only made out with Wade, they didn't have sex. In her eyes, Justin made a lot more of it because of his own insecurities.'

Yet still, all was not lost. During their public break-up, and after the dust had settled, there were discussions between them that encouraged a reconciliation. Justin was wary, but the love was still there. Britney, who'd been left equally devastated by the episode, was desperate to make amends, pledging her long-term future to him. But then, just as relations were getting back on track, 'something else' happened but no one seems prepared to say what. All that is known is that Justin suddenly quit and Britney was once more pleading for understanding.

It didn't matter whether a second suspicion had substance or not. Justin suddenly realised that without trust, he couldn't re-invest his love, and he couldn't afford for a suspicious mind to eat away at him when he needed a professional focus. He made the decision to walk away, and Britney – so close to winning him back – was crestfallen.

When interviewed by Barbara Walters on US television, Justin detailed the sad end: 'When we were going our separate ways, we sat down and I said to her … I said, "If there's ever a moment when you really need me, you can rest assured that I will be there because I love you as a person, and I will always love you."'

Britney the person fell to pieces as Britney the performer threw herself into the 'Dream Within A Dream' tour 2002, which had started the previous November. She was a typical trooper, bravely stepping up and acting like a pro – until the tour's final leg in Mexico City that July.

Halfway through the fifth track, 'Stronger', she suddenly stopped singing and told the crowd: 'I'm sorry, Mexico. I love you. Bye,' and fled the stage, never to reappear. Her management insisted this was due to the risk of thunderstorms and lightning. Back in LA, Justin outwardly remained philosophical: 'You know, we're not perfect and I do not judge anybody ... it's just a situation of "It's just not enough anymore". It was a very intense relationship, that's for sure.'

Privately, he was broken and he decided to reserve his biggest statement for the release of his second solo single, 'Cry Me A River', in December 2002. The song, which spoke of bridges being burned, laid bare both his abject hurt and deep love with opening lyrics that stated: 'You were my sun, you were my earth ...' But it was the accompanying video that caused the biggest stir, using a Britney look-a-like to depict a cheating girlfriend. Justin played himself as the wronged party, but then he imagined a twist, depicting him exacting revenge by breaking into her house and filming himself with another woman on her bed – allowing 'Britney' to return home and find the hurtful footage playing on the television.

'It's not about her, it's about me,' he said of the video but he, like the real Britney, was learning that controversy, however personal, fanned the flames that brought sales. The song won him a Grammy Award for 'Best Male Pop Vocal Performance'.

One year later, seemingly in response, Britney turned to the man who masterminded the 'Lolita' *Rolling Stone* furore, David LaChapelle, to direct a music video for the tragic ballad 'Everytime'. The controversy now involved the enactment of drowning by suicide. She told interviewer Diane Sawyer that the song should 'speak for itself' when asked who was it *for.*

If that was so, then it screamed loudly. First, Britney issued an apology with the lyrics, '... My weakness caused you pain/And this song's my sorry'. More disturbingly, it illustrated the depths of Britney's devastation and regret, making clear that she was haunted by what she had done by depicting her suicide in the bath, slipping into unconsciousness and under the water, lured by light from the after-life. In order to soften these graphic scenes, Britney then rises from the water, resting her head on the bath's edge, suggesting the scene was all in her imagination.

If anything, these unsubtle communiqués conveyed an even deeper, but unintended meaning: here were two musical stars who saw nothing abnormal in taking their woes and heartache into the public arena, barely camouflaged as art – the A-list version of *Jerry Springer*. But for two people whose development had been framed within television since their pre-pubescent years, this was how they chose to communicate and simultaneously relate to their audiences. It brought them attention and success, too. Such was their education in life.

Around this same time, the media intensity on Britney started to increase as pop analysts queried her versatility and longevity. Suddenly, everyone was awaiting the sales performance of her fourth album, *In the Zone*, which included the self-penned 'Everytime'. Could the pop tart make the transition, like Madonna, into a sexually powerful woman? Even CNN asked: 'Is Spears' star falling?' as analysts highlighted the statistics that her third album, *Britney*, had sold 3.7 million copies compared to the 9 million of *Oops! … I Did It Again*. No one, it seemed, was taking into account the invention of iTunes and Internet downloads within a musical landscape moving with the times. Instead, the media kept its focus on the star wobbling on her pedestal, waiting for the giant fall.

There was now more pressure on Britney than ever before at a time when she felt personally bereft. She was still only twenty-two years old, but regarded as a veteran of the industry, who could take what was coming. But those closest to her argue that an arrested development meant that she was, emotionally speaking, still a pre-teen. This is another consistency that emerges when investigating the Britney Spears' story. Everyone who knows her speaks of a woman who has the attitudes – and mannerisms – of a girl.

Behind the scenes, everyone in her camp, management and record label was keeping their fingers crossed that Britney could hold it together for the November 2003 release of *In The Zone*. The schedule involved America, Britain, the MTV Music Awards in Scotland, France, Germany and Spain.

First stop in Europe was London for appearances on *CD:UK*, *The Graham Norton Show* and *Richard & Judy*. This was the time the pop princess's visit coincided with the book promotion of US Secretary of State Madeleine Albright. A producer on the show had previously welcomed Britney to *The Big Breakfast* in 1999, when 'it was obvious she was the product of Disney training', but even in the intervening years, little had changed: 'Despite her stardom, there was no sense of being in the presence of pop royalty.

'Richard and Judy bought her a limited-edition designer handbag and she loved it. She still didn't take such gifts for granted; she remained the girl-next-door type. The only stipulation was that she wanted three different types of mints – and no one could mention Justin.'

Graham Norton was an odd choice for Britney's previously targeted demographic but Larry Rudolph, speaking to *Time* magazine, said they were hoping to 'pick up a gay audience ... in the same way (as) Madonna and Cher.'

One evening, Britney visited the exclusive nightclub, Boujis, in South Kensington, and tabloid spies witnessed her getting so drunk that she had to be carried out by her bodyguards. By now, she was teetering as her label attempted to paper over the emerging cracks.

France was the next stop, but when Britney arrived in her suite at the Plaza Athenee, she didn't emerge for two days. Doctors visited her in her room and the official line was that she had flu, which then escalated into a fever. A decision was taken to scrap the rest of the media tour. Instead, Britney returned to Kentwood to take refuge at Serenity. Concerns about her emotional state were now causing so much concern that Larry Rudolph, a man of few public words, reassured fans that this was not the beginning of a nervous breakdown, but merely exhaustion.

'She is going to stop being the public Britney Spears and start being the private Britney Spears,' he announced.

For once, Britney had screamed 'Stop!' and those around her listened.

Britney's 'break' lasted less than a month. Not surprisingly, she couldn't relax or chill. 'I need to be working all the time. It feels normal to me,' she later told *Time* magazine. It seems that she struggles to cope outside the fantasyland of fame.

She was discovering that she was a really empty person when she wasn't performing. It's what she learned to do to feel better about herself, and it's the one place where she feels free of the pain she feels. But it's almost rendered her one-dimensional, meaning she will struggle to both be alone and sit still. I suspect that she struggles to be content by even relaxing and watching a movie. When a child is raised amid so much fighting and loud anger, their systems are flooded with adrenaline, creating a constant mode of 'fight-or-flight'. Britney's flight was towards performing and whilst it was her coping mechanism, it also served to excite an already nervous energy. Consequently, she would not be able to take a break from performing without taking the fix she gets from performance.

More crucially, without Justin by her side, she was more lost than she'd ever been. Throughout her journey, he'd been her true ballast against the many alien and potentially destabilising realities that success had thrown her way. He'd been a constant presence and source of happiness since 1993, and they had developed as young people and stars on parallel tracks. His was the voice she could ring from anywhere in the world when anxiety gripped her in the night; when she needed someone to understand what was going on with her. No one could identify with Britney like Justin, and she was bereft without him. In her mind, she had nothing stable to hang onto anymore, and she felt deeply traumatised.

There are many reasons for Britney's struggle with personal attachments but one of them is the anxiety transmitted into Britney as a child as a direct result of her parents' difficulties – an anxiety and insecurity based, in part, on whether Jamie would return home or not: 'Was Daddy coming back tonight?' Britney will also have witnessed Lynne's upset when he didn't show and so all Britney's future attachments were in danger of being linked to that trauma from childhood. She, therefore, will be deeply traumatised by break-ups because of the unconscious association with an unstable domestic set-up in which the comings-and-goings of love were deeply upsetting events. So when Justin leaves, it is, in effect, her daddy going, and leaving mum crumpled on the floor.

During the 2008 MTV documentary, *Britney – For The Record*, she explained the situation in her own words: 'With Justin, he was a part of the magnitude of what I had become so when he was gone, I was like, "What am I supposed to do with myself?" I would go out just to keep myself busy. So I became a goer ... A real busy girl ... A party girl. I was devastated.'

Every confusion, anxiety and depression she'd felt since 2001 was compounded not only by a profound heartbreak but also the self-blame that she heaped on herself. Her constant analysis went into overdrive and often triggered the onset of increasing anxiety attacks. *Forbes* magazine named her the 'World's Most Powerful Celebrity' but she couldn't have been more fragile. She continued to take Prozac, and was now taking the diet supplement Zantrex-3 to help maintain her weight, as evidenced when a bottle spilled onto the floor at Heathrow airport.

One year on, her pain was still raw as she promoted the release of her fourth album, *In The Zone*. Once again, Britney's album debuted at No. 1, selling 609,000 copies in the US in its first week. But, during her now-famous interview with Diane Sawyer on ABC, on 13 November 2003, she could not hide the sadness she continued to feel, or the agitations within.

During taping, cameras picked up on Britney unconsciously wringing her hands, pressing a fist into her other palm and popping her knuckles. When Diane Sawyer asked about her 'toughest of years' that involved the break-up with Justin and Aunty Sandra's diagnosis with cancer, Britney started to speak: 'It was pretty rough, yeah … erm … yes, it's kinda weird … oh weird!' and she looked behind to her team, wanting to escape but knowing the cameras were still rolling. In her awkwardness, she tossed her hair and returned her gaze to Diane Sawyer with a random, 'Hello! Erm … Oh my goodness!' She was now struggling to compose herself. 'Hello,' she said again, '… Ewww! Strong, Britney! Yeah, it was weird.' She smiled, but then her face crumpled. Starting to cry, she asked: 'Can we stop for a second?'

Off-camera, Britney broke down.

When Britney appeared on C4's *Richard & Judy* show, the Justin topic may well have been a no-go zone but the general terms of love and expectations were touched upon when she said: 'Love is love. It takes you over ... it's so intense ... but then it shatters you. As much as you love is as much as you hurt.'

Using her arms to illustrate a new wariness, Britney demonstrated that she'd disappeared into self-protective mode, suggesting she was taking cover. As for future love, she spoke about sound judgement: 'I think that you have feelings about things, and you have to have instincts ... and hopefully they are good instincts.'

But sound instinct had little part in her decision-making. From the moment Justin left, Britney responded impulsively, not instinctively. Seemingly random liaisons came and went, and a once-discriminating selectivity was discarded. Britney began to push away and smash out of the rigid framework that she'd hitherto honoured. The self-discovery that her footloose-status suddenly allowed would involve experimentation, in all walks of life, that the imposed halos of Disney and pop stardom had previously disallowed.

From the clean-cut, handsome Justin Timberlake, the rebounding Britney crashed into the arms of the grungy, punk-looking Fred Durst from Limp Bizkit in early 2003. He lived up to his bad boy image when he appeared on the Howard Stern radio show and shattered Britney's carefully constructed saintly image. She partied too much, drank too much, smoked too much, he said, before adding that she also enjoyed 'dirty talk'. He also revealed that she seduced him wearing a see-through top with no bra.

Britney was learning the hard way that her fame made her a sexual conquest that was a trophy to be paraded and boasted about on national radio. The marketing strategy of being made to appear lustful and accessible on front covers now revealed its flip-side – a majority of men, as apes who beat their chests and claim the prize, couldn't resist the ultimate boast: 'I conquered Britney'. It is the law of human nature in a tabloid generation fostered in unison by the media and entertainment worlds.

Now, as well as feeling used as a performer, a commodity and a cash cow, Britney faced the sad realisation – once removed from the trust of Reg and Justin – that not even sex was sacred. It was merely another act to be paraded and reviewed like an album. Now she could never again be sure what men were attracted to: the image or the real person. In this respect, the performer persona rendered the real person almost invisible. Other men would also shout out their conquests, including a blind date she was purported to have shared with a twenty-one-year-old by the name of Tom Witchey. He told the *News of the World* that she invited him back to a hotel suite in Santa Barbara and he was 'taken aback by how spontaneous she was' and 'our clothes just came off at the same time.'

That such careless interactions took place at all is not a surprise. Released from her heartfelt connection with Justin, Britney's love life became all about the freedom she'd never previously explored, and there was also a momentary sense of validation – to feel hot, sexy and wanted in the void left by her first real love. Now sex became the performance but once it was done, the heartache and disillusionment returned.

Britney was sexualising her longings in the same way as she sexualised her image but this, too, was an act that didn't fulfil her. Deep down, she wanted what Justin had provided: something true that made her feel respected, adored, special and wanted.

When Britney realised that Justin was dating actress Cameron Diaz in the spring of 2003, she conveniently hooked up with Diaz's ex, Jared Leto, an actor and musician who also stems from Louisiana. It is hard not to view this pairing as a ploy to annoy both exes. But it didn't matter a jot whether there was motive or sincerity between Britney and Jared getting together. After one dinner, they never again saw each other 'romantically'. Britney was invited out, and went to dinner with action-hero actor Vin Diesel, who told the pop star that, 'they would make a good couple together.' Again, after one dinner, Britney returned home, unconcerned and disinterested.

One individual who did catch her eye, however, was actor Colin Farrell. It was a date orchestrated as Colin filmed the movie, *The Recruit*. Regardless of its Hollywood origins, Britney instantly liked how refreshing he was. Colin was candid, down-to-earth and didn't honour the LA stereotype, she told friends. When she started to hold parties at her Hollywood Hills home, he would be present, together with another actor, Heath Ledger. But these would be the two known faces in a social circle of hangers-on.

Indeed, what started to concern friends was that Britney would go to clubs and invite back complete strangers for random parties that carried on till dawn. Happy strangers from LA's club scene piled up at chez Spears, disbelieving they were partying with the one-and-only Britney inside her home, with not a checkpoint in sight. It was clear that, most of the time Britney was in no state to be aware that photos were often taken. She tried her best to be discreet, inviting tight little groups upstairs in a giant walk-in closet that became a mock VIP room, leaving random people to have the run of her house.

On the hill behind the property, Britney, Heath Ledger and Colin Farrell would sit together at the clubhouse. It was the same spot where she'd often sat with Justin. Two

Hollywood stars and one pop princess would sit and watch the sun come up after a hard night's partying.

This is how Britney coped during the night: holding parties, and surrounding herself with company, forever occupied day and night. Colin Farrell was a brief romantic escapade but Heath Ledger was a platonic relationship. At the time, he was dating actress Naomi Watts. In fact, when Colin wasn't around, Heath spoke with Britney about his love for Naomi – away filming in Australia at the time – and Britney reminisced about Justin, according to those who shared the conversations.

In an interview in *Stuff* magazine before his tragic death, Heath admitted to spending time with Britney and was quoted as saying: 'I want that girl; I can't deny it. I can treat her better than any man around, and let me tell you, I was smitten.'

It never did go beyond friendship, but Britney privately described him as a 'gentleman', whose advice she valued. Here were two celebrities who understood the pressures of fame and built a friendship from that basis. She confided in friends that he 'got the crazy stuff' about the industry and couldn't abide 'the bullshit' that celebrities were asked to do. Both Heath and Colin Farrell were two celebrities who treated her normally, and she liked that, she said. Britney remained friends with Heath until his tragic death in 2007.

By her own admission, Britney partied hard at this time and, stoked by the independent advice from Colin and Heath, she felt defiant against all that she had previously known. No longer was she going to be told what to do, think or how to act. And what better location could there be for a full-out rebellion than sin-city itself, Las Vegas?

In the NBC series *Friends*, Ross and Rachel are in Las Vegas when they become hopelessly drunk, wildly reckless and giddily flee to a wedding chapel to tie the knot. When they wake in the morning, the shocking reality of their stupidity suddenly dawns. 'This is not a marriage! This is the worst hangover!' they scream and they decide to get an annulment. It was a classic episode first aired in 1999 but Britney decided to do her own real-life cover version in January 2004.

In a characteristically impulsive decision, she decided to use her jet-set lifestyle to transfer a New Year's celebration with friends from Kentwood to Vegas. The group included brother Bryan, childhood friends Cortney Brabham and Elizabeth Jensen, and a local young man called Jason Alexander. They were all 'crashing' at the guesthouse at Serenity, which led to a row with Lynne about the level of partying, and Britney yelling about being controlled. Britney's response was to treat her group to Vegas and a stay in the luxurious Palms Casino Hotel for New Year's Eve. As the clocks struck midnight in a nightclub nearby, Britney turned to Jason Alexander and they started making out. That night, according to Alexander, they'd been downing the 'love drug' Ecstasy. What happened next was detailed in a tell-all account that he provided to *News of the World* reporter, Jane Atkinson.

They returned to the hotel, where they proceeded to have regular unprotected sex over the two days, where more pills were popped in between watching the movies *Mona Lisa Smile* and the *Texas Chainsaw Massacre*. Then, in the early hours of 3 January as they lay in bed together, Britney asked Jason if he'd like to get married. By 3.30am, they were up and dressed in casual wear, heading to The Little White Wedding Chapel in a black limo.

They paid $55 for marriage licence number D635363, pulled in two startled witnesses and then the pop princess-turned-bride walked down the aisle to 'Here Comes The Bride'. She staggered in as Britney Spears and wobbled out as Britney Alexander, on the arm of her new husband as dawn broke.

Back in Kentwood, the groom's father, Dennis, was working under the bonnet of a truck when a reporter asked him for a comment about the wedding to Britney. 'What y'all talking about? My boy's not even in Vegas!' was his response.

No one was aware what had happened, not even the best friends back at the Palms Casino, who had carried on sleeping.

Lynne Spears was at Serenity when she received a phone call from Britney, breaking the news that she had indulged in a spur-of-the-moment wedding. Perhaps part of a growing rebellion within Britney was awaiting the reaction. And the reaction was swift.

The Spears were on the first plane to Nevada, together with Larry Rudolph, two bodyguards and an attorney, and a damage-limitation exercise took care of business more quickly than a Vegas casino can take people's cash. Britney and Jason apparently resembled scolded school children as they sat, man and wife, on the edge of the bed. Jason was told how irresponsible he'd been. Britney was told she could ruin her career. They were then told precisely what would happen next: they would apply for an annulment based on 'incompatibility' and 'flawed judgment' – and no one was leaving the room until it was signed.

Such a reckless decision would become a characteristic that Britney would display again in the future, responding spontaneously to life without considering the consequences. As someone naturally excitable with an inherent nervous energy, and as someone with no sense of who she is without fame, she has little capability to regulate impulses that dictate her actions. There is no stable inner-voice to stand back, observe and consider the consequences. In this regard, Britney is someone whose journey through life will be a series of erratic jumps that ponder the consequences after the event. Las Vegas was one such example.

In Jason's version of events, as told to friends back in Kentwood, 'these mean-looking suits and power men from LA' were stood around and he felt intimidated. The upshot was that he and Britney signed the annulment papers and the marriage lasted 55 hours.

Jason departed with, he says, Britney reassuring him that everything would be okay, to trust her people and they would speak soon. This might explain why he says he felt that his three days as Britney's lover would become a proper relationship once the politics and bad press had died down.

But for Britney, it was nothing more than a night of fun that got out of hand: 'That thing was a total ugh,' she later told *People* magazine, 'I was not in love at all.' She was so unconcerned by the brouhaha that she even poked fun at herself during her subsequent 'Onyx Hotel Tour', telling adoring male fans: 'You may be lucky. I could end up marrying you!'

Jason Alexander learned the hard way that what happens in Vegas, stays in Vegas. Four months later, it would all become immaterial anyway, because Britney's next surprise would mean there was no turning back.

10

It's Her Prerogative

'I married for the wrong reasons –
instead of following my heart.'
– *Britney, MTV documentary, 2008*

Britney came to the realisation that, for six years, she'd danced to the tune of everyone around her, being told how to think, speak and function in the interests of career and brand. In her mind, 2004 would represent a turning point; a phase in which she would take command as the performer-in-charge. Within the empire of Britney Spears Inc, its figurehead sought more autonomy and her thwarted Vegas rebellion was the last time anyone would tell her what to do.

'Things are changing ... and so am I,' she announced on her website.

In a telling insight in that same blog, she revealed that she had 'actually learned to say "NO".' Then, in an apparent swipe at those who had previously guided her, she expressed a new understanding on the topic of child stars: 'Going and going and going is all I've ever known since I was 15. It's amazing what advisers will push you to do, even if it means taking a naive, young, blonde girl and putting her on the cover of every magazine.'

From someone who had forever acquiesced in nearly all areas of life, and seemingly posed happily for semi-nude photographs, this was a stroke of defiance against her commercial exploitation, even if one punch didn't quite spell an eternal fight. But her pointed comments were, if nothing else, a fair indicator of a resentment brewing beneath the surface. Larry Rudolph probably knew then that their association was coming to an end.

All manner of gloss and controls – the polish, protocol, restraints and expectations – wouldn't be revered in the same way. She would instead be more raw; seeking to ad-lib and improvise while remaining a consummate professional. Impulses and spontaneity would become the hallmarks of her bolt for freedom. It was perhaps appropriate then that she should choose a stretch of beach between Santa Monica and Malibu to draw her line in the sand.

Adopting a ploy straight from the book of Diana, Princess of Wales, Britney had learned that if she clicked her fingers, the paparazzi came running. Since late 2003, she'd gingerly fostered an arm's-length relationship within media ranks, knowing that one powerful image conveyed a thousand words. The girl whose life had been all about imagery had come to realise that the paparazzi could become a useful means of communicating with the world, without the filter of management. But, as every celebrity eventually learns, the paparazzi is not a dog that will simply wag its tail on being fed a few biscuits. It is an uncontrollable beast, and the more you feed it, the more it grows, until it reaches an intolerable size and devours its subject. Britney would soon learn this salutary lesson but, back in 2004, all she was thinking about was stamping her authority on proceedings. Equally important, she was showing the world that she was strong and happy after all the doubts and heartache of the previous year. Her crown may have slipped but she'd regained her composure.

When cell phones started to ring in paparazzi circles, word spread about a direct tip-off from Britney. A cluster of camera lenses gathered outside the Beverly Hills Hotel. It was 23 April 2004, four months on from Vegas, and six months after her tearful interview with Diane Sawyer.

The sight that represented Britney's next chapter surprised everyone. Out she walked with a young man whose tall, lean frame was hidden beneath an oversized white T-shirt and topped with a back-to-front burgundy baseball cap. As one observer put it: 'We all thought, "What the f***?! Who's this punk?"'.

It was Britney's new man – back-up dancer Kevin Feder-line.

No one knew it yet but they'd met four days earlier at an LA nightspot called Joseph's, a Greek supper club near Hollywood Boulevard, where Britney partied before embarking on the European leg of her 'Onyx Hotel Tour'. No one had the first clue what to make of this anonymous guy but it was evident from her demeanour that Britney was deliriously happy and orchestrating this media event.

From the hotel, the couple drove in her white Mercedes to Santa Monica, trailed by a bemused, but salivating pack, who en route alerted newsdesks that Britney and 'some guy' had stepped out in what seemed like a public declaration of love. The message was clear: Britney was over Justin.

Once at the Pacific Ocean, Britney appeared the picture of carefree happiness in her cropped denim shorts and white summer shirt, knotted above her abs. She jumped on her new beau in a piggyback all the way to the water's edge. They sat on the sand, side by side, taking in an ocean view on a beach crawling with paparazzi, without an advisor in sight. After removing her shirt to reveal a yellow bikini top, Britney said: 'You got your pictures … Can y'all go away now.'

Of course, it was futile. The beast had already been invited to the table. Suzie Jack, a reporter-turned-producer who trailed Britney for six years while working for magazines such as *US Weekly*, said: 'I don't think Britney appreciated that once you've invited in the paparazzi, there's no uninviting them. But that moment was all about her being seen to take control whilst seeking the validation of the paparazzi, and therefore, the watching world.'

But this deliberate picture of happiness was soon juxtaposed next to the news that Kevin Federline was already the father of one, and his actress girlfriend, Shar Jackson, was six months pregnant with their second child. The last time she'd seen Kevin, she said, was when he kissed her goodbye and disappeared to 'work on a commercial for Pepsi.' Kevin denied this. His version, supported by two sources close to him, is that their relationship was 'technically over' before he even met Britney. Nevertheless, the actress accused the pop star of 'not only breaking-up a relationship but a family as well.' Theories doing the rounds were that the photo-call was a clear message to Shar that said: 'He's mine now – back off!'.

It was a bizarre beach scene that involved the paparazzi, love and accusations of betrayal. That same afternoon, with ironic coincidence, the coastguard reported sightings of sharks in the ocean.

Two days later, Britney was required to leave for London to commence her European tour, but she couldn't face leaving Kevin.

'I'm not going on tour unless you come with me,' she told him, 'so pack a bag, grab your passport and get on that damn plane!'

It didn't matter whether the touring schedule could accommodate him; Kevin was joining her, come what may. Britney knew from bitter experience that absence *didn't* make the heart grow fonder; it placed a wedge slap-bang in the middle of intimacy. With this love, she wasn't taking chances. Borrowing a line from the late Princess Diana, she later told *People* magazine that she 'needed to kiss a lot of frogs before finding my prince' and she wasn't letting this one out of her sight.

What made this interview with *People*'s Todd Gold most interesting was not the love she expressed, but the love she dismissed. With a fatalistic view, and putting Justin Timberlake in his place, she said: 'My other loves were like puppy love. They were like practice for the real thing. This is my happily ever after.'

The European 'Onyx Hotel Tour' was a huge success that ended suspicions that Britney's star was falling. She returned with a virtuoso performance widely received as an act transcending the 'teen-sensation' and evolving into an adult performer. Britney remained a powerhouse who pulled in sell-out crowds and sold best-selling albums. On the transatlantic flight back to America from her final date in Dublin, she felt she was back to her best and overjoyed to be next to her new boyfriend. The flight was at cruising altitude midway above the Atlantic Ocean when the couple started a discussion about life and love. They had been in the air for two hours and hadn't stopped talking and laughing since take-off, so the mood was high.

As conversation started to skirt the future, the topic of children cropped up and Kevin spoke of his love for children. He then happened to mention that true love didn't require a certificate because, 'love is love ... Love is the only commitment.'

Britney interrupted him: 'What if you want to get married?'

As he paused and pondered, she then asked: 'Would you marry me?'

Kevin wasn't sure whether she was speaking rhetorically, until the look on Britney's face told him that, after two months mainly spent on the tour, she was serious.

'NO!' he said.

It wasn't that he didn't want to marry her, it was more to do with the fact that he felt there was an honoured tradition that the man should propose to the woman. Britney stared out the window and a couple of awkward minutes passed by.

'Now,' said Kevin, 'will you marry me?'

Britney burst out laughing because she knew he'd ask.

'Yes! yes, I'll marry you!'

Kevin would later tell *People* magazine that his head was spinning because he'd known since meeting her that she was 'The One'. On landing, the couple broke the news to family and friends, and Britney declared on her website: 'this was the happiest time.'

She couldn't wait to show off her new man in Kentwood. When they arrived, they couldn't have looked a more unremarkable couple. She was casual and pale-faced, with an outbreak of spots, shaded by the peak of her baseball cap. He sported a scruffy beard, scraggy hair and his T-shirt showed off the tattoos emblazoned on both arms. As one local who saw them venture near 'The Dub' bar room said: 'This was no Justin Timberlake!'

They wandered near the only bar in town because Britney took him to visit the home of her late great-grandma Lexie. It was here, in a house still owned by brother Bryan, and in rooms still honoured by the current tenants, that Kentwood's favourite old lady kept a museum-like display of Britney's achievements, charting her phenomenal rise from Star Search to super-star. As Britney road-mapped her career, it was as if she wanted Kevin to be proud, and to understand the human story behind the imagery.

The media struggled to understand what its pop darling saw in this ordinary mechanic's son from unglamorous Fresno, California. Britney wasn't following the Hollywood script. But that was almost the point – she wasn't doing what was expected of her, and she wasn't going to pause to read her lines. Not anymore. But it was also much deeper than that, however flawed her judgement ultimately proved to be. Kevin's appeal at this time was obvious: he represented the ordinary and the normal she dreamed about. He provided the key to a normal life and the status of wife and mother, not princess of pop.

Kevin was just the type of person Britney probably would have ended up with, had she not pursued stardom. He was 'non-Hollywood' and, most importantly, seemed to accept her for who she was. No pretence required. She could leave the performer's mask at the front door. The only other person in the world that she'd previously shared that same intimacy with was Justin, and so this was an echo from her past that was magnetic.

Britney had always said that her idea of the ideal man was someone who wasn't fazed by celebrity and 'someone who hasn't seen much of life.' At first, that seems an odd aspect to seek until she expands her reasoning by adding, 'because then I can see it all over again, through his eyes.'

Another huge attraction was that Kevin's passion was dance. He was a key member of the LA dance circuit and knew about life on the road, with stints as a backing dancer to Christina Aguilera and, ironically, Justin Timberlake.

Those who know him from the world of choreography describe him as 'talented without being exceptional'.

Lynne Spears believes that he was great for her daughter because he was the yin to her yang, keeping her grounded with his laid-back manner. What's also important to note is the one quality that Britney's nature needed – her natural anxious state required someone who could, on paper at least, calm her. And Kevin was, undoubtedly, a soothing, stabilising influence during their honeymoon phase.

He even acknowledged himself that he was the antidote to Britney's 'hyperactive ... running around crazy' attitude and he would jokingly compare her temper to that of cartoon character Elmer Fudd: 'where his face just gets red and steam comes out of his ears.' But the media continued to tag him as 'unsuitable husband material' for the darling it had co-created, and this led to Britney attempting to set the record straight, once and for all, in a shared interview with *Details* magazine in February 2005: 'Nothing gets to him ... because he's not a shallow motherf***** Hollywood actor-guy!'

Even her interviews were beginning to find a new defiant voice, unafraid of cussing. She was, she said, fed up with people viewing her as this 'dumb blonde because I'm quote-Britney Spears-unquote ... People are just way too obsessed with celebrity.'

Kevin hugged her as she turned to him and said: 'I miss you when I'm not with you!'

It was a romantic on-the-record moment that was then pierced by the journalist's follow-up question: 'People think Kevin is with you for your money.'

'Oh yeah,' remarked Kevin.

Britney, continuing her non-measured stance with remarks that no longer sounded sweet-girl scripted, laughed it off and said: 'Well, time will tell, mother-chuckers!'

A banana yellow Lamborghini flashed up kerb-side in front of Busby's, an LA sports bar and club off Wilshire Boulevard. Kevin Federline stepped out with a friend and a bodyguard known as 'Big Mike', his equivalent to Britney's 'Big Rob'. (LA is still waiting to find and name a small bodyguard.) Once inside, and after a few beers, the party headed to the patio, where Kevin treated some fellow smokers to shots of tequila. Then they moved it up a gear, downing a drink called an 'Irish car bomb': Guinness, Bailey's cream and Irish whiskey.

This is Kevin's party scene: a sports bar with a good club attached. He knew how to have a good time but also when to stop. That night, as many around him smoked weed, he refused. As everyone else got wasted, he stopped and was home before 1am. This scene has been painted by a female friend, who knows him from LA's dance and club scene; she believes that a false and misleading reputation preceded him. She is keen to show that he is anything but a wild party animal, or reckless gigolo.

Kevin is, she says, the prime example of the man who fails to match a warped celebrity image: 'People think he's a flash gold-digger but nothing could be further from the truth,' says the ally, 'he's humble, honest and actually very quiet. He never gives it the "big-I-am" and isn't a loud mouth. He's real friendly, and a lot more intelligent than people give him credit for.'

Admittedly, this is only one biased view, and it's from someone who has professionally associated with Kevin since the year 2000. But it's an alternative opinion that rarely gets air time. Ask about a financial motive and the defence is swift: 'He called Britney his Goddess. Money wasn't his objective – he adored her and is a true family man. If anything, he was in awe at first but I honestly think he wanted to take care of her, in terms of love,' she said.

Whether Britney appreciated or wanted that, at a time when she was keen to assert her authority after a life of being 'taken care of', is something only she can answer. Kevin himself would later recall his feelings in an interview he gave to *People* magazine in December 2008, and it echoed what both Britney and her mum had said: 'I don't look at her as "Britney Spears". I look at her as somebody that I fell in love with. Everything just seemed so right.'

When he speaks, he often uses that word 'normal'. He wanted a 'normal' life; he wanted 'normality' for the children they'd have; he wanted 'normal' things, not fancy things. Everything about the way he spoke will have resonated with Britney. Within the normalcy that her husband-to-be spoke of, perhaps there was hope …

The big day was set for 18 September 2004, and the planners had organised a low-key, but memorable day. Britney's strapless white satin wedding gown by Monique L'Huiller was ready, as were the burgundy dresses for the five bridesmaids. All the elaborate invites had been issued to attend 'a special occasion' in the sizeable garden of a private house in Studio City, LA. Britney's self-bought, five-carat diamond engagement ring was going to be sealed with the addition of a platinum wedding band.

Everything was planned to precision, even the little twist that Britney and Kevin had organised: that each of the 30 select guests didn't know they were arriving for a wedding, thinking it was merely a special celebration. But when they reached the venue, they would each open a sealed envelope to find the words 'Surprise!' … and a welcome to the wedding.

As things turned out, this wasn't the only surprise.

There was one unforeseen snag – the pre-nuptial agreement negotiations hadn't been finalised in time. Clearly the
lawyers – Laura Wasser for the bride and Mark Kaplan for
the groom – had much to discuss as they waded through a
60-page agreement. Quite rightly from Ms Wasser's position, and in the interests of Britney's fortune, matters could-
n't be hurried and the many branches of the pop empire
needed to be checked. Britney Corporation Inc needed ring
fencing, regardless of the groom's good faith, otherwise the
new Mr Spears could walk away with a 50:50 split under
Californian law. But Ms Wasser's due diligence – and
evident foresight – didn't assist matters of love and
romance, and that's when an extraordinary decision was
taken to solve the flux: Britney and Kevin would 'partici-
pate in a faux wedding ceremony'.

There would be no marriage licence, as required under
Californian law, nor were they allowed to declare before
the officiating minister that they take each other as husband
and wife. This legal hitch meant the ceremony could not be
solemnised. In other words, Britney's wedding would be
just another performance, celebrated in words and pictures
in an exclusive rights deal with *People* magazine.

The legal papers they both signed stated the bride and
groom 'shall not validly marry one another on the said date'
and 'Britney … understands and agrees that the alleged
wedding ceremony in which the parties intend to partici-
pate … shall not be a lawful Californian marriage.'

It was probably one of the only known wedding ceremonies to be accompanied by the prefix 'alleged', as if a
crime both parties would need to deny. But those were the
documents that were signed on the day prior to the ceremony when it became obvious that the cohabitation/pre-
nuptial agreement was finalised 24 hours before the
wedding when Californian law states there should be a 7-

day grace period. This meant the marriage could not become legal until at least 25 September – a week on from the big day.

It is not clear how many of the select guests were informed that the special occasion was legally meaningless, but it would have taken a brave relative to point out that the Studio City ceremony was equally vacuous as the one perpetrated in Las Vegas. What mattered as far as Britney was concerned was that she was declaring her love for Kevin before her nearest and dearest – and to the public. Ironically, the bizarre legal circumstances had transported them back to Kevin's conversation in the plane that had first led to the proposal: who needs a certificate when all that matters is love?

In an idyllic back garden of the private house, there were archways of flowers as Britney walked down the grassy aisle with dad Jamie. It appeared to be every bit the fairytale wedding she had envisioned. She and Kevin exchanged platinum rings in a ceremony lasting little more than 15 minutes, captured by the omnipresent cameras: photographers from *People* magazine and a crew for a documentary that would later showcase the relationship from its start to the altar.

There remains the faint possibility that this media-focused marriage was the *real* reason behind the faux ceremony: to perform one wedding for the public and another in private. Indeed, when the pre-nuptial agreement was finally prepared and signed, the couple exchanged legally binding vows in a formal procedure two weeks later on 6 October with not a camera in sight. But those close to Britney insist the faux ceremony was a force of circumstance, and legal snags. Whatever the reason, the 18 September wedding was a happy celebration and Britney defied the law by changing out of her wedding gown and into a pink sweatsuit that bore the logo: 'Mrs Federline'.

All guests departed with gift-bags containing a pair of Gap jeans, a silver teardrop key ring and a colour photo of the 'newly-weds' before the party transferred to a nightclub off Sunset Boulevard. The boys wore sweat-tops that bore the name 'Pimps', while the girls wore 'Maids', and everyone partied into the night.

Britney proclaimed married life to be 'GREAT!' and said she couldn't wait to start a family. In the meantime, she'd discovered that she was turning into a 'Suzy Homemaker', who enjoyed cooking and cleaning.

Lest anyone suggest that such domesticity would turn her into a pushover, she asserted her control and parted company with manager Larry Rudolph after a 9-year, 5-album collaboration. 'Britney and I simply realized that we have done all that we can do,' he said in a statement. She, in turn, wished him all the best. Johnny Wright's services were no longer required either.

It seems no coincidence the split coincided with the arrival of Britney's new husband, and man and wife now wanted to be in charge of their own affairs.

With that in mind, her cover-version of 'My Prerogative' was released – an original song by Bobby Brown to reflect his bad-boy image. Once again, Britney was using song to speak for her, using the themes of not needing permission, making her own decisions and not tolerating being told what to do.

For those in doubt, she added her own breathy intro to the song, saying: 'People can take everything away from you, but they can never take away your truth. But the question is … Can you handle mine?'

The problem was the line between truth and fiction was becoming increasingly blurred.

In 1999, as the world first started hearing about Britney Spears, director Ron Howard released a comedy movie called *Ed-TV*, starring Matthew McConaughey. It depicts his character Ed having to contend with the 24/7 invasion of a TV-crew filming his life. Suddenly he realises that producers are controlling his life and fame is sucking all his relatives into the spotlight. It could quite easily stand as a claustrophobic metaphor for the life of Britney Spears, but the fundamental distinction is that Ed did all he could to escape the all-pervasive invasion of the cameras. Whereas Britney decided to increase her exposure, inviting more cameras into her life – even if she was holding one of them herself as a videocam.

Since 2004, from European tour to wedding day, behind-the-scenes footage had been compiled, and the mixed format of video-diary and reality-show combined to create a series called *Britney & Kevin – Chaotic*, launched in May 2005 on UPN. Its theme coincided nicely with the intro to 'My Prerogative', which asked whether people were ready for her truth.

Chaotic finally removed the remnants of any velvet curtain that once hung to protect both the sensational and sacred image of Britney. It was, as promised, 'raw and real' – and devoid of star-like gloss. Britney's ordinariness – pulling faces, goofing and off-guard – was willingly exposed. Perhaps this was the truth she wanted people to handle; the truth that screamed 'I'm no different to you – look!' She was now no longer scared of unmasking herself. No pretence was needed in her marriage; no pretence anymore on the public stage.

It is hard to imagine Angelina Jolie and Brad Pitt ever inviting in the cameras for a 'Brangelina' TV-special: seasoned A-listers step back and see the danger in lowering the drawbridge across the moat.

As Britney discovered in the LA Superior Court, the lowered drawbridge can prove counterproductive, especially where the law is concerned. In 2005, her lawyers claimed defamation against the magazine *US Weekly*, which claimed Britney and Kevin had recorded a sex-tape and feared a member of their entourage would leak it. But Judge Lisa Hart Cole dismissed the multi-million dollar lawsuit: 'The plaintiff herself (Spears) has put her modern sexuality squarely, and profitably, before the public eye. The issue is whether it is defamatory to state that a husband and wife taped themselves engaging in consensual sex.' In this case, the judge ruled that it wasn't because the star 'has publicly portrayed herself in a sexual way in her performance, in published photographs and in a reality show.'

The well-worn Britney argument that there's a distinction between her real self and acting won't wash in a court of law. As she grew tired of the shallowness of her own persona, she'd found one place in life where she was guaranteed not an ounce of sycophancy.

Still, Britney would continue to be provocative and sexualise all that she did, despite declaring 'change'. The sleeve for her *Greatest Hits* album showed her wearing a tiny fur jacket that covered her shoulders, but gaped open to reveal a black bra and briefs; it screamed its raunchy tradition. But she didn't know how to be anything or anyone else; she had been conditioned to sell herself this way. A learned behaviour, and years of being programmed to think sexually, was now incorporated into a fully conscious strategy that had her blessing. Times were not a-changing, and nor was she.

How could she when she had been taught that exploitation equalled popularity? That looking good meant playing the seductress? As the psychotherapist says:

> Britney is so split between her real self and exploited self, that she even exploits herself. She has found something – performance, attention, dancing and singing – that makes her feel alive.

This element of control provides the illusion that everything is fine. In fact, it's an anti-depressant in itself, albeit a momentary one.

It's difficult to see how Britney could have rewound the music industry's coaching that planted so many subliminal rules of life. So, if she was making her own decisions, then she'd taken the same ball from her advisors and instead of dropping it, she'd decided to run with it.

As the new marital home in Malibu neared its renovated completion, Britney started to sort through her possessions that had been divided between her old ocean-view apartment on the Santa Monica front and the nearby Fairmount Miramar Hotel, where she and Kevin had occupied a split-level, garden bungalow for $1,500-a-night.

One item definitely ticked for the removal truck was a black trunk that was a gift from Madonna, someone who had turned from idol to friend. It was a mystical treasure trove stacked full of books of the Zohar, described by believers as 'works of unequalled wisdom and spiritual power'. The evident difficulty with this gift was that the books' text was all in Hebrew. But, as Britney explained to anyone puzzled as to how she would understand such indecipherable glyphs, the idea wasn't to read the information but to 'meditate on the mystical shapes and Aramaic text' – and then the spiritual insights are delivered.

'The words become clear as you meditate,' Britney explained.

For some time, this trunk was the source of her spiritual protection against outside forces and it included wisdoms on such matters as 'the 13 Attributes of Mercy' – 13 spiritual forces that 'protect, watch over and defend from judgements decreed against us'. This trunk was all part of the spiritual inheritance gifted to her by Madonna, and friends said the ancient trunk and scriptures 'must have cost thousands'.

In fairness to Madonna, this was her genuine way of reaching out to Britney. Madonna, years ahead in terms of experience and fully aware of her impact on Britney, was trying to help when she sensed her protégée was flailing. The gift was tied to Madonna introducing her to the Kabbalah and, for a while, Britney left behind her Baptist faith. As someone for whom God had been a mainstay in her life, it was a significant switch that illustrated just how much she continued to search for answers in life, and how much she needed *something* to hold onto.

Britney often wore the believer's badge – a red string worn around the wrist. Even at her wedding, guests received a Kabbalah wisdom as a token from the bride. The Kabbalah is, say believers, dedicated to unlocking the secrets of the heart and soul by finding oneness with the Universe, and believing that all humanity is interconnected on both a physical and metaphysical basis.

As news was confirmed that Britney was expecting her first child, she told *Elle* magazine: 'I read the Kabbalah books and meditate on them. Kevin isn't into it as intensely as I am; for some reason I'm thirsting for it. But he looks at the books every once in a while.'

Britney unapologetically sidelined her own faith and embraced the Kabbalah, telling fans on her website that it had helped rid her of negative influences, 'that were guiding me down the wrong path.' She said that she had reached a point in understanding where not even her family or advisors had the answers she needed. But the Kabbalah did. From the shallow world of commerciality, Britney was reaching out for a deeper meaning in life, sensing the laws of spirituality would teach her more than those of supply and demand.

Britney even had the Hebrew letters 'Mem Hey Shin' tattooed on the bottom of her neck which, when translated, means: 'the power of this name brings the energy of healing at the deepest and most profound level'.

In total, she has 9 symbolic tattoos and this trend began in London when she obtained her very first one – a daisy on one of her right toes, planted to suggest innocence at a time when her innocence was her marketable message. Among the others, she has a little fairy with multi-coloured wings and a little yellow dress on her back to be 'protected by the fairy's wings'; a star to the webbed section of her right hand between thumb and finger, à la Noel Edmonds, to denote positive thinking; two pink dice on her inside left wrist, rolling a combination seven to depict luck in marriage with Kevin (he had two blue dice that rolled a five) and a butterfly on a vine on her left foot to denote personal trans-formation. Later she would add a black, white and pink cross on one of her lower hips, and a pair of lips on her right wrist.

In their own way, the tattoos all meant something to Brit-ney and, in the moment and for a time, she derived value from them. But all her priorities and meanings in life would change with the arrival of her two 'boo-boos': Sean Preston, born on 15 September 2005, and then James Jayden, one year later on 12 September 2006. Their arrival signalled the end of Britney's Kabbalah experiment, when she announced that she no longer studied the Zohar because her babies were now her religion, and motherhood was her focus.

Perhaps Britney's most poignant message, summing up where she was in life, was penned by her own hand two weeks before she learned that she was expecting Sean Preston. For it was then that she co-wrote the lyrics for 'Someday (I Will Understand)' and it's clear that she was returning to the God she'd prayed to since being a child, asking to know 'God's plan' for the way ahead.

By the time her first black-and-white video was shot, Britney was heavily pregnant in an elegant, full-length nightgown as she motherly caressed her 'bump'. Her lyrics spoke of a creative depth that few recognise in Britney, and through song, here was a young woman telling the world that, as she embarked on motherhood, she was still searching for her own answers in life, and she was scared, unsure and needed guidance. Asking God for her truth, she sought reassurance that somebody watches over her.

Her lyrics query the fate behind her fame, as she'd continually done since 2000. And the song builds up to a birth that she hoped would provide answers: 'Someday I will understand ... In God's whole plan ... And what he's done to me ... Oh but maybe ... Someday I will breathe ... And I'll finally see ... See it all in my baby ...' Britney has said that her music is 'a reflection' of whatever she is going through.

And through this song, she told us how much she felt like a rudderless victim to her own dream, and she was asking for help before her babies were born. It is evident, from the lyrics and from those who know her, that she was casting hope onto her babies that their arrival, in some way, would be the key to her self-discovery; that her babies would be her salvation, just as she was to Lynne. And so Sean Preston and Jayden James become just like their mother as a newborn – providing hope amid the hopelessness.

On the Pacific Coast Highway in Malibu, heading north, is a turn-off to a private road that leads to an enclave known as Serra Retreat, where a residential community seems to huddle into the Santa Monica Mountains for privacy. It was here in a community where a quaint monastery held weekly spiritual meetings that Mr and Mrs Federline and family called home.

As with all Britney's choice of homes, it was a Spanish-style, two-storey mansion with eight bedrooms and a large swimming pool set in almost two acres of land. It was a place described by Britney as her sanctuary. When her dad first visited, he made everyone laugh when he walked around gawping, disbelieving its size and comparing it to a holiday resort. But he didn't miss the 'country feel' that Britney always tries to bring to her homes with the worn-wood dining and coffee tables she likes, topped with table lamps adorned with crystal-tassels. Naturally, aromatic candles were strewn everywhere.

Her kitchens would always have 'that country vibe' and she liked hanging massive landscape paintings that reminded her of openness and fields; she also placed a mounted stag's head on the wall. Her pride as a mother was illustrated with the professional portraits of her posing with her children. She even installed a trampoline in the never-ending back-yard – a reminder of her own childhood in Kentwood.

'She called home her sanctuary because I think that's the time, married with Kevin, that she found a semblance of control,' said the source close to Britney. 'She had her family around her and felt protected. When no one was around, and there was no intrusion, Britney seemed her most cool. She loved the process of dressing houses and being domestic; it kept her occupied.' Britney, on occasion, had the habit of introducing people to her refurbished rooms – only they were empty. But her imagination had already visualised and decorated its design, and her excitement took her one step ahead of reality. At least, that would be the kinder interpretation.

One of the main renovations inside had been the incorporation of their own inhouse recording studio. As Britney had already demonstrated with 'Someday (I Will Understand)', she had wanted a hand in writing her own material, seeking to be more singer-songwriter than mere performer.

Away from the stunts, the spectacles and the imagery, she wanted to demonstrate the deeper side to her creativity. Indeed, this was reflected in the fact that she contributed, in part, to eight songs on her fourth and most musically diverse album, *In The Zone*. The full extent of her collaboration as a lyricist is difficult to gauge because she received no sole credits.

In the music industry, the contribution of one line is enough to be included in the credits and benefit from the vast royalties that come with having a hit, published song. Inarguably, one of the best songwriters around at the moment in the pop/rock and dance genre is Kara DioGuardi, who now sits as a judge on *American Idol*. Ask anyone in the industry who they'd most like to collaborate with in this genre and Kara's name, together with that of Linda Perry, falls off every tongue.

It is here where the riches lie. The equation is simple: when you own the publication, and that song becomes a hit, you get wealthy very, very quickly. So that might explain another chief reason why Britney wanted a hand in the writing of her songs, aside from a creative motive.

It might also explain why Kevin sought to exercise his dormant ambitions and become a rapper, not a back-up dancer. As a man who wasn't the primary breadwinner in the house, understandably perhaps he wanted to prove to the world that he wasn't exploiting Britney, and that he could become a talent in his own right. He refused to live in his wife's shadow and be ridiculed as a gold-digger.

Initially, Britney supported him wholeheartedly. He would release two singles, 'Y'all Ain't Ready' and 'PopoZao' in 2006, and then cut an album called *Playing With Fire* that same year. But the consensus implored him to stick to the day job. The harsh truth was, musically and personally, Kevin was cast as the joker and America would never have accepted him as a serious artiste. But his foray into the spotlight meant that he became engaged on the promotional treadmill and took him away from home far more than Britney had envisaged.

This wasn't the 'normal' she'd signed up to. It had been Kevin's invisibility that appealed. But there he was, pursuing a path to become more visible, chasing the stars that the music industry offered. Britney wanted a joint presence at home, a father and a husband. Instead, she saw him beckoned by the spotlight, forever away.

His distance dragged up the insecurities she'd felt with Justin. Kevin's absence from the home reminded her of the absent father in her own childhood. It raked up all her abandonment and jealousy issues all over again. And they weren't the only tensions because the cameras refused to avert their gaze, following her journey into motherhood. She would soon realise that her merits and skills as a mother were another performance deemed worthy of review.

Britney was no different from any other daunted first-time mother, struggling with the onset of responsibility and questioning whether she was emotionally ready at a time in her life when she was still struggling with herself. But the difference between Britney's motherly learning curve was that she had to walk and stumble with a multitude of camera lenses in her face. The cutest animal at the zoo was now a mother, and the media pressed its noses to the glass to see how she interacted with her little lambs.

What then transpired was held up like a charge sheet against her.

6 February 2006: Britney photographed driving with Sean Preston behind the wheel, on her lap. 1 April 2006: Sean Preston falls from his high chair and goes to hospital for a check-up. 16 May 2006: an overhead helicopter photographs Sean Preston properly strapped into a rear baby-seat in Britney's Mini Cooper – but it's facing 'the wrong way', frontwards. 18 May 2006: Britney slips and stumbles on damp cobblestones in New York, almost dropping Sean Preston. The media point out that she kept hold of her coffee cup.

On two of these occasions, the LA Police Department of Children and Family Services deemed it necessary to formally interview Britney. The once adulated American sweetheart was now being held aloft, not as a role model but as a bad mother. If she was so determined to retreat into motherhood and would no longer co-create controversies, then the media would create one for her.

In one of the more heartrending episodes, Britney, feeling hungry, took off with Sean Preston in her Mini Cooper, pursued as ever by a tailgating paparazzi. She stopped to get something to eat at the Malibu Country Mart – a village square of exclusive shops and restaurants – and was crowded by photographers as she unstrapped her son, his little face bewildered by the surrounding chaos, and took him inside. Britney looked more like a woman taking refuge from a storm outside than someone who was hungry.

Then, as she turned to face the staff, she noticed they, too, were taking their own photographs; snapped by staff to her right, bombarded by the flashbulbs that popped and pressed against the window to her left. Overwhelmed in this surreal middle-ground, a defeated Britney sat at a table, rested her head against Sean Preston and wept. Whenever she looked up, tears streaming down her face, they continued taking her photos. Britney the weeping mother was now a fresh image to be put out there and dissected.

Britney would later say of this moment that she sat there, looking at the staff taking photos and thinking, 'You know what? You're a mom! Why are you taking my picture right now? And you see that I'm crying. Are you *that* ignorant?'

What the watching world didn't yet realise was that, privately, Britney simply wasn't coping with the demands of motherhood, now exacerbated by a media-induced crisis of confidence. There was a belief among some in her circle that she was suffering post-natal depression after the arrival of Sean Preston.

It was when he cried that she especially found her role challenging: 'She loved him to bits, as she did with little Jay afterwards. She adores her boo-boos, and seemed fine when others were there as support. It's the times when she was alone that proved too much. Brit was emotionally all over the place, and often became frantic,' said the exceptionally close source. There was a distinct lack of confidence in Britney's interactions with her own children and she started to feel that she could do no right. This doesn't surprise the psychotherapist:

We weren't there and cannot know the precise details but this person who's known nothing but adulation, and has tried to hold herself up in that persona, suddenly has a negative review of her motherhood. The baby's crying is a destabilising factor because it further agitates mum's already frayed nerves. So, because Britney has an inability to calm herself, she is effectively an empty mum holding her son in a bundle of nerves that won't offer comfort, and his crying may worsen. Then what happens? Mum feels even more of a failure because she cannot even calm her own child. Britney couldn't cope with her own needs, let alone the needs of a screaming baby, and you can well imagine how overwhelming this was for someone who wanted to be the perfect mother.

More significantly, when her child cried, the angst comes up in Britney because the mere sound of crying is a reminder of her own pain. It also takes her back to the distress she felt in childhood. But now, as a mother, she cannot disappear. She has to deal with it but doesn't know how because her only coping mechanism was to retreat into fantasy or performance. Britney probably has little knowledge how to contain her emotions at times like this, and it's likely she over-reacted because she wasn't shown by her parents' behaviour how to calm a situation. In this mirrored chaos, she will only feel internal chaos. Unable to cope, she could just 'shut down' and not interact at all. This, in itself, would be hugely confusing for a woman with a clear love and bond with her children.

As Britney attempted to bat away all her internal and external pressures, she then discovered that she was expecting Jayden James in an unplanned pregnancy. Friends say Britney was 'freaked out'. Lynne's advice was that accidental pregnancies are 'the Lord's plan.' This was, Britney heard, a disguised blessing. It seemed to matter little to anyone that another child was being born into a chaos that the mother was already struggling to handle – and so a childhood pattern gets repeated.

One day, as her mother babysat Sean Preston, Britney found time to breathe, away from the pressure, away from the paparazzi. She drove to a bar called Moonshadows, off the coastal road in Malibu; a bar known as the place where a drunken Mel Gibson was once arrested and started ranting about Jews. Britney simply wanted silence; she wanted all the noise in her head to stop. She sat on the bar's narrow outside patio, which perches on a rockface hanging over the ocean. According to a bartending source, she downed five Malibu and pineapple juices, one after the other. She engaged no one in conversation and sat alone, staring out at the ocean.

Asked what she was celebrating, she simply said: 'I'm pregnant again.'

That evening Britney left her Mini Cooper in the parking lot and an assistant drove over to collect her. Not one fan recognised her in a quiet afternoon's trade; not one photographer was present to record the moment. It was almost freedom. But nothing was working for Britney. The hopes she had cast onto marriage and motherhood had only turned into responsibilities that racked up the pressure. Her life would never, and could never, be the 'normal' she craved.

A source who Britney confided in during this time said: 'She had a very clear idea of what married life should be like. She's an idealist, but the reality was very different. She felt a husband and father had certain responsibilities, and she was on at Kevin about obligations she didn't feel he honoured. She felt miserable and all she saw was him running after stardom. She took this as an indication of how much he loved her – that she wasn't good enough for him. Whereas Kevin felt he was doing the responsible thing – going out and paying his own way. All this left Britney with a heavy heart, and she realised there was a price to everything, and she was everyone's investment. Even a photo of her with her children, making one error, could make someone money and the funniest thing in all this? None of the money mattered to Britney. She just wanted a tight family and happiness. I think Kevin felt she was trying to control him.'

This led to furious rows and Kevin buried himself in his work. In doing so, Britney felt even more isolated. Friends of Kevin said: 'he was damned if he did, damned if he didn't.' But Britney, the deep thinker that she is, analysed it all. She asked aloud questions such as: 'How do you know if someone really loves you or not?' In her eyes, she wanted Kevin to prove this and, against the high standards she set, he would come up short. She turned to a girlfriend one day, not knowing what to do for the best.

'What do I do? What do I do?' she asked.

The source said: 'When you've seen a mother hold her child so close, so honestly, then you have seen true love in a simple gesture. This was Britney with her kids. She didn't want nannies all the time, even if she relied on their advice. She wanted to watch and learn, and do it herself. Britney has such a beautiful humanity about her but she was so unsure in certain situations. You could tell she was lost by looking in her eyes, and she cried more than anyone will know. What the public saw was a woman under pressure, not a bad mother. Her heart is immense and people need to see that.'

Britney admitted she was 'an emotional wreck' when pregnant with Jayden James. Indeed, as she expected her second son, she decided to speak out and counterbalance the coverage which she said 'had crossed the line'.

'You know what? I know I'm a good mom,' she told NBC's Matt Lauer in a 15 June 2006 interview filmed at the family home, 'but I'm not perfect, I'm human.'

In the same way that she'd been split between 'performer and person', now she was divided between the good mum she wanted to be, and the bad mum she was held up to be. Public and private life commenced a new mental conflict once more.

Britney may have donned the brave face but she was really a raw nerve sitting before the cameras, forced to justify not only the incidents the media cited against her, but the chances of longevity for a marriage which tabloid magazines questioned, week in, week out. She maintained married life was 'awesome' and that Kevin was working away on his album with her full support.

At the end of May 2006, she posted a poem on her website. Just as Lynne had done since childhood, Britney often scribbled thoughts, verses and lyrics into her journal, but this particular poem, titled, 'Remembrance of Who I Am', wasn't afforded the sanctity of her eyes only. It was clearly intended as a barbed message and public rebuke for someone close. Her words spoke of no more pain, no more chains and 'the silly patterns that we follow' in a theme revolving around her being 'pulled down', 'manipulated' and 'swallowed' ... 'by the ones you think you love'.

It would take Agatha Christie to sift the mystery among a potential cast of suspects who Britney could lash out at for different heartaches and bewilderments. But the poem went on: 'Remember the Bible, The Sins of the Father ... What you do ... You pass down ... No wonder why ... I lost my crown'.

The media interpretation was that the recipient was Kevin, but that was probably more to do with its desire as opposed to the reality. Even though relations were strained, this would have been an odd move when, publicly, Britney was papering over the cracks.

The identity of the recipient is perhaps not so important as the message she was cryptically conveying: the guilt that she'd been made to feel, the chains she was given, the pain she felt, being swallowed, feeling manipulated, feeling weak ... But she was awakening, she said, and 'look who's smiling now.'

But she wasn't smiling. Privately, she was weeping uncontrollably.

In her NBC interview on 15 June 2006, she couldn't stop the tears when Matt Lauer asked, 'What it will take to get the paparazzi to leave you alone?'

'I don't know …' she said, crying, 'I don't know … I would like for them to leave me alone.'

Britney the person was struggling. Against this evident misery, Matt Lauer asked how she could still maintain that her life was blessed and that she was 'lucky'.

'Because I have to believe that I'm here for a reason,' she said.

'What's the reason?' asked Lauer.

'I don't know – I keep searching every day.'

Britney was still surrendering to the idea that none of the disorder and upset enveloping her was self-made, child-hood-influenced and industry-heightened. Within all the internal chaos, she wanted to believe – as she had been taught to believe – that Divine Providence prescribed this medicine. She neither understood it, nor was there any meaning she could fathom. But this surrender to events and outside forces suggests she felt there are no choices and everything was predetermined.

More importantly, she *needed* to believe in this morsel of hope. Otherwise there would be no point anymore. And what mattered as she entered that summer of 2006 was the anchor of home, her marriage and her children. Matters were far from perfect, and she was far from happy, but these were the stabilisers and the domestic framework that just about kept her sane.

11

Little Girl Lost

'I did not want to think about the
reality of it … I just ran.'
— *Britney, MTV documentary, 2008*

Where matters of the heart are concerned, celebrities are not immune from playing mind-games and creating drama. Indeed, much PR seems to depend on it. As in real life, however, the subtext of an emotional action needs to be read if the underlying message is to be understood. So when Britney filed for divorce on 7 November 2006 – eight weeks after the birth of Jayden James – it was, apparently, intended as a salvo across Kevin's ambitions; the whip that demanded things must change.

Friends close to Britney insist the filing of her petition, citing irreconcilable differences, was a last resort because her begging, pleading and weeping had failed. It should be viewed, they say, as an ill-considered test of Kevin's love from a wife who was deeply unhappy and struggling to forgive what she viewed as him reneging on their happy ever after.

Taken at face value, this strategy seems a little risqué until it is pointed out that 'she was finding it impossible with him working all the time, so what did she have to lose?' It also happens to be consistent with a Britney whose nature was to act impulsively, without thinking through the consequences. If this beggars belief, then it must also be remembered that this same strategy worked for Lynne Spears in 1980. When she filed for divorce against Jamie, he came running back. Alas 2006 wouldn't repeat 1980.

The very next day, with Britney in New York on 8 November, Kevin's reaction was swift. He accepted it and decided to fight by filing for sole custody of their sons.

Even if she was prepared to lose Kevin, it was unthinkable that he could take their boys. In her mind, she'd been the stay-at-home mum while he was out chasing his ambitions. This was the final insult.

'She was frantic,' said a well-placed source. 'She is someone who showered her boys with kisses and hugs. She may have struggled at times but SP and Jay are her world.'

Back in Louisiana, Britney's Aunty Chanda knew Kevin's legal application was enough to completely throw her favourite niece: 'Family values are at Britney's core despite all the surface stuff,' she said, 'and, by this time, her children are who she is. Knowing that core value within her, I cannot imagine the fear she was dealing with.'

In public, Britney wore the brave mask and coped as best she could: once more turning to the world of performance. It just so happened that the day after she'd filed for divorce she was in New York for a reconciliation meeting with Larry Rudolph – the manager who'd gone by the wayside when Kevin arrived on the scene. Now, Britney turned to her mentor again, stepping out with him in Manhattan, going ice-skating at the Rockefeller Center. Once again, Larry had thrown Britney a rope, this time after her romantic fantasy slapped her in the face. She hadn't felt 'seen' or loved at all; marriage appeared to be Kevin's launch pad. So if normal life wasn't the answer, maybe a return to stardom was?

Two weeks later, she was booked as the first presenter at the 2006 American Music Awards in a 'live' ABC telecast hosted by Jimmy Kimmel in New York. It was her first major public appearance since news of the divorce broke, and the public might be forgiven for thinking she was happy to be rid of her man. As the show went live and the opening credits rolled, Britney waited backstage for her cue, wearing an elegant cream shift dress.

As she did so, she watched a television monitor in the wings – and saw what the rest of the nation was watching: an opening skit in which a fake Kevin was nailed into a box and put out to sea, dropped into the ocean from a crane. The accompanying good riddance message described him as 'the world's first ever no-hit wonder'.

In the auditorium, fans and celebrities howled, knowing Britney was next up. It was a juxtaposition that seemed adorned with her blessing, but backstage 'she was going loopy', according to one of the soundmen. Reps from Jive Records were equally nonplussed, but it was too late – the footage had been aired, and Britney was being counted down for her stage appearance.

Ever the professional, she straightened her dress, fixed her smile and walked into a rapturous ovation that lasted almost 30 seconds as cheers and whistles rang out.

'I'm so happy to be here!' she cooed, as the applause died down and she went on to present Mary J. Blige with an AMA for Best Female Soul/R&B Artiste.

Once backstage again, Britney's graceful gait turned into a furious stomp. No one had told her the skit would happen and she didn't want to be associated with it. Her aides even tried to pull it from a repeat of the show, three hours later, on the West Coast but it went ahead, unaltered. Britney's anger turned to tears because she knew what Kevin would wrongly think.

The spoof had been the brainchild of host Jimmy Kimmel and he defended it by saying that Britney and Kevin 'both have a great sense of humour.' Few could blame Kimmel. Just two months earlier, prior to the split, the couple had made their own sketch for the 2006 MTV Video Music Awards, poking fun at their own parenting, pretending not to know who was looking after Sean Preston.

But the double standard wasn't the point. Britney's upset was because the last thing she needed just then was to further antagonise an already delicate situation. But the damage was done. Kevin felt betrayed and Britney was crushed because she now knew he'd fight her over the children and the mere prospect of losing her boys was as devastating as the reality.

Britney has a place within her that falls apart in crisis, and the mere threat of losing the love and security of her children plays right into traumas from her own childhood. For someone already fragile, and full of anxiety, this prospect will have untethered her from all that she had been holding onto. And as we know, when she feels in distress and overwhelmed by anxiety, what is the only coping mechanism she knows? She runs, and runs towards the performer who keeps herself occupied in a fantasyland because the emotionally loaded reality is something she cannot cope with.

This time, the fantasyland was the Hollywood party scene and she chose to share it with two strangely unique characters: socialite Paris Hilton and actress Lindsay Lohan. She'd previously met Paris on the LA club-beat through old friends in the promoter and stylist worlds. When one is faced with a personal crisis, these two party-girls hardly seem like the ideal Samaritans but all Britney wanted to do was bury her head in the sand. From her point of view, everything she had done previously to restore balance in her life had failed; marriage and children hadn't been her salvation after all.

At such times, her anxieties are too great and she struggles to sit with her own company through the nights. She'd struggled ever since the onset of fame when she slept with Lynne, and since the European leg of her first tour. Stripped of all pretence and left with the raw reality of an uncertain self-worth, Britney by herself is a shadow of Britney the performer. It's as if taking off the uniform removes her identity and causes her to shrivel. So the club scene offers an environment where she finds company and keeps herself occupied till 4am. Then, she is but a couple of hours from daybreak and a new day. On a surface level, her partying reaction, as a mum of two, seemed to defy common sense but this was Britney's way of coping and, by now, living and reacting in the glare of publicity was already an established way of life.

The prospect of a derailing pop star was irresistible to the paparazzi. Lenses trained, they had been waiting for a mighty fall from the pedestal. Morning, noon and through the night, whenever Britney stepped out and drove anywhere, 30 cars followed. Few understand 'paparazzi' is not just a term for a gaggle of zealous photographers; it is also the name of a sophisticated machine, made up of supremely co-ordinated professionals. Each member of this

30-strong pack shares a walkie-talkie type phone; spies working in unison. At a click of a button, this moving network snaps into action, transferring en masse to follow Britney in a shadow that dwarfs its subject. When she walks even ten yards, it won't honour such niceties as personal space – it is a cluster of lenses and blinding flashbulbs that surround and smother her, meaning her only bearings come from looking down and watching her feet. Imagine a busy carriage on the London Underground where everyone around you has cameras, all trained on you in the middle. But this scene moves with you in public at all times.

When she drives, she is the celebrity fox in a Mercedes or Lexus, pursued by the hounds in SUVs and Escalades, packed together, bumper to bumper. It is a block of moving traffic – 30 cars with Britney in its vanguard, hurtling through Hollywood without any regard for traffic laws because the price of a penalty ticket is minuscule compared to the reward of a great photo. And when Britney honours the red lights, this chase suddenly halts; crossroads and junctions resemble the starting grid of a race, vehicles spread three lanes wide and ten deep with Britney revving in pole position. This is the race she declared open when she unveiled her husband-to-be on the beach in Santa Monica.

To place this daily scenario in context, A-listers such as Jennifer Aniston and Charlize Theron will often be stalked by four or seven paparazzi without having actively cultivated that attention. But Britney, in terms of media attention, is the Princess Diana of America and attracts a veritable audience. It doesn't matter if she screams, pleads or begs to be left alone: if she does, this only makes the next dramatic photo.

But Britney did nothing to help herself at this time. She hit Hollywood nightspots, such as Foxtail, Hyde, The Abbey and Area, and the cameras caught *everything*. Infamously, she was caught climbing out of the car, displaying a pantiless crotch and a Caesarian scar. Another time, she was pictured with vomit on her top.

No longer was she the credible performer but a relentless party-girl ordering Jack Daniel's and Cokes; a bleary-eyed and dishevelled princess. None of Larry Rudolph's image straitjackets worked anymore, and he was fast learning not even his expertise could control such reactionary behaviour.

Meanwhile, Kevin Federline was being the stay-at-home dad, liaising with nannies and baby-sitter Lynne Spears. Against this backdrop of the declared custody applications, the juxtaposition was clear. Britney insisted the media 'exaggerated' her every move and created 'a skewed perception of who I really am' but she seemed to forget her primary lesson: perception counts for everything in Hollywood.

Her personal assistant at the time was a 23-year-old called Kalie Machado, who had joined the payroll two weeks after the divorce petition filed. As Britney's shadow from December 2006 to end February 2007, Kalie witnessed life inside the bubble at a traumatic time, and she decided to speak out in 2008 – once released from her contract – because she felt the truth was being warped. She believed that it was the people *who were there* who could provide an authentic, non-skewed version of events if there was to be a genuine understanding of the human, not the brand.

Kalie would by no means be the only assistant to come and go in an erratic turnover of staff, but out of everyone, the 24-year-old was regarded as a firm favourite, without agenda. Parents and management would scoff at such a suggestion, but when Kalie spoke about outsiders misunderstanding what was going on, she included Lynne, Jamie and Larry Rudolph. As will become clear, there were strong

differences of opinion about what was best and most appropriate within a camp that was splintering in the face of an
increasingly distressed and rebellious Britney.

'I was with her for four months when Jay was just three
months old,' said Kalie, 'I was with her everyday and I
would fight for Britney against anybody who says it was
drugs and alcohol that ruined her.'

She stresses crucial timings in the light of events yet to
unfold, saying that Britney was sad, lonely and 'got drunk a
few times' in the December of 2006 and January 2007, but
no more than anyone else dealing with heartbreak. Her
deliberate point being that Britney did not require rehab,
but, 'unfortunately her mother and manager thought she
was going wild.'

It is clear from Lynne's memoir that she believed the
root of her daughter's problems was post-natal depression
and a broken-hearted spirit that 'brought her to the breaking point.' She then wrote: 'What I didn't know then – did
anybody know? – was how much she was truly suffering.'

Privately, Britney conducted her own internal post-
mortem on the marriage, what had gone wrong and what
part she'd played in it all. The answers wouldn't come
immediately, but by 2008 both she and Kevin would offer
their own clear-headed explanations: Britney in her *For the
Record* MTV documentary in December 2008 and, that
same month, Kevin in *People* magazine. When asked what
had gone wrong, he said that he'd been on the road promoting his CD, attempting to be 'the working dad … trying to
provide for my family' when he was 'blindsided' by the
divorce petition. He said he'd done everything he could to
be a husband, a father and work more from home: 'I don't
know; I guess it wasn't enough.'

Meanwhile Britney, speaking of the devastation and her
response, said: 'I did not know what to do with myself. (We

had) built a dream home in Malibu … with a pool and a huge backyard for the kids, and I did everything for them and my world was that. He started doing an album … and started wanting to do things for himself and I just never saw him anymore. When that happened, things just got really weird. When it ended, I felt so alone.'

In the lonely aftermath of the divorce petition, custody posturing and parties, Britney was set up on a blind date with a male model called Isaac Cohen. It was December 2006, and the first comparison made by the media was that his chiselled features and light beard resembled those of Kevin. The second was when the magazines located Isaac's high-school sweetheart Jennifer Sypal and compared her to Britney's look of 1999. Later, Jennifer was reported as saying that Isaac thought she looked so much like the pop star that he jokingly called her 'Britney'.

Six years on, Isaac found himself stepping out with the woman herself in a fling that provided Britney with companionship. Its substance mattered little. She was pulling somebody into the void, and friends say that Isaac was a strong and understanding support, even if the relationship was only destined to last seven weeks. Britney leaned on this new figure in her life and invited him back to the marital home that Kevin had vacated.

It is perhaps not surprising that Isaac would later sell his story to a tabloid newspaper. It was the *News of the World* that benefited from another lover providing a kiss-and-tell, although today, Isaac's friends say he deeply regretted the trade-off.

Nevertheless, he revealed how Britney flew him to Las Vegas and booked them into the $20,000-a-night Hugh

Hefner Sky Villa atop the Palms Casino Hotel. It is a penthouse with views and a decor capable of taking the breath away of even the most spoilt celebrity; it comes with a large living room, full bar, gym, sauna and spa room, and 'for some unexpected panache' has its own glass elevator, revolving bed below a mirrored ceiling and a rooftop Jacuzzi. This is more the size of a small pool, with a glassed wall shielding the spectacular view of The Strip.

Isaac's interview incorporated the usual tabloid fare: how the sex was 'adventurous', 'amazing' and involved an 'alfresco romp', before transferring to the revolving bed. But beneath the titillating detail are nuggets of truth buried within the account that he imparted to both the newspaper and, separately, to friends afterwards. It is here where the real insights lie from a man who however misguided his kiss-and-tell might have been, was clearly someone in whom Britney trusted and confided. In a composite of that article and friends' testimony, we are afforded a sympathetic examination of a frightened girl fighting for control – and with herself.

'Once the sex stopped, Britney was like a little girl lost, unable to cope with life. There were many occasions she wept uncontrollably. She said she would do anything to be a normal girl again. She was convinced that pictures of her partying would mean she was going to lose custody. It was incredibly upsetting, and I just did everything I could to make sure she had my support,' said Isaac.

Removed from its tabloid dressing, Isaac's more sincere viewpoint attempts to foster a sensitivity and understanding of Britney's troubles: 'She realised the partying did not work; it made her even more miserable. Far from being a trashy drunk, the girl I met was shy, sweet and desperately sad, and she was beside herself with fear that her boys would be taken away. She would cry so hard, and cling to me. She was frightened. I knew I was with her because she felt alone but she was romantic, giving and so kind.'

Back at the marital home, it was clear to Isaac that Britney was still coming to terms with the marriage collapse that she had precipitated. In the hallway, her wedding dress was showcased in a glass cabinet next to the bedroom. The invitations were framed on the wall and a copy of *People* magazine, showing her, Kevin and baby Sean Preston, laid out on the coffee table.

'Even as we made love, it was like Kevin was still in bed with us,' Isaac told the *News of the World*.

At the same time, assistant Kalie Machado was also witness to Britney's desperate state. The conversations they shared suggested her boss didn't know where to turn, or what to do. In her sadness, and when she partied, Britney relied more and more on her nannies: 'She had help but she didn't want it – she wanted the father of her children to be there and help her. Britney was hurting a lot, and her only comfort was to have her babies as close to her as possible. She loves them more than anything. The love that Britney projects is there for everyone; even on a bad day she'll say please and thank you.'

But she was beyond agitated. As Britney paced the house, she would call Kevin's cellphone but, according to Kalie, 'he never returned her phone calls,' adding: 'She didn't talk about it, but I knew what was going on. She'd call him every other day and get nothing.'

From Kevin's point of view, it is understandable that he was smarting and refusing to be sucked into a situation that he clearly felt had been irreparably damaged.

As the festive holiday season approached, Britney couldn't face being among her memories at the marital home so headed to Kentwood to be with her mama and family. 'She was incredibly sad and lonely,' recalled Kalie, 'There were a lot of tears around Christmas and New Year.'

Upon returning to LA, Britney and Kalie took off to Las Vegas for two nights to 'see in' 2007. New Year's Eve was celebrated by going to see Prince in concert, moving on to a nightclub called Pure while a nanny cared for the babies at a nearby hotel. Once again, Britney 'had fun but didn't go wild'. Kalie says that when Britney sees a dance floor, she's on it: 'She could dance all night long – it's what she does,' she said. She also admits that Britney got drunk but never in a loud, crazy or obnoxious way. She was, instead, sad and melancholic: 'She would mostly start thinking about Kevin and start crying. All of January she cried like that.'

It was clear that Britney was climbing the walls at home and would often bolt to places such as Vegas, New York and Miami for impulsive changes of scenery. On 16 January, she and Kalie returned to Nevada, where Britney appeared as a special guest back at Pure. A few hours before her 'appearance', she requested the privacy of the adjoining 'Pussycat Doll Lounge' and it was while inside that room that she 'wanted to play the role of a burlesque dancing queen.' With no one but her small entourage for an audience, Britney climbed up on stage, stripped down to her bra and 'put on a performance' wearing her white shorts.

Kalie said: 'There was nobody else around and she was having fun, getting all sexy on stage. That's what she does as a performer.'

It was this type of event that often made the newspapers as evidence of derailing wildness. Years of building a squeaky-clean image now provided Britney with no margin of error. The young woman who was never allowed to let her hair down as a child was now letting it down in heartbreak – and being judged for it.

When she returned to LA, it was obvious that Isaac Cohen's relevance had run its course. One phone call ended that episode in late January. His final say on the matter was: 'I just hope she does not break down. She is far too special for that.'

His tabloid interview, with posed photos, was printed in England the following month.

Meanwhile, Britney agreed a temporary, joint-custody arrangement granting Kevin a three-day-a-week visitation schedule. An uneasy compromise had been reached.

Then, one evening, assistant Kalie's cell-phone rang out. She looked at the screen illuminating and noted it was a restricted number but answered it anyway: 'Hello? ...'

A male voice was on the other end of the line, claiming to be a private detective hired by Kevin, but declaring an interest in swapping camps. Kalie explained: 'He said he had a whole bunch of incriminating evidence on Britney Spears and he was going to hand it over to me.'

Whatever was claimed, Kevin had not hired a private detective nor had he been compiling any incriminating evidence, but Kalie wasn't to know this at the time. She says she asked the man to email the information after providing her email address, and she ended the call. Five minutes later, he rang back saying he didn't feel comfortable committing sensitive information to email. With her boss's interests in mind, Kalie was persuaded to meet – with her roommate as a witness – in a Starbucks in Santa Monica. It was getting late, around 9pm, but an assistant's work is hardly nine to five.

Her roommate stayed in the car as Kalie entered the coffee shop, looking for a man wearing a cap. That's when

she walked over and introduced herself to a Middle East-
ern man called Osama Lutfi, better known to friends as Sam
Lutfi.

In this hastily arranged meeting, she was struck wary by
one of the first things he said: 'As soon as I sat down, he said:
"Don't try and take down my licence plate number – it's
fake." But I wasn't even thinking of doing that. Why would
I?' Kalie spent the next twenty minutes in Starbucks but
noticed that Sam wasn't carrying any papers to support the
incriminating evidence that had been teased in the phone
call. Maybe he hadn't made the call? Maybe it was an assistant or someone else?

Instead, 'he asked all sorts of questions about the house
[Britney's], who was living there, where we went …'. Kalie
reminded him that she wasn't there to answer questions,
but to see his evidence. When this wasn't forthcoming, she
made it clear she was going to leave. 'Then he started telling
me that he knew for a fact I was under investigation. He
told me I was being followed everywhere … and that the
house was bugged,' she revealed.

Sam Lutfi's version of events is that he'd met Britney at a
party and so rang her assistant. But Kalie didn't feel at ease,
quit the meeting and returned to her friend in the waiting
car. She immediately phoned Larry Rudolph, who rebuked
her for going and told her to forget about it. But Sam Lutfi
was not to be deterred: there would be other ways in …

Britney's personal quest for understanding the meaning of
life now moved on from *Conversations With God* and transferred to a collection of books on Diana, Princess of Wales,
Goldie Hawn's *A Lotus Grows In The Mud* and the work of
English poet William Blake.

The general impression of Britney is that she's a shallow, simple girl who knows little. Without doubt, she is unsophisticated, and someone who struggles to keep an attention span for as long as her performances hold the attention of others. She herself knows her limitations. That's probably why she feels best expressing herself creatively, via tailor-made lyrics or collaboration. As she sees it: who listens to her other than when she sings? So she mines her creativity for thoughts, lyrics and poems, and this represents the depth she keeps guarded. It is a depth with apparently little awareness, without any real accommodation, and yet she strives to fill it, forever digging for meaning. When the answers do not come, she attempts to fill it with the diverse life lessons and wisdoms of others. One poem that she came to read and explore at the beginning of 2007 was William Blake's 'Tiger! Tiger!':

> Tiger! Tiger! burning bright
> In the forests of the night
> What immortal hand or eye
> Could frame thy immortal symmetry
> When the stars threw down their spear,
> And watered Heaven with their tears,
> Did He smile His Work to see?
> Did He who made the lamb, make thee?

Britney drew her own analogy, saying on her website that tigers, 'make you wonder what is behind their gaze … behold the beauty of the tiger.' Typically cryptic, it's not clear how much she delved into Blake's true theme, yet it seems apt for the woman who didn't know whether her fame was a blessing or a curse. For her search mirrored Blake's own bewilderment: did God create the gentle lamb and Satan the terrifying tiger – and are they one and the same?

Media reports, quoting 'close aides', said that Britney had started to read, 'every book there was on Princess Diana' because she felt there were comparisons with how the Press treated her. This was, of course, a seed first planted by her camp back in 2000, when besieged by the paparazzi in London.

In exploring the work of Goldie Hawn, she absorbed the actress's take on the 'transitions and transformations' that lead to self-fulfilment. 'The important thing is that we acknowledge them and learn from them,' wrote Goldie. Britney felt so inspired by this work that she often dipped into chapters to draw a strength that reassured her of one thing: the trials she was now facing were all part of a bigger picture and formed a necessary process that would lead to rebirth. Indeed, this was, she said, exactly the type of book she wished to mirror when it came to writing her own auto-biography. Her trials and tribulations as a pop star would one day be a life lesson to others, she hoped.

All mention of 'transition and transformation' from Goldie Hawn led her to believe that she was the caterpillar who would become the butterfly; that she could somehow change, shed her old skin and start a new life. This rang true with what she told friends.

A well-placed source close to Britney said: 'She wasn't just wanting to run away from her problems, she wanted to run away from who she was. She spoke of running away to a remote island but the loneliness would have killed her. This is the thing about Brit – she wants what she can't bear. She's so happy when she's on stage and loves that part of her life. Then she rails against it when off-stage. She spoke about becoming a schoolteacher, a waitress – *anybody* other than who she was. But the truth is that she can't live without the attention she gets when she performs, or the control it gives her.'

This was Britney's wavering mind-set after the break-up with Isaac Cohen. Indeed, that same January 2007, she wrote on her website how the previous two years had been 'enlightening' and added: 'I am now more mature and feel like I am finally free.' Then, in the next sentence, she sought to reassure her fans that she'd been working hard on her next album and, 'I look forward to coming back this year, bigger and better than ever ...'

Seeking freedom one minute, returning to the persona of performer the next; thus demonstrating the very split within her that she struggles to understand. Britney is starved of the simple needs that she mistakenly thought she'd found with Kevin. She yearns to be her own person and to be loved for her true self; but a life of performance has left only a frightening emptiness when she looks away from the stage or recording studio.

So perhaps it was while she entertained a desperate thought to be someone other than Britney Spears – believing in 'transition and transformation' – that she decided to do what she did next.

This wasn't, as has been suggested, a moment of madness; it seemed more premeditated than that. 'She'd said, "I want to shave my head" before and I'm like, "Britney, it's probably not the best idea,"' explained Kalie, providing insight into an incident on 16 February, widely interpreted as 'the melt-down moment'.

'There were two times she wanted to shave her head. The first time, we were driving and she was like, "Pull over at this salon!". She'd been thinking about it, but I said no, and she didn't go through with it. The second time ... I wasn't with her.'

Instead, it was a Friday evening. Accompanied by her bodyguards, Britney was being driven through Tarzana, a suburb of LA, trailed by the paparazzi. She spotted Esther's Hair Salon and said: 'Pull over!'.

She walked in, and sat in a chair before stylist Esther Tognozzi, complaining her hair extensions felt too tight. 'I want my hair shaved off,' she announced, facing Esther's reflection in the mirror as the paparazzi adjusted their focus outside the salon window. The stylist, faced with being an accomplice in the public sabotage of the pop princess, told her this wasn't possible.

'Of course, I tried to talk her out of it,' Esther told US entertainment show *Extra*, 'I said, "You know, maybe you're having a hormonal moment or something ... maybe tomorrow you'll feel differently about it. Let's talk about this."'

As Esther turned to the bodyguard seeking moral support, Britney grabbed the electric buzzer and started shearing. As her mousey locks fell to the floor, there was nothing anyone could do. When she was finished, Britney sat still and looked at her newly shorn head, and that's when Esther noticed the tears welling in her eyes: 'She said her mom was going to be mad ... and she got a little teary-eyed. She all of a sudden realised what she did.'

The stylist tried to make her feel better by complimenting her 'nice shaped head' while photographers outside rushed to their laptops to wire the photos that would, in minutes, be circulated around the world. Later, tufts of Britney's hair were touted on eBay until an auction, said to be reaching $1 million, was pulled because the website admitted the hair could not be authenticated.

Britney walked next door into Body & Soul for a hip tattoo. The look on people's faces registered disbelief. When an employee asked why, she was reported to have replied: 'I don't want anyone touching me. I'm tired of everybody touching me.'

But the star whose fame was propelled by powerful imagery was about to be destroyed by that same force. Unlike the *Rolling Stone* 'making-of-me' moment, this was the breaking point. Naturally, picture editors chose the most vacant-looking, wide-eyed photos for publication. The media, like the record industry, knows all about imagery too. Consequently, it was these moments frozen in time that seared a belief into the watching world that Britney was 'losing the plot' and on the verge of a cataclysmic breakdown.

'BALD AND BROKEN' declared *ABC News* website. 'SHEAR MADNESS' cried *Fox News*. Joy Behar, co-host on ABC's *The View* – the US equivalent of ITV's *Loose Women* – spoke for many when she remarked: 'A lot of people feel this is self-mutilation.'

Media coverage asked one repetitive question: 'Is Britney teetering on the edge of sanity?'

There were theories that she'd shed her locks because of a threat that the courts were going to take hair follicles for drug testing. But with joint custody agreed in February 2007, there was no prospect of such a procedure. The subject wouldn't be mooted until 6 months later so such conjecture was erroneous, but people needed to make sense of what appeared as a maddening act.

The appearance of shaved heads has always had a propensity to make people feel intimidated or uncomfortable. Viewed as a sign of rebellion, illness, fright, violence and, more extremely, madness, it's an image befitting stereotypes: Mods, GI-Janes, hooligans, convicts, cancer and lesbianism, unless a pre-established image from someone like Sinead O'Connor. Outside of that, no one knew how to process the sight of the glamorous princess of pop dethroning herself in public so everyone clutched at any rational explanation to one irrational act.

It seemed few had considered the possibility that this had little to do with self-loathing, more a loathing against the persona that had defined her until then. What few people knew was that Britney was rowing with her mum, Lynne, who seemed to be incessantly reminding her daughter of her motherly duties and responsibilities. What made Britney most irate was that her mama kept mentioning how Kevin wasn't forever on the town. Whether Lynne's instructions on how to be the perfect mother stirred dormant childhood resentments is not known, but it's clear that the mother who'd been transfixed on Britney the performer was now equally focussed on her being the best mother – and it was all being viewed as 'controlling' behaviour.

It seems blatantly evident then that the head-shaving moment was the culmination of an escalating rebellion, heightened by heartbreak, that can be traced back to 2004 when Britney decided she no longer wished to conform, be controlled or take instruction. Indeed, the evidence suggests there is much more of a credible case to be made for someone who shaved her locks to seek empowerment, as opposed to a person who is out of control.

Britney had been well-coached in the messages that imagery conveys and this one dramatic image told her mama, and any other interested controllers: 'So now what are you going to do with the pop star?!' What better way to rid herself of the performer's identity than by losing the very hair she was famous for; sabotaging the act to free the person?

Dr Alistair Roff, social psychologist and 'an expert in celebrity culture', told *The Times* newspaper: 'This is not so much a cry for help as a cry of "leave me alone!"'

This is where another significant factor comes into the story. Two days before the shaving, Britney had felt 'forced' to check into the Crossroads rehab centre while in Antigua at the behest of her parents and management. They had grown convinced that her partying was the manifestation of serious problems. Britney disagreed, and was furious. Twenty-four hours later, still railing, she checked out. Forcing anyone into rehab or therapy nearly always provokes an even bigger anger because the 'patient' feels the instigation of therapy is to meet the needs of others, not them. It was against this background, therefore, that Britney returned to LA and shaved her head. Suddenly, the superficiality of the pop star lay on the salon floor. 'It was like when they pushed her, she pushed back,' said assistant Kalie.

Britney's rebellion wasn't only directed at her parents. The second coming of Larry Rudolph had returned her to the instructions and directions that she'd once tried to escape. At least, that's how Britney viewed it. It was like the year 2000 all over again: Larry wanting to manage her image, her parents monitoring her every move. And they all reached the same conclusion: that the only plausible explanation for a wayward Britney must be drugs, alcohol or both. There was also a genuine concern that she had become dependent on the prescription drugs used to treat her anxiety and depression. Britney didn't know it at the time but it seemed both parents and manager may have been relying on information from sources close to their daughter. Yet there was no concrete proof. Despite suspicions, rumours and allegations, there was nothing solid. Indeed, this would be a consistent thread throughout all the episodes yet to unfold. Britney would be judged on the balance of probabilities, or so it seemed.

Another factor that needs to be taken into consideration is that Britney had also been grieving the loss of her dear

Aunty Sandra. Two weeks earlier, after a long fight with cancer, this fine lady passed away. Britney was obviously devastated and attended a funeral afforded the dignity of no media attention. This favourite aunt and second mother figure had been a true rock in her life, and one of the first people she visited whenever she returned home. The loss meant another rope holding Britney's stability suddenly frayed.

Life's circumstance bombarded her at once, but the testimony of Britney's shadow Kalie Machado is that there were no signs of addiction or mental illness. The problem, she feels, is that a series of visual images led to a collective, snap diagnosis from onlookers.

Lynne Spears had seen the head-shaving events unfold on television. As she watched, the distraught mother asked God to be with her daughter. In her memoir, she said: 'Something inside of her had broken and needed to be healed.'

She, Jamie and Larry Rudolph had made up their minds over a situation with which they no longer felt in control: Britney needed 'to stop running from the pain' and be placed into rehab. The anxiety-ridden girl, who had been placed on Prozac as early as the 'Oops! … I Did It Again' tour was now being told, six years later, that she needed help.

The media labelled Britney crazy and 'bonkers', and the family prescription was rehab. It is hard to believe what would drive anyone crazier than being told you are going crazy, when, deep down, something whispers to you that it's deeper than that, and nor are you to blame. Who could fault Britney if she looked back to her childhood and felt like telling her own parents what the true definition of 'craziness' looked like?

There were angry phone-calls between daughter and parents. Britney considered herself the victim of a gross over-reaction and screamed for understanding. In her eyes, it was normal for a divorcing woman to go out and party, especially since she'd spent the previous two years in a near perpetual state of pregnancy.

But her parents, supported by Larry Rudolph, believed in all good faith that they had her best interests at heart; that she wasn't seeing straight or behaving in the way that a responsible mother – and pop icon – should.

Britney would attempt to explain the head-shaving incident herself in the 2008 MTV documentary when she spoke of going through 'so much artificial stuff' with her marriage and divorce, adding: 'I was devastated. People thought I was, like, going crazy … but people shave their heads all the time. I was going through a lot, but it was like me feeling a form of rebellion, or feeling free, or shedding something that had happened.'

Assistant Kalie believes no one around Britney grasped the distinction between crazy out-of-control partying and a young woman in serious emotional trouble. Near-dawn stumbles, inelegant exits from vehicles and a gallery of media partying photos do not, she insisted, translate into someone going crazy. It would be rehab, she said, that would tip Britney over the edge. As a theory, this in itself is worth exploring.

Rehab on its own wouldn't have the power to send someone crazy but many forces had already caused Britney to crumble: negative review of motherhood, not coping as a mother, a marriage ending, and her aunt dying. Not to mention the collapse of her fantasy of normalcy. All these factors represent a loss in some form so Britney was in a perpetual state of grief, never having the time to recover. The woman who had wanted more control was actually at the mercy of life events. In that fragile state, it could be argued that rehab would send her crazy as the final straw that broke the camel's back, but all that would depend on the truth of any substance addiction.

But, on its own, Britney's coping mechanism – going out as the performer – was her way of numbing the pain and it's a common reaction. In her mind, she was already dealing with inaccurate and negative projections placed on her without people close to her misunderstanding what was going on inside her. The flooding of all the consequent anxiety and anger could definitely tear her apart.

The girl who was perceived as nothing but a performer was now being perceived as 'crazy', 'losing the plot', 'going off the rails'. And she's left screaming: 'Why can't any of you see what's really wrong?' and 'How dare you treat me this way!' It's almost as if no one in her world knew how to relate to her personally when in crisis and so rehab became the ultimate solution.

Privately, Britney could only rail against her Gods. Inwardly, she felt she couldn't trust those closest to her because their one-size-fits-all solution was rehab.

The day after the shaving incident, she decided to leave home and check into West Hollywood's boutique hotel, The Mondrian. She arrived alone and stood at reception wearing a peroxide blonde wig, hoping to check in without a credit card. But she was denied a room and suddenly the name 'Britney Spears' didn't seem to carry much weight in Hollywood anymore. Britney started crying and saying: 'Nobody wants me anymore … nobody wants me anymore'

It took a small group of girls she didn't know to put their arms around her and offer comfort.

Britney then proceeded to the busy patio where, in her bikini, she sat on one of the pool steps and began to shave her legs. Stopped by an attendant, she moved onto one of the loungers, where she continued to make friends with more strangers and started posing for pictures. In her search

for company, she was reaching out to anyone and everyone.
Once again, this random episode would make its way into
the magazines and the world – and her immediate family –
would become alarmed by the symptoms without determining the cause. It almost appeared as if there was a deliberate strategy to stand off Britney, to allow her to hit rock
bottom – and then she'd see the reason for rehab. But whatever thinking went into this period, there seemed a collective avoidance – even by Britney – of all issues at hand. Time
would prove that the end result was an anger that would
make matters far worse.

Assistant Kalie, who has since moved to San Francisco
to work as a hair stylist, watched from the sidelines, equally
helpless. 'Britney tried to get hold of me when they were
trying to get her into rehab but they told me to stop answering her phone calls. They viewed me as an enabler. She
wasn't trusting anybody – that's why she didn't do as they
say and why she appears difficult.'

The last time she saw Britney was the week prior to the
head-shaving episode, when she joined her on a trip to New
York: 'Her mom called me on the phone and said, "What
are you doing? You being there with her is enabling her!
She thinks because she has a friend there she can go out and
party when she should be at home being a mom."'

The next day, Kalie found herself on a plane heading
back to LA. She was asked to take a few days off: 'I still
don't know why she did it [the head shave],' said Kalie, 'she
never had a chance to tell me. She was forced into rehab
before she got the chance.' Like a stubborn horse refusing to
enter the starting blocks, Britney entered rehab again.
Meanwhile, the stranger from Starbucks – Sam Lutfi –
prepared his white horse and shining armour.

'Promises' was the name of the rehab centre lined up for Britney, and it is a facility renowned for its effective alcohol and drug treatment programme.

A visitor's first impression upon walking into the coastal grounds in Malibu is that it might well be a luxurious five-star resort with its fine decor, luxury and panoramic ocean views. That's because Promises is deliberately designed to accommodate clients, 'who are accustomed to luxury, including celebrities, business executives and government officials.' Its tranquil Californian seclusion is all part of the privacy and medicine because, 'the beauty of the natural surroundings inspires a sense of awe and gratitude that encourages the recovery process.'

According to the website: 'Depression, lack of hope, and even suicidal thoughts are more prevalent in areas where a normal day is grey and bleak and may hinder individuals … attempting to overcome an addiction or substance abuse.'

The facility treats addiction to a variety of drugs and substances, including alcohol, cocaine, codeine, heroin, marijuana and methamphetamine.

This was the pre-ordained sanctuary selected for Britney. Its anonymous testimonials from high-profile clients speak of its effectiveness: 'I don't have to put on a facade anymore,' and 'My career was on the line. The more success and fame I received, the more I indulged.'

The precise details of how Britney arrived at checking in to Promises Malibu on 20 February are not known. She seems to have gone willingly, albeit reluctantly. But, just as she did in Antigua, she checked out 24 hours later. She was missing her children, and was frantic because she had learned that Kevin had joined forces with mum Lynne, agreeing with a strategy that the collective focus was getting Britney into rehab. Lynne's intentions were well placed: she thought she was exercising tough love, as did everyone else.

But Kevin scheduled an emergency custody hearing and Britney responded, suspecting she was losing her children in a process aided and abetted by her own mother. This would become an issue that would later fester in Britney's mind. But, at the time, she was confused and angry, and that's why she quit Promises after 24 hours. She bolted for Kevin's house, where he apparently made it clear that if she didn't return and complete the full 30-day treatment programme, he would apply for immediate court orders to grant him full custody because he had the welfare of his sons to consider.

Kevin, with good grace, cancelled his emergency custody application. But Britney retreated, feeling that events – and everyone – had turned against her. She departed from Kevin's house as a passenger in a silver Mercedes. At her lowest ebb, she sat there as paparazzi swarmed the car; cameras lenses and videos to her right, and across the bonnet at the windscreen.

Further down the road, still being pursued, Britney's Mercedes' brake-lights came on. The next thing witnesses saw was Britney brandishing a green umbrella, trotting to a photographer's SUV and attacking his window and door before returning to her own car and driving off. This time, photos captured her looking demonic and raging; now the world was convinced she was in dire need of help. She wasn't the first celebrity to attack the paparazzi and she won't be last, but a sequence of events was now threaded together to build a *prima facie* case against a woman who was all the time screaming injustice.

Britney was becoming the 'car crash' that no one could peel their eyes from. By way of example, mere footage of 'a stoned Britney' attracted 13 million hits on the web site YouTube. The source exceptionally close to Britney says the umbrella incident happened not only because of paparazzi provocation, but because she'd been with her dad Jamie after the head-shaving incident and the message she'd understood was that if she didn't go into rehab, she would lose her kids: 'She felt they were using the kids as leverage to get her into treatment. She went nuts because she wanted her kids more than anything and she no longer knew who to trust.'

Friends maintain an escalating series of circumstances turned the screw on Britney and, 'made her feel as if she was losing her mind.'

A defeated Britney acquiesced and returned to Promises.

By end March, having decided to toe the line, she emerged to be reunited with her sons. When she first saw them, she ran to them and scooped them up into her arms, showering them with kisses and hugs. She had 'done her time' in rehab, supported throughout by her family, management and Kevin. The couple then reached an initial and pending divorce settlement in which child custody was agreed on a 50:50 basis. But behind the apparent truce, Britney's resentment ran deep.

Manager Larry Rudolph was fired. She would later mock him in X-17 photo agency footage, scoffing: 'Like, my management *totally knew* what they were doing when they sent me into rehab.'

The punishment for her mother would wait.

That spring of 2007, Britney posted a heartfelt message on her website that represented the longest public explanation she'd ever given, demonstrating how keen she was to be heard. It was almost as if these writings, of which she now took control, became her one voice and outlet for truth. She described her message as a letter, saying she wanted to reach out and, 'explain all that I have been faced with recently.'

Promises had been a 'very humbling place' and she accepted she'd hit rock bottom.

'I confess, I was so lost,' she wrote, but she specifically denied her problems had anything to do with substance abuse or depression.

Britney likened her behaviour to a bad kid running around with Attention Deficit Disorder and said she 'had a manager from a long time ago come in and try to direct me and my life' but she didn't seek to apportion blame. Instead, she recalled her childhood and reminisced about happy nights watching family movies, dancing and singing. She acknowledged that, 'a lot of insecurities from when I was little are coming up again'.

But most of all, her highly personal letter seemed designed to offer reassurance to those who cared and to place events in context: 'I know everyone thinks that I am playing the victim, but I am not and I hate what is going on right now so much. Maybe this is the reason for this letter. ...' she wrote, before continuing: 'I feel like some of the people in my life made more of some of the issues than was necessary. I also feel like they knew I was beginning to use my brain for a change and cut some ties, so they wanted to be in more control of my life than me.'

And, to finish off, she wrote: 'I am sitting here at home and it is 6.25 and both of my sons are asleep. I am truly blessed to have them in my life ...'

12

The Self-Destruct

'I can do this! I can do this!'
– Britney, before the MTV VMAs, 2007

B y the summer of 2007, it seemed that a domestic peace had arrived. But in an endless story of deceiving appearances, Britney hadn't forgiven Lynne for 'siding with Kevin' prior to rehab. As well as discarding her manager, Britney had refused to speak with her mama, unless there was a new accusation to make.

Her resentment was heightened by an irrational suspicion that Lynne was spending too much time with her estranged son-in-law and grandchildren. There were angry claims of 'back-stabbing' and 'deceit' as relations between a once inseparable mother and daughter broke down.

On 27 June 2007, those relations hit an all-time low.

By now, Britney's younger sister Jamie-Lynn had followed her tracks into showbusiness and embarked on an acting career, starring in Nickelodeon's Emmy-nominated *Zoey 101* – a children's sitcom about an all-boys' boarding school accepting its first intake of girls. Jamie-Lynn, then fifteen, played the protagonist Zoey Brooks and this role earned her a Teen Choice Award nomination for 'Best Breakout Female Performer' before landing the 'Favourite TV Actress' accolade at her network-sponsored 2006 Kids Choice Awards. The theme song for the sitcom was actually co-written by Britney, and sung by Jamie-Lynn.

Britney, therefore, knew where Lynne was most likely to be – on the set of *Zoey 101* in Valencia, north of LA. So, on a baking hot day, she set off in her black CLK 550 Mercedes and encouraged the paparazzi to follow. What was about to happen next needed to be caught on-camera; it *needed* to be made equally public as her own humiliation. When the star and her paparazzi tail arrived at the *Zoey101* location, everyone was waved through, as if Britney had said: 'They're with me.'

The rest was captured on video: Britney pulling up outside her sister's trailer, marching up purposefully in her flip-flops, cropped denim shorts and white top, while hiding her eyes behind sun-glasses. She knocked on the door, Lynne answered and Britney thrust a set of papers into her hand before turning to walk away.

It was silent footage because it was shot at a discreet distance, but it's clear that Lynne says something to appeal to Britney, who turns on her heels to re-confront her mama. As a crestfallen Lynne sits down on the step, she unfolds the papers to read them while Britney continues to speak and gesticulate.

The media made much of this orchestrated moment, speculating that Britney had served Lynne with a restraining order to keep her away from Sean Preston and Jayden James. In actuality, it was a scathing letter, making clear her daughter's feelings that she wanted to be left alone.

Afterwards, Britney made a comment to reporters that mocked her mama's concerns that had previously sent her into rehab, saying: 'I'm praying for her right now. [I hope] she gets all the help she needs.'

Lynne, who was privately devastated by this rift, later responded by simply saying: 'I've got a strong family, and everything is going to be fine.'

Back in Louisiana, friends and relatives who knew of the intense love and bond between mother and daughter were dumbfounded. Britney's Aunty Chanda observed: 'This was when Britney turned into a whirlwind of disaster. It was as if she'd gone so far away from the person she was that she couldn't find her way back so she lashed out, and she lashed out at the person closest to her. Deep down, we all knew how much that one decision would tear her up inside and that became apparent later,' she said.

Jamie had also been banished after publicly apologising for his daughter in a statement released to the *New York Post*'s Page Six column. In it, Britney was admonished and Larry Rudolph was supported: 'When Larry talked Britney into going into rehab, he was doing what her mother, father and team of professionals with over 100 years of experience knew needed to be done. She was out of control. Larry was the one chosen by the team to roll up his sleeves and deliver the message, to help save her life.'

The final insult, as far as Britney was concerned, was when Jamie said: 'The Spears family would like to publicly apologise to Larry for our daughter's statements about him. Unfortunately, she blames him and her family for where she is today with her kids and career.'

Britney was livid. In her emotionally loaded PR counter-attack, she said she was praying for her father: 'We have never had a good relationship. It's sad that all the men that have been in my life do not know how to accept a real woman's love.'

That final sentence clearly spoke of a long-held resentment from the child still within Britney and goes some way to explaining her struggle to forgive a father for all that she had witnessed. But these statements also indicate the size of this undignified rift. A family was now communicating highly personal feelings via the media and websites.

Britney's continued revolt was to show the world who was boss, and she was removing everyone she had previously relied on. She was going it alone, without parents, without manager, without publicist. She even fired the bodyguard, Tony Barretto, who she'd hired after coming out of rehab.

She had thrown the pilots and stewards from the private jet at 35,000ft, and the VIP passenger found herself sitting in the cockpit – angry, defiant and telling everyone that she knew how to fly.

The only person retained was assistant Alli Sims, an old friend from Kentwood and an aspiring singer with clear ambitions of her own. Together, they called themselves 'Thelma and Louise' after the fictional female outlaws. Alli was Thelma; Britney was Louise.

And as they laughed, partied and carried on regardless – together with another new assistant, Shannon Funk, the nose of the plane started to pitch …

The star now wanted to be manager and publicist rolled into one.

The first Britney-endorsed strategy was to request an interview and fashion shoot with the celebrity-friendly *OK!* magazine. This photo-spread would announce 'Britney's

Back!', while still honouring her obligations with the label she was still contentedly and contractually tied to, Jive Records.

Ever since January, there had been talk of a 'comeback' with her first studio album since 2003. The end result would be the 12-track LP *Blackout* that she'd recorded that summer, producing several tracks that would include 'Toxic' and 'Gimme More'. Jive's A&R team was determined to return the focus to Britney's music and away from her personal life. In Britney's own mind, her self-organised *OK!* shoot was a crucial platform to build from.

But the moment the restructured 'Team Britney' arrived for the *OK!* studio-shoot on 19 July 2007, the omens weren't good. If proof was needed that she was charging on with an amateurish operation, then she was about to provide it in spectacular fashion by leaving behind a defaced set and a stunned editorial team. If ever there was a magazine that bent over backwards to accommodate stars and make their images shine, it was the stable with the British journalist Sarah Ivens at its helm as editor. But the behaviour of Britney was something no amount of gloss could clean up and, in a telling departure, the magazine decided to share it with the world: 'It was like a cry for help. It was heartbreaking,' said Sarah, speaking at the time to explain the decision to effectively expose the singer's on-set manner. In the published truth, the sad decline in Britney was all too apparent.

She had put on a diva-like show in which she appeared under the influence of something; she dismissed out of hand the magazine's elite choice of stylists and make-up artists and insisted her own attendants use the available products to make her up. She also complained that her wardrobe 'wasn't sexy, short or tight enough.' From that moment, the one-time pro threw herself into a reckless – and uncharacteristic – 'anything goes' approach, but now there was no one in her team who was capable, experienced or strong enough to advise her otherwise.

Over the course of a 'disastrous' shoot, she regularly disappeared to the bathroom; refused to remove an Alisha Levine pink gown before wiping her greasy hands down its $275 front and back after lunch; and watched as her pet dog London pooped on a $6,000 Zac Posen gown. Britney, who was by now virtually self-combusting, then walked out of the interview still wearing clothing worth an estimated $14,500, including a $1,000 Vera Wang dress.

Editor Sarah Ivens could have chosen to hide this erratic display from the world, but she felt it was more responsible to 'provide a wake-up call for her [Britney] and for the people around her.'

Once *OK!* unmasked Britney, there were media commentators who suggested this was the human behind the brand, but in the circumstances, that seemed a harsh judgement. What the world witnessed was a Britney acting out of pain, not malicious intent, and so her genuine temperament and attitude were obscured. As Sarah Ivens said, this was a blatant, albeit unconscious, cry for help from someone whose actions defied the mature words she'd posted on her website.

Afterwards, assistant Shannon Funk became the scape-goat for this embarrassing débâcle, but Britney seemed clue-less about her role in the episode, or the message she was sending – and the most interested reader of that *OK!* edition would be Kevin. Already he had become concerned by unsubstantiated rumours emanating from Britney's quarters that she was derailing. The *OK!* incident finally confirmed his worst fears, and he would act swiftly in the interests of his children.

Paperwork was filed in Los Angeles Superior Court that sealed the Federlines' divorce on 30 July 2006. Britney's divorce attorney Laura Wasser was reported as saying: 'I think she's okay with the terms. I think both of them would prefer to have more custody [beyond a 50:50 split] and that can be worked out down the line.'

But Kevin wanted to work things out his own way.

Twenty-eight days later, on 27 August, he upped the ante and made his intentions clear: he wanted 70:30 custody in his favour because he felt he was the more responsible parent. In previous months, there had been much hissing and spitting, but this was first blood. In so doing, he also filed legal papers that placed Britney's financial records in the public arena to justify why *she* should foot the legal bill for the action that intended to take away her children. When your ex-wife is earning $737,868 a month and can afford combined mortgage payments of $61,271 for two US homes, he considered this an equitable request. Court documents also showed that he had little income and his spousal support – $20,000-a-month – was due to expire in three months' time.

But in order to support his case that the children would be better off with him, he showed his hand through attorney Mark Kaplan, expressing an intention to subpoena those closest to Britney, including assistant Alli Sims, nanny Christine Hallet, a bodyguard called Daimon Shippen and ex-business manager Larry Rudolph. In the end, it wasn't their testimonies that would matter; it was the testimony of a man who would return from the past.

But as these manoeuvres took place behind the scenes, Britney attempted to keep a focus on the 'comeback' gingerly being built around the *Blackout* LP. At the start of August, she was booked and went into rehearsals for the MTV Video Music Awards in Las Vegas on 9 September. Kevin's legal assault on her 50:50 agreement would be made 12 days before this now infamous telecast but Britney was determined to get out there and prove a point. She'd lined up the song she was going to perform, 'Gimme More', and this time, she pledged, she would show everyone 'that the bitch is back.'

In a meeting held between MTV producers and representatives from Jive Records, everyone was unanimous about one truth: 'if Britney could do one thing with her eyes closed, it was a telecast,' as a record label executive put it.

There were many discussions held well away from the pop star's ears because there was genuine concern about Britney's capabilities to perform in the wake of her rehab. But, based on her past record, this was a girl who had never failed to 'be on it' when the pressure was on. As one source close to the record label said: 'Brit was regarded as such a pro that, regardless of everything else, it was felt she could literally turn up the day before, do a rehearsal and it would be a walk in the park. Television was her one fail-safe.'

MTV wasn't convinced. The mere thought that a wobbling Britney could arrive twenty-four hours prior to its showcase award ceremony and *then rehearse* induced mass palpitations. It needed to see, know and be sure that she was ready. Verbal guarantees from the pop princess were no longer sufficient; Britney needed to be rehearsing five weeks ahead of time and there was one more expectation: she needed the framework of experienced management around her. In this regard, Jive ushered in the services of Jeff Kwatinetz and The Firm talent agency, with his A-list stable credentials in music and film.

'Why do I need management?' Britney asked out loud when told of these plans. She was reminded that a routine was required and that MTV 'would appreciate it' if she didn't try to organise this appearance on her own. She was, after all, the main curtain raiser. Everyone but Britney seemed to know that routine was an imperative ingredient for her stability. After a large dose of ego stroking, and a stern reminder of the hard work involved, she agreed that she 'needed help'.

'Okay, I'll do it … I'll do it,' she said, with a hint of excitement, 'set it all up.'

She no longer wanted to be a slave to her schedules but recognised this was in her own interests. Later on, she would complain to her newly formed team that, 'everyone wants to take me out and party, but I just want to be a normal girl.'

A source close to the MTV discussions said: 'MTV could not have been more motivated to ensure everything ran smoothly, in both its and Britney's interests, and preparation began five weeks before September 9.'

But as an illustration of the lack of confidence around the star, all parties agreed that Britney's sizeable fee would not be paid upfront as usual but released as staggered payments to maintain the incentive throughout the rehearsal process.

By August's beginning, a new infrastructure was in place with MTV, Jive and The Firm working in concert, supported by attorney Laura Wasser, and collaborating with a choreographer. One notable absentee was assistant Alli Sims – who had disappeared in what appeared to be a retreat from the pressures. She even told the team that she didn't think Britney would make it to Vegas based on what she had already witnessed. It seems there had also been 'a small tiff' between star and assistant, and 'Alli was out of the professional picture for most of that five weeks'.

The inference, as established from those intimately involved with this process, is that the new assistant may have been a great ally and party companion, but she also represented a distraction.

'Let's put it this way,' said the source, 'when Alli wasn't there, Britney was 100 per cent focused and worked her ass off. She told us she didn't want to party, she wanted to work.'

Initially, as Britney found herself once more squeezed into a schedule not of her making, she partly kicked back, cancelling a day's schedule at the last minute. But after ten days into this five-week prep – rehearsing or working out every day – she apparently found her groove and was 'in the zone'. A choreography source said: 'You should have seen how excited she got! She started to feel it again and said, "I can do it! I can do it!" The biggest challenge was harnessing that excitement and keeping her going, but her commitment was definitely there.'

With two weeks to go, she had nailed the routine: 'She'd so mastered it that she kept saying it was "dumb" to keep on rehearsing,' said one dancer.

This level of mastery – with 14 days left to kill – left an age-old problem that the camp knew well: how to keep a bored Britney challenged. Few could blame her when rehearsal days normally involved ten run-throughs of 'Gimme More'. But it was imperative they maintained Britney's focus and presence. It was then that the dancers came up with a preoccupying idea. One dancer explained: 'We knew she liked goofing around and having fun. So, en masse, we all joined her in the workouts with the personal trainer and we turned tedious gym-time into playtime. We messed around, kept her spirits up … You know, every one of us was pulling together and rooting for her.'

The dancers weren't the only stabilisers in the camp. For five weeks, a woman called Michelle Dupont, associated with The Firm, had the sole mission of being Britney's ultra-reliable shadow. The dancers said she referred to Michelle as 'my new BFF' and it was clear there was a professional, but easy-going rapport. Michelle slotted into the gap left by assistant Alli and provided much-needed professionalism. In fairness to Alli Sims, she had never wished to be an assistant: she longed to be the pop star.

Britney, who still required hair extensions to disguise her short hair, was then introduced in LA to her appointed hairstylist Ken Paves, a regular guest on *The Oprah Winfrey Show* and once dubbed by the media as 'the hottest hairdresser in Hollywood'. He is the man who Eva Longoria, Jennifer Lopez and Jessica Simpson request for their fashion and magazine assignments. Indeed, the only reason Ken became free was because Jennifer Lopez had dropped out of her appearance at the VMAs. His retainment was therefore seen as something of a steal. But it was decided to introduce him to Britney first in LA because the record label knew from previous experience the 'sensitivities' of new people arriving without notice. Britney and Ken could not have got on any better. Indeed, colleagues of Ken say he couldn't be easier to get along with because, 'he makes it all about the woman and they love him for it!'

Ken wasn't regarded as the only coup in what was fast becoming a highly polished and sophisticated 'comeback' strategy. Celebrity stylist Trish Somerville was drafted in, and she was a regular on *Vogue* shoots as well as working with Christina Aguilera and burlesque dancer Dita Von Teese. In fact, Britney had personally requested, 'the Dita Von Teese stylist'. Trish was asked to design an outfit of 'daring elegance', and what she created won immediate approval with artiste and team. The source said: 'It was a really tasteful, fitted one-piece which was seen by everyone, and it couldn't have been more appropriate or classy.'

At one point, illusionist Chris Angel was also retained to introduce a 'magic segment' into the routine but it was agreed to be too risky for live television. Tricks and illusions would have to wait for another day, and another show.

Ten days before the VMAs, representatives from MTV, Jive and The Firm all gathered for a rehearsal in the dance studio. What they witnessed excited everyone. The source close to the record label said: 'Everyone was psyched; Brit was effectively going through the motions and not at full speed, but she was ready. Was it great? No. Was she back to her best? No. But that girl had turned things around and was TV-ready.'

There had been continued meetings 'at least twice a week' to ensure Britney stayed on track and mission impossible was close to succeeding. Even Kevin's legal salvo seeking 70:30 custody rights didn't seem to sway her. Once Britney pulled it out of the hat and showed everyone what she'd demonstrated to her team, there'd be no doubting her. As the countdown began, the operation shifted from LA to the Video Music Awards venue at the Palms Casino Hotel in Las Vegas, and no one – especially Britney – could have appeared more confident.

⬥⬥⬥

Britney arrived in typical pop-star fashion via private jet, three days ahead of the show. Gulfstream jets, hired through a company called Netjets, were often her preferred mode of transport around America.

Once in Vegas, she was destined for her luxury suite at her hotel and VMAs venue, the Palms, under the protective wing of four bodyguards – and Alli Sims. The stay-away assistant had returned to the professional fold. The reason for this, the camp was told, was that, 'Britney wouldn't get on the flight', without her assistant. Where this impression came from, and what lay behind such a volte-face, is not clear but the annoyance was palpable. As one source who worked with the record label put it: 'The same girl who'd told us Britney wouldn't make it to Vegas now turned up as some sort of indispensable figure when the truth was that everything had run like clockwork without her. Alli stuck to Brit like glue. The moment we pitched up in Vegas, something in Britney completely changed and the whole thing came apart.'

No-one is suggesting that Alli Sims was that catalyst. Indeed, it seems that anyone's company outside of a professional focus is a distraction Britney cannot resist, led by her need to chase 'normal'. But it would be fair to say that Alli's presence would not assist the professional focus that was required. The reunion of 'Thelma and Louise' was not part of the careful strategy.

The Firm's Michelle Dupont found herself suddenly sidelined and, without that guiding influence, the wheels started to come loose on a carefully orchestrated machine.

On the Friday evening before the Sunday broadcast, Britney, wearing a white crop-top and jeans, rehearsed a run-through of 'Gimme More' primarily for 'camera blocking' so that the telecast's director knew her positions on stage. This process is never a full-speed rehearsal but everything still seemed fine as Britney went through the motions.

'The odd person was a little alarmed,' said the source, 'because she didn't seem to be trying but, I'll tell you, had she delivered that rehearsal on the night, it would have been a hit. It wasn't as great as back in LA but it was *acceptable*.'

On the eve of the show, the expected plan was that Britney would leave a pre-VMA party at the Hard Rock Hotel and retire to her suite in preparation for the big day. Instead, she hit the Vegas club-scene with Alli, attending the nearby

Beatles Bar before proceeding to Jet nightclub at The Mirage. Britney, wearing a beige silk dress and Fedora hat, found herself in a VIP area with P. Diddy and record producer Dallas Austin, the same man who'd let go of the song '… Baby One More Time' for her to record in 1998.

After 3am, the group then proceeded to a party in a hotel suite until beyond 4am and, 'it was obvious that Britney had been drinking like a fish that night.' It is known that at around 2am, Diddy suggested to Britney that perhaps she should call it a night. The record label source said: 'I know Diddy was saying, "You should go back, man," but they wouldn't. Britney wanted to stick with Dallas. What could these guys do?'

The next morning, as Britney slept through till noon, the phones were melting with calls between MTV producers, Jive Records and The Firm management about the previous night's antics, but the calmed consensus was that, 'Brit had done the routine so many times she could do it with her eyes closed … She'll be fine.'

But Britney's mood, whether hangover induced or not, was plainly tetchy and she'd told her bodyguards she 'wanted no one near me.' When she withdrew to her dressing room, Alli did her job and obeyed instructions not to let anyone in, not even her record label representatives or Michelle Dupont. The rep who'd steered Britney through an intense five-week preparation was suddenly barred by an assistant who had decided to stay away until the big occasion beckoned.

In the dressing room, Britney's anxieties were raging and she decided it would be a good idea to start drinking shots to calm her nerves. Whatever speculation there may have been about what Britney was taking before her performance, the mystery can now end – it was tequila shots, one after the other.

Her prickliness wasn't helped when Justin Timberlake popped by with a 'good luck' message. 'He was cool and couldn't have been friendlier but that definitely wigged her out more,' said the source.

The camp's spirits slightly rose when the positive influence of Britney's brother, Bryan, showed up but, as one of the team said, 'the writing was already on the wall because she was already f***** and freaking out over the littlest thing'

A low self-esteem hitherto hidden behind convincing facades was now making itself known as anger and a difficult attitude; the sagas of the previous months all stirred by the intense pressure to deliver. In Britney's mind, the negative thinking could only process one thought train: failure in marriage, failure – she was told – as a mother, failure as a daughter, and a failure as depicted in *OK! Magazine*. Suddenly, the prospect of performing offered no escape from her anxieties. Instead, all she could focus on was being a failure in an eagerly hyped comeback. In truth, she was terrified, and the good luck gesture from Justin was the final reminder that this was a huge broadcast to millions of people. Her sense of foreboding contained the prospect of personal failure.

It is important to know this mind-set in order to understand the self-sabotage about to unfold. Unworthy in her own mind, she would render herself unworthy in public. As the source who is assisting with this backstage picture wishes to make clear: 'Brit is someone wanting to be loved, not used, not treated like a robot, not there for everyone else to make money, and not working all the time. She's never known what it's like to make her own choices so she doesn't know what a smart choice means. It was inevitable that she was going to reach the "F*** It, F*** You!" stage. The great sadness is that she reached it in the run-up to this big moment. But people need to understand that this wasn't one moment: it was the culmination of many events that went before it.' Panicking and in fear, Britney started to act out – guided by her twitching impulses.

It was, by now, 90 minutes before the show began, and hair stylist Ken Paves, himself immaculate and groomed, entered the dressing room with an assistant, carrying the golden hair extensions in his little box. After his warm welcome in LA, he wasn't expecting the frost that greeted him.

'I don't like him! I want his assistant,' announced Britney. In the awkward moments that followed, his assistant quite rightly pledged her loyalty to Ken. As he diplomatically tried to smooth ruffled feathers, Britney instructed her bodyguard to eject him from her room. The bodyguard, merely doing his job, forcibly removed the Hollywood stylist. In the corridor outside, observers saw Ken being shoved out the door, remonstrating loudly that 'I've never been so insulted in my life!'

He was still carrying the hair extensions, carefully tissuewrapped in his kit.

Had MTV cameras managed to capture this opening act in the ensuing comedy of errors, it would have surely captured its best-ever behind-the-scenes special. Management and record label representatives were meanwhile on the floor in the auditorium, reassuring one another – and MTV producers – that everything was back on track after the night before.

Then word came through: 'Britney's just fired Ken Paves.'

As the situation was elevated to a code-red, management and record label finally gained access to the dressing room to speak with Britney. She explained that she didn't like Ken's attitude.

'That's great, Brit, but you need him right now. He has your hair extensions,' she was told.

Britney pondered this reality: 'Okay then, he can come back,' she said.

By now an understandably indignant hair stylist was many floors above, after retreating to his hotel room. Ken Paves wasn't answering his phone or his door. Colleagues say he was 'beside himself'. Now, with one headstrong artiste to control, and one upset stylist to calm, the team had a difficult impasse to resolve.

With Ken in lock-down, and expressing his candid thoughts about Britney, a truce wasn't imminent.

In her dressing room, Britney seemed oblivious to the distress she had caused. In the corridor, MTV runners and producers grew agitated with the clock running down.

'Where are her f****** hair extensions?!' asked someone.

'With Ken Paves,' explained the label.

'And where's *he*?'

'In his room … but we're working on it.'

It dawned on MTV that their opening act was playing up – and she had no hair. Suddenly, Nelly Furtado's stylist came to the rescue, offering her assistance – but Britney still needed hair extensions. It was then decided that the only option was to get the keys for the hotel hair salon, open it up and use some of its hair extensions.

The source said: 'It was amazing the curve-balls that were being thrown that night, and even more amazing that we were begging for Britney's hair from the hotel salon, but by now everyone was frying – apart from Britney.'

In her dressing room, Britney was observed knocking back another shot.

Once Nelly Furtado's stylist had saved the day and 'done her best', everyone was asked to leave the dressing room so that Britney could slip into her striking Trish Somerville one-piece.

'I've got it,' Alli reassured everyone, 'but she cannot talk to anyone right now.'

If anyone was accustomed to these temperamental moments, it was Alli, and so everyone decided to back off. The dressing-room door shut, and the lock clicked. Britney was locked away with her assistant and another friend.

With half an hour to go before MTV went live, its producers still found Britney locked inside with her pensive team on the outside. This wasn't the most reassuring sight. The source said: 'Now the producers started freaking out, saying, "Will she come out? Why can't you get her to come out?!"'

Every time anyone knocked, the door remained locked.

'Ten minutes, everyone! We've got ten minutes,' someone shouted.

Seven minutes before going 'live', and to everyone's relief, they heard the dressing-room door unlock. As it pulled open, Britney came into view – but she wasn't wearing the designated Trish Somerville, flattering one-piece.

'What the f***?!' someone else shouted.

Britney, wearing her hotel salon hair extensions, stood there in a black bra, black hot pants and fishnets, showing an unflattering paunch. When her team looked in her eyes, 'it was obvious she was somewhere else but present.'

That perhaps explained why she didn't see the collective look of horror that greeted her from the faces around her. Alli spoke for her instead, announcing Britney, 'had wanted to go for it.' Years of training had misled her that 'sexy sells', and so her low-esteem made a disastrous choice, and the assistant backed her. But the management wasn't having it. Britney's reps insisted she change back into the Trish Somerville outfit.

'It's too late … It's too f***** late! We've got to get her on stage!' shouted an MTV assistant, liaising through an earpiece with the control room, and Britney was led away.

The one prayer that everyone clung to in the madness was that cometh the hour, cometh the Britney of old; that in public, this consummate professional would rise to the occasion and get through the opening sequence. As the broadcast went live, and a crowd of A-list musical stars that included Justin Timberlake and P. Diddy took their seats at white-clothed tables, Britney and her dancers got into position on stage. Her team took their seats in the auditorium, while some waited in the wings.

The source said: 'Everyone knew it all hinged on her hitting the first line we'd rehearsed to a tee: look down the camera on a close-up and lip-synch, "It's Britney, bitch!" – the whole thing about that was to declare "I'm back!". If she could hold that line, and get through, she'd won. But the music started, she stood there and stared at the camera without moving her lips. She missed it completely. At that moment, before she'd moved a muscle, we knew it was over.'

What followed was an infamous performance in which Britney looked more like a wasted clubber in Vegas than a princess 'in the zone'. All her facades imploded as she lethargically walked and wobbled through the next few minutes. In one evening, she had sabotaged her perfect hair, her designed outfit, her choreography and her reputation. If it wasn't deliberate, it was subconsciously driven, but it was sabotage all the same. Britney got the attention she craves, but this time as a laughing stock and an object of pity.

Britney had always gone to performance to feel connected and to feel whole, but here she was disconnected and hardly functioning. She had no real self to start with and now her false self was shattering. It was the moment that pulled back the curtain on even her coping mechanism.

So many traumatic things had happened to her and she had been widely and harshly judged. There was nothing inside of her that was strong enough to withstand it all, and she painfully discovered that anxiety reaches a point that not even performance can hide. If it was possible to get Britney quiet, calm and strong enough to open up, I think she'd probably admit to feeling tortured inside.

Backstage, she knew. There were reports that she asked to see an immediate playback on a television monitor, but all that can be confirmed is that within minutes of leaving the stage, she was in floods of tears as the rest of the show continued.

Outside the auditorium doors, the casino floor – emptied especially for the event – resembled an end-of-party scene, with only cleaners, security and hotel staff in sight. It was then that a fire-exit door from a back-stage corridor burst open. Britney, wearing a hooded sweater over her stage outfit, tore through, shoulders up, head down. One security guard strode alongside, while assistant Alli trotted to keep up behind.

Britney spotted an open-air, but closed, restaurant called Guardino's and dived under its roped-off barriers to escape somewhere, anywhere. She walked upstairs to the second floor and sat on the floor, her back slumped against a stonewall. Speechless, Alli sat across from her as the bodyguard stood. From a distance, Britney was seen using a cell-phone, either furiously texting or repeatedly dialling. An off-duty waiter, seeing her distress, brought her a glass of water and there she sat for nigh on forty-five minutes, crying continuously. She left Las Vegas that night.

Outside the dressing room, representatives from Jive attempted to lift the gloom by looking on the bright side, saying, 'It wasn't a 10, but at least she performed' – but that

was more wishful thinking, somehow hoping that if positive things were said, it would affect the media outcome.
The backstage joke was that Jive was in shock.

'There was so much love and support in that whole place
for Britney,' said the source, 'and the thing that offended
people was that she threw it back in everyone's faces. The
dancers who'd been with her for five weeks, pulling her
through, were gutted – but we also knew Britney was devastated.'

In the aftermath, rapper Kanye West said: 'I felt so bad
for her. I said, "Man, it's a dirty game." This game will chew
you up and spit you out.'

Billie Joe Armstrong, vocalist and guitarist with rock
band Green Day, compared it to 'watching a public execu-
tion.' The instant media reaction was unforgiving, panning
the performance and ridiculing Britney's weight: 'LARD
AND CLEAR' said the *New York Post*. Britney's reps didn't
escape unscathed, either. MTV, Jive Records and The Firm
all stood charged with recklessness, rushing Britney back
from rehab and cobbling together an ill-prepared comeback. Dan Abrams, a television host on MSNBC, asked
aloud: 'How do the people around her allow this to
happen? Why did someone not say, "Hey, you're not ready
to perform"? What do you pay these people to do?'

But she had proved to everyone that she *was* ready. She
was, according to the source, 'hitting it out of the park two
week before' and MTV was as mortified as everyone else:
'MTV is a cool operation full of pros and everyone had gone
out of their way to handle Brit with kid-gloves to create a
rebirth. But she decided to press "self-destruct".'

The travesty was not just that Britney had undone
herself; she'd undone the due diligence and carefully
managed five-week strategy of the entire team around her.
The most temperate, and understanding, reaction came on

that same MSNBC show when celebrity addiction specialist Dr Drew Pinsky said his heart went out to her. He asked viewers to shift their perspective from observing a pop star to seeing a woman; everyone should try to imagine that they were not talking about Britney Spears, but a Britney Smith.

He said: 'Britney Smith is a divorcee ... has two young children ... has a stressful career ... was recently admitted for chemical dependency. There's been speculation about post-partum depression and there's been bizarre behaviours. You add all that up for Britney Smith and you have someone who is in serious, serious trouble, psychiatrically.'

Eight days later, on 17 September, The Firm management severed ties with Britney in a statement that said: 'current circumstances have prevented us from properly doing our job. We wish Britney the best.' That same day, attorney Laura Wasser also stepped down with fond wishes, adding: 'I don't want anyone to perceive that we're dumping Britney. In many lawyer-client relationships, there's a time for fresh blood.'

There was now a void where Britney's management and advisors once stood. But one man had already earmarked that role for himself; the man from the Starbucks meeting: Sam Lutfi. He would tell friends that he was in Las Vegas the very weekend of the VMAs, blending in anonymously. Why he was there, and at whose invitation, is not clear. Time would later reveal assistant Alli to be a strong supporter, and they would meet at a place called Toast on Third Street in West Hollywood. So had he approached her in the same way that he'd approached Kalie Machado?

No one knows – or no one is saying – which door he came through. But within this mystery, one fact is clear: Sam Lutfi was already firmly embedded within Britney's inner circle by the end of August.

It was said, and it has been maintained since, that his motives were pure and honest; that this complete stranger had been hired, 'to place positive stories in the media about Britney' and 'help turn things around.' That he gained trust and access so quickly and so readily tells its own story about how weak Britney was, and how frighteningly naive was the set-up that now laid her bare to all outside influences.

Back in LA, Britney had her hands full dealing with the double-resignation of management and attorney on 17 September. But there would be more bad news that day, too: for the divorce – and the custody negotiations – that had already moved through the gears from amicable to messy was about to shift to the calamitous level with a testimony from her recent past.

Typically, the bodyguard profession is built on the rules of the Three Wise Monkeys: hear no evil, see no evil, speak no evil. It expects a professionalism blind to indiscretion but alert to danger in a duty and code regarded as sacrosanct in Hollywood.

It had been four months since Tony Barretto was fired for allegedly failing to hear an instruction to pick up a hat from the floor, but he felt compromised by indiscretions that spelled danger. For him, maintaining a silence could have had potentially more grave implications than breaching an unwritten code – it would have placed at risk the welfare of not only Sean Preston, then two, and Jayden James, one, but Britney herself. At least that was his justification after filing a legal deposition that was dropped into the divorce-child custody arena of Britney and Kevin, rolling in like an unpinned grenade.

This hulk of a man turned up at Los Angeles Superior Court as, 'a key and secret witness' in the 17 September hearing of the Spears v Federline custody case. By his side stood a face well known on American television screens: celebrity attorney Gloria Allred. On the courthouse steps, she announced that her client had observed Britney's 'behaviour inside of her home, outside of her home and around her children.'

The attorney explained that he was 'reluctant to come forward and become embroiled in the custody dispute' but he was a father, too. Mr Barretto then conducted interviews with the *News of the World*, CNN's *Larry King Show*, the *Today Show*'s Matt Lauer, Fox News' *On The Record* with Greta Van Susteren and *Hollywood 411*, aired on the TV Guide Network.

Barretto had been with Britney for two months and it's not clear what concerns he'd made known, if any, behind the scenes before his dismissal on 17 May. All that is known is that he signed and swore a declaration that contained damning allegations. Regardless of their veracity, it would become a highly significant move because what he alleged alarmed both Kevin Federline and the courts. This one event would prove to Britney that her declaration of power and control was hollow in a situation that was now taking on its own hurtling momentum.

Barretto's eyewitness account alleged Britney had been 'suicidal' and she'd acted 'so strange [and] unpredictable that we don't ever know what is going to happen.' He cited 'mental problems' and 'drug and alcohol issues' as his chief concerns. 'Her home is no place for her kids to be raised,' he added.

His most alarming allegation centred on a date she'd shared with a singer-songwriter he named and whom she'd met in rehab. The date was at the Mondrian Hotel, a favourite haunt of Britney's. In an account later repeated in an interview with the *News of the World*, Barretto said her security team responded to a call from Britney and 'we knew we had to get to her fast'.

The sight, he says, that confronted them was Britney 'completely out of it', looking like she'd overdosed: 'Her skin was all waxy. We thought she was going to die. The hotel room was littered with empty beer bottles, liquor bottles and cigarette butts. I spotted a glass pipe, which is often used with crystal meth.'

The damage was done, and the true gravity of this situation rose above mere matters of perception. Barretto had pitched his ex-client into a legal crossfire that questioned her standing as a fit mother. The added poignancy was that everyone knew what this would mean because his declaration, coupled with Kevin's monitoring of events, compelled the LA Superior Court to take action for the sake of the boys.

The judge, court commissioner Scott Gordon, ordered Britney to undergo random drug testing, counselling and parental classes as a holding order while he evaluated what to do in terms of resolving the custody issues. But it was page seven of his order that proved most damning, saying that, 'based on the evidence presented, the court finds there is habitual, frequent and continuous use of controlled substances and alcohol by the petitioner [Britney].'

Even though it was September, and Barretto's allegations dated back to early May, the law in California takes past conduct as a likely indicator of future conduct.

Strangely, Britney's attorneys chose not to cross-examine Barretto in court, leaving his allegations – and verbal testimony – unchallenged. The task was later taken up by Fox News television interviewer Greta Van Susteren, renowned for being a sharp ex-criminal defence lawyer prior to a television career that began with CNN.

When Barretto appeared on her show, she asked him whether he'd ever actually seen Britney with drugs. The bodyguard replied: 'I've seen her with alcohol … never with drugs.' Van Susteren pressed him on the alcohol, asking whether it was used in an excessive way and/or in front of the children. The bodyguard replied: 'Well, she … you know, this wasn't a behaviour that she did regularly. I have seen her on occasion.'

As this incisive interviewer pointed out, if Mr Barretto's evidence was the central plank to the judge's ruling, then significant doubt was cast over the allegations that threatened to remove Sean Preston and Jayden James from Britney's side.

On a later show, attorney Gloria Allred clarified the situation, saying her client had seen Britney 'use drugs twice, not in the presence of the children' and she had also, 'seen her use alcohol and … seen her in the presence of the children appear to be under the influence'.

But based on all that testimony, none of this fitted with 'habitual, frequent and continuous use of controlled substances and alcohol', and Britney could have been forgiven for feeling wronged. As Greta Van Susteren said: 'I'm deeply disturbed. I hope the judge had other information.'

Had that one episode of Fox's *On The Record* received the same global attention that Barretto's dramatic court appearance attracted, surely there would have been an outcry. A well-placed source close to Britney commented: 'Everyone was convinced that Brit was addicted to drugs, and that drove her mad. Her dad's addiction problems were automatically assumed to have turned her into an addict, so she was addict-diagnosed by association, and that's what her parents were convinced about. That this was in her genes. Brit indulged in drugs, yes, but socially – like half of LA. But her problems were mental and ran much deeper. So that court ruling was a travesty.'

But Britney hadn't helped herself and so the 'habitual' and 'continuous' drug use label was a stain few could remove. As a result, the judge set out a checklist that he ordered Britney to honour. If she failed to adhere to his requirements, the repercussions could prove decisive.

She was to undergo twice-weekly random drug tests that would be sealed; she must undergo therapy once a week and also meet with a parenting coach for a total of eight hours a week. In effect, the judge wanted to see evidence that Britney was determined to put her life back on track, and be a responsible and capable parent.

As the judge gave himself time to consider his options, he also ordered that both Britney and Kevin enroll in a free Parenting Without Conflict programme to educate them in how best to communicate and co-operate without causing a friction that could affect their sons.

Wherever people looked for hard, concrete evidence of addictive drug abuse, this was never found; not from assistants and friends, and not, it has to be said, in one fired bodyguard's testimony, where usage did not amount to addiction. But Britney was still effectively cast as someone with a notorious substance abuse problem. Nevertheless, she still had a 50:50 custody share with her ex-husband and things couldn't get much worse, or so it seemed.

But this saga had not completed its downward spiral, mainly because instead of hiding away, Britney's inexplicable actions would co-produce a Hollywood soap opera, where television crews, paparazzi lenses and video-journalists swarmed around her to ensure that not a development, twist or odd behaviour was missed. All talk of 'Chaotic' or 'Ed-TV' could be forgotten.

This would be 'Britney-TV' at its most raw and unedited, and it would play out 24/7 to its saddest climax.

13

Through
the Lens

'You want a piece of me?'
– Britney, radio interview with Ryan Seacrest, 2008

It is an ironic truism in the life of Britney Spears that the camera never lies, yet she will tell you that on countless occasions it misrepresented and exaggerated her truth. One moment, the lens of the video director or magazine photographer was both showcasing the brand, but she said, distorting the actual person. In another, the lens of the paparazzi or television crew provided the glare of publicity she basked in, but then magnified her every move, flaw, foible and error – and recorded it for posterity.

In the pros-and-cons, love-hate relationship with the technology that could make or break her, Britney never quite knew how to handle the image game. And by 2007, LA had become central to the fiercest paparazzi fest that makes the one-time, much-feared tabloid operation of Britain look tame in comparison.

It is nowadays a King Kong-sized beast and she is the Ann Darrow, both in fear and awe of the attention it provides, and singles her out to receive. It seems the perfect metaphor to describe the way Britney has handled the paparazzi in recent years – running from its power then seeking to be in its clutch and held high.

That chase and invited capture is charted in a building outside Santa Monica in a photo archive held within the offices of Splash News, the biggest paparazzi agency, with more than 100 lenses trained on celebrities, wherever they may roam.

Whatever Hollywood says about this profession, it is fascinated and appalled in equal measure. At the 2008 grand opening of LA's swankiest hotel, the SLS, Splash was granted an entire wall to showcase its work, and there wasn't a single celebrity that night who didn't gawp at its furtive collection of A-list photos. One by one, they all stopped and scanned the gallery as if it were the latest edition of a tabloid magazine. Celebrities watching celebrities is the secret voyeurism of Hollywood.

From the vantage point of Gary Morgan, CEO at Splash since 1989, pop stars like Britney are the Premiership footballers of America: young talent asked to handle enormous adulation and wealth, and held up as role models by a media that sniffs an inherent weakness: 'Agents and managers make the mistake of thinking instruction, direction and having a PR represents guidance. Britney's story represents a pretty standard collapse in these terms and no one knows how to handle it.'

The paparazzi business is as commercially ruthless as Hollywood itself, and Splash News has witnessed celebrity-tragedies like Britney come and go, so Gary might be forgiven his jaundiced outlook: 'This town is an edifice designed to build people up as fast as possible, and make as much money as possible before spitting you out and moving onto the next big thing. Because for every Britney, there'll be Miley Cyrus, Zac Efron or Taylor Swift … until that squeaky-clean generation performs beyond its sell-by-date. What never ceases to amaze me, in the face of decades of evidence, is how much people actually believe in their own fame – and Britney's no exception.'

It is for this reason that Gary – and the other paparazzi operatives – are unapologetic for the news exploitation of a girl who was happily exploited by the music industry. Splash is too big a global operation to solely depend on one woman, but within the battery of photographers and cameramen who follow Britney, many careers and incomes literally depend on her existence.

As Gary explains: 'When she steps outside, there are dollar signs in the sky because every small thing she does represents news with a global reach.'

Robin Navarre, co-owner of photo-agency X17, once told the *LA Times* that, 'X17 can make as much as tens of thousands from one magazine on an exclusive story.' In all the expectations that have been heaped on Britney since the moment she was born, perhaps the heaviest is this substantial slice of a media economy, which in 2007, was said by one estimate to represent 25 per cent.

But her industry import goes beyond just the media sector, it seems. Britney Corporation Inc, with all its branches and tentacles taken into consideration, pumps an estimated $120 million a year into the US economy even when she's derailing, according to *Portfolio* magazine.

An article on 'the Britney industrial complex' – all associated economic activity around her – stated she represents the equivalent of a company employing tens of thousands of people. 'She's a goldmine,' said writer Duff McDonald, a former investment banker with Goldman Sachs. Aside from sponsorships, record sales, concert revenue, merchandise, promotions and $400,000 appearance fees, Britney made the media $75 million a year as an institution consisting of television, magazines, newspapers, websites and photo agencies.

'Whether she's shaving her head or battling for custody of her children, Britney seems to grow more fascinating and, to some people, more lucrative every time she stumbles,' continued Duff McDonald.

Britney herself clearly recognised this reality with the November 2007 US release of 'Piece of Me', the tabloid-bashing hit in which she sings: 'I'm still an exceptional earner … you want a piece of me?'

The precise accuracy of the financial figures surrounding her cannot be measured without a true audit but the minutiae almost seems irrelevant because the over-riding theme provides sufficient indication of the dependency resting on Britney's shoulders. On top of all that, she also happened to be the first major experiment for a new media that became hungrier second by second, feeding constant updates to websites and phones in rolling 24/7 coverage. To wit: Britney enters hair salon. Britney starts shaving head. Britney is bald. Britney leaves hair salon. Britney enters tattoo parlour. Britney has tattoo. Britney drives off in car … and so on and so forth. Her every move was being chronicled throughout a media surveillance that was an everyday occurrence.

'She really was the first major celebrity who provided instant gratification for that unquenchable demand,' said Gary Morgan, 'and no one could control that image anymore, not her label, not her manager, no one.'

But this suffocation would become Britney's comfort blanket. In her loneliness, she started to view the media circus as an arena for a daily performance where she was the star, and the paparazzi was both supporting cast and audience. The young woman who had alienated herself from her own parents and grown distrustful of many others started to regard the paparazzi as an extended family, made up of faces she recognised. As will become clear in examining this life through a lens, she would play, tease and co-operate on a daily basis.

From the very onset of fame in 1999, and after becoming freaked out by her paparazzi treatment in London on her first tour, she had often attempted to 'handle' the paps.

'She would come down to the bottom of the road with a friend,' said Gary, 'and buy the guys coffees. Then she'd strike a deal, saying, "This is what I'm doing today" and ask to be left alone at a certain point. It was her early attempt to cope with it all, I think. But those early negotiations sucked her into believing that this was something she could control.'

She was 'negotiating' without understanding the precedent. Or as Gary Morgan puts it: 'Yet another example of Hollywood never learning its lesson.'

By mid-2007, she'd become expert at courting the paparazzi, granting the public a round-the-clock peephole into a human drama within the arena of show business. And a majority of that audience willed the fallen heroine to get back on her feet, while at the same time fearing a tragic end. As an *Observer Magazine* article asked in its main headline: 'Can Anyone Save the Little Girl Lost?' Part of that answer lay in another key question that held such public fascination: Will Britney end up losing custody of her boys?

On the balmy evening of 30 September 2007, Britney could-n't have appeared more relaxed as she dined with her sons and a nanny at a Greek restaurant called Taverna Tony in Malibu. She probably hadn't given a second thought to being charged with two minor driving offences nine days earlier – two incidents caught by paparazzi camera. In the first, she hit and damaged another car's back bumper while pulling into a car parking space and was filmed walking away. In California, this is classed as a 'hit-and-run' misdemeanour. In the second, she was caught with an out-of-date driver's licence, meaning she was a mother driving illegally with her two sons strapped in the back seat. Court commissioner Scott Gordon, the man presiding over her custody case, cannot have been impressed by this latest blaze of publicity. Further compounding matters, he discovered that Britney hadn't been in 'substantial compliance' with his previous orders to undergo therapy and to honour random drug tests.

The next day, 1 October, he issued a written order instructing Britney to hand over her sons to her ex-husband after a private court session was requested by Kevin's legal team. Without warning, her reluctance to fully engage with the judicial conditions, together with her personal instabil-ity and run-ins with the law, brought its costly punishment. She lost physical custody in the 50:50 joint arrangement, meaning Kevin had primary custody and she was left with visitation rights. If she wasn't going to take charge in her personal life, then the judge would. It was as if Britney was too wrapped up within her own crisis to see the mess she'd caused herself. If this wasn't quite a dereliction of her moth-erly duties, it was a dereliction of common sense.

Nevertheless, a second hearing was scheduled two days later, back at LA Superior Court, and here was an opportu-nity for her to redeem herself and put on the performance of her life; to make a passionate case for parental terms to revert back in her favour. Technically, she wasn't required to attend because the judge's mind was already set. But, as any savvy advisor would know, showing up as the mother who was about to have her children torn from her side would have been the smart PR choice in a highly public custody battle. More significantly, Britney's appearance in court, coupled with some remorse and one major apology, might have demonstrated to Scott Gordon a maternal intent to be taken into account for future hearings.

On the afternoon of 3 October, a shaven-headed Kevin Federline showed up with his attorney for what would become a closed hearing. The cameras waited for Britney's grand arrival, wondering if she'd slipped in a back entrance. But she was a no-show. The hearing, lasting almost three hours, went ahead without her. It was viewed by the media at least as a reckless display of parental ambivalence. With no experienced manager or PR by her side, Britney's choices were once again self-defeating. Sam Lutfi was the one who ultimately persuaded her to obtain a valid driver's licence but it was too little, too late. It's been speculated that Kevin wasn't awarded primary custody because of his shining skills as a father but because of Britney's own careless mistakes.

As this court drama unfolded, and studio commentators asked, 'Where's Britney?', the answer cropped up in Malibu: she was being photographed at Starbucks and then a gas station, smiling to the paparazzi before returning home; putting on the performance. The courts still had to consider Kevin's 70:30 custody application but it seemed events were determining the outcome for him. Los Angeles Superior Court spokesman Allan Parachini told reporters that Britney should get regular visitation but there would be one riding condition by order of the judge: her visitations needed to be supervised. The courts would no longer take any chances.

That week, a nanny met with Kevin to hand over Sean Preston and Jayden James. Between October and Christmas, the custody case would go back and forth between different hearings but nothing changed. Her supervised visitation was restricted to two visits a week: from 12 noon to 7pm on a chosen day, and one overnight from 12 midnight to 10am.

Removed from the general presence of her boys, Britney would now start drowning, slipping further away from any sense of reality – and desperate to hang onto anything, and anyone to save her.

There may come a time when Britney rewinds her life and reviews it in playback; when she will no doubt have a better clarity that will enable her to distinguish fact from fiction, and the sincerity of the individual characters who came – and went – as part of the cast list.

By October 2007 Britney had clearly trusted Sam Lutfi and would willingly submit to his guidance and invite him deeper and deeper into her world. It no longer mattered that people hadn't heard of the man. By holding the hand of Britney Spears and becoming her constant shadow – he became somebody. From the sidelines, Lynne and Jamie Spears understandably felt pushed out and powerless.

Jamie – now 'dry' himself after undergoing rehabilitation in 2004 – could associate with Britney's reckless, devil-may-care attitude. But by standing off, they had let in a stranger whose motivations they could never know, although Lynne had good reason to feel suspicious.

At the end of the summer, and before the 2007 VMAs, she received a phone call from a man who later turned out to be Sam Lutfi, and he was offering her a proposal. He told her that he was a spokesman for a company, 'that wanted to sell high-quality cubic zirconia jewellery on a home shopping network,' she explained in her memoir, adding: 'Talking about jewellery on TV? That sounded like fun.'

At this juncture, she didn't know that Sam had already made inroads into her daughter's life. All the pieces of that jigsaw would only fit into place later. But it does seem incredible that, with all that was going on with Britney, Lynne even contemplated taking the spotlight at such a difficult time. So public was their estrangement that the idea of Lynne even pursuing this option would seem incredulous, had she not admitted it herself in *Through The Storm*. It tends to reinforce the point that here is a mother who, for whatever reason, has the same attraction to the spotlight as her daughter.

Nevertheless, Lynne went with her friend Jackie to meet with Sam Lutfi, who turned up with two attorneys. Sam would prove he was well connected in Hollywood, inviting Lynne, Jackie and Jamie-Lynn to a taping of ABC's *Dancing With The Stars*, and arranging a meeting with a talent agency in Hollywood to assist Jackie's musician son. But in the end, nothing came of those meetings or the TV-jewellery deal.

Lynne later realised that Sam had been 'looking for a back door' into Britney's circle and her suspicions then took root. But, as she points out, there was little she could do because by now Britney had changed all her phone numbers and was determined to keep her mum away. Also, Britney – now well read on all aspects of Princess Diana's life – started changing her mobile phones regularly, thus giving her control over who was in, or out, of her life; a controlling ploy that books on Diana had previously revealed.

Only time will determine Sam's relevance in the scheme of things, but his immediate role seemed to be that of a 'rescuer' – the kind of person who could, perhaps, associate with her troubles, talk the talk and offer salvation to someone at her most vulnerable. Of course, that's the very reason he was allowed in:

> When someone is as vulnerable as Britney was, they can be made to believe anything they are told, and that anyone is good for them. In her desperation, if Sam appeared strong, assertive and gallant, she would believe that he could save her.
>
> When someone's anxiety is so raging – as anyone who has ever suffered a true panic attack will tell you – you'll hang on to a stranger if it makes you feel better. In Britney's anxious loneliness, she just needed somebody, anybody, to be there because, by now, it was about survival. I suspect she was so low and felt so worthless that all anyone had to do was knock on her door and say, 'Let me save you.'
>
> What this strongly demonstrates is how poorly equipped she was at running her own life without having someone responsible running it for her and taking charge. By accepting a stranger into her life like this, Britney was effectively forewarning everyone that her life – its meaning and value to her – meant nothing, and she was at a very dangerous point.

According to people who knew Britney at this time, she kept a scrapbook of friends' photographs, past and present. She also trusted anyone in her social party to carry her black Amex card 'because she didn't like carrying it and knew she had enough money anyway'.

One source even claimed Britney started paying people to be with her by day because she so hated being alone, but didn't wish to be a burden. Alli Sims had already decided to step down as assistant, telling friends that, 'she didn't want to be on the payroll because she felt more like friend than member of staff and didn't want to be paid for that friendship.'

That one decision inevitably allowed Sam to have more control. By September's end, he was effectively installed as assistant, manager, friend and life coach. It appears that not one background check was made and that Britney trusted him on face value or the recommendations of others.

It was left to the media to dig into his background and its findings were of concern because Britney's right-hand man had been the subject of three restraining orders. One, in 2004, was made by a Douglas Snoland, who filed an action on 6 September 2004 after a neighbourhood dispute allegedly led Lutfi to pound on his doors and make late-night phone calls, which were then hung up. In the complaint, Lutfi was accused of saying: 'Your mother [she was 71] is a f****** hag ... You will regret the day you ever met me.'

Lutfi denied making such threats but the judge granted a three-year restraining order. The other granted restraint was to protect ex-business acquaintance Jumana Issa, who, in 2005, accused him of 'harassing me repeatedly with obscene emails, offensive faxes ... and out-of-control telephone hang-ups' which she numbered at between 15 and 30 a day.

But the most recent, and alarming, episode centred on events in March 2007 – the same time he'd been seeking to ingratiate himself with Britney's circle. In this case, a man called Daniel Haines told how they had become housemates after meeting on the website MySpace. But, after a two-year friendship, Sam turned. In his complaint lodged with the courts, Daniel said: 'Sam has expressed his hatred for my mother and my sister. I have received numerous emails where he wishes them dead, (or) to be raped ...' The

Orange County Superior Court, after hearing all evidence, restrained Sam from contacting his former friend for a three-year period.

That same year, Britney happily invited Sam Lutfi into her life, telling associates that he was 'a really great guy with a close family'. He was also warmly welcomed into the social circle that she shared with Alli Sims. One night, for Halloween, Britney dressed up as a tiger being chased by the pretend-paparazzi made up of Alli and three friends, who included *E!* News correspondent Jason Kennedy, someone often used as an on-air expert on the Britney saga. Even with all his experience, he told friends that he couldn't believe the 'pandemonium' he witnessed with the paparazzi that followed his friend-of-a-friend.

Nor could he probably believe his luck when, on a night at an LA hot-spot called The Green Door, he found himself sitting with Britney, Carmen Electra and Heidi Klum. As a source close to that evening's proceedings said: 'Even Carmen and Heidi were taking photos that night. Britney's a big deal wherever she goes.'

In the background, also disbelieving his luck, was Sam Lutfi, who would now be a constant figure by Britney's side, placing a protective arm around her shoulder and guiding her through the media storms that would follow. It was exactly what she had been looking for: an assertive man who was confident enough to take care of her.

If there was one place where Britney was guaranteed respite from her woes, it was the sanctuary of the Millennium Dance Complex, where her journey first began back in 1998. Getting 'in the zone' remained her one fail-safe spiritual connection.

Its director Robert Baker hadn't seen much of Britney throughout her marriage and its subsequent fall-out, but he received a phone call one night at 10pm, in the early autumn of 2007. It was Britney, asking if he would kindly open up the premises. If she couldn't sleep, she would dance. Within the hour, she arrived with Sam Lutfi.

'I didn't realise that this was supposed to be a client-manager relationship,' observed Robert, 'because when they showed up, they acted like they were buddies ... rowing. I would see them argue like an old married couple all the time, even over who would drive the car. Sam tried his best to play the role of manager but when he tried telling Britney what to do, she'd turn round and tell him, "You're not my Daddy!" It was quite amusing to watch.'

But Robert, who is a long-term ally of Britney's, is not a critic and feels that Sam's input at this time of her life did serve some purpose: 'The one thing I'd say is that he did ensure she got to appointments on time. I'll hand it to him – he tried to take on her management but the respect was lost because he was also trying to be her friend.'

Separately, an impartial legal source who observed this working relationship said: 'I know he's been held up as this villain of the piece but, from what I saw, it looked like he wanted to take care of her.'

Britney was desperate to get back in shape and 'feel' her dance again. In her initial weeks, and to facilitate her getting back in the groove, she would arrive without make-up and slip into the back of a regular dance class. Robert Baker said it was funny watching the reaction of everyone else in the room because they were whispering: 'Is that *the real* Britney?', and he added: 'There were no airs and graces from her, and no big deal; and she would be in her own head, in her own space. You couldn't tell a star was in the room.'

She took these classes in 2007, but later, in 2008, she wanted to be a teacher.

Robert was sitting in his upstairs office when he heard the gentle padding of feet rushing up the wooden stairs. Britney entered his office and said: 'I'd like to teach kids. Let me teach, Rob.' The dance studio director didn't need to think twice.

It is this unseen side of Britney that he is keen to promote. 'You know, there's all the craziness, all the bad press, and all the paparazzi stuff but there's another side to Britney that's equal, if not bigger, to all that. Just because it's not seen and put on parade doesn't mean that her qualities – her gentleness and how she wants to give back – do not exist,' he said, speaking in the wooden-floored loft-studio where a pop star became teacher, 'Britney's not all about Britney … she's about other people, too,' he added.

In Britney's mind, there is a rare sincerity to children in which she finds ease and trust because they come to her without an ulterior motive, without wishing to make a deal, and Robert is convinced this is what appealed to her true giving nature. 'It was her heaven – just her, dance and children, and these were the times when I saw her truly light up,' he said.

The private classes didn't even showcase Britney's name. They were simply called: 'The Millennium Junior Programme', and organised for a handpicked group of children, who were all girls (but for the exception of Robert's young son). Twice a week, for several weeks, without fail Britney would arrive to try and pass down what she'd been taught since her own childhood. And Robert will never forget the inaugural class.

'The kids had no idea who this "surprise teacher" was going to be, so we had a warm-up man to get them loosened up and lined up. Then, Britney walked in. When the kids realised what was going down, they were all jumping around! Britney loved it because she saw the happiness she brought those kids.'

No parents were allowed because Britney wanted to create the energy and interaction solely with the children. Wearing a simple black leotard, with her hair pulled back into a ponytail, Miss Spears would lead routines from the front, dancing mainly to Madonna songs.

Robert said: 'She asked what music we had but didn't bring her own stuff. She made it clear that this wasn't about promoting her own stuff but inspiring the kids. In those weeks, she made a huge impact on 12 young lives and she derived a lot of value from it, too.'

At the end of each class, and having ensured her young students had worked up a sweat, Britney would call it a wrap, and provide motivational hugs for each child. As Robert said: 'You couldn't measure the smiles she put on those faces. But they'd all pack up for the night and go home with stories to tell. And Britney would go back outside, where the paparazzi were waiting for her.'

<hr />

Two helicopters hovered in LA's smog, above the 405 Freeway.

On the ground, embedded within streams of traffic, 30 SUVs and Escalades formed a distinct and menacing pack, heading east. To the untrained eye, it always appeared as if something dramatic was going on. Or perhaps a movie was being filmed? But the focus of all this attention was just another day in the life of Britney. This was the paparazzi on her tail.

Within that male-dominated paparazzi entourage was a young English woman whose job, for 18 months, was to track Britney's every move as a freelance reporter whose services were utilised by US magazines. This twenty-something singleton belies the image of the earthy newshound because she, herself, is polished – a slim 5ft 11in tall, strikingly attractive young woman with a fashion sense that is Hollywood chic. Today, her career is taking off in a new direction as a model, which is why she doesn't wish to be named, but she looks back to her Britney-coverage days like someone who has herself recovered from an unhealthy addiction: the professional addiction of following a pop star. When she describes life on Britney's tail, it's a craziness that shows the true extent of the media obsession with Britney, as told from inside the travelling circus.

For those 18 months, her days started at 10am outside Britney's residences, and finished up anywhere between 4–5am, when the star attraction would finally retreat home. This journalistic operator was the only woman who stuck with it, day in, day out, from the start of 2007 to mid-2008: 'I had no social life, no love life and no life outside Britney, because tracking her life consumed mine. Those that followed her were all sucked up into this one energy and every penny I earned for that 18 months was earned because of Britney eating, sleeping and breathing. There was something intoxicating about it, but it was knackering and stressful. I lost two stone in weight, ended up chain-smoking; and lived off fast-food eaten in cars and downed sugar-free Red Bull to stay awake.'

She was part of the convoy that, day and night, hurtled after Britney; each driver liaising by walkie-talkie. And since she'd lost primary custody of her sons, Britney's days were left even more empty. So she filled them by interactions with the paparazzi, driving around for hours on end.

As the female in the pack said: 'She'd do 80mph with 30 of us on her tail. Then, for no reason at all, she'd flip a U-turn and just switch direction to throw us.'

'U-turn! U-turn!!' cackled a collection of walkie-talkie-type gadgets called 'chirps' – instructed by two main chiefs at the head of the pack: paparazzos by the names of Clint Brewer and a British Afghani originally from Birmingham, a man called Adnan Ghalib.

Such was the size of this convoy, that Britney – in her white Mercedes – had SUVs and Escalades spinning around in front and behind her. Then, she'd be allowed out to take the lead again – and the paparazzi chase would be on again. These seemingly aimless pursuits could last up to four hours through all suburbs of LA with what appeared to be nothing more than a pop star running the gauntlet.

The female reporter recalled: 'It didn't matter what else was happening on the road. When she turned, we turned, all 30 of us, all at once. When that happened at 11pm on an unlit coastal road, it's a scary type of mayhem. But she was like the lead dancer and all our vehicles were the backing dancers who followed her every manoeuvre.'

Red lights stopped no one. If she'd gone through on green and then the lights switched, this 'freight train of paparazzi' kept thundering through until every last car remained on her tail. Other cars could lean on their horns as much as they liked: the Britney paparazzi chase ruled the LA roads – dangerously, recklessly and indulgently.

By now, Britney had moved out of the marital home and into a seven-bedroom, beach-front property at the exclusive Malibu Colony, off the Pacific Coast Highway. She had also bought a new mansion in a gated community called The Summit, off Mulholland Drive, overlooking Beverly Park. Her restless nature would flit between the two, taking the paps to and fro, via the winding Malibu Canyon Road.

Sam Lutfi was so embedded into Britney's life, and clearly trusted, that he now became the manager who was

invited to sleep over. He moved into the guest room at Britney's house at Summit, two doors away from the star's
bedroom. This in itself is strange for any 'manager' to do,
but it was no doubt at Britney's behest, to combat her loneliness. Friends say he never slept over at the Malibu Colony
residence but was a regular visitor. Meanwhile, in the three
months from October 2007 to January 2008, Britney
became the creature of habit that the paparazzi could set its
watches by.

By day, she would remain holed-up inside, with either
Alli Sims or Sam Lutfi. On days spent in Malibu, she would
emerge sometime between 1pm and 3pm, heading for a
daily Starbucks, ordering a Mocha Frappucino, large, with
straw.

'Hey y'all! How ya'll doing today?' she'd cheerily ask the
paparazzi.

Then, with a Starbucks visit under her belt, she'd get
back in the car and return home. Sometime between 3pm
and 4pm, she'd head back out and use one of two gas
stations: a '76' on the PCH or the Chevron which was literally 100 yards from the end of the gated community driveway. She'd pull up, use the restroom, buy a pack of
Parliament cigarettes and then drive back home.

As the female reporter observed: 'She'd never send an
assistant. It's like she needed the paparazzi fix as much as
she needed her Mocha Frappucino and pack of Parliaments.
This happened every single day, same time, without fail, for
three months solid.'

Then the night shift would begin. At just before
midnight, Britney hit the LA club-scene, seeing an endless
trail of 60 head lamps in her rearview mirror. Arriving in
Beverly Hills or West Hollywood, she'd attend one club for
45 minutes then take in another till 3am, then it was over to
a friend's house in Studio City till 5am when she finally

retreated home – until the next day sent her into a repeat of the same loop, all over again.

> Everyone needs a routine because it moves us through the days and this was clearly Britney's attempt to bring some certainty to a world that felt all over the place. It may have been odd, dysfunctional behaviour, but this daily pattern brought her a sense of safety and sanity. Many people with anxiety issues install plans and routines into their lives to keep occupied. It is the plan that distracts them from sitting still and dealing with the anxiety and the pain they feel.

Her lost bewilderment was often displayed to the paparazzi on a few occasions when she'd arrive too late to a club and not be allowed entry. The female reporter said: 'This was the time when, after taking a few shots, the guys would put down their cameras because she'd be like, "They won't let me in! They won't let me in!" and she spoke like a child. Her body language changed, she'd look all nervous and stand there, scrunching her hands together, saying, "I don't understand … I don't understand." The photos may have shown pop star Britney, but away from the flashbulbs, we saw an eight-year-old girl stood in the street.'

Her account has been verified by three separate members of the pack: two agency staff and one independent freelancer; each one of them said that the hustle and bustle of the paparazzi scrum was intense, 'but at no time did anyone lose their respect or be rude to Britney, and vice-versa.'

The female reporter said: 'Everyone in that pack cared for this girl and any of us would have reached out to her because we saw what she was going through. She never once lashed out at us. That umbrella attack was a one-off, out-of-character reaction that happened for other reasons.'

In following her on a daily basis, it seems that many in the pack became self-appointed guardians of a prey who'd accepted their presence and purpose. One of them – Adnan Ghalib – had grown particularly fond of Britney and would always be the chivalrous one, filling her car at gas stations, opening doors for her or instructing colleagues to back off. He made no secret of his intentions that he was 'going to get in there with Britney', and the smiles and winks she returned in his direction suggested he had good reason to fancy his chances.

It was around this time that the odd paparazzo from the X17 photo agency was invited into Britney's house with Sam Lutfi. 'Not once did any of them see her drunk or using drugs,' said the female reporter, 'the only oddity they observed was Britney frantically cleaning. They expected a party-girl but found a cleaner with OCD, wanting every surface to be spotless. Apparently, she'd re-arrange the chairs, wash down the tops and polish the kitchen cabinets.'

Another notable observation made was that Britney clearly relied on numerous anxiety drugs to calm her because, Sam told them, 'she sobs uncontrollably about losing her boys and falling out with her mum.'

On countless occasions, Britney needed to escape the confines of both her homes, and this is why she became a regular guest at different five-star hotels around LA. She felt that hotels never closed down and had staff on duty around the clock. This, in itself, was a comfort to her anxieties.

What particularly worried Sam at this stage was that he heard Britney say out loud that, 'life is not worth living without ma boys' and it was then that he decided to act as the peace-broker between mother and daughter. But that would take time and diplomacy. Meanwhile, the strengthening bond between celebrity and paparazzi might have explained why Sam was known to text the chosen few with details of Britney's destination. Indeed, she gave the game away when, one day in October 2007, she headed to a birthday party with Sam, the open-top Mercedes surrounded by lenses.

'Where you going, Britney?' shouted one voice from the crowd.

'You know, you have the address!' and she laughed as Sam drove her away.

Gary Morgan at Splash News could have predicted such behaviour much earlier: 'The moment she picked up with Paris Hilton and Lindsay Lohan, we knew she was derailing. And then she became addicted – addicted to the paparazzi.'

Britney is addicted to the energetic force that plays out between her and her audience, whether that audience is as a child with her mother, a true audience at a concert or the audience of the paparazzi. If she is addicted to anything, it is this.

When she felt alone and abandoned, then she will have felt a certain security in having thirty men outside her home, watching out for her but also watching over her; recognisable faces that, for a lonely woman, create artificial, but familiar company.

Being by herself is extremely difficult for someone like Britney because her anxiety-ridden natural state means that she finds being alone a really horrible experience. At this point in her life, she was wafer-thin brittle and desperate to attach to anyone so she attaches to the constant in her life: the paparazzi. This inevitably leads to observers saying, 'Look how she courts the paparazzi!' but it has more to do with her desperation and need. Morning, noon and night, these became the figures who are guaranteed to be there; so the paparazzi provides both a comfort blanket and a 'fix' for when she needed to become the performance to escape her chaos.

Britney's driving habits, paparazzi pursuits and the odd jumping of a red light to evade her pursuers didn't impress the courts once again. In November, the judge in the custody case decided she wasn't allowed to drive with her children in the car during her supervised visitations – unless someone else was behind the wheel.

In the end, it seems a perverse irony – and shows how desperately lonely she had become – that the paparazzi who had once made her so miserable now became some form of odd support network. Britney had become the archetypal co-dependant: knowing the paparazzi was bad for her, but falling under its spell and direction; dancing to its daily tune in a spotlight that provided both a sense of wellbeing and an identity.

Britney Spears had never forgotten the chivalry of English paparazzo Adnan Ghalib, who'd always assisted her when the media pack became fierce in his five years on her tail. So when she found herself herded and overwhelmed inside Quiznos, an LA sandwich shop, one day in late September 2007, she'd fled to the restroom for some breathing space. Witnesses said the paparazzi crowd 'took over the shop' and 'there must have been 30–35 guys with cameras, videos and flash lights packed around one restroom.' Britney pushed the door ajar and, in a hushed voice, asked: 'Where's Adnan?'

The swarthy man was ever-present, answered the call, barged to the front and slipped into the restroom where, after a few seconds, he re-emerged to lead his damsel in distress by the hand and safely to her Mercedes. And that was how Adnan Ghalib, then 35 and working for an agency called Finalpix, was invited into the world of Britney Spears.

Over the following weeks, the two engaged in blatant flirting from either side of the camera lens until another media storm engulfed her in the middle of the road one week before Christmas.

Britney, flooded with panic, abandoned her car and ran to Adnan's vehicle, demanding to be let in. Before he knew it, he was fleeing the scene with her in his passenger seat, thanking him for 'rescuing' her. It seems being rescued and taken care of were strong magnets for a weakened Britney at this time. But where Sam was a strictly professional association, there was obvious chemistry between the pop star and her favourite paparazzo, and they would now start an intense love affair.

For a girl whose love of England was obvious – with her pet's name, her penchant for mimicking the accent, her admiration of Princess Diana and the heritage through her late grandma – Adnan's appeal was enhanced simply by the way he spoke, even if it was Americanised-Brummie. But what would make this dynamic even more interesting was that there would be no love lost between Sam Lutfi and Adnan Ghalib: two men now engaged in a subtle power-struggle to gain supremacy in Britney's eyes as the wisest advisor and most positive influence.

The paupers were sat at the princess's table, seeking equal attention, and she knew it. The feel-good attention, and reflected importance, would have provided yet another powerful, but short-lived fix for her wellbeing. But such notions were almost irrelevant alongside the lonely truth – that the real reason they were both in her life was because she mistakenly thought they represented her last chance of salvation: Sam in her career, Adnan in matters of the heart. That she looked up to two such figures is probably the most informative insight yet into Britney's own sense of personal value and self-worth. That is not intended as a snobbish commentary on the class or background of these two individuals, it is merely a fact that when the world's most adulated and famous pop star turns to a random stranger and a member of the paparazzi for guidance, there is not much further she can fall.

Valuable insight is also afforded through the lens and through the eyes of Adnan Ghalib. He has never given a detailed print interview about his intimate relationship with Britney but, in one frank conversation, he did confide in one close individual at a time when he was telling friends: 'I'm pinching myself that I'm Britney's boyfriend.'

It was easy to understand his glee. He had been raised in a terraced street in Small Heath, Birmingham, arriving with his family on a batch lottery visa from Afghanistan. The story that he told fellow paparazzi was that he returned to fight for the militia and he was 'a trained soldier' who knew how to handle himself. He swapped the West Midlands for Hollywood, determined to 'conquer America' and worked as a bartender before becoming a self-taught member of the paparazzi. He bought a camera, a motorbike and set to work following celebrities around Los Angeles. For the last five years, his main 'target' had been Britney – and now he was dating her. Up until then, his biggest claim to fame had been his successful gatecrashing of actor Adam Sandler's wedding in Malibu, until his cover was blown and he was arrested for trespassing.

With similar cunning and charm, he now found himself on the inside of Britney's world, at her invitation. It is through an indirect account from a source close to Adnan that the doors can now be opened into the most unlikely relationship in Hollywood.

Once Britney jumped into Adnan's car that day before Christmas, she directed him to the Peninsula Hotel in Beverly Hills, where she'd booked two rooms, a suite for

her, and a second room for use during the day by yet
another new assistant. It was that empty room, with an
office-like ambience, where Adnan was invited.

From 11pm through to 4am, they both sat up and 'talked
and talked and talked'. When he left, walking out into a
stunned group of colleagues, he kept his discretion and
returned home. But within seconds of walking through the
door, he received a text message from Britney, asking him to
return. By now, the intrigued media pack had dispersed,
thinking that all lights were about to go out. So Adnan
walked in unnoticed, second time around, and this time
made his way to Britney's private suite.

'I had never been so nervous in all my life!' he told his
friend.

As he reached the double doors, he realised they were
ajar. When he walked in, he found Britney padding around
in her bare feet, wearing nothing but an over-sized white T-
shirt. It was at this time that Adnan had just had a cast
removed from an injured foot. Britney poked fun at her
reputation for running over photographers' feet and jested
that she hoped she hadn't been responsible.

With that, she undid his laces, removed his socks and
'gave me the best foot massage of my life'. Contrary to speculation or what Adnan may, or may not have boasted about,
they did not consummate their relationship that night. In
the less ego-driven account he gave to his friend, he said
Britney seemed too fragile, and too raw.

Over the next three days, the couple went to great
lengths to hide their affair. Adnan was especially cute at
knowing the tricks of the trade to divert one of his own.
Their subterfuge proved effective because Britney arrived
at his apartment in West Hollywood unnoticed. And it was
there that her glimpses of normalcy from within a basic
man's world proved even more appealing. He made her

turkey sandwiches and they watched *Harry Potter* movies together. Britney was apparently excited that 'this is what normal people must do on first dates!'

According to his friend, she also told Adnan 'that I've never had someone behave so gentlemanly towards me before'. Unlike most of her lovers, she wasn't being rushed into bed. She was, in her eyes, appreciated for who she was, not a sex commodity.

Adnan privately described her as, 'the most naturally sexy, carefree, fun, amazing woman you could ever wish to meet'.

He was adamant, and enraged on her behalf, that she'd been accused of habitual drug use because he 'never once saw her take any drugs and she drank on only three occasions.' His bigger concern, it seemed, was her reliance on prescriptive medication. He believes it was these doctor-prescribed drugs that suppressed, and didn't cure, her anxiety issues. He spoke about anxiety attacks, which were 'debilitating' but the drugs gave her an artificial feeling that everything was okay. It was, he said, this 'false high' that allowed her to keep running away and behaving 'in a manner that didn't look good to the courts.'

But the bigger issue Adnan had to contend with, and something else that didn't look good, was the hitherto unmentioned fact that he was already married to a part-time model called AzLynn Berry, whom he wed in 2005. She would file for divorce when she learned of his betrayal with Britney. Adnan's attitude, told to friends, was a defence that pleaded:

'What married man would say no to Britney Spears?'

Certainly, Adnan found himself incapable of saying no and became besotted, and there's no doubt Britney, in her search for intimate company, made her intentions absolutely clear. But as much as he would boast about his celebrity conquest, he would also impart telling insights about her mind-set at this time.

On Christmas Day night 2007, they again came together at his apartment and Britney was watching television when Adnan's mother called. Apparently struck by the warmth of his interaction, when he placed the receiver down, Britney was in tears.

'I wish I could talk to my mum tonight,' she wept.

She had swung erratically between missing and resenting her parents that winter, but she had never gone a Christmas without talking to her mama, and as 2008 approached, she was perhaps realising the self-created void in her life.

In Adnan's version of events, all Britney wanted was to mend bridges with Lynne, and hold Sean Preston and Jayden James.

'She just wanted her family back,' he stated simply.

14

Rescue Mission

'I look back and I do not see how I got through that.'
– Britney, MTV documentary, 2008

The Britney Spears' story now started its descent into a disorienting web of Kafkaesque proportions, with a ticker-tape shower of legal documents that would include not only custody depositions but also child neglect suits, civil claims, medical orders and, ultimately, restraining orders and conservatorship papers.

Allegations, regardless of concrete evidence, would be held against Britney in an undignified saga where an on-going tussle centred around one theme: rescue. Rescue of the children, the rescue of Britney and the rescue of her brand ...

The probing arm of the LA County Department of Children and Family Services (DCFS) had now entered the fray due to the continued allegations of former bodyguard Tony

Barretto, who added to Britney's woes by lodging an official complaint under the California Child Abuse and Neglect Act. The agency met with him in a two-hour meeting and then announced it was launching a full investigation. One month later, it had requested access to all files in the custody case as court documents revealed the official probe centred 'on multiple child-abuse and neglect' allegations.

In effect, the strength of those claims was a repeat of his evidence, which Fox News' Greta Van Susteren had taken to task. Although Barretto's attorney did say that some details had not been previously revealed in public, stressing that some disclosures to the DCFS needed to be kept confidential. No one seemed bothered to point out that the very word 'confidential' was beginning to lose its meaning and value in this particular case. 'Confidential' started to appear just like any other Hollywood facade that didn't stack up against the painful reality.

Britney's cause wasn't helped when court-appointed parenting coach Lisa Hacker submitted her report to the custodial judge Scott Gordon. Often the services of these coaches are used in US divorce cases as part of the mediation between warring couples. But it seems Britney didn't appreciate the intervention, or being told how to be a mother.

On three separate occasions, she failed to keep a prearranged session, reported Miss Hacker. In a testimony given to the court, she made it clear that Britney, 'loves her children and the children are bonded'. But she then pointed out several areas of concern. She found that the mother's interactions with Sean Preston and Jayden James were 'not child centred' and she 'did not fully engage with them'. It was also observed that the atmosphere in the house, 'ranged from chaotic to almost sombre without any communication at all.' On three occasions, it was noted Britney 'rarely engaged with the children in conversation or at play' and she seemed to pay scant regard to the advice of the parenting coach.

'The problem is that unless Ms Spears realises the consequences of her behaviour and the impact it has on the children, nothing is going to be successful,' Miss Hacker concluded in her report. If only she had been around in the eighties and working in Kentwood. She also made it abundantly clear there was nothing that could be classed as abusive in Britney's treatment of her children.

From the outside, the gravity of the situation seemed to be more of a case for Channel 4's 'Supernanny' Jo Frost than the Child Abuse and Neglect department. But all the agencies had been placed under the same fierce spotlight that follows Britney, and so it was inevitable they had to at least appear as thorough and forensic, lest they were held to public account at a later date. Meanwhile, Britney herself was being held to account. Indeed, her friends said she was being 'publicly flogged'.

As she left her house, the paparazzi would now see her sobbing in the passenger seat as she drove past. She was no doubt in the passenger seat because, in yet another inquiry, the LA Police Department had announced that it was investigating her for allegedly running over an officer's foot as he attempted to navigate her through a routine media storm outside court one day.

Whatever Britney did, and wherever she went, there seemed to be a repercussion. And, of course, within this circus from hell were two truly innocent individuals: two-year-old Sean Preston and one-year-old Jayden James. The effects of all this on them will become known only with time but it wouldn't be a surprise if they grew up with equal sensitivities and anxieties, regardless of the good intentions of everyone concerned, before, during and after these events.

If Britney's childhood represented a disordered chaos, then this was chaos on a whole new level. Often they were spared the glare of publicity and protected as much as they possibly could be, but the erratic nature of this parental structure, the anxieties of their own mother and being torn from the all-important maternal love at such an early age will, without doubt, leave its own long-term legacies.

Meanwhile, Britney's battle was to prove her value as a mother – and prove to the courts that she wasn't using drugs, contrary to popular opinion. Finally, after taking her random drug-testing to the last chance saloon, Britney adhered to the system's spot checks for urine samples. She had to submit to random tests twice a week; she would be alerted by phone call and then had to provide a specimen within six hours.

The results would remain sealed, but a well-placed source close to Britney said: 'Her attitude changed from, "Why the f*** should I?" to "Okay, I'll show 'em". She continued to party, just as she'd always done, and always provided the urine samples – and they were always negative, negative, negative.'

Understandably, this authority-driven scrutiny and onslaught of allegations left Britney feeling besieged and victimised. Her attorneys at the time were from the firm Trope & Trope, and it was decided something needed to be done to safeguard their client's interests.

In this regard, it was Britney's attorneys who drafted in the expertise of a company called Family Care Monitoring Services which, according to its website, sits: 'as a beacon of light in an often dismal situation' – there to protect both child and parent in 'the minefield of hurtful accusations'.

Indeed, it was a bundle of allegations that had earlier led to the judge saying that Britney's visitations must be supervised by a monitor. So this was a court-appointed monitoring, and separate to parental coaching. But Trope & Trope didn't want the courts to select the monitor, which is why it took control of the situation.

As a legal source close to this process said: 'It may have been court-ordered, but it was felt that Britney needed this monitor there to protect her from potential vexatious allegations. It provides the judge with eyes, and grants protection to Britney. She was not just under suspicion of being a bad mother but a neglectful one, and that went beyond the pale in many people's eyes. The monitor was essential to bring a clear and true picture to the whole mess.'

Whether Britney viewed the process that way is doubtful. She struggled to listen at the best of times and had a history of rebelling against any form of instruction. Indeed, for someone whose life had been lived in the spotlight, the sense of intrusion must have felt acute on her precious visits with her sons. For there is no escaping the reality that, at all times, the monitor is this silent witness observing the mother in her own home. There is no escape from the eyes that followed Britney, and it was a system that would be in place from October 2007 to the start of January 2008.

As the source said: 'Can you imagine how hard it is to be yourself and feel relaxed when your motherhood and interactions with your own children are being watched under the hawk eye of a monitor who says, "Pretend I'm not here" but doesn't miss a trick, a gesture or a nuance? It didn't matter that Britney tried her best. She felt that everything she did, and everything she said, was being interpreted and reported back to the principal.'

Of course, the system itself would counter-argue that its presence was there, not in the interests of Britney Spears, but the children. But the company's own website does make clear that, 'it observes and notes all that is seen and heard'.

Unlike a parenting coach, no advice or assistance can be given by a monitor. Had Britney looked to this body for help, none would be given. If she asked for advice, she would simply have been met with silence. But a note would have been made. Within all the realms of human nature, it is an inherent characteristic that we all act differently in the company of strangers, especially if that stranger happens to be monitoring us. The pressure on Britney must have felt intolerable, yet it was inescapable.

As the source said: 'This isn't an assistant, a nanny or a coach. It's just this uncomfortable, forceful presence until Britney got her ducks in a row.'

Britney's reality was that she was now being watched whenever she stepped outside her home (by the paparazzi) and watched whenever she was indoors (by the monitor). Equally, it was a suffocating reality of her own making.

If there was one saving grace in this entire process, it was this: the monitor had the power to end any visitation if there was any hint of Britney being under the influence of drugs or alcohol, or indeed if she even played up and demonstrated anger.

As the source said, and to Britney's credit, not a single visitation would be cut short. The monitor's observational reports on these crucial visitations were never made public, and would only be seen by both sets of attorneys and the judge. But the over-riding aim of this measure was clear and direct towards Britney: regardless of your childhood, fame, troubles and privilege, it was now time to step up and become accountable as proceedings moved into a new year, 2008.

The legal source said: 'It had reached the point when her public display as Britney Spears was immaterial compared to her private display as a mother.'

Lynne Spears was in Kentwood when she received the call that she'd been waiting for in October 2007. Alli Sims relayed to her that Britney was ready to resolve their dispute. After catching a flight to LA, a tearful reunion took place at the house in Malibu, in the presence of Sam, Alli and a new assistant. According to Lynne's memoir, mother and daughter 'just held on to each other for the longest time.'

It is abundantly clear, from both Lynne's book, and subsequent events, that it riled her that the apparent architect of this emotional reunion was Sam Lutfi. There is no love lost in this department, and she wrote that the level of control that she witnessed him exert over her daughter was 'bewildering'. Indeed, to many people, Sam made no secret of the fact that people listened to him: attorneys, security guards and paparazzi.

When one is viewed as the trusted right-hand man to one of the world's most famous pop stars, the vicarious power is obvious. Sam was the one man in a professional sense who had the ear of Britney and helped orchestrate her every movement; even a reunion with her mother. He was the crutch that she leaned on, and that inevitably afforded him influence, but it was an influence that Lynne and Jamie Spears observed through gritted teeth.

Lynne called him 'The General' and few would disagree because everyone needed to first go through this self-appointed, Britney-endorsed protector. Maybe it was this truth that *really* rankled with Lynne after her period of estrangement? The one question that would start to occupy the Spears family was how they could reconnect with their daughter when Sam was so deeply entrenched in her life and sleeping at her house. Suspicions had long festered in their minds, and with Britney demonstrating a reckless and misguided judgement, they worried about the extent of her surrender to Sam's advice. It almost didn't matter whether his intentions were good or bad, the origins of his access into Britney's world were cause for justifiable concern. She had known this man for less than four months and yet he seemed her chief advisor, guru and confidante. All shareholders within Britney Corporation Inc looked aghast at the figure sat beside the CEO; the *Meet Joe Black* moment in Britney's world, without the spirituality.

From a parental point of view, from the sidelines they'd been forced to occupy by Britney, all they could do was witness her rapid decline via the media, and what they witnessed alarmed them. A lifelong friend in Kentwood said: 'They had hoped Britney would come to her senses, but she was *losing* her senses. Jamie and Lynne were worried sick, worried that they were going to lose her either by suicide or a car accident.'

Fears about Britney's state of mind had heightened real concern about the prospect of her one day taking her own life. Indeed, this concern seems to have been first mooted by Alli Sims, who was better informed by her close observations of Britney.

A source close to Alli said: 'I think it's fair to say that when Alli first mentioned "suicide", she was dismissed for being over-dramatic but Alli was witnessing everything first hand, and Jamie and Lynne were not. Britney had reached the point where she feared losing the kids forever and she didn't know how to stop the slide.'

What concerned Alli were comments from Britney about how she'd 'just like to go to sleep and never wake up again' and, one occasion, she threatened to hang herself.

Alli continually urged Jamie that the situation required kid gloves. Whereas the Spears felt that people like Alli were fellow party-girls and, therefore, 'enablers'. Clearly there were differences of opinion as to how a precarious situation should be handled and the truth is that no one knew what to do for the best. Although, from Jamie's previous statement to Page Six, it seems he felt they were acting on informed advice.

The one conversation that disturbed Jamie was when he suggested that Britney needed the threat of losing her children because, as he well knew, hitting rock bottom is the moment when you decide to help yourself. But it was then that Alli screamed her fears.

'I swear to God, Jamie,' she said, 'she will kill herself. You've *got* to listen to me!'

Perhaps it was those alarms that created a shift in Jamie's mind. This was no longer a situation where a rebellious daughter was simply derailing. She was, or so he was told, suicidal.

Jamie knew that the whole set-up around his daughter was a joke that was leading her down a destructive avenue. Now, he had to contend with the fear that she might take her own life. For years, he had sat on the sidelines and felt out of control. This time, if it was down to him, things would be different. As his lifelong friend said: 'What's the guy supposed to do? Sit back and do nothing? Back here, we all knew that he was biding his time, waiting for his moment.'

Whatever his inadequacies as a father in childhood, he was determined to make amends. He was a changed man and a better man for undergoing treatment for alcoholism in 2004. Now, he was determined to be a better father.

The barrier to that intervention was the harsh reality that he was definitely regarded as *persona non grata* by Sam Lutfi, and seemingly Britney herself at this time. Sam, both then and in later court hearings, expressed his belief that Britney was scared of her father. Only Lynne had been granted the 'in' and so she would maintain that crucial foot in the door. Despite the reunion, mother–daughter relations did not immediately thaw. Britney's moods lurched between seeking peace and flashes of anger, and so she often banished Lynne into the wilderness again, such as the time over Christmas 2007.

In Lynne's written account of this time, she depicted Sam as the puppeteer, manipulating the situation for his own ends. But a very different picture is painted by two independent sources – one paparazzo and one legal worker – who witnessed Sam's interactions with Britney when Lynne wasn't present ... and when Lynne attempted to make contact. Unbeknown to Sam, he has two unlikely allies whose separately-given accounts verify each other.

Taking one of them, the legal source said: 'Lutfi was the peacemaker, and cheered on behalf of Lynne so her suspicions of him are without foundation. One text message from Lynne was enough to get Britney yelling, calling her mum all sorts of names. But it was always Sam who calmed her down and made her see reason. Without doubt, he was Lynne's chief diplomat.'

On one occasion, in November 2007, Lynne arrived at the front-gate to see her daughter and grandchildren. She pressed the buzzer and asked to be let in. Britney point-blank refused. It was Sam who privately persuaded her to let her mother in, encouraging her to talk and build bridges. This perhaps explains why Lynne got the impression that Lutfi was 'the gatekeeper', as she described him.

The ultimate and impartial truth no doubt lies in the
secret files of the appointed monitor. That person was duty-
bound to note all such flashpoints when the children were
present.

Far from keeping Lynne at arm's-length, the evidence to
date suggests that Sam was keen to invite her back into the
fold. It is, of course, impossible to know his private motivations and the manner of his arrival on the scene was strange,
to say the least. But those who witnessed this domestic set-
up speak more of a facilitator than a manipulator. And when
the evening of 3 January 2008 came around – with Britney
in another non-speaking spell with Lynne – there was only
one person Sam turned to.

With 2008 just three days old, Sean Preston and Jayden
James had spent a seemingly happy few hours with Britney
on one of her supervised visitations at her house at the
Summit gated community. It was, apparently, an uneventful
afternoon, which saw Sam discussing business on his cell-
phone while Sabi the housekeeper tidied the house. Britney played happily with her boys under the ever-watchful
eye of the monitor.

But she was keeping a tight lid on her emotions after a
tension-filled morning in which she submitted to a legal
demand to visit her ex-husband's attorney offices to answer
questions for a legal deposition as part of the custody case.
Accompanied by Sam, an embittered Britney reluctantly
honoured this appointment at the behest of the judge. She
was indignant at sitting in the company of an attorney from
the opposing side, providing answers that justified her
motherhood skills. After she left the offices, she broke down
in tears. Then, that same afternoon, she learned from the

authorities that a trial date was set for her driving misdemeanour offences.

What effect these circumstances had on Britney's mind
can only be guessed at, but the tensions were vibrating. The
true impartial version of events and the run-up to what
happened next are also contained within a sealed file, as
submitted by the monitor who witnessed everything. But
the following account is what has been verified.

As the scheduled 7pm handover neared, there were
reports of a telephone row with Kevin. Britney was crying
and became frantic and shielded her boys, not wanting them
to leave. Propelled by that day's events, she was convinced
Kevin was not going to let her see the children again. At least,
that's what she kept screaming at the point of handover. A
bodyguard managed to scoop up Sean Preston and place him
in the back of an SUV outside. In the meantime, Britney had
bolted with Jayden James in her arms to a bathroom, locked
the door and refused to come out. Kevin and his attorneys
were informed, and the monitor used the telephone to make
an emergency 911 call in line with this required danger.

Under the terms of the supervised visitation, one of the
children was now deemed to be at risk. By 8.30pm, police
had arrived on the scene.

By 10pm, the scene that surrounded Britney's house
resembled a siege stand-off with an armed intruder: ten
police cruisers, two ambulances, and one fire truck in attendance, red, white and blue lights flashing silently. In the night
sky, six media helicopters beamed their spotlights onto the
mansion. Inside the bathroom, an already distraught Britney
cowered in a corner, hugging a distressed Jayden James.
Breaking news on the television and news websites reported
that she had taken one of her sons 'hostage'.

In Kentwood, Lynne's cellphone rang. It was Sam Lutfi,
in tears.

Feeling helpless, she then rang Jamie and Britney's brother Bryan in LA, only to be told, 'that Sam was blowing things out of proportion'. Both ex-husband and son were firm, saying they must adopt a 'wait-and-see' attitude. Lynne forced herself to watch events unfold on TV.

LAPD officer Jason Lee was reported from the scene saying: 'The officers are still there. They are trying to resolve this peacefully and legally, according to the court order. They've been there since 8 pm, and it is in regards to Britney Spears' custody battle.'

Inside the house, a bewildered Britney was finally persuaded to open the door. Whether this coincided with the arrival of Kevin's attorney Mark Kaplan cannot be known, but his presence certainly seemed to help. Britney was found huddled in the bathroom, her body shaking with near grief. Jayden James, who was unharmed, was handed over to the bodyguard.

At home, Lynne saw what other viewers watched: an ambulance pulling into the driveway, waiting. Half an hour later, Britney was carried out on a stretcher and secured with tie-downs and placed into the back of the ambulance; her wide-eyed and dazed look became the haunting image broadcast around the world. Under a heavy police escort, she was transferred to the Cedars-Sinai Medical Center and placed under a Section 5150 – an involuntary 72-hour psychiatric holding order.

Kevin Federline arrived at the hospital, followed separately by Sam Lutfi – and then Jamie Spears. Meanwhile, a fraught Lynne was on the phone to someone she'd been liaising with over the past year: American talk-show host and CBS psychologist, Dr. Phil McGraw.

As he would later detail, he said the phone rang '… and it was Lynne – she has a very close relationship with my wife

Robin – and, clearly, she was very upset, which you would expect, as any parent would be.'

In Santa Barbara, new boyfriend Adnan Ghalib was visiting his sister when a friend called to alert him. His calls to Britney's cell-phone went unanswered, and the next morning he headed to LA. That same morning, an extra dose of celebrity arrived when Dr. Phil called in to see Britney. Later reports said that she 'responded unenthusiastically' to his arrival but that most certainly had everything to do with him being a Spears' family appointee, and its associated politics, than anything else.

In her hospital room, there was only one person Britney wished to speak with – Adnan. In an account provided by his friend, she called him as he headed south and reassured him everything was fine and 'there had been a big misunderstanding.'

He arrived to find Britney sitting on the bed, wearing a black gown and talking calmly with Jamie. If anything, this one incident had broken the ice as far as father–daughter relations were concerned.

'Adnan, don't look so worried … there is nothing wrong with me,' she told her beau. Later that day, against doctors' wishes, she discharged herself from hospital.

Under the terms of this enforced confinement, Britney would have been evaluated by a mental health professional to determine if psychiatric admission was warranted. Once that assessment had been carried out, and no admission deemed necessary, she would have been allowed to voluntarily discharge herself. Britney's 'hold' lasted 24 hours.

On the CBS *Early Morning Show*, Dr. Phil appeared to explain his much-debated visit. Everyone, of course, was curious to know how the television star had come to assist the pop princess and he said: 'I went to see Britney at the request of her family … they were very frustrated that she apparently wasn't going to be held for a longer period of time.'

He also issued a statement to the show-business television programme *Entertainment Tonight*, in which he referenced how Britney was in 'dire need of both medical and psychological intervention.' And he also appeared on ABC's *The View*, where he said: 'I think the whole purpose in going was to have a meeting and start a low-key dialogue that in some point in the future might make her open to some suggestions about getting some help.'

He flatly refused, on all occasions, to disclose the contents of his limited conversation with Britney but the mere fact that an experienced psychologist would go on television and even discuss the parameters of his visit says much about how no one seems immune from being sucked into the buzz of the Britney fame machine and its attached media circus. Having stepped away from this vortex, it was clear that Dr. Phil regretted speaking out in such a fashion. He issued a statement of apology, saying: 'Was it helpful to the situation? Regrettably, no; it was not, and I have to acknowledge that, and I do.'

Meanwhile, the 30-strong paparazzi crowd that followed Britney had now mutated to include an estimated 70 photographers and cameramen. With her house under siege, and concerned fans arriving to offer support, Britney was desperate to escape the glare. In the early hours of the morning, when everyone had decamped, she drove with Adnan to a holiday home in Palm Springs, seeking seclusion two hours east of LA.

It was here – he revealed to friends – that the couple first consummated their relationship.

'She felt like the world was off her shoulders,' he told them. By now, he freely admitted to his closest friends that he was 'absolutely infatuated with the girl.'

However intense this fling might have been, it seemed both parties might have entertained separate delusions. Adnan, with his head in the romantic clouds, was the paparazzo pinching himself that he was enjoying passionate interludes with Britney Spears – just days after her harrowing breakdown. For him, such liaisons contained meaningful substance.

Meanwhile, Britney seemed to view Adnan as the escape from all her troubles. If anything, this relationship, and her reaction to it, was yet more evidence of her state of mind. But Adnan wouldn't listen to the friends who advocated caution. He was desperate to be the hero whose love would rescue the fallen pop idol.

Back in LA, there was no escaping the cold reality of the implications on Britney's custodial rights. All her chances had expired, and Kevin Federline was granted immediate sole custody under an emergency order. His attorney Mark Kaplan was reported as saying: 'Kevin doesn't want to keep his kids from being involved in her life. But foremost is that the kids be in an environment of structure [and] stability.'

It is doubtful Britney watched this news as it broke on the television. She remained locked away for two days with Adnan, preferring to bury her head in the desert sand. After 48 hours at their secret retreat, she headed back to LA. But it was clear, one hour into the journey, that she was unable to face reality. En route, in one of her impulsive needs to escape into a fantasyland, she turned to Adnan and said: 'Let's drive to Mexico!'

By now, Britney could have expressed a desire to travel to the moon and Adnan would have taken out a loan for a rocket. Eager to please, without questioning the wisdom of this escapism, he agreed to the detour and drove four hours to the village of Rosarito, south of the US border, checking into a cheap $110-a-night hotel. In Mexico, at least,

Britney could pretend to be somebody else. She donned a pair of spectacles, wore a pink wig and adopted a London accent, as rehearsed in childhood.

Adnan Ghalib and Britney Spears passed themselves off as English tourists taking in the gift shops. Of course, the one thing Britney couldn't escape was the reality that her boyfriend of one month was a paparazzo who knew the value of her image, especially if it happened to be exclusive. His bravado – or his professionalism – couldn't keep secret their destination, and news soon swept media circles that, 'Adnan and Britney are getting married in Mexico.' This was a Chinese whisper without foundation, but it meant that his photo agency obtained 'exclusive' video footage of a day-trip to Mexico.

Even in her darkest hours, and even when on the arm of her boyfriend, Britney brought instant profit. It was later reported that she would row with Adnan about him tipping off colleagues but that seemed rich coming from a girl who'd consistently co-operated with the media pack. The whole thing merely confirmed a truth she already knew: Britney was everybody's cash cow.

The fantasy escape to Mexico soon wore thin. Seven hours after arriving, the couple decided to return to LA, where she would now have to face the music. Among those who were furious was Sam Lutfi, no doubt because Britney had gone running to his adversary in her hour of need. Of course, no one was happier than Lynne Spears to see Adnan come out on top in this game of one-upmanship. She might not have liked the fact that her daughter was dating a paparazzo, but as long as there was another man in Britney's life other than Sam, that could only be a good thing in her eyes.

Meanwhile, Jamie Spears was hatching his own smart manoeuvre on the sidelines. He would start discussions with lawyers about instigating a legal intervention under the auspices of a conservatorship that would compel his wayward daughter into his custody and under his control. This nonsense was going to end.

As friends point out, the man who couldn't save the life of his mother when he was fourteen years old was now alert to the ever-present dangers of his daughter's mind-set, and he was determined to do everything in his power to look after her.

But first, Britney prepared for the next scheduled custody hearing on 14 January 2008.

The scene outside the LA Superior Court was something not even experienced news reporters had witnessed before. MSNBC correspondent Janet Shamilan couldn't contain her puzzlement over the story she was covering. In a 'live' feed, she was previewing the day's events with the anchor in the studio. Behind her, an estimated 100 camera crews and photographers from around the world awaited the imminent arrival of Britney Spears. As the reporter spoke, a black Cadillac Escalade swept up kerb-side, and all bedlam broke loose as reporters, paparazzi, TV-cameramen and many hangers-on started jostling and sprinting with the madness of a panicked evacuation.

Shamilan was clearly taken aback: 'It's a zoo. Is this not just embarrassing? I mean ... at a time when we're covering really important presidential campaigns and issues ... it's just astounding as a reporter, for me to be here to see this ... and see the resources that are dedicated to this. There are at least 30 to 40 LAPD officers for security outside, for arrivals and departures. It's just a spectacle.'

In the midst of that spectacle, the inexperience of both Adnan and Sam was exposed as Britney exited the car from the pavement – and into the heaving scrum. Manager and boyfriend looked like two men who'd won a competition to look after Britney Spears for a day, seemingly with not a plan in place for her arrival. For a woman whose anxiety-issues were known to anyone close to her, it was obvious she would soon feel panicked.

Within seconds of finding herself surrounded, she was heard to say: 'I wanna get back in the car … Let me get back in the car!'

All three scrambled back into the car and drove off.

As Shaliman then observed, the Escalade started to circle the building, 'trying to figure out a way of getting in', but in the end, they drove off and Britney never appeared at the hearing. A court spokesman was equally perplexed because 'she wasn't ordered to attend' so no one knew why she was there, or what purpose it served. Unless, after the last no-show, it was an ill-prepared PR attempt to at least show willing?

Meanwhile, a suited Kevin Federline, sporting a mohawk and chewing gum, turned up on time with his lawyers in more civilised and well-handled arrival. Once more, a clear PR message was issued: Kevin represents order and calm; Britney is in disarray and chaos, with two people flailing with her.

The outcome inside the court was a formality: Kevin's emergency sole custody was continued until further notice, and Britney was not allowed to see her children. On the court steps, her former husband's attorney Mark Kaplan told news crews: 'There is no victorious view of the results and his [Kevin's] goal, his hope for the future, is that at some point, he will be able to parent the children in partic-ipation with their mother.'

Meanwhile, Britney's media circus moved en masse to the suburb of Studio City where, for some odd reason, Sam and Adnan led her into the Little Brown Church in the San Fernando Valley. Not even God could be spared this Hell's circus but, of course, no one could miss the photo opportunity of the pop star sitting down to pray. Maybe it was all a PR stunt? If so, then even the Church was happy to play along, or so it seemed, with a spokesman saying: 'The Church is a place of prayer, open 24 hours of day for people seeking peace.' The circus then moved to a restaurant on Ventura Boulevard for lunch, where a fellow diner told *OK!* magazine that Britney 'had cried all of her make-up off.'

In an increasing farce, Britney and Adnan went into a Rite Aid store in Studio City, where they started to scour the shelf containing pregnancy test kits. It just so happened a photographer was there to 'spy' the moment and 'exclusive' images were released through Adnan's agency, Finalpix. In the circumstances, this was a crass PR stunt, but according to the friend of Adnan, 'Britney was convinced she was pregnant', saying she 'knows what my tummy feels like and I'm pregnant … I know I am … I'm pregnant!'

The couple bought one kit, went home to do the test together and it came back as negative. Britney sat on the toilet seat and sobbed, according to this source, who said: 'It wasn't about having Adnan's baby, it was about having a replacement for Sean Preston and Jayden James, and he knew it. He was equally gutted because he wanted to be seen as the father of Britney's child. The whole thing was getting sick.'

That same week, Adnan appeared on *Entertainment Tonight*, where he spoke of Britney's pregnancy scare, but it seemed there may have been another motivation. The friend said: 'that there was an expectation of him to tell the truth about Sam Lutfi and tell the world that Britney would be fine' following a phone call with Lynne Spears. As someone who was not a fan of Sam himself, this would have been the ideal opportunity to publicly embarrass his adversary, but in the end, he didn't go through with it, 'because he didn't buy Lynne's suspicions of Sam'; suspicions that would later emerge in her memoir; suspicions that would motivate the Spears' legal conservatorship bid that sought to wrestle Britney from the control of the manager to whom she had submitted.

Ultimately, Adnan Ghalib would tread the same path as many before him and liaise with the *News of the World* to discuss a deal, but instead it seemed to turn the tables on him by exposing him for touting video clips of Britney. Suddenly, he didn't appear quite so chivalrous as he had at first.

The article's content made it clear that reporters had viewed the footage for sale. One clip showed Britney sitting on a bed wearing a nightie, talking about herself in the third person, saying: 'When Britney was a child, she had to work really hard.' The second showed her wrapped in a white bath towel, telling the camera how she has angels watching over her. And the third piece of footage was deliberately aimed to reflect well on Adnan himself when Britney referred to his pet name and said: 'I'm really happy: Bubba's here for me now. It's all good.'

Britney would not be made aware of such dealings until later, nor would she seem overly perturbed. Maybe in her mind it was just another version of 'Chaotic', as once formatted and sold with Kevin Federline?

With delicious irony, her topical single 'Piece of Me' had its UK release and its chart performance demonstrated that, as far as her music was concerned, Britney's strength and enduring success remained unrivalled. From a No. 19 position on 7 January, one week later the single shot to No. 2 and would go on to sell almost 150,000 copies. The gulf between the dual personalities of Britney the performer and

Britney the person had never been wider. One was strong and soaring, the other was lost and rapidly deteriorating. At her lowest moment, her brand was embraced.

By January's end, matters would come to a head in typically dramatic fashion.

With so many different undercurrents, agendas and power-struggles going on within and around Britney, it was inevitable the bough would break. Never had so many professed to be in control of such an evidently out-of-control situation, and tensions spilled over on the night of 28 January 2008.

Sam and Britney had one of their usual rows, but this one was more loaded than usual and his jealousies over Adnan surfaced when he accused her of caring more about her new boyfriend than she did about her babies. Witnesses said there was a screaming match in which Britney was reduced to tears.

Britney stormed out of the house, carrying her pet dog London, and sat down on a stone wall. She looked beleaguered, disoriented and appeared almost nonchalant to the paparazzi that took their dishevelled photos. Asked if she was okay by a concerned female reporter, Britney looked up and said: 'I'm fine ... just sitting for once having a nice time with my dog.' After twenty minutes, she returned to the house, only to drive away with another paparazzo friend, Felipe Teixeira, because she wanted to be away from Sam.

Now word leaked out to the awaiting media crowd of a tremendous row between Sam and Britney. As it did so, one paparazzo slipped away to place a discreet phone call to Jamie Spears, tipping him off about this opening. For it seemed there was a concerted effort within the split ranks of the paparazzi to help the Spears family find a way of breaking Sam's iron grip on the Britney Spears operation.

One or two Spears-friendly photographers knew that Jamie 'was waiting for the right moment' and so a discreet agreement was reached that would keep him abreast of any intelligence or dramatic developments. As one source within the paparazzi ranks said: 'I think you could say that Jamie had wised up about how to use us to his advantage. The upshot was that they normally had Adnan on the inside and us on the outside. There was a consensus among many who cared for Britney that Sam Lutfi needed to go. So when that row happened, we knew relations were weakened and Jamie needed to get in there. That's when the call was made.'

It was a paparazzi-inspired coûp d'état aimed at over-throwing Sam Lutfi and reinstalling Jamie and Lynne to their rightful place as parents. They both felt a desperate need to step in and take care of their daughter. When the news was received, the Spears mobilised. Lynne jumped in the car with her friend Jackie; Jamie leapt into his truck. In the fog of subsequent claim and counter-claim, it is not clear what truly transpired inside the house. Sam claimed Britney was afraid of her dad; Lynne claimed Britney was only afraid of Sam. Heated words were exchanged between Sam and Jamie, leading to bodyguards asking the father to leave, and that left Lynne, her friend Jackie and 'The General' waiting for the one person they were all fighting over.

Britney then walked into the house, accompanied by Adnan.

In a sworn legal document later submitted to the courts, Lynne then outlines what happened next: 'Sam then told Jackie and me that we needed to do whatever he tells us. I objected. He then told me, "I'm the one who spends 24/7 with your daughter."' After some time, Adnan – who was apparently made to feel unwelcome by Sam – left the scene.

Outside, a crew from Hollywood.tv caught the text message that Sam then sent Adnan: 'You need to cease all contact with her completely. I've tried to work with you helping her, but you didn't do as asked. The only way to help now is disappear. She's never been this way before.'

Suspicions and paranoia abounded in the house. Sam had convinced himself that he was the victim of a conspiracy to mount an 'intervention' to wrench Britney from him. The Spears had convinced themselves that Sam was controlling their daughter by all manner of sinister means, including sedation.

As with many aspects to this story, hard evidence would be sorely lacking.

Amidst all this tension, Britney stood, becoming increasingly agitated. According to Lynne's statement, she could not stop moving, cleaned the house incessantly, changed her clothes 'many times' and then changed her dog London's clothes.

'Britney spoke to me in a tone and with the level of understanding of a very young girl,' said Lynne.

Later that evening, and according to Lynne, Sam made it clear that without his influence, Britney would kill herself. Lynne's statement added: 'Then he said to me, "If you try to get rid of me, she'll be dead and I'll piss on her grave."' Sam Lutfi denies saying this. Her account continued: 'At one point during the night, Sam was screaming at me and Britney said to me, "Sam treats me like that."' In her memoir, Lynne remarked that her daughter said this, 'as if it were the most normal thing in the world.' But, of course, to Britney's mind and ears, it was – because of the distressing echo from her childhood. It was absolutely normal. And if

Britney's weakness was to tolerate such treatment, then it was a learned behaviour.

There were clear hostilities simmering during a drawn-out drama that lasted from 7pm to 3am, with Britney never sitting still. She was, 'meandering around the house ... but she was out of it.'

It is through Lynne's statement that perhaps a true measure of Britney's troubles can be gleaned because of the prescribed medications on the kitchen counter top: Risperdol, Seroquel, Aderol.

The existence of these pills suggests Britney's sufferings are complex, challenging and long-term.

According to FDA guidelines, Risperdol is an anti-psychotic mainly prescribed for the treatment of mental health disorders that can cause delusions, hallucinations and any other false belief. Tellingly, it can also be used for the short-term treatment of mania, as associated with bipolar disorder – a long speculated diagnosis often attributed to Britney's anxieties, mania and erratic mood swings. Seroquel can also be used to treat bipolar, as well as OCD and deep anxiety issues. Interestingly, it is regarded 'as the most sedating of all anti-psychotics', which might lend an explanation as to why Britney would appear sedated in Sam's presence. Thirdly, Aderol is a stimulant – and 'upper' – used to assist alertness and concentration. On top of all these, Britney continued to take her anti-depressants.

Aside from any diagnosis, what was abundantly clear that night was that Britney's condition rendered her incapable of being the performer she once was. She was barely functioning, hardly sleeping, and seemed propped up on medication and not much else. Publicly, the cause of her troubles remains undiagnosed and it is not even known whether there is a professional consensus that these were 'the right medicines' for her.

Based on the conversations that night, there may have been some doubt for Britney told Lynne that night: 'I don't like the pills and I don't like the psychiatrist. Can't I see another psychiatrist so I can see my babies?'

It was then that family friend Jackie reassured her: 'Britney, your parents can help you find a psychiatrist [who] needs to get to know you to give you the right medicine.'

'I'll do anything to get them back,' said Britney, exhausted but unable to sleep.

By 4am, she started asking for her 'Daddy'. Lynne ensured she put him on the telephone there and then. He promised his daughter that he would come round at noon the next day.

According to the statement: 'Britney never went to sleep … and was very agitated most of the night'.

When noon arrived, Jamie did indeed come to the house and Sam was now powerless to prevent a meeting requested by Britney. According to Lynne's account of events, Jamie gave his daughter a big hug.

'Baby, you okay?' he asked.

'I'm fine,' said Britney, and then she burst into tears.

Three days later, Jamie's rescue mission would be complete – but not without a fight.

Lynne and Jackie were back at the house with Britney. It was Wednesday, 30 January 2008. Lynne had gone to sit with her daughter because Sam had started talking weirdly about receiving a tip-off that 'somebody was going to try and commit Britney again'.

Within the hour, there was a furious pounding on the door. The next thing Lynne knows is that 'twenty police officers stormed into the house', declaring Britney was being detained under a 5150 involuntary psychiatric hold.

When a startled Lynne asked to know on what grounds, she was told that they were just following their orders. Britney, bewildered and docile, was loaded and strapped into a gurney to be transported away from her house for the second time in a month.

'Mama? Mama?' she called out.

'I'm here, baby!' said Lynne, running after her daughter, and then being denied the chance to ride with her in the back of the ambulance. In the sky above, helicopters hovered.

At the gates a battery of camera lenses were raised once more. It was a mystery why the 5150 was now in place but, according to Lynne's memoir, the admittance slip at UCLA Medical Centre mentioned 'driving recklessly' and 'not taking medicine as directed'.

When the family arrived at the hospital, Sam was with Britney in her hospital room. Lynne screamed at him: 'YOU put her in here!' Sam denied such a thing. He felt such an accusation was illustration of the conspiracy against him. In the shouting match that ensued, it was Britney who asked everyone to calm down. Neither Lynne nor Jamie could bear being in the same room as 'the man who inserted himself into my daughter's life (and) home ...'

But the upshot of this episode was that Sam, it seemed, was now back in control, and the Spears had lost the grip they thought they once had; denied by the system that so easily applied a 5150 order against their daughter again. Outside, Britney's second mental breakdown was being reported on the news. Meanwhile, Sam nipped out for a bite to eat. In that moment, Jamie and Lynne 'pleaded our case' to be heard by the doctors, rushing through their reasons, suspicions and arguments before Sam could return. One doctor heard them and, under the terms of a mental health evaluation, he decided to assess Britney to obtain further information. In so doing, he ordered that no one be allowed in her room. The Spears were barred access – but so too was Sam when he returned with a fast-food takeout.

This time, Britney would be kept in hospital for the full 72 hours permitted under a 5150 holding order. That duration provided Jamie Spears with ample opportunity to get his already prepared conservatorship case before the courts, armed with the depositions detailing the shenanigans of the previous few days. After the divorce hearings and custody cases, the LA courts would now be the arena to determine whether Britney Spears was mentally 'incapacitated', had a flawed judgement that rendered her susceptible to 'undue influences' and whether she was capable of looking after herself and her own affairs.

In a closed hearing at LA Superior Court, court commissioner Reva Goetz approved the conservatorship with Britney still admitted in the UCLA. From that moment on, the pop star who had rebelled against instruction, direction and being told how to live her life was now enforced into the care, custody and control of her dad Jamie.

Sam Lutfi's pretensions of control were over, even if the legal battle was not.

After almost 10 years in the spotlight, Britney's once cherished dream had turned into a hellish nightmare, but even if she didn't quite realise it at the time, her dad would now be the hope amid the hopelessness. He had answered the SOS that her actions issued.

In the interests of her own welfare, she lost the freedom in a life that was effectively going into regression, and she would be left with the rights of a pre-teen all over again. But few would disagree that after her self-sabotage and erratic behaviour of 2007, Britney desperately needed love, guidance and stability from the family she'd deserted.

The healing process would be a challenge in itself, but after reaching her nadir, it was Britney's time for a personal recovery – and the resurrection.

15

The Resurrection

'When can I tour again? I want to tour again!'
– Britney, 2008

lash forward 12 months into the year 2009. As Britney surveys the scene around her, she might be forgiven for thinking she's gone back to the future. It's like the year 2000 all over again. An African-American bodyguard called Rob is standing in the corner; there's the happy influence of assistant Felicia Culotta, returning to her side after a stint with the Jonas Brothers. Elsewhere in the room, there's Larry Rudolph, smiling and confident; back for his third stint as manager. Scattered around this scene are a jovial and upbeat bunch of backing dancers, regaling a night of yet another 'Circus' performance in the bag, another rung of the ladder achieved. This is life back on the road again, back inside the golden hamster wheel – cheered, encouraged and supported by the classic version of 'Team Britney'.

It's as if the star of the show has woken up from a bad dream to find nothing has changed. Until, that is, the differences come into focus.

For there, in a corner, acting as the chef of these private proceedings and standing over a mobile stove, is the ever-present guardian of Jamie Spears, someone who once relinquished control of his daughter's dream but now holds the court-installed reins. Not Lynne, not Larry, but Jamie. He won't make the mistake of surrendering control a second time as he turns over a new leaf for both himself and Britney within a rigid and disciplined framework.

As Britney continues to scan this condo-suite inside a luxury five-star hotel, the new rules and disciplines are stark: *everyone* is drinking water. There's not a drop of alcohol in sight; not even a can of Red Bull. It's a strictly water-only event. Which probably explains why the dancers have given it the nickname of 'The Sober Tour' ever since the official 'Circus Tour' kick-started in New Orleans, Louisiana, on 3 March.

The scene, on a day in late April 2009, is jovial and good-spirited; Britney 'neither seems up nor down.' It's the day after one of her performances and she is holding a contented equilibrium. Then, as Jamie continues to rustle up a brunch just like he used to make a crawfish boil in Kentwood, Britney steps outside onto the patio. She fancies a cigarette – one of the things she is permitted to indulge in. She exhales the smoke into the air, which is feeling a little chilly at night in the Nevada desert. It feels good to be back in Las Vegas. Her ignominy of the 2007 VMAs is buried in a shallow grave like the turncoat who dared pull back the curtain on a massive Vegas gamble. Few can forget that self-betrayal but 'Sin City' is a forgiving place, and past losses are never mentioned.

What makes this return particularly poignant is that the VIP party is taking place inside the venue of that same VMAs gamble: the Palms Casino and Hotel Resort. As Jamie mans the stove, he keeps an eye on his daughter, chatting with the dancers. Most probably, he can't believe the leaps and bounds she's made since those haunting days of January 2008.

From the moment she came out of hospital and into his court-sanctioned care, he remained with his broken daughter, nursed her and fed her – assisted by Lynne – on a near 24-hour basis. Britney was virtually down and out between February and March, and rarely left Jamie's side. During that month, it could be argued that she received more parenting from him than she'd ever experienced in childhood; he truly was attempting to make amends, giving up his catering job to dedicate his time to Britney.

He ran errands, bought the groceries, cooked every evening and ferried his daughter to see both friends and medical professionals at the Neuropsychiatric Institute at the University of California, where she underwent evaluation, receiving the help she had always needed.

Clearly it was a renewal for father–daughter relations, and a small insight was provided in the conservatorship court papers he submitted: 'I received numerous telephone calls from Britney. I spent a good deal of every day conversing with Britney. After she was released … I brought her home and secured her living and care situation.'

Suddenly, on this day in 2009, it all seemed long ago. Whatever was going on inside her head at this stage, no one will ever know but her appearance now is that of a reformed character: with life restored to the eyes that once formed a deadened stare. His attorney-advised conservatorship – to rescue her from 'an immediate and substantial medical emergency' – seems to have been her saviour.

The pop princess has since dusted herself down and picked herself up for a much-hyped 'comeback', at the age of 27, and she is now midway through a meticulously choreographed and controlled professional resurrection. This return to the stage, to the only persona she knows, appears to be her prescribed salvation. At least, for Britney the performer. Such a quick verdict is not so easy to reach for Britney the person. The jury cannot rush such deliberations.

Britney the performer is most definitely toeing the line these days.

Britney the person seems to be keeping her cards close to her chest.

After two quick cigarettes, she wants to lark about with her backing guys on the dance-floor within this luxury, giant condo in a hotel complex owned by the Maloofs. Jamie, in his new career as a caterer before he became Britney's conservator, used to cook for Phil Maloof, chairman and CEO of Maloof Productions, and a son of the Maloof business and entertainment empire, which not only owns the hotel resort but the NBA's Sacramento Kings. If Britney is looked after and protected anywhere in America, it is by her supporters within the Maloof family. 'Phil regards Brit as a special kid, and he'll lay out the red carpet for both her and the Spears family,' said a source. Indeed, it is Mr Maloof's brunch that has been held to honour Britney. This scene of sobriety is as 'wild' as Britney's Vegas days and nights will get for the near future. Her wheels are not allowed to leave the straight and narrow – and sober – tracks.

Soon enough, after socialising and eating, she leaves the soirée of around 35 people. Once she's out the door, the restrictions can slacken a little and a drop of alcohol is allowed to be seen. It seems that Bloody Marys are a particular favourite on this occasion.

Britney retired to her room, knowing she was in the home straight of the American leg of her tour, after telling us her clubbing days are over. She much prefers to be tucked up in bed watching television or reading a Danielle Steel novel, she told *Glamour* magazine for its January 2009 edition.

Not that quiet nights in were an immediate option because she knew that this same tour schedule loop would send her on to the United Kingdom, and London's 02 Arena and the MEN in Manchester before conquering the rest of Europe. It seems a familiar echo.

She had, of course, the comfort of her 'family' this time. Sean Preston and Jayden James shadowed this all-important tour, Kevin Federline having agreed that he would join her on the road, knowing the presence of her sons was a crucial support. Tensions in the custody battle had calmed since a resolution was reached – out of court – between Kevin and Jamie Spears, as the conservator. A judge had earlier allowed Britney's visitations to recommence after noting her new 'business-like approach'. The couple's 'modifiable' agreement granted Kevin primary custody, with Britney having regular visitations, with an in-built aim of moving towards a point of co-parenting. Kevin Federline also emerged with a financial package: Britney footed his $250,000 legal bill, agreed to pay him $20,000 a month in child support and an extra $5,000-a-month for joining her on tour.

Britney also had her extended family of dancers on tour. But, as an indication of the obsessive controls now put in place around Britney, each one of those dancers was bound into the tightest retainer contract because, this time around, the star's welfare would be put far ahead of any dancing ability.

As one source from within the troupe said: 'When auditions were held in the New Year, every dancer had to agree to be drug-tested and there were other stipulations – no one was allowed to drink alcohol in the presence of Britney, and no one was allowed to even discuss alcohol or drugs in front of her. Never in a million years had any of us come across this before. Management were not just concerned about undue influences on the outside, they were bothered about undue influences on the inside, too.'

This strict filtering process was designed to sort the wheat from the chaff to protect the interests of the star. Those whose choreography impressed the team, and then passed the drug tests, were welcomed on board as professionals joining the collective push to maintain Britney's personal recovery. All the razzmatazz and spectacles of the 'Circus Tour 2009' cannot disguise the kid-glove measures and tough restraints that were taking place behind the scenes. Such necessary mollycoddling is an indication of not only how seriously Jamie is taking his role as protector, but how vulnerable Britney remains. Her circle doesn't want a sniff or mention of alcohol or drugs in her company. And the water-only brunch at the Palms resort was further evidence of that.

But the mere fact that she was standing as a picture of health back in Vegas in 2009, having performed to a sell-out audience at the MGM, was a Herculean achievement on its own.

Certainly, with Jamie Spears at the helm and his appointee Larry Rudolph back in the wings, there was no doubt the old team had restored order to the chaos and revived a career from its flatlining state. Once more, Britney was making headlines, but this time for professional reasons alone.

On the professional front, it no longer mattered that the mask and the crown had so infamously slipped, and smashed into pieces on the ground. Manufactured stars can always be repaired in Hollywood. A period of quiet and proper rehabilitation, together with ongoing mental health evaluations, had rebuilt the broken persona, and put the person back on her feet. The young woman who was hardly functioning by the start of 2008 was certainly back on form come the start of 2009.

It wasn't all plain sailing. There would be legal wrangles, practical difficulties and emotional dramas but Britney wouldn't – or couldn't – stay away from the spotlight for long. Her star may have dulled but, despite everything, she remained a highly marketable commodity with an audience baying for her return, and with contracts that had to be honoured.

But with the star boxed and stalled in the starting gate, she would inevitably act up, struggle and wrestle on occasion – demonstrating that a reluctance to conform was still very much part of her nature. With tough love and a firm grip, Jamie had a fight on his hands, and from more than one quarter, before he could relax and enjoy cooking up brunches in Vegas. For the road to recovery was a challenging one throughout 2008.

A seat inside Los Angeles Superior Court was the hottest media ticket in town where Britney Spears was concerned. For pure entertainment value, the showbusiness gossip correspondents found an endlessly rich supply of insight and material from, first, the divorce case and then the custody battle. Throughout 2008, this would also become the scene of an intense power struggle for ultimate supremacy – for the right to take care, and take charge, of the superstar's life.

Courtrooms have always been venues of pure, unedited theatre. In Hollywood, they remain the one place where even the most skilled publicist cannot deflect, bury or obfuscate the truth. Jamie Spears, flanked by his attorneys, had to become accustomed to the spotlight and he soon realised that the 'everything-is-under control' reassurance would not be so easy to deliver within the raw testimony required by the courts. Over time, there would be no hiding Britney's changing moods, or her struggle within the conservatorship straitjacket. But he was determined to maintain his parental control on her life and career – even when the matter was referred to the California Department of Justice Attorney General, Edmund Brown.

As Mr Brown's deputy attorney acknowledged in legal correspondence, 'conservatorships can be difficult and emotional undertakings ... since cherished personal freedoms are at stake.'

Ultimately, the attorney general refused to intervene because he was satisfied, 'the court is appropriately supervising the evaluating process ... of Ms Spears'.

That letter, of 22 August 2008, was written to attorney Jon Eardley, who argued the law chief should intervene because Britney hadn't been given prior warning of her father's intentions as she lay in hospital, and this went against her wishes. Furthermore, he told the Department of Justice that 'Ms Spears ... personally opposes the conservatorship'.

He based this assertion on an undisputed claim that he was 'orally authorized by Britney Spears to file for a Notice of Removal' to release her from her father's temporary conservatorship. This apparent instruction came after the attorney had written to Britney on 28 January 2008, offering her a legal strategy that would benefit her. There was no known professional link between Jon Eardley and Sam

Lutfi so it seemed a strange coincidence that this approach coincided with Sam's escalating power struggle with the Spears. Court papers would later reveal email exchanges between Mr Eardley and Sam in relation to challenging Jamie's conservatorship. This link would become significant later.

Sam had been sidelined ever since the conservatorship began because the first thing Jamie did with the powers invested in him was to take out a temporary restraining order, approved by the courts.

Mr Eardley wasn't the only lawyer raising a hand to contest the conservatorship, for Britney had also retained counsel Adam Streisand, from the law firm Loeb & Loeb, to represent her interests instead of the court-appointed counsel, Samuel Inghams. Mr Streisand argued in court that 'Ms Spears has expressed a strong desire that her father not be appointed conservator. He has been estranged from her, and this has caused her stress.'

But, caught by the power of a conservatorship order, Britney is effectively viewed as not being able to think for herself, and the finding in the LA Superior Court ruled that she 'lacks the capacity to retain counsel' – even if others might disagree.

It was to this end that the efforts of both Mr Eardley and Mr Streisand were thwarted. Yet, as the correspondence from the attorney-general's office stated, she wasn't legally powerless: 'Ms Spears still retains the ability to challenge the notice … by filing a petition.'

Within all the convoluted legalese, no one seemed able to explain the crux of her helpless dilemma. For how is a country girl from Kentwood, whose inabilities were obvious in negotiating the simpler responsibilities of life, supposed to mount a legal challenge if she is not deemed mentally capable of appointing her own attorney? Especially when a subsequent plea from Jon Eardley to the Court of Appeal was thrown out on 24 March 2008 because, 'orders were not appealable'.

This predicament is exceptionally rare for an adult who is not deemed gravely ill. Many would rightly argue that the process stripped Britney of a core civil liberty – her very freedom. But the counter-balance is that she is, as clearly demonstrated, ill-equipped to cope in the normal world on her own, and her bolt for freedom was in danger of costing her the even bigger liberty of a right to life. Jamie was, therefore, doing what any parent would do – saving a daughter from herself.

In a statement, Lynne and Jamie had described their daughter, 'as an adult child in the throes of a mental-health crisis' which must have been a hard thing to admit from two people who had only ever held Britney aloft as a shining, happy talent.

The final, and most interesting, word arose at the end of the attorney-general letter, when his deputy James Root sympathised with Mr Eardley's concerns: 'Based on the information you have shared with this office, it is clear that the conservatorship proceedings ... have touched on intense emotional and financial issues within the Spears family, and that Ms Spears believes the conservatorship to be unlawful, onerous and contrary to her best interests.'

It has to be stressed that this impression was based on Jon Eardley's assertions, not Britney's personal opinions. Also, Britney had reached out in the initial weeks of her conservatorship so it may have been a rash and premature reaction. Indeed, Britney was reported as telling the *Daily Star* in September 2008 that, 'My father saved my life. I probably wouldn't be here if it wasn't for him.'

In her MTV documentary, *Britney – For The Record*, she reflected on all that she had been through and admitted: 'I look back and I do not see how I got through that.' Without naming names, she said she had allowed 'bad people' into her life and she'd been 'taken advantage of' in the past year because she had lowered her guard out of loneliness. Her trust had been 'battered', she said.

She was also aware that a rebellious nature motivated her actions and she attempted to explain this by saying that she, 'never wanted to become one of those prisoner people.'

Ever since 2004, and an interview with *Seventeen* magazine, the words 'prison' or 'prisoner' were often used by Britney as an indication of how supervised her life had felt. The irony was that she alluded to this in a documentary filmed under the auspices of the very conservatorship that contained her freedom.

In October 2008, after various extensions to the original order, LA Superior Court commissioner Reva Goetz made the temporary conservatorship permanent, granting Jamie Spears indefinite control over every aspect of Britney's life: her finances, career, medical files, choices of residence, choice of friends. Everything could be monitored and controlled, from her access to a phone and its itemised bill, permission to drive a car, usage of a credit card and the granting of pocket money.

'BRITNEY'S GOING TO BE DADDY'S LITTLE GIRL FOREVER,' announced one media headline. 'It's official – Britney's no longer in control of herself,' said the NBC news website.

In the MTV documentary, Britney described her life as a 'Groundhog Day' and couldn't hide how stifled she felt. The 'prison' analogy was turned out again when her tempered frustrations said: 'Even when you go to jail, you know there's a time when you're gonna get out. But in this situation, it's never ending. If I wasn't under the restraints I'm under, I'd feel so liberated.'

Technically, she could be forever under her parents' control if she never contests the conditions of the conservatorship, or if she doesn't prove she's capable of surviving on her own. But ask anyone who knows her and they're all agreed on one prediction: she'll be contesting it soon enough, the moment she's proved that she's back on top.

In the meantime, for his role as conservator, the courts awarded Jamie $10,000-a-month plus an $800 office allowance as a salary to compensate for the loss of his catering business. In a sign of how the conservatorship was also looking after Britney's welfare, the judge authorised her psychiatrist to hire two other doctors by paying them retainers. This financial authorisation is a factor many forget. Jamie Spears does not have carte blanche over his daughter's finances. It is a carefully managed process carried out under the watchful eye of the courts.

For Britney, life had gone full circle: supervised at Disney, supervised as a teen pop sensation and now supervised by her dad, the once most distant figure in her life. Much as she has kicked and screamed, it seems strikingly evident that Britney is the runaway horse that needs strong control, otherwise everything within and around her falls into disarray. Ironically, the enforced stability is probably the most stability she has ever yet known.

Jamie had sole control over Britney's personal affairs but a co-conservator was appointed in relation to both her finances and business empire in the shape of former attorney Andrew Wallet. This due prudence was to illustrate both transparency and the fact that Jamie's past bankruptcy would not hinder his new responsibilities.

The co-conservators had some audit to undertake, especially because Britney had been in the habit of allowing friends to use her credit card. Her generosity is known to be one of her weak points; her spending habits are lavish, if court papers served as part of the divorce proceedings remain a true measure. Since her divorce, she had spent $102,000 on entertainment, gifts and holidays, and was burning through $122,0000 a month (roughly $1.4 million a year), and this did not include her $86,000 health insurance premiums plus hefty mortgage and rental payments.

In 2008, Britney was declared 'substantially unable to manage her financial resources or resist fraud and undue influence'. Court papers also added that she 'is unable to properly provide for her personal needs for physical health, food, clothing and shelter.'

The court and the media were told, 'that Ms Spears did not object to the arrangement' and perhaps there is a deeper benefit to this whole scenario, as the psychotherapist explains:

> This is a loving and responsible parental act from a father who can administer care, unobstructed by his alcoholism and no longer denied by any estrangement. The truth is that a conservator lends a power and direction that Britney personally did not have. It installs necessary boundaries, stability, protection and a fortress. In effect, Jamie becomes the authority figure that he was unable to be in her childhood. He's not coming in as a disciplinarian. He's coming in out of desperation. If Britney was seeing this objectively, then she'd see a father stepping in to make sure she was okay.

> For Jamie, knowing how his mother died, he saves the life of the daughter he couldn't bear to lose in the first place. It's now a chance for him to prove himself, and heal his own wounds. This conservatorship offers them both an opportunity for mutual healing based on lessons that are there to make them stronger.

Meanwhile, now that the conservatorship had put her back on track, Britney Corporation Inc powered its engines. Because, in an odd juxtaposition to her need for personal care due to evident incapacitation, she was deemed mentally fit enough for a comeback tour. After traversing America, next would come dates in London, Manchester, Dublin, Paris, Germany, Denmark, Sweden and Russia. Britney will have been on the road from March to August 2009.

Only in the world of Britney Spears could someone be deemed so docile as a person, and yet so vibrant as a performer to resurrect and revitalise her brand. Once again, 'the show must go on ...'

In May 2008, as Britney headed into meetings with Jive Records, Larry Rudolph and various producers to choose songs for the winter release of her sixth album, *Circus*, the debate began about the motivations behind returning her so suddenly to the recording studio and stage.

A great deal of the reaction was rooted in a collective concern for Britney's welfare, but the most significant dissenter to emerge was the man who'd initially helped launch her career 10 years previously: co-manager Johnny Wright.

In the current day, this man of few words was more pre-occupied with the latest 'teen sensations', the Jonas Brothers. But when asked by the US version of *OK!* magazine for his reaction to Britney's return, his candid view carried weight not only because of his music industry pedigree but because he could genuinely say he understood the mind-set of the young woman in question: 'A comeback is not what I wish for Britney ... she is being pushed back into being a money machine. In the beginning, in her mind, she could stop at any time. Now she's thinking, "I've got 170 people on payroll, my dad quit his job, my mom relies totally on me and I can't take a break." Seeing Britney do it by the numbers isn't a good sign," he remarked.

According to the psychotherapist engaged on this book, the majority of 'shrinks' would back Johnny 'because I cannot think of one therapist who, after all Britney had gone through, would advocate a return to such pressures as being the wisest choice.' She added:

All this does is reinforce the facades, repeating a potentially damaging pattern. Patterns represent a challenge to be broken, not repeated. It's almost as if every time she cries for normalcy, she is returned into an endless loop of the Britney machine. It seems the justification is that, 'this is what she identifies with'. I think the wider problem might be that everyone around her identifies Britney with it, too, and doesn't really know of another way forward. So the performer persona is put back together and strengthened whilst the person on the inside remains fragile and just about held together, having had no time to undergo real and lasting inner-work.

The better alternative in my opinion would be to stop, retreat from the limelight and find personal healing before even attempting to re-build the career. Someone would be required to stand up and say 'No' to either the machine or Britney because I suspect she cannot imagine any alternative either. For her, returning to performance will feel like the only answer. But someone needs to assert that 'No', back off, take her away, leave her alone, and announce that no one is going to know about Britney for a while; giving her the chance to be a person in her own right.

Returning her into performing is the path of least resistance, and that's what an addictive person is always seeking, and so this 'comeback' plays into that need to perform, escape and occupy her anxieties. This option allows Britney to keep running to performance without facing the issues that she needs to address in isolation, away from the spotlight.

A source who once worked with Jive Records said that it would be a 'very brave commercial decision' to create a lengthy hiatus in the career of Britney and he sympathised with her management's dilemma: 'In many respects her crisis made the demand for her return even more compelling, but believe me, everyone around her knows the help she needs and is doing all they can to help her. What do you do? It's precarious because there's potentially more of a risk to remove her from the performing world because she simply doesn't know the basics of living in the normal world. The truth is that Britney doesn't get hurt going into the recording or dance studio; it's the one place where she doesn't fall apart.'

This insider also says that the voice of Britney will have carried weight (even though it doesn't seem to in her personal life) because he says the first person rushing towards the stage door is the pop star herself: 'Brit was constantly asking, "When can I tour again? I want to tour again!" She always wanted to be touring right away, and it's an enthusiasm that's commercially hard to resist when you know you've got sell-out arenas and beyond 40 dates. Do the math.'

Mathematics and number crunching are an inescapable reality of the music industry. Record labels like Jive are there to make hit records, not fix people. But a close ally of Britney, dance studio director Robert Baker, said that his information suggests it wasn't the prospect of huge profits that was the compulsion behind the tour, but the prospect of a debt that might have 'finished' Britney Spears. As someone who always had his ear close to the ground with his clients, and remained close with the Spears camp, this is a strong suggestion that potentially changes the entire preconceived picture.

'If Britney didn't go on tour, she could have been hit for around $100 million,' he said, 'It might be lower but I've heard it's around this figure because she was contractually obliged for another album and another tour – and there was a deadline.' The precise nature of Britney's contractual clauses and penalties is not known, and Robert declines to expand into precise details, but his informed theory suggests that – as is the norm for the pop star – Britney didn't have much of a choice when the financial reality dawned. And for someone whose worth is valued at $65 million, we are asked to believe that many lawsuits could have wiped her out.

As Robert explained, expectant concert venues and sponsors, as well as Jive, don't just write off a contract if a mega-star worth millions simply decides to walk away: 'The whole contract set-up and a timetable was in place before Britney had her meltdown. Had she quit and walked away, then the recouped advances, penalties and accrued interest would have been near the $100 million mark.'

When that financial prospect is thrown into the equation, and combined with Britney's need for some semblance of her 'normality' after all the craziness, then it's easier to better understand the thinking and the necessity behind the birth of the *Circus* album and tour, well away from Britney's natural passion to perform.

In Robert's version of events, the 'comeback' was clearly designed to protect both Britney's short-term sense of well-being and her long-term financial position: 'You've also got to factor in that a routine is all part of restoring stability to someone's life,' he said, 'and she finds routine in

performance. It was important to get her back into the environment which, to her, feels like "home".'

Inevitably, Britney headed to the Millennium dance
studio as part of this same process and he remarked that it
was 'heart-warming to see Britney emerge from this groggy,
foggy place and start to become herself again.'

Britney has always said dance is her guaranteed spiritual
experience, but this time, it was also her therapy. Robert has
had many doctors prescribe dance as part of a patient's
rehabiliation: 'Dance is scientifically proven to be therapeutic because of its repetitive nature and it provides a routine,
getting the neuros reconnected.'

He added: 'Whatever Britney had gone through, it was
obvious she'd not lost the head of a performer. It's almost
like a source of energy that she plugs into. You can't doubt
the girl.'

If ever there was one demon that Britney had to banish, it
was her VMAs experience. After her televised disaster of
2007, few could have blamed her for running to the hills
whenever MTV or VMAs was mentioned. But, with her
comeback in the pipeline, she was invited by producers to
provide the introductory speech to open the 2008 VMAs,
this time held in Los Angeles and hosted by Russell Brand.

One year on, she strode with gusto into an all-too-raw
memory and laid her ghosts to rest in spectacular fashion.

Throughout the summer, she had effectively laid low,
getting herself back in shape. The image transformation was
already obvious in a pre-taped promotional skit with the
British comedic host, as she sat, demure and cross-legged, in
a black halter-neck dress on a leather chaise-longue. Behind
them, in a warehouse lot, an elephant flapped its ears and

curled its trunk – the subtle reminder of the great unmentionable and 'the elephant in the room', and a display of Britney's self-deprecating humour. With this television commercial teased in the week before the broadcast, it was the ideal icebreaker to pave the way for her return.

On the day of the show, on 7 September, Britney's understandable nerves were later revealed in her MTV documentary, as she was filmed at home and backstage.

'This is a really important moment for her,' Larry Rudolph was heard to say, 'because this is the official beginning of the comeback.'

Wearing a silver Versace shift dress, a radiant Britney bit her nails as she stood in the wings, awaiting her cue. As she walked on stage, the resurrection began among friends from the music industry. In a clearly rehearsed, but gently delivered message, she said: 'I want to thank God first and foremost for just blessing me like this. I want to thank my beautiful family, my two beautiful boys for just inspiring me every day. And my fans ... thank you so much!'

The audience, made up of music industry types and other artistes, remembered all too well the pain of the previous year and acknowledged Britney's return by getting to its feet and treating her to a standing ovation.

Over the next hour, she turned a notorious event into a memorable occasion, by receiving the MTV Awards for Best Female Video, Best Pop Video and Video of the Year for her tabloid-bashing hit: 'Piece of Me'.

In the photo-call afterwards, she looked every inch the American sweetheart once again and the message was clear: Britney was back, and meant business.

With three more trophies added to the cabinet and as winter approached, Britney didn't wish to entertain talk of a 'comeback' after a summer of preparation. Already the pressure was sufficiently loaded without repeating the language that preceded the VMAs of 2007. 'Comeback' had almost become a dirty word in her mind, and yet everyone else was hooked by the mere prospect of her public redemption. A world fan-base willed its idol not to just come back, but to arrive with an impact that proved she was still No. 1.

'This is going to reinforce her icon status,' declared Barry Weiss, chairman and CEO of the BMG Label Group, which includes Britney's label. He was talking about the release of the *Circus* album, but such expectations were also applicable to the tour scheduled for the spring.

In her MTV documentary, *Britney – For The Record*, she professed not to know what all the fuss was about, saying, 'I've been here the whole time … and, you know, I've been recording for a while.' It was as if she didn't want to understand that people used the word 'comeback' because it was viewed as bringing her back from a tipping point of no return.

But it was her response to the debate on her readiness for the spotlight that proved the most telling moment of the entire documentary, even if her 'answer' was open to interpretation. Filmed in a hotel suite at The Mondrian, Britney's eyes were fixed on the off-camera interviewer as he asked: 'So, do you feel ready to put yourself back into the spotlight?'

If this probe was meant to elicit passion and enthusiasm then it wasn't forthcoming. Instead, Britney's stare fell, she blinked twice and her eyes dropped away as she dipped her head.

It was the one question she didn't answer on-camera.

Reading her silences is like reading her moods – it's a subjective analysis based on the prevailing conditions at any one time. On-camera, she couldn't have looked any less enthusiastic, as if staying silent was the more diplomatic choice. Or maybe, just maybe, this was PR orchestrated, too? Either way, it wasn't a resounding 'Yes! I'm ready for the spotlight'. Far from it. But then people like Robert Baker, and the source who has worked with the record label, had observed her privately buzzing for the spotlight again, eager to dance, keen to tour.

Happy versus sad; enthusiastic versus 'not feeling it' Crying one minute, laughing the next ... seeking an authority figure then looking to rebel. There are many inherent splits within the thoughts and moods that Britney entertains and one wonders what can quell her inner conflicts to bring her the balance she needs. It seems an impossibility to nail where she stands, and what she truly thinks, under the auspices of such a micro-managed brand and conservatorship. What *would* Britney say if freedom was hers?

Jenny Eliscu, a contributing editor for *Rolling Stone* magazine, attempted to find out in October 2008, in a 'comeback' interview. She'd first met Britney in 2001 when nothing was off limits. It was so easygoing that they effectively hung out together, even discussing the possibility of writing a frank book one day.

But the micro-managed interview of 2008 was a whole other experience. In the magazine's 'Conversation with Writer Jenny Eliscu', she said she was allowed to see Britney 'several times' over two months but was 'only allowed to speak with her on two occasions' – and never alone. Talking in-depth was an impossibility, and only pre-approved questions were allowed. 'Britney today has about as many legal rights as when she was in Mickey Mouse Club,' wrote Jenny.

'Comeback Week' prepped the world for the launch of the album *Circus*, released to coincide with her 27th birthday, on 2 December 2008. She appeared on ABC's *Good Morning America* – without being interviewed – and then hit Germany, France and Japan as part of a whirlwind publicity promotion.

En route, she headed to London and ITV's *X-Factor* where she'd meet – albeit briefly – the true example of pop star level-headedness in Cheryl Cole. If ever the industry needed a dignified role model to demonstrate steel and sincerity, then look no further than this down-to-earth Geordie with a mum, Joan, who stays firmly in the background whilst maintaining a bed-rock of support. If Simon Cowell gets his way, America will soon be introduced to Cheryl, voted *FHM*'s 2009 Sexiest Woman in the World … with Britney in fourth place.

For Britney's *X-Factor* appearance it seemed fitting that all contestants had to sing one of her hits from across the years, and her presence resulted in the show's best audience with 12.8 million viewers tuning in. There was much ridicule about her performance and criticism that she'd not met the contestants, or even spent time with Simon Cowell et al. But the truth was that Britney had flown in for a whistle-stop appearance, arriving late from Frankfurt. Time didn't allow for pre-recording or social meet-and-greets, such was the rush of events. And ITV weren't complaining. Besides, it was all a warm up, anyway, for the main touring event, four months later: 'The Circus Starring Britney Spears'.

A definite momentum was building that suggested the dark days were in the past. At least, that's what people were saying, their fingers firmly crossed. The year 2008 would end on a high, and return Britney to a pedestal where failure wasn't an option. For her *Circus* album sold more than

500,000 copies in its first week in the US, and debuted at
No. 1 in the Billboard 200. Then, the album's first single,
'Womanizer', went straight to No. 1 in the Billboard Hot
100 – her first chart topper since her debut hit '... Baby
One More Time'.

History, in a good way, was now repeating itself and
Hollywood heralded its latest comeback kid as Britney
prepared for life once more back on the road ...

16

Britney ...
One More Time

'Touring is my favourite thing.'
– Britney, 2004

The wheels of the private jet touched down, and Britney no doubt felt instant trepidation, excitement and comfort in finding herself on home soil in Louisiana. She'd done this journey countless times before, but this time the return home was more loaded than usual. This particular return placed all her career's poker chips on black.

The Britney Spears juggernaut had hit the road in preparation for a 32-city, 52-date US and UK tour that would add further European dates but start in New Orleans, USA, on 3 March 2009.

Back in LA, 16 monster trucks left in convoy for the 1,900-mile trip to Louisiana, stacked with the set, props and costumes needed to stage a musical three-ringed circus.

Britney travelled ahead, touching down on the small apron at McComb airport on Friday, 27 February – three days ahead of her opening night.

She had returned home to her childhood playground; to the people who knew her best, knowing that at least 20 friends and family would be centre-stage in the first two rows.

On the far side of the small terminal building in McComb, a gaggle of press waited to catch the homecoming moment. On the plane, sons Sean Preston and Jayden James were all smiles and giggles as Mum and her entourage gathered themselves. After a three-hour flight, Britney was keen to get off the aircraft for a smoke to ease understandable apprehension.

She stood from her leather seat, donned a pair of sunglasses and stepped outside. As she came down the rear steps of the jet, there was a rapid flutter of camera shutters, capturing the brisk wind blowing her hair and billowing her black skirt.

She wore Christ's crucifix as earrings, just as she had done at the *Mickey Mouse Club*. As the jet's engines wound down, Dad gave her a kiss on the forehead, and the scene couldn't have appeared happier. Then, Britney walked off for her cigarette, warming her lungs in the chilly breeze. All this was captured on-camera: every movement, every gesture. As ever, all eyes were on her. It may have crossed her mind that many of the onlookers would be waiting for her to mess up on tour, waiting to see if she still had 'what it takes'.

She was well aware that the pre-production saga of meltdowns, custody battles and conservatorship hearings would be poured into one pressure-cooker tour, with all judgements held in abeyance. This was a personal and professional revival that had America riveted.

'BRITNEY HAS THE WHOLE WORLD WAITING AND WATCHING' declared the on-line site *Thaindian.com*. Gary Bongiovanni, editor-in-chief of concert trade magazine *Pollstar*, said: 'From the moment tickets went on sale, the buzz was strong that this wasn't going to be a failure. We've got to believe Britney is ready and will do a professional show. If she doesn't, it's over.'

One person convinced she'd be ready was her first choreographer, Wade Robson. Originally he'd been hired as the man to guide Britney through the 'Circus' but, like everyone else, he was concerned that she was rushing back or wouldn't be capable, come the offing. But Robert Baker, who witnessed the choreographic chemistry between the two of them, said: 'There was a one-on-one meeting with him and Britney. He wanted to make sure her head was in this, that she was prepared and knew how much work was entailed, and they sat for about an hour. It was Britney who enthused *him*! He came back, saying, "She's ready to! She's ready for it!"'

Ultimately, Wade would step aside in a decision that disappointed Britney, but it seems the controlling conditions of the conservatorship brought with them restrictions that he found himself unable to work with. No doubt he expected the same freedom as the olden days but, he felt his creative space was impeded under the tight conditions laid down by Jamie.

A source close to the dancer said: 'Initially, Jamie was obsessed about which dancers were talking with Britney. Every conversation felt monitored and everything felt too controlled. Dance requires freedom. Wade's at the point in his career where he can do exactly what he wants, and picks and chooses. It wasn't working for him to work in such an environment and, amicably, it was agreed to find someone else.'

Another departure was Andre Fuentes, the choreographer television viewers had seen in the previous year's MTV documentary. Apparently, it had always been the long-term plan to replace him, 'because they were looking for a different style'.

The fresh injection of cutting-edge choreography was provided by the new man, Jamie King, a tour director and choreographer whose name is usually synonymous with Madonna concerts. It represented an old school reunion because it was Jamie who had directed the 2000, 'Oops! ... I Did It Again' tour so Britney remained in safe hands.

On the eve of the opening date, there was a full dress rehearsal at the New Orleans Arena. In fact, it would run right through until 2am the next day but now there was nothing more Britney could do or give. She knew the routines so well that she could pull it off with her eyes closed; as she always could. But that wasn't the point. What mattered was the finesse of the delivery, the slickness and the entertainment value, and whether Britney was back to her best.

No one was more confident than the mastermind himself, Larry Rudolph, who described the 'Circus' concert on radio as 'an extravaganza of spectacular-ness' and a 'full-blown, full-out Britney Spears' show.'

No circus had ever heard such a thundering drum roll and it was typical that Larry should be the one providing it, but no one knows Britney's capabilities and moods better than he, and he knew she was buzzing – and believed she was ready.

He said: 'She has this nervous energy; she's got this way of channelling it. I've said to her before that if you were on a football team and were going to the Super Bowl, they'd want you to be the quarterback. When it comes to game day, nobody brings it like she does.'

Britney had extra reason to be top of her game because two special VIP guests would be sitting front row centre: Sean Preston and Jayden James would be sat with their grandparents, seeing their mama perform for the first time.

A fleet of black SUVs swept into the New Orleans Arena, and Britney arrived at 18.28, two minutes early and 90 minutes before stage-time. She was escorted straight to her dressing room, where she remained until it was time to walk out.

Britney's mind races at the best of times, and her self-doubt is no stranger. Even though she'd trod this concert road hundreds of times before, not even she could have been immune to the immense pressure. Her last 'come-back', her last 'live' attempt, was the VMAs of 2007. She had so much to put right – and an army of critics to prove wrong.

In a packed stadium, the anticipation was at fever-pitch as 16,000 fans chanted her return: 'BRITNEY! … BRIT-NEY! … BRITNEY!'

As the ringmaster appeared from her dressing room, she was 'in the zone'. She linked hands with her dancers and prayed for God to bless the show and make it great. Outside in the arena, a three-ringed stage was the centrepiece of a show split into four acts: Circus, House of Fun, Freak-show/Peepshow and Electro Circi in a spectacle that many critiques would describe as 'very Cirque du Soleil' or 'Vegas revue'. The audio-visual circus-themed extravaganza began with a high-energy dash of clowns, acrobats, jugglers and illusionists – all following the support act of the Pussycat Dolls – before Britney made her grand entrance in a ring-master's uniform. As before, she lip-synched, of course, but few in the arena would care. They were there to witness Britney's revival, to see whether she could hold it together ... and cheer her on.

On the night in New Orleans, she could not have been more amped or ready; her old excitement was back. Whatever trials and tribulations she'd faced during this first tour in five years, there was no outward sign of any distress. Britney gave her all, turning in a performance that few would have credited when they viewed the broken woman being loaded into the back of an ambulance. As one in the Kentwood party in the first two rows commented: 'That bitch tore the house down, and showed everyone that she's never down for long!'

As the *LA Times*' Anne Powers observed, she 'looked hearteningly happy as she took on the role of ring mistress, clearly relishing the chance to prove herself healthy and in control.'

And Britney was still delivering her power-packed messages, most notably with an audio-visual on the giant screens that covered a costume change: Britney on video covering Marilyn Manson's haunting version of 'Sweet Dreams' by the Eurythmics with the loaded lyric: 'Some of them want to use you ...'

As the concert reached a flawless climax just before 9pm, Britney took her final bow in front of a curtain of falling sparks. She danced on the spot and had the widest smile on her face. She'd not interacted much with the audience in the way that she might have previously done, but after the encore of 'Womanizer', she punched the air and saluted her home crowd: 'Thank you, New Orleans! I love you guys. Did y'all have a good time?'

That night, and the following day, the general consensus of the reviews was that Britney was hardly back to her best and her dance moves might not have been as slick as they once were. But few could measure the performance without taking into account the depths from which she'd hauled herself back, and in the main she was heralded a hit across America. The artistic purists would complain about the by now standard lip-synching, while harsher critics would say Britney was propped up and excused by the dancers, who created a manic illusion to disguise her decreased tempo. But overall, this was an impressive comeback, where the die-hard Britney fans were treated to what they paid to see: the wow-factor of a performer who, even when her back is against the wall, can prove the indefatigable spirit that prevents her star from waning.

In the *LA Times*, Anne Powers set a consistent theme when she said that 'Spears can safely call this performance a success' and she pointed out: 'Anyone who thinks her lacklustre would do well to remember what she really is: a burlesque performer, a carny's dream born a century or so too late ... but able to fulfill the spectacle of blond ambition now.'

Britney was guaranteed a thumbs-up from show-business blogger Perez Hilton because he delivered the audiovisual introduction welcoming everyone to 'the circus of the bizarre.' His review described it as 'an exhilarating assault on the eyes', but his main point, away from all the brouhaha was that 'Spears seemed to be clear-headed. She did not appear heavily sedated or lethargic. She was on point!' The VMAs 2007 started to fade into black ...

Perez wrote about that intangible quality that ensures the general public remains hooked to a bizarre fascination: 'There is *something* about Britney that makes her truly special. She has that indescribable "it" factor. People are always rooting for her, even when she was at her lowest lows. We genuinely want to see her succeed! And she's back, bitches!' And despite the fact that he could be regarded as 'on-side', that was probably the truest thing any reviewer said, because whether you're a fan of her music or not, there was a global goodwill spurring Britney on. If it wasn't the most sensational of returns, then it might rank as one of the more sensational fightbacks since Rocky bounced back off the ropes. Britney: The Sequel was set to be a box-office smash.

Of course, this was only the first night and *People* magazine's Chuck Arnold rightly urged restraint: 'Don't call it a comeback quite yet. Britney Spears still isn't all the way' – and he pointed out that she seemed 'laboured at times' and 'never really hit her stride.'

But 10 days later, she had the *New York Times'* Jon Caramanica raving as he depicted the scene of 'blunt-force imagery: Ms Spears locked in a cage ... suspended in a picture frame ... and as a ringmaster wielding a whip.'

He wrote: 'Throughout, Ms. Spears appeared radiant and unfettered, often smiling and never uncommitted. Mid-show she briefly erupted into a military shout. "I don't know what you've been told," she said. "This mama is in control!" She seemed certain of it.'

Britney, of course, is her harshest critic. Even within the on-stage blur of the non-stop action, she doesn't miss a trick. According to a source among the dancers, one night she saw herself on one of the giant video screens. The source said: 'She looked up at one point, saw herself and didn't like what she saw. There was this big thing about not wanting anymore video. Brit puts a lot of pressure on herself, performance-wise and image-wise, and there were a few dramas here and there. But the girl's under pressure and needs to blow. Most of us were real impressed that she's kept it together because, let's face it, everyone was doubting her.'

As America continued to embrace Britney's performances through March and April, none of her success surprised Robert Baker at Millennium. He knew Britney was determined to climb the mountain and that tenacity began soon after she'd left hospital, when she arrived at his dance studio with Jamie: 'She was wanting a focus back then because she, more than anyone, knows the routine she needs.'

Robert thinks the proudest member of the audience would have been Jamie Spears, as the man who picked his daughter off the floor, 'removed the dead wood' and cracked the whip: 'Britney and Jamie have had their difficulties, that's known. But I saw them here together and they're moving on. Whatever mood she was in, he was able to talk her down, bring her round and explain things. Without doubt, Jamie's arrival on the scene became Britney's turning point – she'll thank him one day.'

City to city, Britney the ringmaster continued to put on a spectacle and pull in the crowds, while splitting opinion among reviewers. Meanwhile, there was one legal sideshow that needed to be resolved.

When Britney's rebellious streak, impulsive nature, struggle with being controlled and past form are taken into account, it all raises one question that only time can answer: Is she happily toeing the line because she accepts her fate? Or is she playing a cute game and biding her time, contemplating her Great Escape?

Within this unknown debate, there does seem a part of Britney that continues to rebel and kick back against the conditions of the conservatorship. It is not hard to understand why: she's a 27-year-old woman who has never felt in ownership of her life. Having been told that she's an incapable mother, the final and public insult is to be told that she's an incompetent adult on her own; one more failure to add to her self-worth, another 'management' of her life. Old resentments are bound to be stirred. For she is now pigeon-holed as a performer, and pigeon-holed as a private individual. The frustrations and sense of powerlessness must feel maddening within the new calm, regardless of the order such a drastic measure has introduced.

In late 2008 and early 2009, Jamie Spears – in checking her phone bills – discovered text message and phone call contact with Adnan Ghalib. Sources say there 'were literally hundreds of texts' between the ex-lovers. Meanwhile, on 28 December 2008, Sam Lutfi sent a text to Britney's hairdresser saying: 'I've done everything I can to free her from this. Very close to getting her free now.'

Jamie sniffed out a plot between Sam, Adnan and attorney Jon Eardley to mount a challenge to the conservatorship. Indeed, evidence submitted to the courts demonstrated that counsel, John Anderson, had been lined up to represent an ex parte application until he withdrew because of a non-specified 'conflict of interest'. All of this, it was argued, was causing Britney emotional distress. Sam Lutfi and his legal team argued Britney was 'crying for help'.

Having seen Britney derail in Sam and Adnan's company, Jamie viewed the intended legal challenge as undermining Britney's mental and physical recovery so he applied for restraining orders against the ex-manager, the ex-lover and the campaigning attorney.

The ensuing case at the Los Angeles Superior Court in February 2009 provided the only clear window into Britney's new conservator-controlled world as Jamie, in the witness stand, admitted his daughter was 'sometimes allowed to use the cellphone ... sometimes not.'

It was in the January, he said, that a nanny heard Britney having a whispered phone conversation 'in the wee hours of the morning.' So when she went to dance class, the head of her security retrieved her cellphone from her bag so the call register could be checked. Caught red-handed, Britney explained that someone acting on behalf of both Adnan and Sam had slipped her the phone at the Peninsula Hotel, Beverly Hills, one day.

At a later hearing, Sam's sister, Christina Lutfi, said she smuggled a pre-paid cellphone to the singer in the sauna room of the hotel because Britney repeatedly called Sam's cellphone, seeking help to hire a lawyer. So even as she prepared to go on the road, Britney still seemed unsure which life situation is best for her.

> Because of Jamie's alcoholism, and the arguments Britney witnessed as a child, she may well struggle to respect the father who has arrived in a position which demands respect. This is a conservatorship embedded with historic issues that are liable to tweak Britney's anger. But this does not necessarily constitute a 'cry for help'. Britney is someone who can act impulsively and not consider the consequences. Her actions come more from a desperate, knee-jerk place than an SOS call. Nor should we forget the pressures on Jamie in all of this, who faces a daily challenge with his own issues. He's being the responsible father whilst trying to keep himself together, Britney together and the conservatorship together.

If Harriet Ryan's court reporting in the *LA Times* is any guide, the pressure was already taking its toll as she described Jamie's second hour in the witness stand at the February hearing: 'Britney Spears' father was the picture of resigned misery. His shoulders sagged like he was carrying buckets of cement ... His eyes were puffy and cast down, and his mouth dropped in the pronounced frown of a bulldog,' she wrote.

On 29 April 2009, the defence of his fortress proved worthwhile. Judge Aviva Bobb granted restraining orders that barred Sam Lutfi and attorney Jon Eardley from making contact with, or acting on behalf of Britney until 2012. In an earlier hearing, Adnan Ghalib was legally restrained for the same period.

Mr Eardley's counsel, Roger Diamond, said his client had only tried to be 'a good Samaritan'. Sam Lutfi's attorney Bryan Freedman added: 'Never before in the history of the world has a restraining order been issued against someone who did nothing more than answer a cry for help.'

But these views were clearly not shared by the judge overseeing the conservatorship hearing. Judge Reva Goetz said it was 'shocking' that anyone was seeking to change representation for Britney, especially in light of 'her remarkable' improvement. Also, Britney's court-appointed counsel, Samuel Ingham, said his client 'expressly repudiated' all attempts to involve attorney Jon Eardley.

Robert Baker at the Millennium, who has known Britney for 10 years, believes she will look back on this episode and see the wisdom that might not be currently known.

'No one can argue with the one fact that when Jamie came in, everything calmed down,' he said. 'He's got rules but also incentives in place. "If you do this, you can have this ..." Or, "Do this now, and we'll do that later." It's like watching a responsible father in charge of a rebellious teenager, and it's a battle of wills at times. But all Britney has to do is look at the before and the after. When someone is sick, and doesn't realise how sick, they have to take medicine, and it's a tough medicine. But Jamie is administering it from a place of love, and sooner or later the world will see what a good and positive influence he's been.'

This belief is corroborated by an associate of Jamie's in LA, who has spent time with him, both in California and

Louisiana, and says that he is under no illusion about the dramas that may lie ahead: 'He realises that Britney might not appreciate what he's doing right now, but in time, she'll see it eventually. He knows he's doing right by her: it's tough love. Jamie's attitude is that she can hate him now, and kick and scream as much as she likes, but she'll thank him in the end.'

Within the ever-changing moods and understandable sensitivities that Britney experiences, few would take bets on the outcome within a saga known for its unpredictability and its deceptive appearances. Britney's *Circus* comeback has banked the money, and archived the good reviews. And a performer in crisis seems just as popular with fans as one on the top of her game. The reverberations of her latest world tour and imposed fatherly restrictions may not be known until the travelling circus rolls out of town and all parties take stock. But Robert Baker considers Britney will probably have a fresh outlook on life and says he has already witnessed great change within her since the wide-eyed, naive girl walked into his studios back in 1998.

He commented: 'She's growing all the time and is a lot wiser than the media give her credit for. Fame has been one of the major contributors of her having to go through this thing. It destroys people but she's strong enough to bounce back. You know, I think many other people would have folded under the pressures she has faced, and never made it out; it would have been curtains, fade to black. It takes tremendous strength and resilience to go through what she has and still find yourself able to go back on tour.'

If there is one thing that Britney is guaranteed to do, it is to keep searching and Robert says that these days, she's more aware than she's ever been. 'The best way to describe it is this,' he said, 'for a long time, Britney had her eyes closed. Now, her eyes are being opened, and the roles of people around her and the responsibilities she has are dawning. She's woken up to find herself as the CEO of a billion-dollar corporation where everyone, to varying degrees, makes money because of her. That has led to a lot of resentment. Personally, I think she wants to be free of all this stuff but that's a difficult transition. She wants to be her own person but she doesn't know who that person is As much as there is a fight for control around Britney, there is a fight for control within Britney and it's a mind screw.'

He will never forget the moment when, during a conversation before her hospitalisation, Britney reflected on her life when there seemed to be no direction. She had finished a dance class and had put a smile on many children's faces, as she does when her fans buy her records; just as she does when a sell-out concert screams her name. But it's when the performance is over that she struggles the most.

Robert said: 'I think Justin Timberlake was the last true ballast she had, and as we were speaking, she turned to me and said, "I'm the loneliest person in the world." She was so tired of playing the person everyone wanted her to be. But I can promise that she tries to figure it out everyday, and she will come out of this stronger. I'm convinced that she'll prove to Jamie with her actions that she's fine, and then she'll stand on her own two feet, find her own liberation and then, hopefully, the happiness she deserves.'

In her final word on the matter, the psychotherapist believes the challenges ahead are immense but says that Britney's salvation will not be found on the stage:

She will learn as she gets older that the things that are fake or inauthentic will not work as well, and I think she's reaching the point where she's realising that being the performer all the time is not the answer. It is only when she takes away the drug – the performance – and goes cold turkey that she can hope to find the salvation that she is clearly searching for. Perhaps this is a stage-by-stage withdrawal, and maybe that's the professional evaluation, but a withdrawal from the spotlight – for a considerable amount of time – is what Britney really requires, and certainly once her current tour is over.

When she does retreat and come face to face with the emptiness inside, it will be harrowing and will require courage because she'll feel more lost than ever and will have to sit with her anxieties, but with the help of a professional therapist.

If it is truly her dream to find her identity away from fame, then that dream is just as attainable as becoming a pop star. The therapeutic process requires the same dedication, stamina and perseverance.

In order for it to be effective, Britney will need to be as far away from the performance – the stage, industry and attention – as possible. It is taking all the mirrors away, and the one drug she cannot do without. But in that isolation, and facing that emptiness, she gets the opportunity to construct and develop the person that has hidden away to accommodate the performer; the chance to find that person within.

After years of giving, I hope for Britney's sake that she knows that she, too, deserves to receive what she seeks away from the industry. She seems a sweet girl who is generous to a fault, who gives open-heartedly. Britney has given since the day she was born, brought happiness and helped the lives of others. But who is actually giving for Britney the person? Who is seeing and valuing Britney the girl? She needs to be 'seen' for who she is because she's starving for someone to get her, love her, and protect her. But most importantly, it is now her value as Britney – not the pop princess – that matters above all else. When she is recognised as the person first and foremost, that's when her best interests are being served. After the inner-work that she needs to do, she will be able to look forward and ask herself what she really wants? And if it is still a life of performance,

then she has a person that's never been there before to walk
with her on that journey – her true self.

This, certainly, is a story with so many unwritten chapters
and so many twists and turns to come. And yet it is impossible not to draw a conclusion in the interests of this young
woman that she needs considerable time out, away from
the pressures and expectations. Britney's pop-star status
doesn't make her invincible. Her identity with performing
doesn't equate to a power of veto over the identity she
doesn't yet know. And one day, maybe someday soon, someone will see the human wisdom of allowing her to step off
the golden hamster-wheel – even if she objects – and allow
her to hang up her cape for a while to begin a journey that
doesn't involve tour buses and hotel rooms.

Iconic fame like Britney's does not diminish; her name
will endure and will stand the test of time, just as her character has somehow withstood all that she has faced. But if she
continues to be commercially flogged, promoted and over-
hyped, then the danger is that the person inside *will* further
diminish and become lost again. Returning her to 'performance' merely feeds an avoidance of the real issues at hand.

The Circus Starring Britney Spears has proved that she is
back, and the contracts will hopefully have been honoured.
As Larry Rudolph said in December 2008, in launching the
same titled CD: 'I think she is America's pop princess, and
the world's pop princess, and this just reconfirms it to
everyone who doubted it.'

He's right; it does. The professional doubts have gone,
the comeback has been achieved, she's proved the point; as
has everyone else. Britney is back on the throne, where she
belongs.

I hope Britney reads this book. More to the point, I hope
Britney is *allowed* to read this book. And I hope the people

around her read it, too – especially the insights from the psychotherapist – in the hope that a penny or two will drop within the impossible wealth swirling round Britney Corporation Inc.

Now, let a new expectation form, wishing for her long-term wellbeing and personal happiness in retreat. Big hearts, permanent smiles.

We must assume Britney is receiving all the appropriate and professional guidance and support she requires. But one regime of conservatorship and one year of evaluations cannot – and will not – be enough to resolve undercurrents, issues and conditioning that have influenced her entire life. Such matters take time to be unravelled and understood before healing can be achieved. And that is a process she must face away from the stage, away from the spotlight.

Let us not forget that Britney is human, seeking a self-fulfilment and true identity while dealing with common insecurities that hide behind her mask.

In this respect, perhaps she's just like the rest of us after all.

With the exploration of Britney's life, career, dreams and crises over, I returned to The Mondrian to meet the music-industry man who'd been good enough to hear me out when this journey first began.

A few months earlier, we sat in the same booth on the pool patio when he gave me his brief take on Britney, when he didn't give much away. Instead, he slipped me a couple of names of people he thought I should contact, writing them down on the back of his embossed business card.

It's now end April 2009, and he's curious.

'Ya get anywhere?'

So I recounted the journey in summary, tossed in a few anecdotes from Kentwood, and told him that I'd tried hard to understand life from Britney's point of view.

'What's the dramatic conclusion then?' he asked

So I told him.

I told him there are no conclusions because this story's unfinished. Britney remains something of an enigma, but my admiration of her has increased ten-fold.

Now he's intrigued. 'Why?' he asks, not associating 'admiration' with the pop tart.

'Read the book, stand in her shoes and then see if you'd be still standing at the end,' was my reply.

He said he respected my attempt at compassion but then reminded me that we're in a town which pays lip service to such empathy – although his banter was actually more barbed than that.

'But power to you for trying, bro',' he said. Half an hour later, he picks up the tab, wishes me well and rushes off to his next meeting, leaving me in a social setting where people are too busy trying too hard.

I leave, get in my car and head for Venice Beach.

En route on the 10 Freeway, heading west, I look for the one must-see landmark in the distance, resting on a hillside: 'HOLLYWOOD'.

In 1923, the sign originally read 'HOLLYWOODLAND' as a real estate advertising hoarding, but the last four letters deteriorated and dropped away in the forties. Now the rest of the sign remains as a Californian emblem of the great white hope hanging over this town. What an irony that even this emblem of dreams sits and hopes that no one will realise that it's imperfect, not whole; flawed, and broken – and has been for years. But it's more than just an ageing facade: It is the symbol for an intoxicating drug called fame; the world's most chased and addictive substance.

Go on, try it; you've little idea what it contains, and no idea of its power.

But go on, take it; the rush it gives and the lasting sensation it provides are out of this world.

Go on, you know want to.

It will change your life.

It will make you feel better.

Just ask Britney.

Author's Research Note

In compiling this biography, several research tools and informed sources were utilised. Much material pertaining to the current life and times of Britney Spears had already been well documented in the print and broadcast media and other previously published works. In this regard, I particularly used the following books and publications for reassuring research, reference points and timeline guides: *Britney Spears' Heart to Heart* by Britney & Lynne Spears; *Stages* by Britney Spears; *Britney* by Sean Smith; and *Through The Storm* by Lynne Spears. The thoughts and feelings of Britney have, in part, been deduced from her personal writings on her own website, especially those she put into the public domain during 2006–07.

There was an extensive use of court records obtained from the records office of the Los Angeles Superior Court in downtown LA, and the legal archives at the Court of Tangipahoa Parish in Amite, Louisiana.

I also consulted the archives within the LA offices of Splash News, visited the Kentwood Museum and relied on the online newspaper archive, HighBeam Research.

Many people have assisted and contributed to this project, and I've looked from different vantage points throughout. Some of the invaluable sources requested anonymity for understandable reasons. Most notable are those I deliberately emphasised in order to separate their accounts, namely 'a source exceptionally close/close to Britney', 'a well-placed source', 'a source who has worked with the record label', 'the lifelong friend of the Spears family', and 'a legal source'. The insights these discreet sources provided greatly informed this project. The authenticity of these people is, I hope, found in the detail and proximity of their accounts that gave me eyes where I couldn't see. I would like to point out that no sources received any payment or gift for their co-operation. This deliberate policy allowed me to sort the wheat from the chaff, making a clear distinction between those who wanted to co-operate in the best interests of Britney, and those who seemed to think that their accounts were worth money. The accounts you have read, therefore, represent a truth untarnished by inducement.

As explained in the Introduction, I worked with a psychotherapist to assist a deeper understanding of Britney, and this lady's expertise is ratified by her credentials: MA, MFT (Masters in Clinical Psychology and Marriage Family Therapist). She has been a psychotherapist with a private practice for twenty years in Los Angeles, and one of her speciality areas works with psychosomatic issues arising out of complications due to anxiety, depression, stress and stress-related illnesses.

Acknowledgements

When the publisher first approached me about writing a book on Britney, I looked at my music collection of Missy Higgins, Deacon Blue, Coldplay and Rod Stewart and immediately wanted to say 'No'.

So, for turning me around, for having this idea in the first place and for sharing with me the aim to understand the human story of Britney Spears, my first, foremost and sincere thanks go to publisher Carole Tonkinson, who has been an enthusiastic joy to work with. My gratitude invested at Harper UK also goes to Victoria McGeown for sharing the pressure and pulling this operation together, Michelle Brackenborough for creating such a stand-out stunning cover, and Faith Booker for the book's photographic interior design. It's enough to make a man like pink! And then thanks to: Belinda Budge, Eleanor Goymer, Simon Dowson-Collins, Arthur Heard, Steve Burdett, Laura Summers, text editor Jane Donovan, whose editorial support and sharpness was much appreciated, and counsel Victoria Shore.

When I rang literary agent Jonathan Lloyd at Curtis Brown, he was understandably overjoyed to hear I'd be doing the Britney book. Until he realised it wasn't a ghost-writing gig. But, as ever, he watched my back and provided true guidance and support throughout the all-consuming months of writing, together with the 'what would I do without you?' assistance of Camilla Goslett, whose reassuring port of call I've now relied on since 2003. Thanks also to Anna Davis, Felicity Blunt and Craig Dickson.

When I rang home to mention the Britney project, Mum and Dad – a.k.a. Shirl and Cliff – pretended to be huge fans. I wasn't fooled. But your immeasurable love, support and belief defy the distance, and continue to be my bed-rock, tied into the support from my twin, Ian, sister, Nic, and cousin Donna.

In starting this project I could not have imagined the indispensable collaboration from the psychotherapist. This kind heart sat with me, educated me, guided my pen and took this book on a compassionate journey that I hope does its intentions justice. I cannot name you but I can thank you for an invisible but massive contribution. Dr Phil, move over …

I would also have been lost without my two 'Britney experts', Suzie Jack and Sophie Forbes. Suzie's leg-work with me in Kentwood, combined with the doors she opened and the tireless thoroughness she brought, provided a major input to this work. Sophie's insights from LA gave me eyes where I had none, and her guidance and contribution were equally valuable.

Of course, immense gratitude goes to those individuals who, either on or off the record, agreed to speak with me and share their insights of Britney's world, from this story's beginnings to its current day. Thank you to: Chuck Yerger, Myles Thoroughgood, Chanda McGovern, Nigel Dick,

Michael Caplan, Gary Morgan, Robert Baker, Matt Shaw and Hazel Morris. I reserve a special thank-you to the parents of the late Robin Wiley, Bill and Shirley, for allowing me to at least acknowledge your daughter's memory with a nod to her contribution to Britney's career, as well as her own enduring talent.

For those individuals – in both LA and Kentwood – who asked not to be named, my gratitude is for trusting me. You took time out to help shape an account that could not have been told without you.

Special thanks also to Michelle Hughes, Rebecca McKinney and John Smith at the records offices of the Court of Tangipahoa Parish in Amite, Louisiana, for your time and patience.

I would also like to acknowledge, for support and help, past and present: the late Brian Lynch for everything, Stephen White for giving me a chance, the late Jack 'Echelon' O'Neill for sharing the passion, Phil Spencer for your guidance, 'PB' for opening the door, Ali Gunn for putting me on this path, Ausieblond for your inspiration, Hazel Orme for your education, and also: Janine, Chris and Barry Mort, attorney Brad June, Eugene Duffy, Harris Mendelson, Angela Reynolds, Mark Wagman, Mike Harold, Gina-Raye, Elisa, Alan Nevins, Tom Jones, Graham Cauliford, Steve Ginsberg, Mike Savage, Teresa, Carola Eastwood, Lynne Beaudoin, Chetan Parkyn, Jo Malone, Gary Wilcox, Charlotte McCarthy, Rob Barnard, Tom and Helen Williams, Ben Lack, Sally Annetts, the guys at Infinity Wireless in Santa Monica, Alan Franks and Andrew Bean at MGR, Paula Whitworth and Jenny White at Splash, and Dan 'Danno' Hanks, whose research and digging pointed me in the right direction and led to breakthroughs.

Finally, I'd have floundered without Erzuliee's creative refuge and support, and the 'just-checking-you're-not-dead'

calls, coffees and sounding boards of Petey's Mum
'Marjorie', Paul Tetley, Simon Townsend, Claire Fordham,
Suzanne Foss, Denise, 'Bean', Jenette Nowakowski and the
long-distance Jeremy Armstrong.

I promise to talk about something else now …

Steve Dennis